The Point:

Journey to Life

THE POINT

Journey to Life

Randy L Allen

Nella Publishing House
A Division of Nella Limited Liability Company
Tuscaloosa, Alabama

For additional information address: 500 Main Avenue, Suite 201, Northport, Alabama 35476

www.RandyLAllen.com

ISBN: 978-1-7344159-4-0

First Edition: April 2022

Additional Books by the Author

God's Glory Revealed: 52 Devotionals
ISBN: 978-1-7344159-0-2

For the Praise of His Glory: 52 Devotionals
ISBN: 978-1-7344159-2-6

Weekly devotionals are available at www.RandyLAllen.com

CONTENTS

Part II. Spiritual Realm

Part III. Connecting with God

14 | MY JOURNEY WITH PRAYER (SO FAR) 377

Part IV. Our Purpose

15 | GOD'S GLORY REVEALED....................................... 393

"Very truly I tell you, whoever hears my word and believes him who sent me has eternal life and will not be judged but has crossed over from death to life. Very truly I tell you, a time is coming and has now come when the dead will hear the voice of the Son of God and those who hear will live. For as the Father has life in himself, so he has granted the Son also to have life in himself. And he has given him authority to judge because he is the Son of Man."

John 5:24-27

INVITATION

I recently met with an attorney in Texas. He knew my professional background. He knew I was a petroleum engineer and an attorney, and that I had worked in a law firm and as general counsel to an oil and gas company before creating and managing private equity investment funds. He knew all that, so when I mentioned that I am now a pastor, his face suddenly twisted with a puzzled expression. He wanted to ask a question but required some time to formulate the words. I guess he was trying to phrase his question without offending me. He asked, "So what happened that made you want to go into the ministry?" emphasizing "what happened." I may have misinterpreted his expression and emphasis, but it seemed that he expected me to explain how the bottom fell out, how my life went bad, how I was thrown in jail, how I became homeless and face down in the gutter.

But so far, my story includes none of those things. I did not really have an answer for him, because no huge event happened, it was just the next logical step along the path. As I pondered how to respond, he filled the silence saying, "Because I have a friend who was very successful, but along the way he made some bad choices that cost him everything, his possessions, his family, and after that he went into the ministry. So what happened to you?" I explained that nothing dramatic happened; rather, I finally stopped ignoring God's call. I simply started listening. My friend seemed disappointed that my story offered no juicy satisfaction.

Actually, as I progressed through my career I regularly studied Scripture and was actively involved in church. My Bible traveled the world with me, and over the years I had some incredible opportunities to tell people about my faith in some amazing and some unlikely settings. In my experience, business is based on relationships and relationships take time. I spent a lot of time over the years getting to know business associates including lots of early morning breakfasts, lots of meetings in conference rooms, lots of dinners and lots of after dinner discussions. I cannot recall ever bringing up faith in any of the conversations, but faith often came up. And I was so glad when it did, because it is painful to discuss matters of insignificance for too long, and genuine probing inquiry into matters of importance and depth is much more interesting.

Shortly after earning my pastor's license, some of our closest friends invited Lori and me to Augusta, Georgia to watch the weekend rounds of the Masters. Sunday at the Masters was a magical day at an amazing place – spectators treat the course with reverence normally reserved for sacred spaces. We walked the course, stopping at different holes to watch play for a while before moving on. We happened to be at the 8th green when Bubba Watson overshot the green. His ball landed a few feet from us, providing the perfect view as he chipped to begin his charge to take the green jacket. We stayed until the final group walked to the 18th green, then we started our long walk to the cars. The sun was setting and the pine tree shadows were long on the perfectly manicured lawn. Azalea perfume filled the air, peppered with an occasional waft of cigar smoke, which was surprising in a place with so many rules. It had been a great day spent with good friends watching incredible things at a magical place. As we walked, Peter asked me about my decision to become a pastor. Before I could answer, Casey embellished Peter's question (and please do not read anything negative into her question because she is wonderful and dear and there was no negative intent whatsoever in her question – merely honest curiosity) asking, "Why would you possibly want to be a pastor?"

I tried to explain, but I failed miserably. I'm not sure what I said, but I was filled with a sense of inadequacy and later I longed to get the opportunity back. I pondered my failure and thought about different answers I might have used. While my imagined answers would have communicated my thoughts to Peter and Casey, they would have failed with an audience unfamiliar with Christian catchphrases. For instance, had I talked about meeting Jesus and my relationship with Him and the experience of hearing His call – all things Christians might say to one another – each statement should lead to more questions. What do you mean by His call? How can you meet Jesus, didn't He die 2,000 years ago? And if He lives in the spiritual realm, how did you meet Him and how do you have relationship with Him, and how do you hear His call?

As I pondered this I realized the answer had (and still has) many layers and foundations would need to be established before a meaningful answer could be articulated. Casey's question implied deeper questions that caused me to peel the onion, one layer at a time seeking the foundation. I recalled the many times in my life when I have wondered what is the point of it all? Why am I here? Why are any of us here? Are we here simply to gather as much pleasure as possible or is there more? If personal pleasure is our purpose, why does it fail to satisfy? What is the source of satisfaction?

Early in life I struggled with the notion that all living things die; that death is the natural conclusion of life; and the question occurred to me, "If we are just going to die anyway, what is the point?" A little later I pondered more about the meaning of life – why are we here, what is our purpose, and do answers to these questions exist? As I started my career at the law firm, I often thought about the long, hard path that had carried me there. I had worked hard as a student in engineering school and law school, striving to do my best and struggling to graduate and pass the bar exam, and for what? As I drove the clogged freeway before sunrise and after sunset working at a job I disliked, I often wondered why had I worked so hard for so long? I quickly allowed the rhythm of my orderly, scheduled life to dig deep ruts where each day was just another day in a long stream of waking up early, going to work, working late, struggling to find time to eat and to attend to life's necessities, only to get to bed late and wake up unrested to start over the next day. Driving the clogged highway to work often caused me to wonder, "What is the point of it all?"

Our time on earth is pretty short. If the average lifespan is 80 years, on average each person has 29,200 days. I started calculating how many days on average I had left, checking off one at a time, but the thought caused me to wonder whether I will do better or worse than average. And I realized, I was pondering the wrong question. It seemed better to consider quality than quantity, so I began to contemplate, "What will I do with today?" What will I do of significance today? The question caused me to think about what it means to succeed. I pondered the possible sources of satisfaction and fulfillment. We have so little time, understanding the point of it all is important because, while I was running full speed ahead I wondered whether I was running in the wrong direction. If I desire satisfaction and fulfillment, it will help if I am on the path leading there.

It might be cliché to discuss the one who sought satisfaction through his or her career, only to find that each promotion, each pay raise, each new car and each bigger house caused satisfaction to be farther and farther away. It might be cliché to discuss the man or woman who searched for satisfaction from sex, alcohol, cocaine, marijuana, heroin, chocolate cake, tennis, running marathons, CrossFit or countless other pursuits, only to find deeper emptiness. To label these "cliché" does not mean they are inaccurate. Status as cliché is often the result of accurate repetition.

What is the point of it all? I wish the answer was short, concise and easy, but it is not. What provides joy in your life? What makes you feel spiritually whole, satisfied, and complete?

That day as we walked off the Augusta National course leaving the Masters, Casey's question was sincere and my answer was woefully lacking. Years later, here is my answer.

Part I. Life

<<<<<<>>>>>>

1 | LIFE

*"The thief comes only to steal
and kill and destroy; I have come
that they may have life, and
have it to the full."*
John 10:10

Until then Nicole[1] had little experience with death. Her smile warmed the space around her. When she entered a room she instantly filled it with optimism. She genuinely cared about people, was extremely compassionate, and was always ready to say something to brighten the mood. Having recently graduated with a geophysical engineering degree, she was intelligent, educated and quick-witted.

As Nicole watched cancer and chemo steal life from her mother, she grew increasingly sad, angry and desperate to help. She was angry at the cancer because it was in her mother doing what cancer does. She was angry with the doctors because the treatment plan, chemotherapy and the supplemental cocktail of chemicals designed to negate chemo's harmful side effects, only increased her mother's suffering. She was angry with the priest who visited the hospital each day. Her mother loved the priest, was happy that he took the time to visit, and enjoyed his conversation and prayers. Her mother was glad the priest came,

---

[1] Nicole is not her real name.

but as Nicole watched her mother's skin grow increasingly ashen and her head grow bald, and as she saw the sparkle leave her mother's eyes and her body reject every form of fluid and food, her anger focused on the priest because he came and prayed each day but his prayers produced no noticeable effect.

After months of daily prayer, her mother's life continued to leak out of her. If God really existed, if God was really capable of doing all things, if God really had power over life and death, and if the priest was really God's representative here on earth, why were his prayers not working? She concluded that Christianity was the wrong path to help and she was desperate, so she looked to eastern and new age philosophies.

She read books on eastern philosophy and visited new age healers. She visited a store that sold healing crystals. Glass cases displayed small rocks in a manner similar to a jewelry store. Most of the rocks were quartz crystals about two inches long. The man who ran the shop explained that each crystal has a frequency and each person has a frequency, and when the frequencies mesh, the crystal will heat up. That is how you know the crystal is right for you. Much to her surprise, she found a few rocks that actually heated up in her hand. Hoping that her frequency and her mother's were similar, she bought a few and took them to her mother.

Nicole's mother appreciated her daughter's love and concern and effort, but was troubled by the unorthodox gifts. God made the crystals, so they seemed good, but was it okay to use them for healing? Were crystals like Epsom salts in bath water or closer to black magic? While Epsom salts use physical properties for health, crystals use some form of energy and they seemed related to occult practices. Were the so-called healing properties from God or demons?

After her mother's death Nicole returned to church for her funeral. She thanked the priest for his kindness, but her faith in God was broken. She continued searching for answers and peace, but I believe she only returned to church for weddings and funerals.

Twenty years later I urged her to take another look at the Bible. She was surprised that I openly professed faith in Jesus

Christ. She smiled and in her joking way she ridiculed me saying, "I always knew you were spiritual, but how can you believe the Bible? You really believe all those stories from Sunday school? It's so old-fashioned. You sound like my grandmother." It was gentle and teasing, but derision nonetheless.

She was raised in the church, but when her faith was really tested it did not provide the support she needed. Jesus did not appear in the way she wanted. Jesus promises eternal life to people who believe in Him. Her mother believed, her mother followed Christ, yet she died. In my friend's mind, Jesus did not appear at all and if He did not appear when her mother's life was on the line, why would she desire a relationship with Him?

Another friend's faith was tested in a similar way, but her faith was strengthened by the experience. Freddie was in her 50's and she had the reputation of being a prayer warrior. She was actively involved in Christian church, she studied Scripture daily and she prayed all the time. When she prayed, God responded. She emitted the sort of glow that helped me understand medieval paintings depicting holy people with light around their head. Her adult son struggled with many issues throughout his life. Shortly after making tremendous strides towards stability, he became sick and fell into a coma. Freddie prayed and prayed and prayed that God would restore her son's health. She knew with confidence that God exists, that He is the Creator of all things and that He has the power to heal everything and anything. She knew that God could heal her son, so she prayed for complete healing.

Her son died. Life left his body while he was still in the coma. As she grieved her faith was shaken. Why did God not heal her son? Why did God choose not to answer her prayers?

A young man visited Freddie. He had been in a coma at the same time in the same hospital as her son. The man described his experience and explained to Freddie that God gave her son a choice. Her son could either return to his physical body or go to heaven, and apparently her son was ready to move on. The young man explained that God heard her prayers, but her son had a choice in the matter. The situation was not exclusively between Freddie and God.

Freddie believes the young man was a messenger from God giving her His holy guidance when she needed it the most, and her faith was strengthened by the experience.

Similar situations take place each day in hospitals around the world. They cause us to ask many questions about God, like whether He exists, does He get involved in the world, how much power does He have, if He does exist and He has power to change things, why does He allow people to suffer with cancer and in comas, why does it seem that He chooses not to answer prayers? They cause us to question God and His nature. As we ponder God, we must consider ourselves in contrast or by comparison.

Life and death situations cause us to contemplate our existence. What is important to you? What does it mean to live a life of substance? How do you define success? Why are we here? As we peel the onion, layer after layer, asking questions such as these, we come to the fundamental question, what is life?

People involved in situations such as these often long for more time with the people they love. But outside the hospital the world continues moving, people go to their jobs, take their kids to school, watch movies, enjoy physical health, and many go through each day failing to appreciate the health that they have and failing to see the glory of each new day. Most of us, while we are healthy, fail to ponder life. We live day after day after day through a routine that does not include introspection or regular analysis of significant matters.

To ponder life together we must begin by agreeing on what it is we are pondering. The word "life" has many meanings. It means the events occurring between birth and death. As we ponder whether we are living lives of substance, this is the definition used.

It also means the quality separating living things from nonliving things. In this sense, what is life? I sit at a desk writing, I am breathing and thinking. I am alive. The desk and chair and computer are not alive. And one day the life currently propelling my body will leave and my body will die. In that instant, what is it that will leave my body? Or maybe nothing leaves the body. Maybe the body simply runs out of whatever the life force is, like a car running out of gas or a battery losing its charge. In either case something changes. Something alters the body from living to non-living. What changes? This is the most fundamental aspect of life.

What causes life? We are alive and someday our lungs will stop breathing, our hearts will stop pumping blood, and our bodies will die. We have vague notions about what life and death are. If the quality, principal or state that causes life happens to be an element, death would be the result of that element leaving the body. If it is a force, death would be the force expiring or running out. Death is the absence of life. This is similar to the scientific notion of hot and cold. Science discusses heat but not cold; reducing the amount of heat causes a drop in temperature. Cold is not a property; it is merely absence of heat. And science does not discuss darkness, only relative amounts of light. Before we can understand what death really is, we must first know what life is. We must first identify the quality, principle or force causing life, the absence of which results in death.

I first encountered these questions one day in high school zoology class.

Our teacher was a giant. As I recall the scene, and my memory may slightly exaggerate, Mr. McCollum had to turn his shoulders to fit through the doorway. He did not need to duck, but with twelve-foot ceilings the door was really tall. He was not fat, but everything about him was big and he dominated his domain, the high school science lab.

We sat on tall circular stools at elevated black counters adorned with chrome natural gas valves on the far side and a sink in the middle. The room's air held formaldehyde and cleaning solution with an occasional hint of natural gas from kids playing with the valves. Wooden cabinets lined the side and back walls of the room with glass doors revealing glass beakers, flasks, test tubes and ring stands. The floor was a chessboard of one-foot-square black and white linoleum tiles.

Mr. McCollum slowly paced in front of the class lecturing. His hands were enormous. Each finger was like a Churchill cigar. He frequently used his right index finger to push black plastic eyeglasses up his nose. Even when he was calm his voice roared and when he was upset he was quite intimidating. On the first day of class he lectured. And lectured. And lectured. He had to stoop to write at the bottom of the blackboard and he struggled not to break the chalk. Not long into that first lecture my back started an annoying ache from sitting on the tall stool with no backrest. I sat wondering how much longer I needed to endure the ache. The clock was on the wall behind me, but his presence was so intimidating I was afraid to turn and look.

Angela sat next to me. She must have been wondering the same thing as she glanced at her watch. Mr. McCollum immediately stopped his lecture, pointed his giant index finger at her and roared, "You, you there. Do you have a problem? [long pause] Do you need to take medicine? [long pause] Is there something else you need to be doing right now? [long pause] Well then ... leave. If I am boring you then just leave. [long pause] Leave."

Angela was horrified, shocked and embarrassed. She mumbled something like, "No, I don't have anything else to do." He did not acknowledge her statement. He only stared and waited for her to comply with his command. In horror, confusion, embarrassment, and by now a little anger, she gathered her belongings and left, only to stand in the hallway with nothing to do until the next class started. The class sat in horrified silence. There was no laughter.

Note to self: keep eye contact with Mr. McCollum and do not, under any circumstance, look at your watch.

I noticed the size of his feet and I was in awe. As he stood in front of me I noticed that his foot spanned the length of two floor tiles. Unbelievable. I wondered, "Where did he buy his shoes?" And where did he buy his giant pants, which were pulled up high above his waist? Awful thoughts when you are trying not to smile or, horror of horrors, laugh.

Mr. McCollum never really lightened up, but as the semester rolled along he gradually showed elements of humanity. One day we each sat before a starfish. Our job was to separate the nerves from other tissue without severing the nerves, and to map the nervous system. The class was silent as everyone struggled with the job at hand. For no apparent reason, Mr. McCollum started talking.

He described how he had served as a medic in World War II. He had dreamed of being a doctor, "but these hands were worthless with scalpels" he said holding up and staring at his giant mitts. He indicated that his enormous size robbed him of his dream of becoming a doctor, so he settled on serving as a medic and later becoming a high school biology teacher. He discussed doctors and his respect for the profession. He described the wonders of medical science and its growing ability to save lives. He contrasted the knowledge and tools available to doctors with the tools he had used helping soldiers in combat settings many years earlier. He discussed the deaths he tried to prevent. He said that at times soldiers lived whom he thought would die, and that at times the reverse happened. And he continued saying, "while we scientists know a lot, we have no idea what the stuff of life is. We have no idea what causes life. We understand death. We are good at killing, but we have no idea what the stuff of life is."

Before that moment, I had never thought about the source of life. I had considered causes of death, but never the cause of life. The notion that some substance or force animates the tangible components making up our bodies had never occurred to me. I never imagined that what Mr. McCollum referred to as the "stuff of life" existed.

What is the stuff of life? What causes life? It is likely that people have always pondered these questions.

2 | Searching for the Cause of Life

> "Then the Lord God formed a man from the dust of the ground and breathed into his nostrils the breath of life, and the man became a living being."
> Genesis 2:7

> "Life. n. [4] spiritual existence transcending physical death."
> Merriam-Webster Online Dictionary [1]

Something causes life, but what is it? Where does it come from? If it leaves, why and where does it go? If it is a force, what causes it to expire or run out? As we seek to identify the source of life – the thing or force or whatever it is that causes life – where should we look?

I like visiting libraries and bookstores because I love books. I am filled with awe, wonder and excitement as I walk down aisles surrounded by shelves loaded with books because each book houses thoughts, dreams and the imaginations of the authors. I am amazed by the time and energy represented by the written pages. Descriptions of authors' most intimate, innermost feelings and their wildest imagination may be found in books, connecting us to the writer and to places and times we may never be able to visit. Many contain glimpses of people, places and times that survive only through recorded memories, and as I walk down the aisles loaded with books I am excited by the worlds waiting to be explored.

When I was little I loved going to the library, pulling old books off the shelf and inspecting brittle pages tanned and yellowed with age. Old books sitting closed for a long time have a certain smell – it is not musty or dusty, but the sad smell of decaying paper. I often selected a book, flipped to the copyright date and then looked at the last date the book was checked out. I looked at how many times it had been checked out and imagined who read the book. I was holding pages housing the author's thoughts and memories, and I was also holding the very book that another had held and read, absorbing the thoughts and memories of the author. Books represent an intimate exchange between author and reader, and library books are special because they represent the intimacy shared by many different readers.

One day as my mother, brother and I were leaving the library we walked past a table loaded with books and a sign reading "Book Sale." I saw a thick old book with a tan hard cover. It was about three inches thick. I picked it up. It was a Webster's Dictionary from 1930. I asked if I could spend my allowance money to get it. My mother allowed it and I lugged the beast of a book home with both hands. It had that smell, and it contained words and definitions no longer used.

On occasion I consulted the old Webster's, and as I pondered the cause of life I opened it to see how life was defined in 1930. I looked at Google Books to see scanned images of older and newer Webster's; I looked at newer versions from my bookshelf, and Webster's dictionary online to see how its editors had modified the definitions over the years.

In 1828, Webster's stated with confidence that human life is caused by joining a body and a soul, while the 1930 version contains no reference to soul. At some point during the century separating the two, confidence regarding the cause of life was deleted and not replaced, leaving a void that continues in current versions. Life is defined by the characteristics exhibited when it exists, like growth, response to external stimuli, the ability to convert fuel into energy, etc. When certain characteristics are seen, life is presumed and the critter exhibiting the characteristics is presumed to be alive, but silence surrounds the void relating to cause.

What causes life? The question is not posed in Webster's, at least not since some date in the late 1800's or early 1900's.

PONDERING SCIENCE

Bios is one of the Greek words translated as life, and biology is the study of life. It seems that biology would be a good place to look for an explanation of the cause of life. Webster's mimics biology, which does a terrific job of describing what life looks like by listing physical characteristics exhibited by living things. For instance, living things use fuel. They convert fuel to energy, which is why we need to eat to survive. But if conversion of fuel to energy were the only attribute of life, an automobile would be alive because it also converts fuel into energy. Living things also respond to external forces. If you poke a living thing, it responds. If you leave it in darkness and shine a bright light on it, it responds. Living things grow, their cells replicate, and the list of physical traits exhibited by living things goes on and on, and science has done a remarkable job of refining and expanding the list.

As scientists propose adding to the list, debate typically follows. There appears to be debate regarding whether viruses are alive. Viruses force consideration of whether a living being must be independent. Viruses typically live within a host. They seem to be alive until removed from the host for some period of time. Viruses are alive if independence is not a requirement in the definition of life; if independence is required they are not alive, or at least not for very long. While this is a very interesting puzzle, and there are many more like it, biology avoids discussing the cause of life.

This makes me wonder, is science the proper tool for considering the cause of life? Science strives to understand nature and natural phenomena through reasoning, observation and experimentation. It is a closed system. It intentionally limits itself to natural elements, natural forces and natural phenomena because if it were to allow consideration of the supernatural realm, its progression would halt. Supernatural explanations are an easy cop out when solving puzzles so complex that they seem impossible.

Imagine Marie Curie pioneering the path toward understanding radioactivity. As she began her inquiry she noticed that certain elements emitted magical energy, but why? She was engaged in difficult, complex and risky work. It would have been easy for her to simply conclude that the rocks possessed some unexplainable magic quality, some supernatural power. Had science allowed explanations incorporating supernatural phenomena, the complex and risky work would have detoured, the progression of science down the difficult path would have halted, our understanding would still be bound by then existing barriers, and we would not understand radioactivity. Science must limit the box within which it operates to ensure continuation of difficult work and to prevent copping out. It must limit itself to natural phenomena.

This is a good thing accomplishing good results and improving lives. Through improved understanding, scientific endeavor saves and improves human lives in many, many ways. While science must limit its realm of consideration to natural phenomena, does that mean all human endeavor and all intellectual pursuit must be similarly limited? The scientific method is appropriate for many pursuits, but is it appropriate for all pursuits?

When considering the cause of life, is it appropriate to consider the existence of souls and spirits? What about God? If the realm available to consideration is limited to the natural box, these considerations are off limits.

We are products of the Age of Enlightenment, the Industrial Revolution, the Space Age and the Age of Information. We live in our intellect focusing on the physical realm, yet we are comprised of both physical and spiritual components. If we ignore our spiritual self, we separate ourselves from the possibility of full existence.

Our schools explain the scientific method, the rigors of rational thought, and the life-enhancing wonders of science. They also teach about Greek mythology and gods worshiped by ancient people, and the contrast leads to confident assurance of our intellectual superiority over ancient people. As a result, at an early age we begin to envision two categories of thought. We envision the intellectually superior category containing mathematics, science, the natural realm, and rational thought. The other category, the less advanced category, includes superstition, mythology and irrational thought. It is the stuff of uneducated, uninformed, irrational people and ancient societies. For many, supernatural phenomena are placed in the second category alongside superstition, mythology and irrational thought.

Is the entire supernatural realm equivalent to ancient mythology or do some elements of it actually exist? Is it possible that life has a supernatural cause? Given the limited box in which it operates, is science the best place to ponder the cause of life? Or does this puzzle require a larger box?

I think about efforts of scientists across the ages to better understand our world and our existence. Until around 350 years ago, many events like weeds growing in fields where only good crop was sown and tadpoles growing in wheat field ponds were seen as evidence of spontaneous generation. But lens technology advanced in the late 1600's, allowing scientists to view the microscopic realm. They saw things like tiny seeds, tiny eggs, bacteria and cells for the first time, and suddenly a new realm of understanding emerged. As a result, many believed that cells would provide answers allowing us to understand the cause of life. But our understanding of cells led to new puzzles, such as DNA and genomics. As with advanced lens technology 350 years ago, advanced computing technology allows big data sets to be analyzed allowing scientists to see previously hidden connections between data, and our understanding of genomics is rapidly expanding. Technology advances science and science advances technology. As we continue to peel the onion of scientific understanding, new puzzles emerge with greater complexity. Our understanding is evolving but as we learn more we seem farther away from solving the ultimate puzzle – what is the cause of life? – than ever before.

Science is not the proper tool to consider the cause of life. The cause of life does not fit within a box containing only natural contents – it is beyond the realm we have defined as natural. It is supernatural. Similar to Roy Scheider's famous line from the movie, *Jaws*, "We're gonna we need a bigger boat."

FIGHTING FOR LIFE

We wake before the sun, much earlier than usual, drive across town, park in a multi-level concrete garage, walk across the street and enter a building housing a war zone. The world within the building runs with militaristic protocol, battle plans, documentation, and a unique language. Workers wear clothing indicating rank and area of expertise. Sights, smells and sounds of the hospital are unique; each designed for a specific role in the battle to save lives.

The lobby contains the first sign of the many battles fought there. Near the door a kiosk displays hand sanitizer and a sign urging people to apply the gel generously. A few steps down the hall another station holds hand sanitizer, surgical facemasks, Kleenex and a sign commanding "Cover your cough. Clean your hands." Inside the building bacteria, viruses and other microscopic critters are among the enemies.

Lori discovered a lump in the back of her thigh diagnosed as soft tissue sarcoma – a cancerous mass that needed to be removed. After zapping it with radiation over the course of 25 sessions, we arrive at the hospital to remove the rebellious growth.

The pre-op room smells like disinfectant. A jug of anti-bacterial gel hangs on the wall beneath a sign saying, "Every patient, every time." Fastened to the wall next to the sink is a large container of orange anti-bacterial soap. A nurse hands Lori a pile of antiseptic wipes, instructs her to take off all her clothes, and explains in detail how Lori should scrub her entire body before putting on the patient's version of a surgical gown, which strips away feelings of modesty or thoughts of personal privacy.

After scrubbing and putting on the proper clothing designating her role in the procedure, Lori lies in bed. A nurse arrives, pokes a needle into a vein on the top of her right hand, and attaches a tube leading to a bag of salt water hanging a few feet above the bed. Another person pokes her left forearm to collect a blood sample, while a third person stands at a computer asking questions about her medical and physical history – so many questions about things that would never have occurred to me. Afterward, a series of people stop by. Each introduces themself by name and function, and asks more questions, many of which repeat questions previously asked by others.

Finally the surgeon and anesthesiologist arrive to discuss their plans. They explain the plan and all the things that could change the plan. For instance, based on the MRI they believe that the mass is separated from the big blood vessels and the large nerve running down her thigh, but if the mass actually touches either, the plan would suddenly take a complicating turn, which the surgeon describes in detail.

As Lori lies on a bed in the pre-op room, nurses cover her with a blanket connected to a small heat pump. It is so nice for her to have hot air pumped through the blanket enveloping her like a warm hug. A doctor explains that the hospital's blood supply comes from employees at the hospital who are regularly tested for diseases of concern, and the blood is genetically scanned for foundational signs of diseases to ensure, to the extent possible, it is safe. The hospital and staff are attuned to meticulous details in an effort to keep patients comfortable as they fight to prolong life.

Each person, each tool, each machine, each chemical serves a specific role in the battle against the rebellious mass and death. The smell of disinfectant, jugs of anti-bacterial gel littering the halls and mounted in every room, and anti-bacterial soap next to every sink are strong indicators that bacteria and viruses and other microscopic critters are viewed as death's foot soldiers, and they must be continuously destroyed.

In the hospital, battles are fought to prolong life and in the battles, doctors, nurses and janitors focus on the physical realm.

The hospital covers six city blocks and holds hundreds of beds. The surgery waiting room is large and well lit with comfortable chairs, nice TVs, a dozen computers linked to the Internet, Keurigs for free fresh coffee, and room for over a hundred people. The facilities hold state-of-the-art equipment with the latest technology managed by professional technicians who are guided by doctors with the highest education and pedigree. Everything reveals meticulous attention to detail.

Just past the admissions area and waiting room, around the corner behind a locked door is an interior room labeled "Chapel." I do not know how big it is or how it is decorated or whether it has windows, but windows are doubtful because it appears to be an interior room, because each time I try the door it is locked.

The hospital focuses on the physical realm while many patients and their families struggle with both physical and spiritual needs. Most nurses are truly human versions of angels doing their best to show patience, kindness, gentleness, compassion and genuine love to each patient while serving on the front line in the war against physical death. Compassion is not their primary job, but it is wonderful when they show it while doing their primary job. Many patients and their families confront mortality, some for the first time. As a result, some pray for healing while others struggle with spiritual needs. They are in the hospital because of physical needs, but many also suffer spiritually.

In contrast to the awesome facilities, state-of-the-art equipment, expert personnel and many detailed measures taken to protect and prolong physical life, the hospital does not focus on spiritual needs. While individual nurses reach out in love, the organization is designed to focus on physical needs, and I say this without any hint of negative judgment because the hospital is a wonderful place doing a remarkable job. And I am not arguing that its focus is misplaced. I am merely making an observation. Spiritual needs are an afterthought highlighted by the chapel, a small locked room hidden out of the way.

PONDERING SCRIPTURE – PHYSICAL LIFE & SPIRITUAL LIFE

As I ponder this I wonder, does the contrast reveal society's focus on the physical realm while ignoring spiritual needs? The hospital may be a metaphor of our society.

Scripture invites us to consider life in two unique ways, each possessing an independent cause. We are part physical and part spiritual. We each have the type of life that I have been referring to so far – the force animating our bodies, the quality allowing our hearts to beat, our lungs to process oxygen, and our brains to flow electricity – which I will refer to as physical life. We also have the possibility of a different type of life, which I will refer to as spiritual life.

Scripture suggests that physical life continues so long as our bodies are united with our soul. It does not explicitly say this, but the suggestion is clear from both the Old and New Testaments that a spiritual force animates our bodies and the force leaves the body at the point of physical death. Scripture uses words translated as soul, spirit and heart in reference to a person's spiritual self, which comprises the spiritual force delivering physical life.

Similarly, Scripture suggests that spiritual life is the union of our spirit with God, the union of our spirit with the Holy Spirit. Spiritual life occurs when a person's spirit is united with God and spiritual death occurs when a person's spirit is separated from God.

Viewed from a certain angle, spiritual life and physical life appear to be independent. It is possible to be physically alive yet spiritually dead. A person may have all aspects of physical life – they may walk, talk, think and carry on with all physical attributes of life – yet be spiritually dead because he or she is separated from God. It is also possible to have spiritual life while physically dead. However, if we seek a full, satisfying, rich life, we need both physical and spiritual life, rendering them interdependent.

Through Scripture, God appears to be concerned about our entire being. He is concerned with the quality of physical life and He concerns Himself deeply with spiritual life and the notion that spiritual transformation is available to everyone through relationship with Him. The transformation from spiritual death to spiritual life is invisible. While we cannot see the transformation, metamorphosed people reveal subtle evidence of their change. They experience wholeness, satisfaction, new life, and they know the change is real. Like a caterpillar turning into a butterfly, a person transformed with spiritual life is a new being possessing new beauty shown indirectly through patient, gentle, loving, kind interaction with others.

ADAM & EVE INTRODUCE THE CONCEPT OF SPIRITUAL LIFE

Modern Webster's dictionaries no longer say a soul is necessary for physical life. In fact, Webster's no longer discusses the cause of physical life. They do, however, discuss spiritual life. The 2015 edition includes, along with many other definitions of life, a definition relating to spiritual life. It says, "Life. n. [4] spiritual existence transcending physical death."[2] Webster's is aligned with Scripture on the notion of spiritual life.

The availability of spiritual life through union with God is one of the themes running throughout Scripture, from Genesis to Revelation. It is introduced in the second chapter of the Bible – Genesis chapter 2. As God tours Adam around the Garden of

Eden they arrive at one particular tree. God explains that Adam can eat anything from the garden except fruit from that particular tree. God continues saying "for when you eat from it you will certainly die."[3]

Adam and Eve eat the fruit, but they continue to breathe and walk and look alive. Had they walked into a hospital, any examining doctor would have pronounced them physically healthy. But God said they would die. How can they be physically healthy yet dead?

They suffer spiritual death. They are separated from God and they are suddenly aware of their separation. Just as the serpent promises, their eyes are opened, they know good and evil,[4] and in that instant their behavior changes. Before gaining knowledge of good and evil their naked bodies were no problem, but suddenly they feel the need for clothing. Before they gained knowledge of good and evil they communed freely with God, but suddenly they are separated from God and feel the urge to hide from Him. They are spiritually dead and their behavior reflects the condition of their spirits.

So we have physical life and spiritual life. Physical life is the union of body and soul, and spiritual life results from the union of human spirit and God. Spiritual life does not depend on the body, but it influences the body. This definition of life may be satisfied even after physical life stops and the human body stops exhibiting tangible attributes of life.

Choice was involved in that first spiritual death, that initial separation from God. Adam and Eve chose to eat the forbidden fruit. Yes, they were tempted, but they made the choice and the fruit did not satisfy like they thought it would. They sought satisfaction, they bought into the lie, they chose to eat it, and then they discovered that the forbidden fruit was not that great after all.

And here is the crazy thing: they lived in the land of satisfaction when they sought satisfaction. They lived in open communion with God. They walked and talked with God. They knew the quality of life that Jesus refers to as life abundant.[5] They experienced full life, whole life, and they were the only people (other than Jesus) who ever knew real, complete, total satisfaction, yet they believed the lie and they sought that which they already possessed.

They had exactly what they sought, but they did not realize it until it was too late. It is like the Joni Mitchell song about destroying paradise. She wrote (and sang) in her song *Big Yellow Taxi*: "Don't it always seem to go, that you don't know what you've got til its gone...." Since Adam and Eve ate the forbidden fruit, mankind has sought return to that place of satisfaction, and there is only one way. Satisfaction is only available through spiritual life, through spiritual union with God.

Isn't that the way it is with each of us? We are tempted and in our temptation we sometimes make bad choices. Sometimes we believe the lies and we make bad choices. Spiritual life always involves a choice. It is available to everyone, but each person must choose to either accept it or reject it.

Adam and Eve possessed spiritual life when they were created, but they suffered spiritual death as a result of their choice. We were each spiritually dead at birth. If by God's grace we choose spiritual life, we will gain it because of God's grace and our choice. The barrier separating spiritual life from spiritual death is each person's choice by God's grace. Since the beginning, spiritual life has been a matter of personal choice combined with God's grace.

NEW TESTAMENT TEACHING ABOUT SPIRITUAL LIFE

The Bible contrasts physical and spiritual life beginning in the second chapter and continuing through the New Testament. Let's look at a few of the passages, but first a word of caution. They are not light reading. To some extent, this is heavy sledding because the same words are used for both physical and spiritual life, so we need to slowly pick our way through each passage to understand what it says. That being said, once again, physical life results from the union of a human soul with a body, and spiritual life results from the union of human spirit and God.

And if you are not interested in reading that is as tedious as this will soon become, please move on to the next chapter. This is the 'no judgment' zone. But before moving on, please understand that Jesus taught a great deal about spiritual life. While people around Him focused on the physical realm, more often than not Jesus was focused on the spiritual realm. He came to tell us about spiritual life, He came to show us what spiritual life looks like, and He conquered death to provide a path for each of us to gain and experience spiritual life. If you will, let's look together at some of His teaching.

John the Apostle

John[6] writes,

> "Whoever *believes* in the Son *has eternal life*, but whoever *rejects* the Son *will not see life*, for God's wrath remains on them." John 3:36

The hypothetical person already has physical life because the person must breathe, think, and choose whether to believe or reject. If the person rejects Jesus, the person "will not see life." Since he or she is already physically alive, "will not see life" only makes sense if viewed as spiritual life. By rejecting Jesus, the person rejects God, chooses not to commune with God and will not experience spiritual life. His or her spirit will continue to be separated from God, thus they will be spiritually dead – John describes spiritual death as "God's wrath."

Jesus – "Very truly I tell you"

In another example, Jesus says,

> "Very truly I tell you, whoever hears my word and believes him who sent me *has eternal life* and will not be judged but *has crossed over from death to life*. Very truly I tell you, a time is coming and has now come

when *the dead will hear* the voice of the Son of God and those who hear *will live.*" John 5:24-25

Jesus is the truth.[7] Everything He says is true. When He begins a statement by saying, "Very truly I tell you," He is not indicating that the next statement is truer than the rest. This is Jesus code explaining that what He is about to say is very important, and He says the phrase before each of the two sentences quoted. What is He saying that is so important?

Jesus refers to life three times and death twice. He presumes physical life while discussing life and death in the spiritual sense. The first sentence refers to a person who hears and believes, so the person must have physical life. The second sentence says, "the dead will hear," which also presumes physical life and spiritual death.

In the spiritual sense, death is separation from God. When a person hears Jesus' word and believes God, that person instantly gains new spiritual life. Jesus describes three aspects of the new spiritual life. He calls the new spiritual life "eternal life," He says the person will not be judged, which correlates to forgiveness, and He says the person has moved from spiritual death to spiritual life.

The second sentence provides a very similar message. The "dead" refers to a person who does not know God and is spiritually dead. Such a person who hears Jesus' voice suddenly gains spiritual life. How does a dead person hear Jesus speak? They must be physically alive yet spiritually dead.

"Very truly I tell you... Very truly I tell you...." The quote is doubly important.

Later, Jesus introduces two very similar statements about spiritual life with the same words. While Jesus teaches in Capernaum, He compares Himself to manna from heaven, the bread-like food that God provided the Israelites during the Exodus. He says,

"Very truly I tell you, the one who *believes has eternal life.* I am the bread of life. Your forefathers ate the manna in the desert, *yet they died.* But here is the bread

that comes down from heaven, which a man may eat
and *not die*. I am the living bread that came down from
heaven. If anyone eats of this bread, he will *live forever*.
This bread is my flesh, which I will give for the *life* of
the world."

...

Jesus said to them, "<u>Very truly I tell you</u>, unless you
eat the flesh of the Son of Man and drink his blood,
you have *no life in you*." John 6:47-51 & 53

Again, the statements presume physical life. The person
must have physical life to be able to believe and belief leads to
spiritual life, referred to here as "eternal life." Jesus is the bread
that sustains this new spiritual life. Just as physical bread
supports physical life, believing in Jesus leads to and supports
spiritual life.

Jesus compares the sort of bread that He is to the sort of
bread that God provided to the Israelites during the Exodus.
Manna sustained physical life, but the Israelites who ate manna
still suffered physical death. Jesus says that if a person partakes
of Him, meaning if a person believes in Him, follows Him and
lives in relationship with Him, that person will not suffer spiritual
death – they will enjoy spiritual life from that moment forward
forever. A person who eats the living bread of Jesus Christ "will
live forever."

After that, once again Jesus says, "Very truly I tell you,"
and once again the phrase introduces a very important statement.
Jesus says that a person must consume Him to have spiritual life.
Once again, the statement presumes physical life because the
person must be breathing and thinking to make the choice. And
if the person fails to choose Jesus, that person has no spiritual life
in them. The person is spiritually dead.

Jesus & Lazarus

In another example, Jesus returns to Bethany to see His
good friends Martha and Mary. Their brother, Lazarus, had
recently died and had been in the tomb four days. Jesus meets

Martha on the road where she grieves and expresses strong belief that Jesus would have saved her brother had Jesus only been in Bethany before Lazarus died. She has full confidence that Jesus could have healed her brother physically and prevented his physical death.

Jesus responds discussing spiritual life, physical death, and spiritual death saying,

> "I am the resurrection and the life. The one who believes in me *will live, even though they die;* and whoever lives by believing in me *will never die.* Do you believe this?" John 11:25-26

Jesus *is* the resurrection and the life. We know He *was* resurrected on the morning of the first Easter, but He said, "I am." He embodies power over life and death. He is that which brings life to the dead. Spiritual life is only available through Jesus. He *is* the resurrection and the life.

How is it possible that the one who believes in Jesus will live even though he dies? The person who believes in Jesus has spiritual life, which continues even after their body dies. While the person who believes in Jesus will experience physical death, he or she will not experience spiritual death. The person's spirit lives through communion with God even after the body dies.

Jesus & Nicodemus

One night Nicodemus, a member of the Jewish ruling council, visits Jesus. Nicodemus greets Jesus with respect, calling Jesus "Rabbi." He also describes Jesus as a teacher sent by God. As they speak, Jesus says,

> "Very truly I tell you, no one can see the kingdom of God unless they are born again." John 3:3

Nicodemus is confused. With images of physical birth in his mind, he asks how is it possible to be born again? "How can a man be born when he is old?" Nicodemus asks. "Surely he cannot enter a second time into his mother's womb to be born!" (John 3:4).

Jesus distinguishes spiritual birth from physical birth saying,

> "<u>Very truly I tell you</u>, no one can enter the kingdom of God unless they are *born of water and the Spirit*. Flesh gives *birth* to flesh, but the Spirit gives *birth* to spirit. You should not be surprised at my saying, 'You must be *born again*.' The wind blows wherever it pleases. You hear its sound, but you cannot tell where it comes from or where it is going. So it is with everyone *born* of the Spirit[2]." John 3:5-8

Twice in the brief passages above Jesus says, "Very truly I tell you..." Each time He draws a connection between the kingdom of God and new birth.

We have physical life and the possibility of spiritual life. Early in His conversation with Nicodemus, Jesus discusses the notion of physical birth and spiritual birth, saying spiritual birth is a prerequisite to experiencing the kingdom of God. But Nicodemus is confused with the imagery of being born again. Focusing on the physical, he wonders how it is possible for a person to be born again. Nicodemus focuses on the physical while Jesus discusses the spiritual.

The setting is full of contradiction. Keep in mind that Nicodemus is a high-ranking religious official. He travels to meet with Jesus. He has sincere questions to ask. He treats Jesus with respect. But he meets Jesus at night, which might suggest a desire to keep the meeting secret, or it might suggest that they were both busy all day and the night was the only time to be alone for deep, uninterrupted conversation. Jesus responds by speaking in riddles.

As the conversation continues, Jesus' riddles turn to ridicule. Rather than providing a clear explanation, Jesus derides Nicodemus for not understanding:

---

[2] Spirit with capital "S" refers to the Holy Spirit.

"You are Israel's teacher," said Jesus, "and do you not understand these things? <u>Very truly I tell you</u>, we speak of what we know, and we testify to what we have seen, but still you people do not accept our testimony. I have spoken to you of earthly things and you do not believe; how then will you believe if I speak of heavenly things? No one has ever gone into heaven except the one who came from heaven – the Son of Man. Just as Moses lifted up the snake in the wilderness, so the Son of Man must be lifted up, that *everyone who believes may have eternal life in him.*" John 3:10-15

For the third time in the conversation, underscoring the importance of the statement, Jesus starts by saying, "Very truly I tell you..."

During the Exodus as the people of Israel traveled in the desert, they often went through times when they were impatient and they grumbled about God. During one low point, they complained about being in the desert rather than back in Egypt. They complained about the food and lack of bread and lack of water. During that time poisonous snakes entered their camp. People who were struck by the snakes died. Moses prayed to God. God told Moses to make a bronze snake, to place the bronze snake on a pole, and to hold the pole. When a person bitten by a snake looked at the bronze snake they were cured; they lived.[8] In that time and place, the bronze snake prolonged physical life.

As Jesus speaks to Nicodemus, He says, "Just as Moses lifted up the snake in the wilderness, so the Son of Man must be lifted up, that everyone who believes may have eternal life in him." The bronze snake extended physical life for those who looked to it. Similarly, Jesus provides spiritual life for those who look to Him and believe. By combining concepts of physical and spiritual life in a single sentence, this probably confuses Nicodemus more.

Jesus continues speaking about spiritual life saying,

"For God so loved the world that he gave his one and only Son, that *whoever believes in him shall not perish but have eternal life.* For God did not send his Son into the world to condemn the world, but to save the world through him. Whoever believes in him is not condemned, but whoever does not believe stands condemned already because they have not believed in the name of God's one and only Son. This is the verdict: Light has come into the world, but people loved darkness instead of light because their deeds were evil. Everyone who does evil hates the light, and will not come into the light for fear that their deeds will be exposed. But whoever lives by the truth comes into the light, so that it may be seen plainly that what they have done has been done in the sight of God."
John 3:16-21

People who believe in Jesus "shall not perish but have eternal life." But our experience tells us that everyone dies. How can Jesus say, "shall not perish"? Some day, your heart will stop pumping blood, you will stop breathing, and you will experience physical death. Jesus is referring to spiritual life and spiritual death. Jesus is the source of spiritual life, which continues after physical death.

While he struggled to understand Jesus during their meeting, Jesus' words must have ultimately made sense to Nicodemus. When he first approached Jesus, Nicodemus did so with respect. Later, as religious leaders plotted to arrest Jesus, Nicodemus tried to temper their emotional condemnation[9] and after Jesus was crucified, Nicodemus helped prepare His body for burial. With Joseph of Arimathea, the two men carried Jesus' body to the tomb. Nicodemus brought seventy-five pounds of myrrh and aloes, and the men anointed the body with spices and wrapped it with linen strips, and placed it in the tomb.[10] While Scripture tells us that Joseph of Arimathea was a follower of Christ, it does not say the same of Nicodemus, but I wonder whether he was then or whether he soon came to be a follower of Christ.

CONCLUSION

Scripture invites us to consider life in two unique ways, each possessing an independent cause. We are part physical and part spiritual. We have physical life and the possibility of spiritual life. Physical life exists so long as our hearts beat and blood flows through our veins and electric current flows through our brains; it continues so long as our bodies are united with our soul. Spiritual life is the union of our spirit with God, the union of our spirit with the Holy Spirit, and this happens through Christ Jesus.

When Jesus spoke with people about spiritual life, the people He spoke with did not understand. Their worldview was so focused on the physical realm they had no idea what He was saying. He prefaced many of His statements with "Very truly I tell you," indicating the words He was about to say were of extreme importance, but they still failed to hear.

I'm afraid people today repeat their mistake. Our society is a hospital, fighting death while focusing exclusively on the physical realm. We are products of the Age of Enlightenment, the Space Age and the Age of Information. We live in our intellect focusing on the physical realm and many fail to realize that, while physical life is important, the quality of physical is enhanced when spiritual life is gained.

I realize that I have written much more about spiritual life than physical life. Please do not interpret the balance of my words as a suggestion that spiritual life is more important. Both types of life are important. My imbalance of words is an effort to bring balance to our thinking. With that in mind, let's dive deeper into the spiritual realm.

3 | SPIRIT & SOUL

"For the word of God is living and active. Sharper than any double-edged sword, it penetrates even to dividing soul and spirit, joints and marrow; it judges the thoughts and attitudes of the heart."
Hebrews 4:12

BODY, SOUL & SPIRIT

"You are not your hair. You are not your body. You are so much more. You are beautiful because you are you, and you will still be beautiful without hair." These are the words I planned to say to Lori as she prepared to start her chemotherapy treatments. I am not sure how the words actually came out.

Along with Ifosfamide and other ingredients, her regimen was designed to include three days of continuous Adriamycin drip, six times. Nicknamed "the red devil," it guarantees hair loss within two weeks of initial contact. The chemo cocktail would destroy her bodily functions, her mental functions, and her emotional functions. It would cause unimaginable pain, weakness, exhaustion, mouth sores and angry intestines. It would destroy her immune system, and make her dizzy and unable to eat or drink. It would take her body to that line between life and death repeatedly on the premise that cancerous cells are less able to recover than good cells. And she volunteered for this. Actually, she sought it. She traveled a great distance to obtain it because, given her diagnosis, it improved her odds of destroying the cancer before the cancer spread to other parts of her body and she believes the tradeoff will be worth the pain.

I traveled from Alabama to Colorado and was with her during her first cycle. As she recovered I went home planning to be back in Colorado for the start of her next cycle. While I was away from her she developed mouth sores, suffered extreme intestinal issues, lost energy, and started losing her hair. I wanted to be with her when it was time to shave her head, but I was about 1,500 miles away. She texted me photos of the procedure and the result. I am not sure what I said. I was torn. I wanted to be with her. I needed to be with her. But I needed to be at home attending to responsibilities there. And I was not there when she needed me. I just wanted to assure her that my love for her is unrelated to her physical appearance because she is so much more than her hair or body. She is her beautiful soul and spirit, and because they are beautiful everything about her is beautiful.

Physical life is important. It is glorious. We must guard it, protect it and do what we can to preserve it because without physical life it is difficult for us to do much on earth and it is difficult for God to reveal his glory through us. While our physical existence is amazing in so many ways, it does not define you or me or us. You are not your body. You are your soul influenced by your spirit. Our bodies and our physical lives are amazing gifts from God, and we should each care for our body, but you are much more than your physical self.

As said many times before, physical life results from the union of body and soul, and spiritual life results from union of spirit and God. If we want a healthy spirit, we must allow it to commune with God, the source of life. Separation from God is death to our spiritual self. God is spirit[1] and our connection with God comes through Christ Jesus by the Holy Spirit.

As discussed in the previous chapter, Jesus is very concerned about our spiritual self. In fact, one of the reasons He came to earth as a human was to provide the path for the spiritual transformation that He prescribes.[2] It should be no surprise that much of His teaching has to do with the health of our souls and spirits. Jesus offers spiritual refuge, but before digging deeper into His teaching, we should make sure we are on the same page regarding the soul and spirit. What do the words mean? A firm understanding may help us see the meaning of Scripture more clearly and may help us along the path towards transformation.

IDENTIFYING FLAVORS

Vocabulary clarifies communication, and refined words are mechanisms to new insights. It is similar to how people who have been trained to taste are able to experience flavors that others miss. By training their ability to perceive data detected by their senses and by focusing their attention to detail, certain people appreciate and enjoy flavors in food and drink that others overlook. Others fail to fully appreciate the same food and drink, not because they lack the physical ability to detect the flavor, but because they have not properly trained their perception. The training involves breaking up a flavor into individual components, learning to identify each smell and taste in isolation, then identifying each specific flavor as part of a larger assembly of flavors. It involves focused perception, attention to detail and vocabulary.

I roast coffee beans. Freshly roasted beans make better tasting coffee than coffee beans roasted weeks or months earlier: it is not bitter or acidic and it has better flavor. Some beans, when consumed within a week of roasting, have extremely sweet fruity flavors unexpected from coffee. I buy unroasted beans from a place in Oakland, California over the Internet. I was first attracted to the site because it offers detailed tasting reviews of each lot and it mentions that many lots are rejected and returned. I am amazed at the tasting reviews. I recently read about a crop harvested in Honduras. The tasting review said,

> This coffee shows extremely well... striking balance between sugary-sweetness and bittering cocoa tones, with a top-note complexness that caused it to stand out on a table of offers from the region. The dry fragrance... is perfumed with brown sugar and fruit smells, along with a grainy-chocolate flavor that reminds me of carob. The wet grounds have a honey and raisin scent, cooked pear, with an herbaceous touch.... This coffee shows hefty sweetness, pleasant herbal notes hanging overhead, and black tea-like acidity providing a mouth-cleansing effect.[3]

I love the detail of the description. While I cannot taste cocoa overtones or smell the honey or cooked pear, the coffee tastes good to me. I love that the taster is able to taste each flavor and I find comfort knowing they reject some beans. If any lot is good enough for their refined palettes it will certainly taste good to me.

But I know I am missing out on some of the pleasure available. If I could taste each individual layer of flavor it would probably enhance the experience. If I work to refine my palette I will discover a new realm hidden in plain view in front of me.

The opposite is also true. I am confident that my unrefined taste is less offended by awful coffee than the taster's is. Recently on a road trip I stopped at a truck stop and bought a cup of coffee. It was burned from sitting on the burner way too long. It was acidic and bitter. It was awful, but I drank it because it was warm and I needed to stay awake as I drove. It served its purpose, but it did not taste good. My taste was much less offended by the burned cup of bitter acid, which I referred to as sewage at the time, than a person with refined taste would have been.

By refining our understanding of spirit and soul we discover a new realm in plain view yet hidden, we open ourselves to perceive our spirit and strengthen our personal connection with it, and we open ourselves to the spiritual realm in new ways. Similarly, as we refine our spiritual perception and our connection with the Holy Spirit, we will be more offended by the sewage surrounding us in the world. As with tasting and smelling, it involves focused perception, attention to detail and vocabulary. So what do we mean by spirit and soul?

SPIRIT & SOUL

I have been discussing spirit and soul as two separate things, but to be fair, not everyone sees them that way. Some see spirit and soul as two parts of the same thing. Others see them as synonymous terms, two ways of discussing the same thing. Soul and spirit are either two parts of one thing, the same thing, or separate things that are very, very closely related.

Some passages use the two words to represent very similar concepts, so close that they appear to be synonymous. Think about Mary's song known as the Magnificat. She responds to God's blessing saying, "My *soul* glorifies the Lord and my *spirit* rejoices in God my Savior…" (Luke 1:46-47). Both words are used, but it is difficult to distinguish them. It seems like two ways of expressing the same thought. The words could be swapped without altering the thought communicated.

Other passages treat soul and spirit as separate concepts. For instance the writer of Hebrews says, "For the word of God is living and active. Sharper than any double-edged sword, it penetrates even to *dividing soul and spirit*, joints and marrow; it judges the thoughts and attitudes of the heart" (Hebrews 4:12). Soul and spirit are closely related and are very difficult to separate, but two distinct entities.

As another example, Paul writes, "May God himself, the God of peace, sanctify you through and through. May your whole *spirit, soul and body* be kept blameless at the coming of our Lord Jesus Christ. The one who calls you is faithful, and he will do it"

(1 Thessalonians 5:23-24). Paul discusses spirit, soul and body as three distinct parts making up a whole human.

So which is it? Are soul and spirit two words representing one entity or two distinct entities? It is a little like a box of air. I am looking at the Amazon box that was delivered yesterday. I have removed the goods delivered in it and, because of my laziness, the box sits on the floor waiting for me to do something with it. It contains only air. In grade school science we learned that air is comprised of something like 78% nitrogen, 21% oxygen, and trace amounts of a bunch of other things like argon, neon, helium, carbon dioxide, water vapor, methane and ozone.[4] So consider the box. Does it contain air, or nitrogen, or oxygen, or one of the other gases? Yes. It contains the combined mass called air and it contains each individual component. Given the right equipment and training it is possible to separate the individual components. But the goal of possessing each individual gas in purified form is only worth the effort for unique applications, like providing pure oxygen to people with breathing difficulties.

Is the soul and spirit like the air in the box? Are soul and spirit synonyms each representing our entire spiritual self? Is the soul the whole of our spiritual self with our spirit comprising one component of it, like air and oxygen respectively? Using this analogy, the spirit would be a separate commodity yet part of the larger whole and almost inseparable. And if it is like oxygen, the spirit is the stuff that sustains life.

Or are the soul and spirit like nitrogen and oxygen? Are they two separate components, each with a unique identity, which when combined form a greater whole? Does the combination comprise our spiritual self, analogous to air, with our soul and spirit like nitrogen and oxygen, respectively?

Is the exercise of separating soul and spirit worth the effort? That depends on how you use the product. Our goal in looking at soul and spirit is to improve our understanding, gain vocabulary, begin focusing on various aspects of our spiritual self, gain deeper understanding of Scripture, seek God's transformation of our spiritual self, and through this transformation allow His glory to shine through us impacting the world. So it is definitely worth the effort.

But which is it? Are people comprised of three separate parts: body, soul and spirit, or two parts: physical and spiritual with the spiritual part made up of spirit and soul? Some people way smarter and way more educated than me will argue I am wrong, while others may agree with me, but by visualizing and discussing soul and spirit as separate and distinct entities, our understanding of our spiritual selves is enhanced, and our vocabulary for communicating about our spiritual side is strengthened.

SCRIPTURE

Scripture is God's word. He is the author of life. He created us as physical and spiritual beings. He provides His word to help us. What does Scripture tell us about our soul and spirit?

OLD TESTAMENT

The Old Testament concepts of soul and spirit are not fully developed. Nonetheless, it is useful to look at the foundational thoughts. The Old Testament was written in Hebrew. The Hebrew word "ruah" is often translated as spirit, and "nefesh" is often translated as soul, but not always.

This is one indication of the breadth and depth of the soul. While the Old Testament uses the word "nefesh" 754 times, the English NASB version only translates the word as "soul" 251 times, indicating the word is used to convey many different thoughts. Consistent with our understanding that the soul creates physical life when joined with a body, "nefesh" is translated as derivatives of the word "life" 181 times. In other places it is translated as "person," "passion," "appetite," "emotion" and other thoughts.[5] Sometimes it refers to entire living creatures and in other places it refers to an entire living human being. Nefesh

[soul] is used to represent the vital life-giving force providing physical life to animals[6] and people.[7]

While people and animals have a nefesh [soul], only people possess ruah [spirit]. From the many uses, the Old Testament conveys the thought that God gives life, but the mechanisms are not fully developed. Genesis unveils the soul as the vital source of life; it is an intangible, spiritual phenomenon; it is from God; and it is distinct from the body. Scripture says,

> "The Lord God formed the man from the dust of the ground and breathed into his nostrils the breath of life, and the man became a living being [nefesh or soul]."
> Genesis 2:7

From this we know that God breathes life into people, God's breath contains the spirit of life, and somehow when God's breath combines with a human body, the body becomes a living being. The word translated as "living being" is "nefesh" or soul, and the passage is silent on the mechanism.

Later Scripture says,

> "Then the Lord said, "My Spirit [ruah] will not contend with man forever, for he is mortal…." Genesis 6:3

God's "ruah" or the Holy Spirit contends with, governs or regulates man for some period of time, but not forever because man is mortal. This says that God's ruah or the Holy Spirit stops contending with man after some time, presumably when the man dies.

The Old Testament also suggests that each person has a ruah or spirit that leaves when the body dies, and it explains where the ruah goes. When a person's body dies, the spirit returns to God.

> "Remember him – before … the dust returns to the ground it came from, and the spirit returns to God who gave it." Ecclesiastes 12:6-7

The Old Testament indicates that each person has a spirit, which is a gift from God that returns to God when a person's body dies.

NEW TESTAMENT

Originally written in Greek, the New Testament provides greater clarity on the concepts of soul and spirit. The Greek word "pneuma" is often translated as spirit, and "psyche" is often translated as soul. While both psyche [soul] and pneuma [spirit] refer to parts of our intangible self, and they are certainly related, the words refer to unique concepts.[8] As with the box of air, the Greek words are very closely related and evoke images of air and breath, which makes sense because they each refer to intangible parts.

Pneuma has to do with air and serves as the root word for pneumatic. In Scripture it is used to communicate the concept of spirit. It often represents God's Holy Spirit and at times is used to represent that portion of a person's intangible self capable of communing with God. It is that part of a person that directly experiences spiritual life or spiritual death, and that experience influences the soul.

Similar to the Hebrew word "nefesh," psyche is also related to breath – its root word, "psycho," means "breath or to breathe." Psyche refers to the intangible, immaterial portion of a person's being that gives life to our tangible bodies and comprises who we really are. Psychology literally means study of the soul.

The psyche [soul] houses our mind, memory, will, self-consciousness, reasoning, conscience, desires, affections, passions and appetites.[9] It holds our personality, character, temperament, and sense of humor. When you consider all the things that make up a person, the intangible parts of the soul are what really make us who we are. As with the Hebrew word "nefesh," because psyche [soul] refers to so much of a person, it is at times translated in English using words other than soul. In places the word is translated as an entire person, a person's life, mind or other intangible components.[10]

Another word, heart, is also used to describe a person's spiritual self. In Scripture, heart rarely refers to the physical organ pumping blood through a person's body. More often it refers to a person's spiritual self, either as a synonym for soul or generally broad brushing the total spiritual self.

As mentioned earlier, the soul and spirit are very closely related. The soul provides physical life to the body. God provides the possibility of spiritual life to the spirit. The character of a person's spirit influences the soul and reveals itself through action.

So how do I reach these conclusions? I studied uses of psyche, pneuma and derivatives of the words in Scripture in an effort to understand the concepts each word seems to communicate. Let's look at some of the passages leading to the conclusions stated above.

Psyche / Soul

To be clear, the words printed in italics below were each written as psyche or a derivative of psyche in the original Greek.

Psyche Translated as "Life"

Scripture records Jesus saying each of the following:

"Do not worry about your *life (psyche)*...." Matthew 6:25

"The Son of Man came ... to give his *life (psyche)* as ransom...." Matthew 20:28

"If anyone comes to me and does not hate ... his own *life (psyche)*, he is not able to be my disciple." Luke 14:26

"Whoever finds their *life (psyche)* will lose it, and whoever loses their *life (psyche)* for my sake will find it." Matthew 10:39

In these passages psyche is translated as "life" referring to the state of animated existence, the condition separating us from death. Life is the union of body and soul. The soul is what makes people living beings. It is the source of physical life. Re-read the four verses above and replace the word "life" with "soul." Does your understanding of each passage change?

Psyche Translated as "Soul"

In Revelation, John describes his heavenly vision. Twice in the book he describes seeing psyches, translated as "souls," that have become separated from physical bodies and are in heaven. This leaves no doubt that souls are spiritual entities. The descriptions indicate that the psyche or soul leaves the body when the body dies, and at least some go to heaven.

"I saw under the altar the *souls (psychas)* of those who had been slain because of the word of God and the testimony they had maintained." Revelation 6:9

"And I saw the *souls (psychas)* of those who had been beheaded because of their testimony about Jesus and because of the word of God." Revelation 20:4

Psyche Translated as "Mind"

In places, a derivative of the word psyche is translated as "mind," representing the part of a person with cognitive function, memory, intellect, and the ability to think, reason and discern. It is the part of a person with perception tied to a person's emotions, passions and feelings.

"All believers were of one heart and *mind (psyche)*." Acts 4:32

"But the Jews who refused to believe stirred up the Gentiles and poisoned their *minds (psychas)* against their brothers." Acts 14:2

"We have heard that some went out from us without our authorization and disturbed you, troubling your *minds (psychas)* by what they said." Acts 15:24

Psyche Translated as "Heart"

Derivatives of psyche are translated as "heart" in several passages. The word is not used to represent the physical organ pumping blood through arteries and veins; it represents the intangible part housing our feelings, emotion, sympathy and affection.

"Obey them not only to win their favor when their eye is on you, but as slaves of Christ, doing the will of God from your *heart (psyches)*." Ephesians 6:6

"What ever you do, work at it with all your *heart (psyches)*, as working for the Lord, not for human masters." Colossians 3:23

Psyches Need Rest

The psyche is the place where a person's desires, senses, affections and passions exist. And psyches need rest.

"Take my yoke upon you and learn from me, for I am gentile and humble in heart, and you will find rest for your *souls (psychais)*." Matthew 11:29

Psyches Respond to Influence

Psyches may be purified, they may be seduced or enticed, they may be overwhelmed with sorrow, and they may glorify God. They respond to influences around them.

> "My *soul (psyche)* is overwhelmed with sorrow to the point of death. Stay here and keep watch with me." Matthew 26:38

> "And Mary said, 'My *soul (psyche)* glorifies the Lord.'" Luke 1:46

> "Now that you have purified *yourselves (psychas)* by obeying the truth so that you have sincere love for each other, love one another deeply from the heart." 1 Peter 1:22

> "With eyes full of adultery, they never stop sinning; they seduce *the unstable*; they are experts in greed – an accursed brood." (a literal translation of the original Greek, shown here as "seduce the unstable," is "enticing souls (psychas) not established."). 2 Peter 2:14

Translated as Entire Person

Souls have attitudes, which reveal themselves through a person's actions. Souls learn, rest, think, reveal and believe. They may be poisoned, can be strengthened, may be troubled, may inspire work, may be weary, may be tormented and may be purified. They sound a lot like people. In fact, the soul encompasses so much of what makes people who they are, in many places the word psyche is used to represent the entire person.

> "And I will say to *myself (psyche)*, 'You *(psyche)* have plenty of grain laid up for many years. Take life easy; eat, drink and be merry.'" Luke 12:19

"Because you will not abandon *me (psychen)* to the realm of the dead, you will not let your holy one decay." Acts 2:27

"*Everyone (psyche)* was filled with awe at the many wonders and signs performed by the apostles." Acts 2:43

"*Anyone (psyche)* who does not listen will be completely cut off from these people." Acts 3:23

"There will be trouble and distress for every *human being (psychen)* who does evil: first for the Jews, then for the Gentiles." Romans 2:9

"So then, those who suffer according to God's will should commit *themselves (psychas)* to their faithful Creator and continue to do good." 1 Peter 4:19

"But my righteous one will live by faith. And I *(psyche)* take no pleasure in the one who shrinks back." Hebrews 10:38

Our soul is who we are. In fact, if it is possible for you to separate your vision of yourself from how you look in the mirror, you might realize that you are your soul. Your soul houses your character, your personality, your memories, your ability to think, your passions, your desires and your sense of humor. You are not your body. You are your soul. And your spirit influences your soul.

Pneuma / Spirit

While Scripture interprets "pneuma" as "breath" in a few places, in the vast majority of places the word is interpreted as "spirit." Scripture does not say this directly, but after studying Scripture – I wrote passages translating the word pneuma in a notebook covering 12 pages and read them over and over seeking clarity, looking for connections, trying to understand each one – I see the spirit as a separate entity very closely related to our soul. Our spirit takes residence within us, it influences our soul, and is influenced by the realm surrounding us including the world around us, situations in our lives, the people we come into contact with, the Holy Spirit and evil spirits. It all influences our spirit and our spirit influences our soul and our actions.

While Scripture does not really tell us what the spirit is, it provides clues.

Mind and Spirit

Our spirit is closely connected with our mind, but they are separate entities. Paul wrote,

> "For who knows a person's thoughts except their own spirit within them? In the same way no one knows the thoughts of God except the spirit of God." 1 Corinthians 2:11-12

Our minds generate thoughts. In certain situations, the Greek word psyche is interpreted as mind, suggesting that the mind is part of the soul. Paul's statement above indicates mind and spirit are closely related but separate. If the mind and spirit were the same thing, the statement would simply state the obvious – of course the mind knows thoughts that it generates itself. So, the spirit is not the mind but a separate entity so closely related to the mind that it knows what the mind is thinking.

Spirits Leave the Body at Death

Like the soul, the spirit leaves our bodies when physical life stops. Four verses indicate this. According to Matthew and John, when Jesus breathed His last breath, "he gave up his spirit" (see Matthew 22:50 and John 19:30). According to Luke, "Jesus cried out in a loud voice, "Father, into your hands I commit my spirit." When he had said this, he breathed his last" (Luke 23:46). While a crowd of people stoned Stephen, he prayed, "Lord Jesus, receive my spirit" (Acts 7:59).

Spirits Experience Emotion

Passages above suggest that the soul is the seat of emotions. Scripture also indicates that spirits feel emotions and influence our demeanor, attitude, mental state, and emotional state, which influence our actions. Spirits become troubled, distressed, and fervent. People's spirits become joyful through contact with the Holy Spirit. The spirits of some people find peace and some become refreshed. We (our souls) are influenced by the condition of our spirit, and the condition of our spirit reveals itself through our actions. Our soul is the seat of emotion, yet our spirits experience emotion.

> "At that time Jesus, *full of joy through the Holy Spirit*, said, "I praise you, Father, Lord of heaven and earth, because you have hidden these things from the wise and learned, and revealed them to little children." (Luke 10:21

The Holy Spirit interacted with Jesus in a way that made Jesus joyful. Jesus was full of joy through union with the Holy Spirit. His joy must have revealed itself in a way that people around Him observed. He must have acted joyful, otherwise how did the observer know that He felt joy? The Holy Spirit conveyed joy and Jesus responded by joyfully praising God.

"When Jesus saw her weeping, and the Jews who had come along with her also weeping, he was deeply *moved in spirit* and troubled.... Jesus wept." John 11:33 & 35

Again, Jesus was influenced by the emotional state of His spirit. He was "moved in spirit." His spirit was troubled. It grieved. While in the presence of mourning people, His spirit felt sadness. As a result, He wept. He grieved. The condition of our spirit influences us and our actions.

On the evening that Jesus gave Himself up for us, as He and the disciples shared the Last Supper, Jesus spoke with the disciples. He taught at a frenzied pace. He knew what was about to happen and He knew His time with the disciples was drawing to an end. John records part of the conversation like this:

"After he said this, Jesus was *troubled in spirit* and testified, 'Very truly I tell you, one of you is going to betray me.'" John 13:21

Jesus was troubled in spirit and He explained why. The combination of events surrounding Him at that particular time and His knowledge of what He was about to experience influenced the condition of His spirit, which influenced His actions. Similarly, the conditions surrounding Paul while he was in Athens influenced his spirit.

"While Paul was waiting for them in Athens, he [his spirit] was greatly distressed to see that the city was full of idols. So he reasoned in the synagogue with both Jews and God-fearing Greeks, as well as in the marketplace day by day with those who happened to be there." Acts 17:16-17

The literal translation of the original Greek says, "Paul, the spirit of him in him..." The NIV interprets this as "he..." Paul's spirit was distressed or provoked. In response, Paul preached to everyone who would listen. He preached in the synagogue and in the marketplace. In response to his spirit's distress and provocation Paul went to work.

Similarly, Luke describes Apollos as "fervent in spirit."

"He [Apollos of Alexandria] had been instructed in the way of the Lord, and he [being fervent in spirit] spoke with great fervor and taught about Jesus accurately, though he knew only the baptism of Jesus." Acts 18:25

Apollos had a fervent spirit, so he spoke with enthusiasm. In another example, in his letter to the church in Rome Paul urged his readers to maintain "spiritual fervor" as they serve the Lord.

"Never lacking in zeal, but keep your spiritual fervor, serving the Lord." Romans 12:11

Spirits feel emotions that influence our demeanor, attitude, mental state and emotional state – the condition of our souls. Spirits may be joyful, fervent, distressed, provoked or troubled. They grieve. The emotional state of our spirit influences our soul, and our soul influences our actions.

The World Influences our Spirits

The world around us, including other people, and the pressures, situations and chaos of life, influence our spirits. Passages quoted above describe Jesus as joyful in response to the indwelling of the Holy Spirit, grieving in response to people mourning around Him, and troubled in response to the torture and separation from God He was about to endure. Paul is described as "greatly distressed" over the many idols worshiped in Athens. One passage describes Apollos' spirit as fervent for the Lord. The situations we encounter along the path of life and the people around us influence our spirits. Paul mentions this in his letters to the church in Corinth.

"I was glad when Stephanas, Fortunatus and Achaicus arrived, because they have supplied what was lacking from you. For *they refreshed my spirit* and yours also. Such men deserve recognition." 1 Corinthians 16:18

"I still had no peace of mind [rest for my spirit], because I did not find my brother Titus there. So I said goodbye to them and went on to Macedonia." 2 Corinthians 2:13

"By all this we were encouraged. In addition to our own encouragement, we were especially delighted to see how happy Titus was, because *his spirit has been refreshed* by all of you." 2 Corinthians 7:13

External forces influence our spirits, and our spirits influence our souls revealing themselves through action. I provide the examples above because they include spiritual greats like Jesus and Paul, and some more normal sounding folks like Apollos, Stephanas, Fortunatus and Achaicus. Jesus was filled with the Holy Spirit, yet His spirit suffered from the world around Him. His spirit felt the joy of the Holy Spirit, but His spirit also felt grief when He saw Mary and others weeping, and the grief in His spirit caused Him to weep. His spirit was troubled just before He gave Himself up for us. In that context I imagine "troubled" means an awful combination of sadness, anger, disappointment and anticipation of the ugliness, the evil weight of sin He would soon experience.

Paul was also filled with the Holy Spirit. This is probably why his spirit was greatly distressed when he saw people worshiping idols. Based on his response to the distress, I imagine he was filled with compassion, sadness and anger for the people who were being mislead, so he set to work to correct the wrong.

If Jesus' and Paul's spirits, filled with the Holy Spirit as they were, were influenced by the world around them, how much more likely is it that our spirits will be influenced by the world around us?

Spirits Possess Personal Qualities

Scripture mentions that the human spirit possesses knowledge, and it describes some spirits as strong. Scripture tells us that Jesus knew in His spirit what other people were thinking, and it describes John the Baptist as being strong in spirit, indicating he had God's wisdom and temperament.

> "Immediately *Jesus knew in his spirit* that this was what they were thinking in their hearts, and he said to them, "why are you thinking these things?"" Mark 2:8

> "And the child grew and became *strong in spirit*; and he lived in the wilderness until he appeared publicly to Israel." Luke 1:80

Spirit, Soul & Flesh

Our spirits seem to be fighting to be recognized so that they might influence us (or our souls) and, through us (or our souls), our actions. As Judas received his payment and gathered the guards, Jesus went with the disciples to the garden to pray. Jesus asked Peter, James and John to keep watch with Him, but they fell asleep. Jesus woke them and said,

> "Watch and pray so that you will not fall into temptation. The spirit is willing, but the flesh is weak." Matthew 26:41 (see also Mark 14:38)

"Flesh" is neither good nor bad: it is judged by its spiritual connections. In places, Scripture uses the word "flesh" to describe positive things, like when John writes,

> "The Word became flesh and made his dwelling among us. We have seen his glory, the glory of the one

and only Son, who came from the Father, full of grace
and truth." John 1:14

John is using the word "flesh" to describe a living person
– a body with a soul. It refers to the combined entity of body and
soul – a body made alive and activated by a soul. Here, the "flesh"
refers to something positive because the flesh described is united
with a pure soul and a spirit connected with God. In other places,
"flesh" has a negative connotation because it is connected to an
impure soul. "Flesh" is neither inherently good nor bad. It
becomes good or bad based on its spiritual connections.

When Jesus speaks to the disciples in the garden, "flesh"
has a negative meaning. Here the flesh is our worldly self,
separated from God and not aided by God's spiritual
transformation. In contrast to the spirit, flesh is weak.

Jesus says this in the context of prayer. He urges the
disciples to pray "so that" they will be able to overcome
temptation. Prayer connects people with God; prayer connects
the human spirit with God's Holy Spirit, and gradually our
transformed spirit transforms our soul. But we have to pray and
we have to open our flesh to the influence resulting from prayer,
from God and from the resulting transformed spirit.

Transformation of Spirit & Soul

This is similar to Paul's writing. He frequently contrasts
heavenly, righteous and Godly characteristics against worldly,
sinful, selfish characteristics, and he describes the transformation
of a person's soul as a gradual process. The Holy Spirit flows into
the human spirit at the moment of belief, but the transformation
of the soul is a gradual process starting at that moment and
continuing for the rest of the person's life. This means followers
of Christ live in some level of conflict – they experience the Holy,
the Divine, the Pure, yet they still experience desires that are
anything but holy and pure.

How can this be? How can a person have the Spirit of
God dwelling within them, yet still be subject to sinful desires?

This is one place where the division between soul and spirit is critical, at least to my understanding. The Holy Spirit dwells within the human spirit at the moment of belief, and the transformed spirit gradually works on the human soul. Little by little, day-by-day, the Holy Spirit's influence works on the soul.

Paul, who was most certainly filled with the Holy Spirit, describes the conflict in a somewhat psychotic sounding tirade writing,

> "We know that the law is spiritual; but *I am unspiritual*, sold as a slave to sin. I do not understand what I do. For what I want to do I do not do, but what I hate I do. And if I do what I do not want to do, I agree that the law is good. As it is, it is no longer I myself who do it, but it is sin living in me. For I know that good itself does not dwell in me, that is, in my sinful nature. For I have the desire to do what is good, but I cannot carry it out. For I do not do the good I want to do, but the evil I do not want to do – this I keep on doing. Now if I do what I do not want to do, it is no longer I who do it, but it is *sin living in me* that does it." Romans 7:14-20

As a quick ancillary comment, the word translated as "unspiritual" in the first line above is "fleshly" in a literal translation, further connecting this quote to the discussion above. Paul is filled with the Holy Spirit, yet he still has "sin living in [him]." While his spirit knows the Holy Spirit, the transformation of his soul is a gradual work in progress.

I have made four assertions about the Holy Spirit without support. Please allow me to restate them, and then provide the support below.

1. The Holy Spirit dwells within believers;

2. The Holy Spirit enters a person at the moment of belief;

3. The Holy Spirit dwells within the human spirit; and

4. The Holy Spirit gradually transforms the soul in a process that likely takes the remainder of a person's life.

A lot of verses stand for the idea that the Holy Spirit dwells within believers. Four are provided below, one from Jesus, two from Paul and one from Peter.

On the evening of the Last Supper, Jesus spoke a great deal about the Holy Spirit. During the evening He said,

> "And I will ask the Father, and he will give you another advocate to help you and be with you forever – *the Spirit of truth*. The world cannot accept him, because it neither sees him nor knows him. But you know him, for *he lives with you and will be in you*." John 14:16-17

In two of his letters to the church in Corinth, Paul wrote,

> "Do you not know that your bodies are temples of the *Holy Spirit, who is in you*, whom you have received from God?" 1 Corinthians 6:19; and

> "Now it is God who makes both us and you stand firm in Christ. He anointed us, set his seal of ownership on us, and *put his Spirit in our hearts* as a deposit, guaranteeing what is to come." 2 Corinthians 1:21-22

49 days after Jesus' resurrection, Peter preached his first sermon. He stood in the Temple in Jerusalem and publicly proclaimed the good news of Jesus Christ to many of the same people who only seven weeks earlier called for His crucifixion.

During the sermon people were convicted of their sin, and they asked Peter what should we do?

> "Peter replied, 'Repent and be baptized, every one of you, in the name of Jesus Christ for the forgiveness of your sins. And *you will receive the gift of the Holy Spirit.* The promise is for you and your children and for all who are far off – for all whom the Lord our God will call.'" Acts 2:38-39

So when does this happen? When does the Holy Spirit take residence within the believer? The quotes above are vague with respect to the timing. Peter says, "And you will receive the gift of the Holy Spirit" and Jesus says "he ... will be in you" but neither specifies when it will happen. In Paul's quotes above, he presumes the indwelling has already happened and the Holy Spirit is at that moment abiding within his readers. Paul clarifies the timing by writing,

> "And you also were included in Christ when you heard the message of truth, the gospel of your salvation. *When you believed, you were marked with a seal, the promised Holy Spirit,* who is a deposit guaranteeing our inheritance until the redemption of those who are God's possession – to the praise of his glory." Ephesians 1:13-14

At the moment of belief, the Holy Spirit is deposited in the believer. Following is an additional passage supporting the conclusion:

> "You, however, are not in the flesh but are in the realm of the Spirit, if indeed the Spirit of God lives in you. And if anyone does not have the Spirit of Christ, they do not belong to Christ." Romans 8:9

People who do not have the Holy Spirit dwelling within them do not belong to Christ. It seems logical to conclude that the opposite is also true – people who belong to Christ have the Holy Spirit dwelling within them. The moment of belief, the moment a person accepts Jesus as his or her Lord and Savior equates to moment of belonging to Christ. Based on the verse, logic suggests that followers of Christ have the Holy Spirit dwelling within them.

Okay, so here is my question. If the Holy Spirit dwells within a person the moment he or she believes and accepts Jesus Christ as their savior, why do we still struggle with sinful desires? The Holy Spirit is God, who is pure, divine and holy. If purity and divinity and holiness dwell within a person, wouldn't the person be made pure? How can sinful desire and holiness exist within the same person at the same time?

And if you wonder whether this really happens, begin by considering your own experience, then consider Paul's somewhat psychotic tirade above. If that does not convince you, consider this verse,

> "Brothers and sisters, if someone is caught in sin, you who live by the Spirit should restore that person gently. But watch yourselves, or you also may be tempted." Galatians 6:1

Paul urges Spirit-filled believers to proceed with caution because they are susceptible to sin and temptation. So how is this possible? If sin is the absence of God or the state of being separated from God, how is it possible for a person to have God's Holy Spirit dwelling within them yet still have sinful desire?

To me, the answer only makes sense if the spirit and soul are separate entities. The Holy Spirit dwells within the person's spirit. While the Holy Spirit transforms the human spirit at that time, the transformation of the soul takes a long time. It is a long, gradual process. Many passages discuss this as a gradual transformation. Here are three.

After discussing the lifestyle of nonbelievers – their sinful lives, focus on selfish pleasure, and separation from God – Paul discusses the gradual transformation of a believer's soul. As you read the following passages please keep in mind that Paul writes to believers – people who have the indwelling Holy Spirit. In his letter to the Ephesians, Paul writes,

> "That, however, is not the way of life you learned when you heard about Christ and were taught in him in accordance with the truth that is in Jesus. You were taught, with regard to your former way of life, to put off your old self, which is being corrupted by its deceitful desires; to be made new in the attitude of your minds; and to put on the new self, created to be like God in true righteousness and holiness." Ephesians 4:20-24

The Greek word psyche is interpreted as soul and mind. Mind is part of the soul. The believer's mind and soul are being made new in righteousness and holiness. It is a process that is underway. It is not a one-time event that happened in the past, at the moment of belief; it is happening and will continue to happen. He writes a similar message to the Colossians:

> "Put to death, therefore, whatever belongs to your earthly nature: sexual immorality, impurity, lust, evil desires and greed, which is idolatry. Because of these, the wrath of God is coming. You used to walk in these ways, in the life you once lived. But now you must rid yourselves of all such things as these: anger, rage, malice, slander, and filthy language from your lips. Do not lie to each other, since you have taken off your old self with its practices and have *put on the new self, which is being renewed* in knowledge in the image of its Creator." Colossians 3:5-12

Similarly, the new self "is being renewed" and is being transformed into holiness like God, the Creator. In his letter to people in Rome, Paul wrote,

> "Therefore, I urge you, brothers and sisters, in view of God's mercy, to offer your bodies as a living sacrifice, holy and pleasing to God – this is your true and proper worship. Do not conform to the pattern of this world, *but be transformed by the renewing of your mind.* Then you will be able to test and approve what God's will is – his good, pleasing and perfect will." Romans 12:1-2

The "renewing of your mind" or soul is an ongoing process.

Of the four points mentioned above, I have provided supporting Scripture for three. I have not supported the third point, namely that the Holy Spirit dwells within the human spirit. Scripture says the Holy Spirit dwells within humans, but it does not specify the location within humans. Nonetheless, I believe it is a true statement because it helps me make sense of the subtleties described above.

CONCLUSION

> "For the word of God is living and active. Sharper than any double-edged sword, it penetrates even to *dividing soul and spirit,* joints and marrow; it judges the thoughts and attitudes of the heart." Hebrews 4:12

The living Word of God divides soul and spirit. The Holy Spirit transforms our soul and spirit, but at different rates.

I have heard people quote C.S. Lewis as having said that we are a soul and we have a body. I have not found the statement in his books, but I have heard the statement attributed to him.

Whether Lewis said or wrote this or not, it stands for the notion that our soul is who we really are, that our soul contains the essence of our beings, and that our bodies are mere vehicles for our use while we have physical life on earth. The statement accurately reflects the importance of our souls, but it neglects our spirits and possibly understates the importance of our bodies. But given the inflated value often attributed to bodies and the physical realm, perhaps the latter point is an intended consequence. We have a body; we are a soul; our spirit influences us; and our spirits are influenced by the world around us.

4 | IMAGE OF GOD

"Then God said, 'Let us make mankind in our image, in our likeness, so that they may rule over the fish in the sea and the birds in the sky, over the livestock and all the wild animals, and over all the creatures that move along the ground.' So God created mankind in his own image, in the image of God, he created them; male and female he created them." Genesis 1:26-27

FOUNDATIONAL THOUGHTS

Our understanding of God and who we are in relation to Him drive our worldview. Our view of humanity, the world and our standing are dependent on our view of God. For example, if we believe God is nonexistent, our basis of morality is diminished, possibly erased, we begin to see humans as the ultimate authority on earth, and we begin to craft rules bound only by our desires. Scripture presents God as eternally present with characteristics beyond our ability to describe or understand. His power is beyond the capacity of our language to describe and our minds to comprehend – He created all matter in the universe out of nothing by uttering the word making it so.[1] He is holy, pure, divine, love, wrath, and the standard upon which everything rests, but each word rings hollow because our language is too limited to communicate the heavenly, our points of references are restricted to this world, and our minds lack the bandwidth.

The most meaningful way to consider God and His majesty is through the lens of people who encountered Him, survived the experience, and wrote about it. They are left trying to describe the indescribable. The colors are more vivid, the sounds fuller, the brightness brighter than anything on earth, and God's heavenly glory has no earthly counterpart. So they resort to the tools they possess to communicate the heavenly to other earth dwellers, feebly comparing God's heavenly glory to the brightest gems and His voice to the loudest sound.

The prophet Ezekiel suddenly sees heaven and he describes "an immense cloud with flashing lightning and surrounded by a brilliant light. The center of the fire looked like glowing metal" (Ezekiel 1:4).

One day Peter, James and John were on a mountain with Jesus when suddenly two long-dead prophets, Elijah and Moses, appeared and talked with Jesus, and Jesus' appearance was transformed. They said His "face shone like the sun and his clothes became white as the light" (Matthew 17:2).

Years later, John prays in a cave on the island Patmos when suddenly his eyes open and he sees a throne in heaven. He tries to describe what he sees, and he says the one sitting on the throne looks like "jasper and ruby" (Revelation 4:3), and something like an emerald rainbow encircles the throne, and it flashes like lightning. He describes the sound of heaven "like the roar of rushing waters and like a loud peal of thunder" (Revelation 14:2). As he tries to describe God's glory in heaven, John resorts to the brightest and loudest things on earth, and they undoubtedly pale in comparison.

Scripture makes it clear that God's heavenly glory is without earthly comparison, and that those who encounter God instantly know they are nothing compared to Him. Some throw themselves to the ground in awe and worship Him and they know they do not belong in His holy presence because for the first time they are exposed to holiness, and they realize how sinful they are.

The prophet Isaiah suddenly peers into heaven and sees God sitting on a throne surrounded by angelic creatures unlike anything on earth continuously singing "Holy, holy, holy is the Lord of hosts; the whole earth is full of his glory" (Isaiah 6:3). Isaiah knows he is unworthy to be in God's holy presence and he says, "Woe is me! I am lost, for I am a man of unclean lips and I live among a people of unclean lips; yet my eyes have seen the King, the Lord of hosts!" (Isaiah 6:5).

Similarly, John's eyes suddenly open and he sees Jesus Christ in His heavenly glory, and while John knew Jesus as a man on earth, His appearance was different in heaven. John writes, "When I saw him, I fell at his feet as though dead" (Revelation 1:17).

Walking along the road leading to Damascus, Paul encounters Jesus Christ through a heavenly bright light.[2] Paul falls to the ground in awe and immediately changes his life entirely and starts following Jesus.

Even the most righteous people are impure, unholy and sinful in comparison to God, and when mere humans encounter Him, they instantly know they are too sinful to survive His holy presence. We are nothing compared to Him and His appearance is without earthly comparison, yet Scripture says God creates humans in His image. What does that mean?

When I hear the word "image" or "likeness," I think of appearance. What does God look like? If we look like God, then

He must look like us. Is God male or female? Does God have dark skin or light skin? What color are God's hair and eyes? When I think of the word "image" my mind races in the direction of physical appearance, and it is the wrong direction.

So does image have more to do with character or personality? Considering it from this angle, different questions arise. God's presence and character are incompatible with sin, so if every human is created in His image, why do humans harm one another? Why does evil exist? Or perhaps the better question is, how is it possible for evil to exist? Let's consider the image of God and sin.

SPIRITUAL FOCUS

Spiritual Presence

God said to the prophet Jeremiah, "Do not I fill heaven and earth?" (Jeremiah 23:24). God fills heaven and earth. God is everywhere all at once.

In 1990 NASA sent the Hubble telescope into orbit. It has since been serviced several times and has transmitted amazing images of distant galaxies. Information from Hubble has allowed scientists to identify the rate at which the universe is expanding, to identify dark energy, to identify over 900 planets outside our solar system, and to accomplish many remarkable things.

Since 1990, NASA has launched other satellites into space. They regularly transmit images and information back to NASA where scientists analyze the information. In 2003, the WMAP satellite sent an image of what is believed to be the most distant part of the universe that can be observed using light. The image is of a galaxy 14 billion light years away. There may be, and likely are, galaxies farther away, but we cannot see them because the light has not reached us yet. Our ability to observe distances in space are limited not by distance, but by time. By simply waiting we will be see light that originated farther away.

Imagine the galaxy observed in the WMAP satellite image, the galaxy 14 billion light years away. God is there. God fills heaven and earth. God is everywhere. God's Holy Presence is not limited by time or space. He can be and is here and there and everywhere all at the same time.

If God is omnipresent, if He is everywhere, if He is not bound by time or space, it seems impossible for God to have a physical form. God must be 100% spirit without physical form. Jesus confirms this saying, "God is spirit" (John 4:24). So saying God created us in His image must mean something other than physical appearance.

The passage first quoted above says God created mankind in His image "so that they may rule…" This suggests that the passage has something to do with authority. God is the Creator. He has all authority, including the authority to delegate. The verse suggests a limited assignment of authority to mankind. But are the assignment of authority and God's image related? The concepts are discussed together. Did God need to create people in His image before He was comfortable delegating authority to them?

The fact that God is spirit suggests the words refer to our spiritual selves. Does the verse mean that our soul and spirit are created in God's image? If so, what does that mean? If God's image or likeness includes no physical attributes, what attributes does it cover? What do we know about God's character, nature or being? What do we know about God?

Spiritual Time

God is eternal, without beginning or end. He exists outside of time. If our souls and spirits are created in God's image, does that mean that our souls and spirits are eternal? Do they age? Are they bound by time? So long as our physical bodies bind them, they are bound by time. But do they, in and of themselves, age?

Apart from physical aches and pains, do you feel like the same person you were when you were much younger? If I close my eyes and don't look in the mirror, in some ways I feel exactly like I did a long time ago. When I am watching a major league baseball game or a video of people skiing extreme snowy slopes,

I catch myself thinking, "I can do that" before laughing at the absurdity of the thought. My father who is in his 80's says, "In my mind feel just like I did when I was 20." When he was younger he was a Golden Glove boxer, and today as he watches a boxing match and becomes engaged in the action, his body twists, turns and jerks as if he is in the ring. Maybe our souls and spirits have not aged as quickly as our bodies have, or maybe the notion of age is irrelevant to the soul and spirit.

Our concept of time is tied to the physical realm. Einstein made famous the connection between time and space in the Theory of Relativity. Travel fast enough and the passage of time slows. Space and time are not simply two independent features of our reality here on earth; they are inseparably linked. And time is not an absolute. It is not fixed. It is variable depending on an object's relationship to space – rate of travel alters the passage of time, but time seems like a constant because we are all on this ball called Earth traveling through space at the same speed. If time and space are inseparably connected, it follows that time is a physical concept, and that time does not exist in the spiritual realm.

Are souls and spirits eternal? The best answer is sort of. They are immortal, their existence continues forever, but each had a beginning. God is eternal – He had no beginning and has no end. God has always been and always will be. If you imagine a timeline, God's existence goes to eternity in both directions, backwards and forwards without end. Souls on the other hand are created by God, so they have a beginning and are not eternal because the timeline for each only goes from the point of its creation forward. Jesus teaches that souls have everlasting existence, saying that some souls will go to eternal punishment and some will go to eternal life. Jesus says,

> "They also will answer, 'Lord, when did we see you hungry or thirsty or a stranger or needing clothes or sick or in prison, and did not help you?'
>
> "He will reply, 'Truly I tell you, whatever you did not do for one of the least of these, you did not do for me.'

"Then they will go away *to eternal punishment,* but the righteous *to eternal life."* Matthew 25:44-46

While Scripture uses the word translated as "eternal" in places referring to quality of life, here it refers to time. The passage indicates that souls are immortal while posing a question regarding where each will spend eternity. Jesus describes two eternal resting places, each option involves time without end. Jesus also teaches that a sentence of eternal punishment is equivalent to death for the soul saying,

> "Do not be afraid of those who kill the body but cannot kill the soul. Rather, be afraid of the One who can destroy both soul and body in hell." Matthew 10:28

A soul that spends eternity in hell is a destroyed soul because it is separated from God from that point forward forever without the opportunity for reconciliation. Jesus says,

> "Truly I tell you, whatever you bind on earth will be bound in heaven, and whatever you loose on earth will be loosed in heaven." Matthew 18:18 (see also Matthew 16:19)

Choices, actions and the underlying condition of our spiritual selves while we are alive on earth have an everlasting impact. "Whatever you bind on earth will be bound in heaven."

Characteristics of God

Scripture tells us that God is spirit.[3] God is the Creator of all things.[4] God is the standard of justice, His judgment is perfect, His work is perfect, and He is faithful.[5] He never lies.[6] God is love.[7] He is merciful, filled with grace, slow to anger and forgiving.[8] He is righteous and He loves righteousness.[9] God provides the standard for perfection in reasoning, love, clarity of thought, crystal clear judgment and wisdom. He sees truth as truth and falsehood as falsehood. God does not make mistakes.

If our soul and spirit are created in God's image, and if that means that mankind has God's capacity to love and God's clarity of judgment and soundness of mind and crystal clear discernment, why are we such a mess? Why do we get confused? Why do we make bad decisions and poor judgments? Why do we mistake falsehood as truth? And why do we fail to treat each other with love? How can we possibly represent the image of the Incorruptible, the Divine, the Holy Creator?

The Hebrew word translated as "image" in the passage above is transliterated as "selem," referring to "spiritual, intellectual and moral likeness"[10] of God, but it does not refer to an exact duplicate. When we think of images today, we are familiar with super-high definition photographs and video that, when combined with giant high-definition screens, allow us to see images in greater clarity than we could see if looking at the real live thing directly in front of us. But "selem" refers to something more like a shadow of the original, "representing the original in an imprecise manner and lacking the essential characteristics of the original"[11] and it refers to spiritual qualities.

Our souls and spirits have spiritual characteristics that are similar to God's spirit, but they are like shadows of the real thing. We have a rational mind and we have some clarity of thought, but we cannot think as clearly as God. We have the ability to discern and judge, but we make mistakes. We have emotions, passion and appetite, but often for things we should not desire. When we commune with God, when we allow His Holy Spirit within our spirit and we allow that indwelling to gradually transform our soul, we gradually replace selfishness with concern for others and we convey what Paul refers to as fruit of the Spirit: "love, joy, peace, forbearance, kindness, goodness, faithfulness, gentleness and self-control" (Galatians 5:22-23).

SEPARATION FROM GOD

In the beginning, God created people in His image and they communed freely with Him in the Garden of Eden. They spoke with God and He responded. They were comfortable with naked bodies. They knew nothing of evil or sin because they lived in communion with God. But evil was in the world and suddenly, as a result of horrific personal choice, God banished people from His presence and cursed the earth,[12] and death came to humans.[13]

The separation of humans from God began with the act in history referred to by some as original sin. Adam and Eve tasted forbidden fruit, their eyes were opened, they suddenly had knowledge of good and evil, they were separated from God, and the earth started producing painful things.[14] With respect to creation, Scripture says as a result of the fall the serpent was cursed, enmity existed between the woman and the serpent, childbearing became painful, conflict arose between husband and wife, and God cursed the earth, setting in motion death, natural disasters, storms, earthquakes, diseases, viruses, bacterial infection and other pain-causing things.

Scripture discusses sin as thoughts and acts contrary to God's will, missing the mark of God's standard, or rebelling against God and His design for humanity.[15] It also discusses sin as a power enslaving humans saying,

> "Jews and Gentiles alike are all under sin. As it is written: 'There is no one righteous, not even one; there is no one who understands, no one who seeks God.'" Romans 3:9-11, and

> "Therefore, just as sin entered the world through one man, and death through sin, and in this way death came to all men, because all sinned – for before the law was given, sin was in the world." Romans 5:12-13

Sin is a presence, force, or state of being, and every human is under it. As a result, sin impacts our thoughts and actions, but what is this thing labelled "sin"? Sin is separation from God, and thoughts or actions are sinful if they enhance our separation from God. Adam and Eve's choice in the garden was the first separation, or the original sin. By tasting the fruit they became sinful and every person after them inherited sin as part of their DNA. All of humanity is under the power of sin, yet people are still created with some of God's image. The original version of God's image that was revealed through people was slightly unclear or shadowy, and it became even less clear and more shadowy when people were separated from God.

I have had many conversations in which people discuss the concept of sin exclusively as actions violating a moral or legal code, and the label "sinner" is often used as a synonym for "bad person," and when some are referred to as "sinners" they hear an expression of judgment indicating the speaker's belief that the "sinner" is going to hell. If our view of sin and sinner focuses exclusively on conduct and thoughts, and if we confuse sin and salvation, we miss the point. Sin is the state in which we live while here on earth because we are separated from God. Our choices, actions and behavior influence and reveal the condition of our soul and spirit, and they lead either toward or away from God, but, with the single exception of Jesus Christ, we are each a sinner and we are each sinful. To be labelled a sinner is to be labelled a human.

Whether you go out of your way to do everything right (you are kind and generous, never judge, never speed, never curse, never gossip, never harm others, never consume harmful substances purely for pleasure – you refrain from every "bad" activity all the time), or whether you have participated in evil few can imagine, we all share certain characteristics: (i) we are each created in God's image; (ii) we are each sinners separated from God; (iii) God loves each of us; and (iv) we each have the possibility of redemption through Jesus Christ.

This leads us to consider the concepts of good and bad. Scripture makes it clear that only God is good.[16] Choices leading us toward God are good. Other choices are bad and may be referred to as sinful choices. But no matter how bad your choices might have been, you still possess the four traits mentioned in the previous paragraph.[17]

Conversations like this often lead to questions relating to whether people are inherently good or inherently evil, which is a fool's game. It is laden with traps. If you say people are good but learn evil we are confronted with Scripture saying that only God is good, but if you say people are born evil we are confronted with the heart-wrenching question, "how can a newborn baby who just started breathing and who has not done anything possibly be evil?" Before we can have that discussion we must define our terminology because if "good" is established by Godly standards, no mere human can possibly be good, ever (unless of course that human is also God). But if "good" is established by some range of relative human standards, where some people are good and others are bad, then the question is much more debatable.

To be clear, traps notwithstanding, only God is good and compared to Him even newborn babies are sinful because they are humans carrying post-Adam DNA. But the question wrongly focuses on action rather than the frailty of the human heart and the need for spiritual transformation. From birth we are in dire need of spiritual transformation.

I have a friend whose occupation is front man for a rock and roll band. He has a long blond ponytail and he wears tights, boots, a tank top showing his guns and lots of make-up while performing. During a recent conversation he mentioned that his grandfather was a Methodist pastor and described fond memories growing up in the church and going to summer church camp in Arkansas. He mentioned his grandfather's favorite joke about how Arkansas is the only state referenced in Scripture (punch line – Noah looked at the ark and saw). He expressed a desire to renew his relationship with God, he said he has been attending a local church with his wife and kids, but shrugged, smiled, mentioned his rock and roll occupation and laughed about all the awful things he has done. He used the words "sin," "sinner" and "sinful" as if his actions and experiences were the fundamental problems, rather than our shared humanity, the condition of our hearts, and our shared desperate need for spiritual transformation by and through Christ Jesus.

I am sinful. You are sinful. Every person you see as you travel through life is sinful. This is true whether you are looking at _____(fill in the name of the vilest most evil person you can imagine) or _____(fill in the name of the holiest person you can imagine except Jesus Christ). Every person is a sinner. Sin is part of every person's DNA. We each find ourselves in this mucky, murky realm loaded with contradiction. God exists. His Holy Spirit is all around us. His holy grace is showering over each of us, yet we are separated from Him and His grace. The question is not whether we are sinners (we are); the question is whether we are moving toward God or away from God.

Why Does Sin Matter?

Given the entirety of that discussion about sin, you might be wondering why does it matter? If everyone is a sinner and I inherited that condition at birth, why does it matter? And if it matters, why did God make me this way?

Here's the thing – God hates sin and sin is death. God is holy and holiness is incompatible with sin. We need God to live full and complete lives. He designed us to live in communion with Him, our purpose will be fulfilled through His will, and He desires for us each to be with Him, but sin blocks all that and corrupts our vision and thinking.

God is the Creator of life, and Jesus Christ came to earth to give life, but sin is death. Before Adam and Eve ate the fruit, God promised that if they ate it, they would die and through that act of rebellion death became reality for all humans.[18] Paul writes,

> "Therefore, just as sin entered the world through one man, and death through sin, and in this way death came to all men, because all sinned ..." Romans 5:12, and

> "For the wages of sin is death, but the gift of God is eternal life in Christ Jesus our Lord." Romans 6:23

Through sin we are spiritually dead and separated from God, and we will die apart from God if we do not correct the situation, and the only path to life is through Christ Jesus.

Why did God make us this way? He respects human will enough to allow the consequences of our choices to play out. He allows the consequences of Adam and Eve's choice to continue, and He respects each person's choice to either enter communion with Him through Christ Jesus or not.

SPIRITUAL TRANSFORMATION

How do we know which way we are heading? God gives us tools to help with this dilemma. He provides Scripture, His holy living word including the Law of Moses, as a guide to proper behavior and as a tool with sanctifying power.[19] He sent Jesus to earth for many reasons, one of which is to provide an example of righteous behavior. And He sends His Holy Spirit to transform our spirit and to convict each person of sin,[20] which means to gain new insight or knowledge identifying something in your life separating you from God, or identifying certain behavior increasing the separation between you and God.

How do we do it? How do we change direction? This is the question implied by my rock star friend. While we can make choices with our physical body that help – we can go to places where other people who are making good choices surround us and make similar choices – ultimately the change is spiritual.

Spiritual transformation lies at the heart of Scripture. Beginning with creation and moving quickly to original sin, Scripture reveals many ways God communicates the availability of and the importance of spiritual transformation. Through Genesis, Exodus, the Law of Moses and the prophets we see, like the rhythmic rise and fall of ocean tide, the rise and fall and rise and fall and rise of God's people. And through Jesus' teaching and Paul's writing we see the continuation of this message – our spiritual transformation is of extreme importance and the first step in the process is believing in, intimately knowing and identifying ourselves with Jesus Christ. Original sin was the first separation from God, and Jesus Christ is the only avenue back to God, the only path toward regaining increasingly more of God's image in our spirit and soul, and the way to spiritual life, and life abundant.

By describing Himself as "the way and the truth and the life" (John 14:6), Jesus is describing Himself as the path to God – the bridge between sinful people and the holy One. And just to eliminate any doubt, Jesus follows that statement by saying, "No one comes to the Father except through me" (John 14:6).

But we need not do it on our own. In fact, we cannot do it on our own. Our choices matter and we have responsibility, but we are unable to start the process of moving toward God on our own, we need the Holy Spirit's help. God showers us with His holy grace, stirring our hearts, causing us to question, opening our eyes and ears to see and hear. Faith is a gift from God, but how do we access His help? We respond to His stirring and believe that Jesus Christ is who He claims to be, and accept everything that comes along with that belief, and ask the Holy Spirit to help us. It begins with God and His holy grace, followed by belief and faith, followed by spiritual transformation leading to changed behavior.

Who Am I?

The thought of being created in God's image makes me consider "who am I?" and "who do I want to become?" What is my identity? What is my identity tied to? When someone asks me to tell them about myself, how do I answer?

If you meet someone for the first time and they ask, "what do you do?" do you answer with your title at work? Many asking the question may expect an answer describing a person's occupation, and people who work spend a significant percentage of their waking hours at work, so for many it may be the most accurate answer. The answer might be "I am a mechanic" or a fireman, attorney, professor, stay at home mom, stay at home dad or another appropriate description. But if you are asked to "tell me about yourself," is your answer the same?

Years ago I heard or read a story about a man visiting a school on career day. When it was his turn to speak, the teacher asked the man to describe his occupation. He said, "I am a follower of Jesus Christ and I serve Him by working as a doctor." He continued to explain what he does as a doctor. But his answer clarified that his self-image was tied to his faith, not his occupation.

Is your identity tied to work or position? Is it tied to social status, power or education? Is it tied to your role as a parent or spouse, or to your spouse's position? Is it tied to your status as a son, daughter, brother or sister? Possibly the answer depends on the setting, who is asking the question and the context of the conversation.

We place ourselves at great risk when we tie our identity to things that change. Companies change, positions change, people get fired, sometimes for reasons that have nothing to do with personal performance. Imagine the top salesman at the company that made the best manual typewriters. He was the best at what he did and he worked at the best company doing what they did, but the world around them changed. If we replace the typewriter with some other once common but now obsolete item like photographic film, buggy whip, or payphone, we see how fluid the world is. And if our identity is tied to a moving target we never know who we are.

The business model of our oil and gas focused private funds involved purchasing wells that were producing and selling product, and forming a new company to operate existing wells and drill new wells. We were always looking for the right people to build new companies around. Some people moved up quickly within large companies before seizing the entrepreneurial spirit and launching a new company with private equity funding.

One of my good friends had spent most his career as a chief officer of publicly traded oil and gas companies. He had negotiated countless transactions involving acquisition of companies and assets. His deal making experience was blended with his position at large companies, and his negotiating power was tied to the authority of his position and the company's power. He left the publicly traded company and went to work with a private-equity-backed startup.

A few months later we met for breakfast and he laughed at how his ability to negotiate had changed. He once was a master negotiator, always able to get the best deal for his employer. But at breakfast he explained that in his new position he was being forced to accept terms that he would have never accepted before, and he understood that his negotiating skills had been aided by the business card he previously carried.

Please don't get me wrong; I am not being critical of my friend at all. He is extremely smart, thoughtful, hard working, good at his job, and a good guy, but while he was in a high position at the larger company, in certain situations he had allowed his self-image to merge with his position and it took a change of position for him to realize it.

And I wonder if he experienced what I felt even at a much lower elevation than he enjoyed. There was a time when I walked with an expanded air of confidence and dignity because of the respect and deference my position afforded me during meetings and professional encounters, and my newfound dignity influenced my demeanor outside of work. I wonder whether he fell into the trap also. I have seen it happen to many others. We spend so much time at work, we must guard against tying our self-image to our professional lives.

It is common for people to grieve the loss of position because their self-image is tied to it, and when the position is gone they do not know who they are. For many men, retirement starts a long grieving process. They feel as if they have lost themselves and their purpose. They no longer know who they are. For many women, particularly stay at home moms, a very similar situation arises when the youngest child moves out of the home.

Connecting Identity with God

Who are you? What is your identity tied to? If it is tied to something fluid, please consider connecting yourself to the only One that will not change – God. You were created in God's image. Does this influence your view of yourself?

Three of the four Gospels tell the story of Jesus speaking with a rich young man. Here is Matthew's version:

> Now a man came up to Jesus and asked, "Teacher, what good thing must I do to get eternal life?"
>
> "Why do you ask me about what is good?" Jesus replied. "There is only One who is good. If you want to enter life, obey the commandments."
>
> "Which ones?" the man inquired.
>
> Jesus replied, "Do not murder, do not commit adultery, do not steal, do not give false testimony, honor your father and mother, and 'love your neighbor as yourself.'"
>
> "All these I have kept," the young man said. "What do I still lack?"
>
> Jesus answered, "If you want to be perfect, go, sell your possessions and give to the poor, and you will have treasure in heaven. Then come, follow me."
>
> When the young man heard this, he went away sad, because he had great wealth.
> Matthew 19:16-22 (see also Mark 10:17-31 and Luke 18:18-30).

The man's identity was tied to wealth and he was unwilling to give it up, even if by doing so he could be a disciple of Jesus Christ. He was a good guy. He followed all the rules and he sought advice from Jesus, but he knew something was missing from his life. Jesus told him the things he needed to do, but he was already doing those things and he lacked the fulfillment that he sought, so he asked "What do I still lack?" He knew something was missing from his life, but when he heard the cost of obtaining the satisfaction he sought, he was saddened because for him the cost was too high. He was unwilling to give up the basis of his identity. As a result, wealth separated the man from God and prevented him from following Jesus Christ. What in your life causes the same affect?

Who are you? I laugh as I write the question because it reminds me of the night before our wedding. Lori and I sat next to each other at our rehearsal dinner surrounded by our closest friends. As the evening rolled along and everyone grew more comfortable and the conversation relaxed, my closest friends told stories about things we had done together over the years. They were funny and we laughed and enjoyed remembering our times together. Given my history, I was relieved at how tame the stories were and in my mind I applauded my friends' discretion. I thought everything was good, but after a while Lori looked at me and said, "Who are you? I don't even know you." My friends laughed at her apparent joke, but she was not joking. She still asks me that question from time to time. While it is certainly important to know who you are about to commit the rest of life to, it is also important to know yourself.

What is your identity tied to? Tie it to only permanent One, the only One that will not change. Fortunately, if your identity is not tied to God, you can change course and make it so. A good example is the doctor at career day who described himself as a follower of Jesus Christ who serves Jesus by helping other people.

WE ARE UNDER ATTACK

Attack on the Soul

Evil surrounds us; we are tempted, tested and attacked; and the choices we make matter. We were each created in God's image and we each either, by God's grace, choose to move closer to God or not. Whatever we do, we choose. We may choose to stay where we are, or move in one direction or the other. Either way we make a choice. Our choice to do nothing causes us to continue in the place of separation. If we want life abundant, we must choose that and move in God's direction to attain it. Let's consider a few things hindering people's progression toward God.

Distractions

We are so busy. Our lives are crazy. I struggle deciding where to begin discussing such a loaded topic. Some of us feel the constant need to perpetuate the self-image we have created for others to view, often at great cost. Perhaps images of driving a nice car, living in a nice home in the right neighborhood, sending kids to the right schools, or going on the right vacations force some to work harder than they otherwise might. For some, striving to get more and better things, status and power destroys the ability to find enjoyment from the things they already possess. For others, the effort of creating and maintaining an appropriate online image squeezes joy from daily events.

While for some busyness is tied to trappings of self-image, for others different drivers create the sense of chaos. Do you have too little time to sleep? Do you need to be continuously plugged in to and through electronic devices and the worlds they reveal to us? Do you need to be continuously informed or continuously entertained or continuously posting about yourself and lack the discipline to deny yourself constantly available access?

Can you recall the last time you were bored – the last time you could find nothing to do? With our smart phone in hand, we face endless possibilities. We also have a lot of work to do just to keep a home running, and while I fail to do my fair share at home (Lori does it all), the little that I do allows me to realize how much work it really is. For many, evenings and weekends are packed with events for their children: the grind of homework, sports practices and games, dance lessons, music lessons … the list goes on and on. A friend with five children maintains a whiteboard in his kitchen with a detailed list of the week broken into hours coordinating the logistics of transporting each child to and from each day's events.

We even over-schedule vacations. We often return from vacation more exhausted than before we left. While each vacation might have been filled with fun that was fully documented for Facebook, Instagram and Snap Chat, it may not have been relaxing and we may not have used the time to recharge our batteries, which are desperately in need of recharging.

Are we so caught up pursuing things of the world, seeking acceptance from others through the self-images we create, and distracted by the chaos swirling around us that we fail to seek God? If we want to bridge the gap separating us from God we must choose to do so. Jesus Christ is the bridge, but we must take the steps along the journey toward God. Are you so busy, so distracted with the demands and desires each day that you fail to take the step? You were created with the image of God imprinted on you, but for your sake, God wants His image to grow.

If we desire God, we must be intentional about taking time to seek Him. It requires scheduling time for God. If we are not intentional about it, it will not happen. Set aside time in your schedule for prayer and reading Scripture. The health of our souls and spirits depend on communion with God. Some of our busyness is necessary and some of it is caused by our choices. Regardless of cause, the sheer busyness of lives prevents many from communing with God.

Worry, Fear & Doubt

What do you worry about? What causes you to stay awake at night? What do you pray for over and over like the persistent widow?[21] There is no shortage of things to worry about, and we tend to worry most about things beyond our control. Do difficult situations draw you closer to God or do they create greater distance between you and God?

I have seen it go both ways. I have seen childhood illness and death drive parents closer to God, and I have seen similar situations destroy faith. I have seen a spouse's illness lead to the same divide. I have seen unemployment and financial ruin devastate marriages, individual lives and the faith of all involved. I have also seen people who suddenly lost their career find new time to grow toward God and they discover new satisfaction, fulfillment and life in the process.

Over the past thirty years or so, Lori and our children have taken top spots on my list of worries. For years I prayed that our children would grow to know God deeply. I prayed for their health. I prayed that they would make good decisions and that their bad decisions would not destroy their lives. I prayed for their future spouses. And I continue praying for them and their families, and as I pray, I gradually entrust God with my concerns. Prayer draws me closer to God and confidence in God's sovereignty and love softens my worry.

I have been involved in prayer groups focusing on a wide array of issues. One involves a group of local pastors deeply concerned with the youth of our community. They are concerned with the proliferation of gangs, the ready availability of drugs, the many young men who believe dealing drugs represents the best opportunity for upward mobility, the many young women who find acceptance through sexual promiscuity, and the many high school students who fail to graduate. They are deeply worried about our community, and they pray and pray and they cry and pray more. And they act within the community to solve problems.

What do you worry about? Does it draw you closer to God or does it create greater separation?

Physical Health

Our bodies, souls and spirits are united. The condition of each impacts the other. Our souls suffer when our physical health fails, or when our loved ones suffer. While insufficient sleep may be a symptom of our busy lives, it may also be a symptom of physical illness or it may lead to physical illness.

When you enter the hospital as a patient, you enter a separate world: a world where time does not matter, where fluorescent light replaces the sun, where a unique language is spoken, where a unique social hierarchy exists identified by the color of hospital gowns, where the predominant smell is that of sterilization chemicals, where unusual sounds of machines beeping and carts rolling and people whispering echo down long halls, and where personal privacy, personal space and, to some extent, personal dignity cease to exist. I have met human versions of angels working in hospitals offering a calming spirit, humble love, and compassion to patients under their care. I am amazed by their ability to show kind, patient love regularly in the midst of trauma. I have also met people hardened by many years of long hours filled with suffering patients, and a few doctors who have allowed the power of their position within the hierarchy to go to their heads. It is a microcosm depicting all elements of the larger world: some people overflow with love, grace, compassion, patience and kindness while others do not.

If you have lived very long, you have probably experienced the wonders of modern medicine. Many of us would have expired a long time ago had we lived in an earlier era. The day I was born, the doctors told my parents that I would not survive my first night. They told my parents to fill out the birth certificate and go home, and that I would die that night. My first name is Randy rather than Randall or Randolph because, as my mother tells the story, she could not imagine an infant's tombstone bearing an adult-sounding name. I did not die, so the doctors said I would probably never walk and would likely have severe mental problems. My mother worked with me relentlessly during my early years, encouraging me to play games and solve puzzles and otherwise trying to stimulate my brain and muscles. Nearly 60 years later, I am still defying the odds. While we now joke about how the early mental diagnosis answers many questions, the early years of uncertainty were traumatic for my parents.

Health issues affect each of us. We pray for healing from cancer, for healing from heart issues, for healing from liver and kidney problems. We pray for physical healing from so many ailments, and even if the root matter involves physical health, this sort of problem puts our souls at risk because of the associated worry, fear, doubt, frustration, depression and general associated emotional trauma.

How do you react when your loved ones suffer physical needs? Do you draw closer to God, or does their suffering cause anger or greater doubt?

<u>Financial Matters</u>

You may be experiencing financial issues; you may be looking for work. The job search attacks your soul continuously and ferociously. When Elizabeth was 6 months old, I worked at a law firm in Denver. Here I was with an engineering degree and a law degree and I was practicing law in Denver. I thought I was set. But our senior partner and largest client had a disagreement, the client left, and demand for the firm's services declined. As a result, I, the lowest on the totem pole, was suddenly unemployed. One of the low points was standing in line at the unemployment office. I was the only person in line wearing a suit. I sent out hundreds of resumes and filled out countless applications only to be rejected over and over and over. We had a mortgage and a young family, and I could not support them. Lori still reminds me how it felt when she could not afford to buy diapers for our little baby. The rejection and fear and humiliation were awful, awful attacks on my soul. It was exhausting. But the situation ultimately led us to a different state, a new home, a new job, and a new life. It was not easy and I never want to go through it again, but it drew me closer to God.

<u>Pornography</u>

Jesus said,

"You have heard that it was said, 'You shall not commit adultery.' But I tell you that anyone who looks at a woman lustfully has already committed adultery with her in his heart." Matthew 5:27-28

Peter wrote,

"Dear friends, I urge you, as foreigners and exiles, to abstain from sinful desires, which wage war against your soul." 1 Peter 2:11

Sinful desires wage war against our souls. For a single snapshot regarding the condition of our society, and this is not even the tip of the iceberg, consider this. If it is a sin to look at another person lustfully outside of marriage, and if sinful desires wage war against our soul, pornography is destroying multitudes of souls. According to a report published by NBC, the global porn industry makes $97 billion annually, including $10 to 12 billion in the US.[22] The Internet and video streaming technology fuels the growing industry. Porn is readily available to anyone with a computer or smartphone and Internet connection.

I have heard it argued that pornography does not hurt anyone. I have heard it said, "its just me, by myself enjoying this form of entertainment. I am not hurting anyone. So I do not understand what the problem is." The problem is that you are voluntarily doing something that wages war against your soul, enhances the separation between you and God, and harms your ability to improve God's image implanted within you.

Your soul needs to commune with God, and that activity hinders your ability to do so. Porn also alters relationships between people. It alters the viewer's perception of other people, and creates unhealthy expectations regarding relationships. First, it dehumanizes and objectifies other people. It causes a person to see other people as objects. And after a while that distorted view becomes even more distorted as the viewer begins to imagine that other people, now objectified and dehumanized, exist for his or her pleasure.

This evil spirit of dehumanization sets in motion a series of vicious, evil thoughts, which are of the same nature that lead people to see slavery as acceptable. It is the same evil spirit that led to the awful, evil, vicious atrocities of the Holocaust, the Killing Fields of Cambodia, the ethnic cleansing during the Bosnian War, the Rwandan genocide and many other similar events over the course of history. After individuals or groups of people are seen as objects, after they have been dehumanized, demonized and vilified, they may be treated with far greater cruelty than imaginable towards people.

Please do not get me wrong. I am not saying that viewing porn will cause you to start killing people. But pornography unleashes the same evil dehumanizing and objectifying spirit that destroys respectful, reverent interaction between people.

Each person is created possessing a portion of God's image. You were created in God's image. Every person you see was created in God's image. God loves you and every other person on the planet. There is nothing you can do to make God stop loving you. And He calls us to love one another. We cannot build respectful, loving relationships with other people if we have dehumanized or objectified them, or if we view them as existing simply to satisfy our personal pleasure. We must realize and embrace the thought that each person was created by God in God's image, loved by God, and is important to God, and it should necessarily follow that we treat each other with the level of respect and love appropriate for a person loved by God.

Pornography pollutes our souls. It unleashes evil. It leads to dehumanization, objectification and unhealthy pursuit of personal pleasure. It taints relationships. It separates us from God. It destroys unity. And people are making billions of dollars annually generating porn.

Addiction

Issues relating to addiction touch virtually everyone. Even if you do not personally struggle with addiction, your life has probably been touched by it. Like a stone tossed in a pond, the ripples carry across the entire pond. Addiction is at times revealed through innocent avenues, like patients following doctors' orders after injury or surgery, taking prescribed medication that, in certain situations, reveals the disease and leads to an addictive cycle. But substance abuse does not always begin innocently, and it is a plague destroying our youth as they encounter many temptations and whispers, like "Try this and you will feel better" or "Try this and it will remove your pain" or "Try this to forget" or "Try this and you will feel closer to God." But they are lies.

I recently met an angel of a woman as we checked in at a doctor's office. During that process I began to talk with the receptionist and after a few minutes she shared her story about her battles to save her son. He is in his thirties now and leading a good productive life. But when he was in his teens and twenties he struggled with many issues, including depression and drug and alcohol use. She described how they went to many clinics and doctors and psychologists and support groups seeking help. She said the only thing that really worked was prayer. She prayed continuously. She prayed in his room while he was away and while he slept. She prayed in her own room and while she was at work. She prayed and prayed for years. She says looking back, she felt like she was in battle. She was battling for her son's survival. And her son is now doing well.

She pointed to the empty seat next to hers, saying that the woman who normally sat in that chair has struggled with similar issues with her son. And she mentioned others struggling with the same issues. Based on the conversation combined with many others like it, I believe the problem is reaching pandemic proportions.

It is a silent pandemic. Parents do not talk about their pain because it involves their children. When our children suffer and other loved ones suffer, we suffer. When the addiction belongs to children, it is difficult for parents to seek the help they need for themselves because the problem does not really belong to the parents. For instance, the mothers mentioned above struggled. Their souls suffered, but while they suffered, they did not want to talk about problems openly because that would have involved talking about personal matters of other people, their children. For them to fully explain why they were suffering they would have needed to discuss their sons' addictions, and it did not feel right to openly discuss their sons' problems. It would feel like a violation of trust or something nearing gossip, and could harm society's view of their children after the problems are overcome.

Dr. Sterling Shumway is chairman of the Department of Community, Family and Addiction Services at Texas Tech University. The Department is conducting remarkable research on the brain related to addiction and is using the research to design recovery programs implemented in its recovery clinics. Many, many families have been helped by the combined effort of research and implementation. During a recent meeting with Dr. Shumway, he said, citing a study conducted at Harvard, that the most stigmatizing word in the English language is "addict." He continued explaining that, based on several surveys in the US, when a person is described as an addict they are viewed more negatively by others than people described as murderers, rapists, arsonists, and a host of other awful sounding labels. Addicts are viewed more negatively than people who intentionally harm other people.

This may, to some extent, explain the shame that some parents feel when discussing their children's addiction, and why many parents choose not to discuss it. For some, the decision may involve parent's pride and concern about how their children's problems will impact their own social standing. For others the decision to remain silent involves a sense of loyalty to their children's privacy. Regardless of the underlying reason, each person, the addict and family members, must reach their version of rock bottom to shatter the fundamental niceties causing silence. The silence must be broken for true healing to begin.

Openness removes the worry, guilt and fear associated with perceived stigma. Our souls cry out for honest interaction with other people. As long as we hide our true selves, worry, fear and guilt will hold our souls and spirits hostage.

Scientific studies have led many to conclude that addiction is a disease. Certainly, choice is involved in identifying who has the disease – a person with the disease who chooses to never use substances that would trigger it will never know they have it. However, once a person with the disease uses a substance of concern, the substance affects the diseased person differently than others, revealing the disease. Science will go a long way to reduce the stigma associated with addiction, and to some extent alleviate some of the associated suffering. But drugs and alcohol will continue to attack the souls and spirits of addicts and their families.

Union of Physical and Spiritual

God is spirit; His image is imprinted on our spiritual selves; and at its most fundamental source each attack is spiritual, yet each of the attacks has a physical element. Addiction, pornography, financial matters, physical illness – they each cause physical consequences while attacking our spiritual being. For many, the attacks prevent them from realizing the full benefit of God's image within them by enhancing their separation from God while also causing physical pain.

While spirit, soul and body are all important and they are interconnected, we often only consider physical consequences while overlooking the spiritual foundation of the attacks. It is similar to the way Jesus was attacked in the wilderness. The story is filled with supernatural characters as it seamlessly blends the spiritual realm with the physical realm. The Holy Spirit leads Jesus to the wilderness where He is tested, tempted and attacked by another spiritual entity described by Matthew as "the devil" and called "Satan" by Jesus. After Satan leaves, angels attend to Jesus.

The attacks occur when Jesus is hungry, alone and vulnerable. Physical needs create spiritual vulnerability. On the surface the attacks involve the physical realm – physical needs, physical safety, possessions and the pursuit of power – but Jesus responds focusing on the spiritual aspects of each attack.

> Then Jesus was led by the Spirit into the wilderness to be tempted by the devil. After fasting forty days and forty nights, he was hungry. The tempter came to him and said, "If you are the Son of God, tell these stones to become bread."

Jesus answered, "It is written: 'Man shall not live on bread alone, but on every word that comes from the mouth of God.'"

Then the devil took him to the holy city and had him stand on the highest point of the temple. "If you are the Son of God," he said, "throw yourself down. For it is written:

"'He will command his angels concerning you, and they will lift you up in their hands, so that you will not strike your foot against a stone.'"

Jesus answered him, "It is also written: 'Do not put the Lord your God to the test.'"

Again, the devil took him to a very high mountain and showed him all the kingdoms of the world and their splendor. "All this I will give you," he said, "if you will bow down and worship me."

Jesus said to him, "Away from me, Satan! For it is written: 'Worship the Lord your God, and serve him only.'"

Then the devil left him, and angels came and attended him. Matthew 4:1-11

After fasting for 40 days, Jesus is hungry and the devil encourages Him to satisfy His physical needs in an improper way. Jesus focuses on the spiritual aspects of the attack. He recognizes physical needs but balances physical needs with spiritual needs. Jesus acknowledges both physical and spiritual aspects of His existence, quoting Scripture saying,

"It is written: 'Man shall not live on bread alone, but on every word that comes from the mouth of God.'" Matthew 4:4

Certainly people need to eat, and Jesus acknowledges the importance of physical needs, but we need more than physical food. We need spiritual food also.

When we are attacked we must recognize the spiritual element. Pornography seems purely physical but it enhances the chasm separating us from God. Cancer seems purely physical, but it attacks our spiritual selves also. Financial stress threatens our basic physical needs, leading us to worry about keeping a roof over our heads, having food to eat, and other basic needs. At first glance each seems like purely a physical problem, but it impacts our spiritual side, and is like other seemingly physical problems – many have spiritual components revealed through physical symptoms, and the impact diminishes our ability to enhance God's image within us.

BALANCE

Undoubtedly physical needs are important. They are important to each of us, and the physical needs of people around Jesus were important to Him: think about how many of Jesus' miracles involved provision of basic physical needs. Jesus fed thousands with five loaves of bread and two fish.[23] On another occasion, Jesus fed thousands with seven loaves and a few small fish. [24] He healed sick people, [25] paralyzed people, [26] blind people,[27] lepers,[28] and He raised people from the dead.[29] He showed concern for people's livelihood by providing miraculous fish catches to commercial fishermen.[30] Jesus showed concern for our physical selves, and we should too.

It is, however, possible that our focus is out of balance. Many of us give much more attention to our physical selves than our intangible selves. We might need to give more attention to our souls and spirits in search of balance.

We spend an enormous amount of time, energy and money on our physical health. Most of us try to eat the right foods. We take our vitamins, a lot of them. The food supplement industry exceeded $30 billion in sales in 2011 and is a growing industry.[31] We are concerned with our weight and physical appearance: the weight-loss industry earned $20 billion in 2012 with 108 million people on diets.[32] We try to get physical activity – in 2012 there were 267,000 fitness instructors in the US[33] – but many of us fail to make it a part of our long-term routine. Think of how large the cosmetics industry is and of how many magazines dedicate cover articles to physical appearance. We try to get enough sleep, but as a nation we are chronically sleep-deprived – 2.5 million people suffer from chronic fatigue syndrome in the US.[34] We go to the doctor and we follow doctor's orders. Most of us want to live longer and we want to feel better during the days that we have. We should take care of our bodies and this takes time and energy, but by comparison, most of us probably spend much less time and energy on the health of our spirits and souls. We need to achieve balance.

The interconnected nature of spirit, soul and body becomes clear when considering the mind. The mind is part of the soul and is spiritual. The body influences the mind, and of course, our brain is physical. Infants do not have the same mental function as fully functioning adults. As the brain matures, complex circuitry is formed enabling the brain to function with increasingly higher capacity. As certain neurons and axons communicate across synapses using electro-chemicals, connections become stronger. A person's mental ability improves to the extent certain components of the brain are used, and unused neurons and axons diminish.

The brain uses chemicals to communicate through electrical impulses. The ability of our brain to communicate within itself is dependent on chemicals and transmission and reception related to those chemicals. It is possible to alter our brain's ability through chemistry. While certain chemicals are in our body, our ability to think is impacted. For instance, alcohol, marijuana, cocaine and a host of other drugs alter what is communicated at the synapse between neurons and axons. The altered chemistry changes how our mind thinks and how our body responds to external stimuli. At the point of the synapse the mind and body are so closely connected it is difficult to separate the two.

We know that brain damage through injury or disease impacts a person's mental state. Damage can influence memory, personality, cognition and many other aspects of the mind. With technological advances over the past twenty years, understanding of the brain has advanced tremendously. Advanced scanners are able to simultaneously record EEG and functional MRI information, and big data computer technology allows comparative analysis across enormous data sets. Scientists are continuously gaining new understanding of physical characteristics associated with autism, addiction, epilepsy and many other brain-related conditions that influence mental function. Advances in genome sequencing are leading to continuously improved understanding of many brain disorders like Alzheimer's disease, Huntington's disease, Parkinson's disease and a host of other damaging conditions impacting many, many lives.

Brain development and damage influence a person's mental state. They influence the operation of our mind while body and soul are united. But will the influence continue after the body dies? Will physical impairment imposed on a person's mind by the body continue to impact the mind after the body dies? While we do not and cannot know, I firmly believe the answer is no.

Our soul houses our mind, personality, memory, emotions, will and other intangible characteristics, and it is connected with our body while our body is living. Our physical brain lights up the fMRI in response to certain stimuli and the stimuli alter our intangible condition. Our soul matures from experience. But when our brain is damaged and as a result our memory fails or our mental state otherwise falters, it is an indication of a physical limitation rather than a spiritual one. If the damaged body is unable to translate or transfer the spiritual into the physical, it is a physical problem. When the body dies the need for that translation or transfer is no longer necessary and the body will no longer constrain a person's spirit and soul.

Our physical senses limit the quality of our experience. We can only see the specific wavelengths of light that our eyes are capable of seeing. We can only hear the sounds within a relatively small range of possible wavelengths, and as dog whistles reveal, sounds exist that we cannot hear. Just as our existence is restricted by time and space here on earth, our experience is restricted to that which our senses are able to perceive. I have heard and read stories about people who have had near death experiences including descriptions of heavenly scenes. They try to describe sounds that are more wonderful than any sound they have heard on earth, and colors that are brighter, clearer, more vivid and more beautiful than anything they have seen on earth. Sound and sight were described as being more glorious than words can convey, beyond earthly description. Is it possible that the sights and sounds are beyond imagination not only because they are in an amazing place, but also because the sights and sounds are no longer filtered by physical senses?

Paul wrote to the church in Corinth,

"For we know in part and we prophesy in part, but when completeness comes, what is in part disappears... For now we see only a reflection as in a mirror; then we shall see face to face. Now I know in part; then I shall know fully, even as I am fully known." 1 Corinthians 13:9-10 & 13:12

In Paul's time, mirrors were not the finely polished, crystal clear tools that exist today. They created blurry images. Are we now seeing as in a mirror circa 50 AD, filtered through physical senses, but "when completeness comes" we will see clear and unfiltered version?

Our bodies are amazing gifts from God. They are wonderfully designed and they are important and we must take care of them, but they are not the most important things. They are important, but our souls and spirits are also important. That is were we house, to the extent we possess it, the image of God. I urge you to spend as much time on the development and care of your soul and spirit as you do on your body.

GOD'S GLORY

"It was the best of times, it was the worst of times..." This is how Charles Dickens launches *A Tale of Two Cities*. Apparently it was. It certainly is. The world is a realm of contrast.

God is holy, divine and pure. We are surrounded by God's glory and His holy healing grace and love, and we are surrounded by evil. The world is the place where God places people whom He creates in His holy image, and it is filled with the wonderful beauty of His creation. Today started with a beautiful sunrise and as I write, spring is popping out around me and I am reminded that God is the source of life, that God created everything out of nothing by simply speaking, and that life is only available through God. I think of all the beautiful, loving people I know – people who will do anything to help another person in need.

Isaiah records a vision of heaven and describes heavenly beings saying over and over,

> "Holy, holy, holy is the Lord Almighty;
> The whole earth is full of his glory." Isaiah 6:3

The world is full of God's glory, yet it is also the place Paul describes as "this dark world" (Ephesians 6:12) and the "dominion of darkness" (Colossians 1:13). It is the place where God allows Satan and his demons to roam. Job describes Satan roaming the earth[35] and Peter writes,

> "Be alert and sober of mind. Your enemy the devil prowls around like a lion looking for someone to devour." 1 Peter 5:8

There is evidence of great evil all around us. Today I see the news of people suffering in Egypt, Syria, Iraq and across the Mideast, and reports of people suffering in Africa, and across the United States. Yesterday, I read a horrific article in the *New Yorker* about human trafficking and sex slavery. We know people suffering in our hometowns. And I bet you suffer because we each suffer. We each know pain. We know torment. We feel the influence of sin and evil within us and around us.

No doubt, earth is a place of contrast. I urge you to reach out for God, seek God, and worship God because He is love, light, life, and the source of satisfaction, fullness, abundance, peace and joy. God is the glory. He is holy, divine, and pure. He is all-powerful. He has all authority everywhere – in heaven, the heavens and on earth. He created all things and He breathes the breath of life into you and me and every living being. He knows all things, and His judgment, reasoning and intellect are flawless. He does not make mistakes.

And He creates each human in His glorious image. A chasm separates us from the image He wants us to have, so we must move in His direction through Christ Jesus and the choices we make and with the Holy Spirit's help. He stirs our hearts, but we must respond. He offers the gift of His holy grace, but we must accept the gift and unwrap it. May you know God through Christ Jesus, may you allow His holy image to grow within you, may you allow His Holy Spirit to transform your spirit and soul, and may you allow God's glory to be revealed through you in ways that impact the world.

As you accept the inward reality of God's image, you must also accept that everyone else is also created in God's image. Every person is created in God's image and God loves every person. It is true for you, me and everyone else. It does not matter what they may have done. We must pray to see the world through God's eyes, pray for God to fill us with His transforming love allowing us to see others as He sees them – as people created in His holy image. When we see people as bearing God's image, we are suddenly able to treat them with honor, respect, love and compassion that the bearers of God's glorious image deserve.

Father, may it be for your glory that you fill us with your Holy Spirit in a new and refreshed way. Enlighten the eyes of our spirits that we may know you, see you, experience you, hear you as never before. Give us your power, your wisdom, your discerning spirit. And please heal each of us. We ask for total, complete physical and spiritual cleansing. We know you created all things, we know you have all authority everywhere, we know there is nothing you cannot do, you know everything about each of us, and we know you hear us, you listen to us, and you love us. And we ask for your healing. Thank you for the healing you have done, are doing and will do. In Jesus' holy name we pray, Amen.

5 | ABUNDANT LIFE, ETERNAL LIFE & THE KINGDOM OF GOD

"The thief comes only to steal and kill and destroy; I have come that they may have life, and have it to the full." John 10:10

"Now this is eternal life: that they may know you, the only true God, and Jesus Christ, whom you have sent." John 17:3.

"Do not be afraid, little flock, for your Father has been pleased to give you the kingdom." Luke 12:32

The world is a place of terrific contrast. It is a place where people reach out to one another in love and compassion, and a place where people plan and commit acts of horrific evil. The world is full of God's glory,[1] yet it is a dark place where Satan roams.[2]

Jesus came to earth for a number of reasons, but the most significant reason was to provide a bridge between we mere humans and God, thereby exposing mere humans to a previously unknown and unavailable quality of life – life lived in communion with God, spiritual life. The world is a place where evil exists and roams; yet it is also the place where God's holy grace is available to mere humans.

Somewhere in Alabama, I do not recall exactly where, I saw a sign near the highway. It was not really a billboard – it was not the sort of sign that a billboard company would erect. A landowner had cleared trees and erected a large sign that said, "Where Will You Spend Eternity? Heaven or Hell?" I was struck by the effort and commitment the sign required. An individual landowner cleared trees allowing the sign to be viewed from the highway, planned the sign, created the sign, erected the sign, and maintained the sign and the clearing, all in an effort to invite thousands of unknown people each day to consider physical mortality and spiritual life.

I have seen billboards with a similar message in many places across the US. Many have an image of flames with words asking similar questions. One is a slick, professionally designed campaign installed on professional billboards. The sign has a black background with white letters saying, "Life is short. Eternity isn't. – God."

The signs remind me of conversations I have had with many people over the years. One was with a friend from Switzerland. We were in St. Moritz. After skiing and dinner we sat talking. He told me about his daughter. She had recently confessed faith in Jesus Christ and was very active in her church. She told her father about her faith and urged him to join her in her faith. She was terrified for the eternal fate of his soul, and he was concerned that his daughter was possibly being brainwashed by a cult.

As we talked, he described his daughter as being happier than he could ever recall. He described how she was making good decisions for her life, and how she was getting her life in order. He described that her life was better now than it was before. With the positive facts in mind, he relented that the, in his words, "Jesus thing" might actually be good for her. As he thought about his daughter's desire for him to consider Jesus, he said, "But I just don't know. I don't know about this whole thing. My life is good. Why would I want to change?" But then he remembered his daughter's concern for his soul and where he would spend eternity. He jokingly concluded that it might be best to wait until the last possible moment, then accept Jesus Christ into his heart. That would allow him to live his life without change and still receive the benefits of a good eternity.

The words "eternity" and "eternal life" often lead us to think about our eternal resting place – where will our souls go after our bodies die? While this is important, it misses the present component of the concept. The quality of life described in Scripture as "eternal life" is not exclusively about whether our souls will go to heaven or hell. Scripture presents it as a quality of life available here and now, while our souls still dwell within our living bodies, while we still experience physical life.

This is very significant. As I tried to explain to my friend in Switzerland, and to many others in many different places, if you wait until the last minute you will miss out on the quality of life that is available for you here and now. You will miss out on experiencing the wonder of spiritual life. You will miss out on the quality of life that is only available when life is lived in union with God, the quality of life that Jesus described as "abundant life" (or "life, and have it in full," depending on the translation of John 10:10), the quality of life referred to as the "kingdom of God," the quality of life referred to as "eternal life."

As Jesus suffered on the cross, the thief hanging on the cross next to Him said he believed that Jesus was the Messiah, and he asked Jesus to remember him. Jesus responded saying they would be together later that day in paradise.[3] Like the thief on the cross, it may be possible to wait until the last minute, but wouldn't life be an improved experience if lived in communion with God?

Had the thief lived, like the disciples, as a follower of Christ living in communion with Him, experiencing His holy presence, experiencing His teaching, and experiencing His miraculous qualities, would the quality of his life have been better while his body breathed on earth? Would he have enjoyed life more? Would he have experienced rest, satisfaction and wholeness? Would he have felt complete?

Abundant life, eternal life and the quality of life described by Jesus as the "kingdom of God" or "kingdom of heaven" are different ways of describing spiritual life: the quality of life that is available by living in communion with God. It is rest, satisfaction, wholeness and shalom. It is genuinely full life.

ABUNDANT LIFE

Jesus describes the quality of this new life by saying, "I have come that they may have life, and have it to the full" (John 10:10). Jesus discusses spiritual life available to people who are already physically alive ("they" in the quote already exist). He came to earth so people will be able to experience spiritual life and more – He desires that they, we, you experience as much of it as possible. He desires that you experience an over-heaping measure of spiritual life. Different translations describe the life Jesus offers as rich, satisfying and abundant life. Through Jesus Christ, the kingdom of God, life abundant, life eternal is available now to everyone who believes.

ETERNAL LIFE

Two passages discussed in chapter 3 mention eternal life. At John 3:36, John the Baptist says, "Whoever believes in the Son *has eternal life*, but whoever rejects the Son will not see life, for God's wrath remains on them." At John 5:24 Jesus says, "Very truly I tell you, whoever hears my word and believes him who sent me *has eternal life* and will not be judged but has crossed over from death to life."

I have heard many people discuss eternal life as something that begins as soon as physical life ends and continues forever into the future. But Scripture says eternal life is something possessed at the moment of belief. John 3:36 says it is possessed at the moment of belief in the Son, Jesus. John 5:24 says it is possessed in the moment of belief in "him who sent me" or God. In each statement, eternal life is a present quality of life.

The word "eternal" refers exclusively to time and means without beginning or end. It refers to time, but Jesus and John the Baptist used the term to describe a quality of life. And the quality of life described has a beginning – it begins at the moment of belief. It may last forever into the future, but because it has a beginning it is not really eternal. So here we have a word, eternal, that exclusively refers to time when used accurately, but is used in Scripture to describe a quality of life, and even as it relates to time it is misused. So we have problems. Has something been lost in translation? What is the original thought translated in English as "eternal life"?

John wrote his gospel in Greek. Two Greek words are translated as "life" in English, bios and zoe.[4] Bios refers to the course of life, the business of life, the affairs of life, or the events occurring between a person's birth and death. It refers to a person's accomplishments and experience. Zoe refers to the life force or the vital element that creates life. It is life in spirit and soul.

Where English translations say "eternal life," John used the Greek words zoe aionion. The Greek word translated as "eternal" is aionion. The root word is aion, a noun meaning a period of time related to some person or event with a beginning and an end, such as the time a person is alive, or a period of historical era. It is similar to era, epoch or eon. For instance, if we were discussing the time when Rome controlled lands surrounding the Mediterranean Sea, we might talk about the Roman aion. An aion does not denote a set amount of time, but varies with usage: a person's aion may be a day or a hundred years, a nation's aion may be much longer, and the Obama aion would refer to the eight year period of Mr. Obama's presidency. God's aion is eternal. It has no beginning and no end. It is the only aion without beginning and without end.

Aionios or aionion are adjective forms describing a period of time or historical age. Zoe aionion means life of a new age or new period. As used in the New Testament, it means new life through relationship with God, Jesus Christ and the Holy Spirit. It is spiritual life. It is life connected with the Divine, and in the instant of connection, a new aion or new age or new life begins.[5]

Where does the notion that the new life is everlasting or eternal arise? Derivatives of the word aionion and aionios appear 71 times in Scripture.[6] Each time they are translated as "eternal" or "everlasting." The literal translation of zoe aionios is "life relating to an era" and it refers as much to the quality of the era as the length. The length of time of an aion is derived through association based on the context of the statement. An aion associated with God depicts the time of God's life. God has always been and always will be. He existed before time and will exist forever. God's life never ends, and this logically leads to the conclusion that the new life associated with God, God's aion, is without end. But God is really outside of time. God is not bound by time. Time does not apply to God. So it really means life beyond time or life unbounded by time, which may be thought of as eternal.

If we focus purely on word studies comparing eternal with aionion or its derivatives, we might conclude that the translation requires a leap. We might conclude that while eternal is one possible interpretation of aionion, it is not the only possible translation. But we have other evidence that the word eternal is the appropriate choice because Scripture refers to a quality of life that lasts forever.

Scripture provides examples of people whose spiritual selves live longer than their bodies, supporting the conclusion that eternal life extends longer than physical life, presumably forever. One is the thief on the cross, mentioned earlier. Jesus and the thief were crucified next to one another. They had been tortured and nailed to crosses, and they each knew that their bodies would stay on the crosses until they experienced physical death. While on the cross the thief asked Jesus to remember him when Jesus was in His kingdom, implying his belief that Jesus was indeed the Son of God and that His kingdom was not reliant on His physical body. Jesus said, "I tell you the truth, today you will be with me in paradise" (Luke 23:43). Their bodies would die soon, but they would soon be in paradise – their spiritual selves would continue living.

Matthew records an event known as the Transfiguration.[7] Jesus traveled up a mountain with Peter, James and John. While they were on the mountain, Jesus was transfigured. He glowed, His clothes turned bright white, and a cloud enveloped the men. Suddenly Moses and Elijah appeared in physical form. They spoke with Jesus in the other men's presence. Moses died around 1,400 BC as the Israelites prepared to enter the Promised Land.[8] Elijah was lifted to heaven in a whirlwind by chariots of fire around 800 BC.[9] The Transfiguration occurred around 30 AD, hundreds of years after Moses died and Elijah departed earth. For Peter, James and John to see Moses and Elijah, Moses' and Elijah's spiritual selves must have still been alive.

At a different time, Jesus spoke with religious leaders about the resurrection. He mentioned three patriarchs of Israel – Abraham, Isaac and Jacob – who had each died hundreds of years earlier, and His statement unmistakably indicates that the men are still alive. Jesus said,

> "But about the resurrection of the dead – have you not read what God said to you, 'I am the God of Abraham, the God of Isaac, and the God of Jacob'? He is not the God of the dead but of the living." Matthew 22:31-32

Jesus acknowledges that God is "the God of" each of the three men. When Jesus says the words, He and His listeners all know that the men had died, yet Jesus says God is "the God of … the living," which suggests that the men are still alive. They are not alive physically, so they must still be alive spiritually.

On another occasion Jesus spoke with a group of religious leaders. During the conversation He made three statements suggesting spiritual life is eternal. John records the following conversation:

> The Jews answered him, "Aren't we right in saying you are a Samaritan and demon-possessed?"

> "I am not possessed by a demon," said Jesus, "but I honor my Father and you dishonor me. I am not seeking glory for myself; but there is one who seeks it, and he is the judge. I tell you the truth, *if anyone keeps my word, he will never see death."*

> At this the Jews exclaimed, "Now we know that you are demon-possessed! Abraham died and so did the prophets, yet you say that if anyone keeps your word, he will never taste death. Are you greater than our father Abraham? He died and so did the prophets. Who do you think you are?

> Jesus replied, "If I glorify myself, my glory means nothing. My Father, whom you claim as your God, is the one who glorifies me. Though you do not know him, I know him. If I said I did not, I would be a liar like you, but I do know him and keep his word. *Your father Abraham rejoiced at the thought of seeing my day; he saw it and was glad."*

> "You are not fifty years old," the Jews said to him, "and you have seen Abraham!"

> *"I tell you the truth,"* Jesus answered, *"before Abraham was born, I am!"* At this, they picked up stones to stone him, but Jesus hid himself, slipping away from the temple grounds. John 8:48-59

In the single conversation, Jesus says (i) people who keep His word will not die; (ii) He interacted with Abraham and saw Abraham rejoice and appear glad; and (iii) Jesus claims to be eternal – he was alive before Abraham and by saying "I am!" Jesus says that He is God, which is why the religious leaders reached for stones. Jesus claiming to be God was, in their minds, blasphemy and grounds for the death penalty.

History and experience suggest that everyone dies physically. Every body eventually stops breathing and stops pumping blood, and every brain stops producing electrical currents, yet Jesus promises that people who keep His word "will never see death." This tells us two things: first, the statement must refer to spiritual life; and second, spiritual life never ends.

As mentioned before, Abraham died about 1,400 years before Jesus walked the earth. Jesus' first statement about Abraham – that he rejoiced and was glad to see Jesus' day – suggests that Abraham was still living at the time of Jesus' day, which means Abraham still experienced spiritual life.

Jesus' second statement about Abraham – that Jesus was alive before Abraham was born – tells us that Jesus was alive before He experienced physical life on earth. His spiritual life started before His physical life. The last two words of His declaration communicate a claim to eternal divinity. By saying "I am!" Jesus tells His listeners that He is God and He clarifies that His spiritual existence is eternal – He always has been and always will be.

Jesus made a similar statement revealing that His spiritual life predated His physical life. When His 72 missionaries return from the mission field, excited that demons submitted to them in Jesus' name, Jesus says, "I saw Satan fall like lightning from heaven" (Luke 10:18). It is generally believed that Satan was represented on earth in the form of the serpent in the creation story, meaning Satan fell from heaven before God created humans. So if Jesus saw that, His spiritual existence predated His physical existence by a long, long time. We know, because Scripture tells us, that Jesus is God.[10] As God, He is eternal – He has always been and He always will be.

The passages of Scripture above provide examples of people who suffered physical death yet continue to live spiritually. The passages suggest spiritual selves live forever, at least the spiritual selves of Jesus, Jewish patriarchs, the thief on the cross, and people who keep Jesus' word. Scripture includes additional examples, but this seems to be enough to communicate and support the point that spiritual life continues forever, it does not die when the body dies.

Our physical life here on earth is most certainly bound by time: unlike God, we must live life one moment at a time. Zoe aionios, eternal life, is important. Yes, it lasts forever and that is extremely important, but the present quality of life available through Jesus Christ is even more significant because Jesus Christ offers richness, satisfaction and abundance to our spirit, and wholeness to our life. It is, first and foremost, life connected to God, the Divine, the Holy, the Righteous. Eternal life, a new aion or a new age of living is available to everyone and this is really significant. The new aion is a life connected with God. With this connection, the importance of worries associated with time should fade. And the new spiritual life is available here and now. It begins in the instant of belief with repentance and the desire to follow Christ. The everlasting nature of the new life, eternal life, is secondary to the present connection with the Divine.

Jesus predicts our confusion over the terminology, so He explains it very clearly for us. On the evening of the Last Supper, Jesus prays and in the prayer He says,

> "Now this is eternal life: that they may know you, the only true God, and Jesus Christ, whom you have sent." John 17:3

Once again, Jesus describes eternal life as a quality of life available now through relationship with God. Eternal life happens when a person shares intimate relationship with God the Father and Jesus Christ.

KINGDOM OF GOD

When you think of a kingdom, what comes to mind? Many kingdoms had occupied the land Jesus travelled. When Alexander the Great's kingdom occupied the land, his kingdom came with a new language, new currency bearing Alexander's image, new laws, new customs, new taxes and new soldiers. When Rome occupied the land, the kingdom came with new currency bearing Caesar's image, new laws, new taxes and new soldiers. So when Jesus spoke about the kingdom, His listeners had certain concepts in mind. The word kingdom implied certain notions of power, control and change. It may have implied government, bureaucracy and politics. But Jesus spoke about the kingdom in a strange new way, a way that confused His listeners. It was almost as if He was using the wrong word.

In chapter 3 we discussed Nicodemus, the Jewish leader who met with Jesus late one night. When Jesus spoke with Nicodemus, he said in order to see or enter the kingdom of God a person must be born again.[11] Spiritual life, eternal life, abundant life and new life are in many instances equivalent to the way Jesus spoke about the kingdom of God or kingdom of heaven.

Scripture records Jesus speaking a lot about the kingdom. Time and time again He describes the kingdom as a quality of life available while a person experiences physical life – it is available now. Consider the present or past tense of the following passages quoting Jesus:

> "Blessed are the poor in spirit, for *theirs is* the kingdom of heaven." Matthew 5:3

> "Blessed are those who are persecuted because of righteousness, for *theirs is* the kingdom of heaven." Matthew 5:10

> Jesus said, "Let the little children come to me, and do not hinder them, for the kingdom of heaven *belongs* to such as these." Matthew 19:14

"Do not be afraid, little flock, for your Father *has been pleased to give you* the kingdom." Luke 12:32

Once, on being asked by the Pharisees when the kingdom of God would come, Jesus replied, "The coming of the kingdom of God is not something that can be observed, nor will people say, 'Here it is,' or 'There it is,' because the kingdom of God *is in your midst*." Luke 17:20-21

Another quote that is in future tense suggests the kingdom is available while people are on earth experiencing physical life:

"So do not worry, saying, 'What shall we eat?' or 'What shall we drink?' or 'What shall we wear?' For the pagans run after all these things, and your heavenly Father knows that you need them. But *seek first his kingdom and his righteousness, and all these things will be given to you as well.* Therefore do not worry about tomorrow, for tomorrow will worry about itself. Each day has enough trouble of its own." Matthew 6:31-34

The quote begins by discussing eating, drinking and wearing clothes – activities that people do while they live on earth. Jesus says God is concerned about our physical needs before advising us to "seek first his kingdom... and all these things will be given to you as well." If we seek first His kingdom, He will provide – He will provide the kingdom and physical needs also. The statement suggests that the provision happens at the same time. When do we have physical needs? We have physical needs while we are on earth experiencing physical life. So the kingdom must be available while we are on earth experiencing physical life.

When you think of the kingdom of heaven or the kingdom of God, what thoughts come to mind? Heaven? The place where God reigns? God's spiritual realm? Where is it? What is it like? What are its geographic limits?

Jesus said He came to earth to "proclaim the good news of the kingdom of God" (Luke 4:43). He described the kingdom as something that "is near" (see Matthew 4:17, 10:7 and 12:28) and He told others that they were "not far from" it (see Mark 12:34). He discussed it as something that may be entered (see Matthew 5:20, 7:21, 19:23, 21:31). He tells us that it belongs to children and people who are like children (see Matthew 19:14), and that certain people will see it (see Mark 9:1, Luke 9:27), though people must be born again to see it (John 3:3). Jesus also said that its coming may not be observed because it is within us (Luke 17:20-21), and God the Father is pleased to give the kingdom to us (Luke 12:32).

So the kingdom is something God the Father gives to us and Jesus came to "proclaim the good news of the kingdom." Very interesting. The kingdom is around us and is possessed by certain people. Jesus also urges us, commands us really, to seek first the kingdom of God (Matthew 6:33). How do we do that? How do we seek the kingdom of God?

This is quite a riddle. What is the kingdom and how do we go about seeking it? While we may not be much closer to knowing what it is, we know that it is something people are able to possess while they live on earth in a human body. The kingdom is not only a place where our souls and spirits go after our bodies die. It is available here and now.

The kingdom is very much like eternal life, and it sounds a lot like the abundant life that Jesus promises. It sounds like life lived in communion with God. It sounds like life lived with the Holy Spirit dwelling within us, like spiritual life.

What is the Kingdom?

The word "kingdom" is used in this context 119 times in the gospels. When Pilate questioned Jesus, he asked whether Jesus was the king of the Jews. Jesus said,

> "*My kingdom is* not of this world. If it were, my servants would fight to prevent my arrest by the Jews. But now *my kingdom is* from another place." John 18:36

Jesus has a kingdom. It is not of this world. It is from another place. Twice in three sentences Jesus says, "my kingdom is," speaking about the kingdom in present tense. "Not of this world" and "from another place" are powerful clues. Scripture frequently contrasts the worldly and Godly, flesh and spirit, darkness and light. God is light; the world is dark. It might be in this context that Jesus says His "kingdom is not of this world." Or He might mean that His kingdom is not of the natural realm and it is from heaven.

"From another place" is an interesting phrase. His kingdom started in another place and now it is here. He does not say His kingdom is in another place, He says it is "from another place," indicating its location has changed.

His kingdom is spiritual life dwelling in the heart of each believer. The life is of God and from God, and it exists in this world in and through followers of Christ.

Jesus tells nine parables describing God's kingdom. He begins each one by saying, "the kingdom of heaven is like...." It is like a man who sowed good seed in a field.[12] It is like a mustard seed.[13] It is like yeast.[14] It is like treasure hidden in a field.[15] It is like a merchant looking for fine pearls.[16] It is like a fishing net.[17] It is like a king who wanted to settle accounts,[18] a landowner who hires workers,[19] and a king who prepared a wedding banquet.[20] Matthew chapter 13 contains the first six mentioned here.

Early in the chapter, the disciples ask Jesus why he speaks in parables. He answers explaining that He knows some people will understand the parables and others will not understand. He says that parables explain the "secrets of the kingdom of heaven" and that some will hear and understand while others will not understand. Jesus says,

> "This is why I speak in parables: 'Though seeing, they do not see; though hearing, they do not hear or understand.'" Matthew 13:13

While Jesus explained why He spoke and taught through parables, it is unclear why He told nine parables discussing the kingdom of heaven. Such a large number causes me to conclude two things: 1) the subject is extremely important, and 2) the concepts do not translate easily into our language or thinking.

Jesus tries to help us understand the kingdom of heaven through parables, each saying what the kingdom is like. It is like a man who sowed good seed in a field.[21] An enemy came and sowed weeds in the field. When weeds and wheat sprouted workers suggested that they pull the weeds, but the owner told them to let both grow and to separate the weeds from the wheat after the harvest. He was concerned that pulling the weeds would harm the crop, but separating them at harvest would allow the crop to grow. The kingdom is like a man who sowed good seeds and spoke wisdom. The kingdom plants seeds.

It is like a mustard seed,[22] which is a tiny speck of a seed that grows into a large tree. It starts out small and grows into something very large.

It is like yeast.[23] We know that so long as it is handled properly, after yeast is mixed into a large amount of dough, a tiny amount of yeast changes the character of the dough. It causes the dough to rise. Yeast is an agent of transformation whose identity and usefulness are exhausted in the process. A small amount of yeast changes a much larger volume of dough making the combined whole better. The kingdom is like yeast transforming the much larger realm in which it is mixed.

The kingdom of heaven is like treasure hidden in a field.[24] The man who discovered the treasure sold all he had to buy the field and secure the treasure. The kingdom has great value to people who recognize it as treasure. To that person, the kingdom is more valuable than all his possessions. Here the kingdom is like the treasure.

It is like a merchant looking for fine pearls.[25] When he found the right one, he sold everything he had to buy the pearl. The merchant had to discern the good pearl from bad ones. He had to recognize the right one, he had to understand its value, and when he saw it he had to act. He had to secure it into his possession. But the kingdom is not the pearl. Here, the kingdom is like the merchant who recognized the pearl to be of great value.

The kingdom is like the person seeking pearls. Perhaps you are the pearl the merchant seeks.

So the kingdom is like a treasure and it is like a person seeking something of value. It is a treasure to the person who finds it, and it seeks things of great value.

It is also like a fishing net that caught all sorts of fish.[26] After the fish were caught the good ones were kept and the bad ones were thrown away. The kingdom is like the net that caught both good and bad fish.

Jesus tells four parables describing the kingdom to be like objects: mustard seed, yeast, hidden treasure and a fishing net. In two the kingdom is like people: the man who planted good seed and the merchant seeking fine pearls. This suggests the kingdom has both impersonal and personal qualities.

WHO POSSESS THE KINGDOM?

We have been considering descriptions of the kingdom explaining what it is like. Other passages describe people who possess the kingdom while they are here on earth in bodily form. Who are these people?

Jesus begins the Sermon on the Mount[27] by giving the Beatitudes. The first and last are:

> "Blessed are the poor in spirit, for theirs is the kingdom of heaven." Matthew 5:3 and

> "Blessed are those who are persecuted because of righteousness, for theirs is the kingdom of heaven." Matthew 5:10

What amazing statements! "Theirs is the kingdom of heaven." It is a present tense possessive statement. The first and last Beatitude each describe people who currently possess the kingdom of heaven – the poor in spirit and those who are persecuted because of righteousness. "Theirs is the kingdom of heaven."

The Beatitudes describe blessings for many other categories of people, such as those who mourn, the meek, those who hunger and thirst for righteousness, the merciful, the pure of heart, and the peacemakers. People such as these receive special blessing from God. They are present tense possessive statements.

Poor in Spirit

"Blessed are the poor in spirit..." What does "poor in spirit" mean? Matthew used the Greek word ptokhos, translated here as poor. He could have used several different words had he desired to communicate the wide range of economic condition captured by the English word poor. The word poor may be used to describe people who work everyday but who cannot afford some basic necessities, people who are utterly destitute with no possessions and no means of earning, and various points along the wide spectrum separating them. Had Jesus meant slightly poor or working poor or people who had some earning power but not much, Matthew could have used the word "penes." But he chose the word "ptokhos," which means absolutely destitute, the poorest of the poor, a person who is at the lowest economic level, a person who has no resources and no ability to earn an income. Ptokhos refers to a person whose only means of survival is begging.

But Jesus is not discussing economic poverty. Jesus says "poor in spirit," ptokhos in spirit, or the lowest of the low spiritually. Jesus is referring to a person who has abandoned all arrogance, a person who is completely humbled. It means a person who has reached the point of complete desperation, a person begging for the spiritual sustenance that is Jesus Christ, a person recognizing that he can do nothing on his own and that Jesus Christ is the only answer, the only solution to what ails him. When a person reaches the point of need some may describe as "rock bottom" and in that place reaches out for Jesus Christ, that person at that time is ptokhos in spirit.

We live in a broken world. The evil in our world is on display daily across the headlines of major newspapers. I recently saw a list of news articles I recorded years ago, which are tragically like current articles. Headlines included 82 men, women and children slaughtered in a Nigerian village. After survivors fled to a local shelter, suicide bombers fleeing alongside survivors triggered suicide vests killing more. The Islamic State claimed responsibility for a suicide bombing in Kabul killing at least 41. A man with a rifle slaughtered people as they watch a concert in Las Vegas. A two-year-old boy in Jacksonville, Florida was killed in a by drive-by shooting. Nine worshipers were killed while worshiping in church in Charleston, South Carolina. The list goes on and on – tragic examples of the broken world we live in.

And we are broken people, each of us. But Jesus Christ provides us with the opportunity for wholeness. Jesus is the cure for brokenness, and for many of us, it is through brokenness that we are able to feel His holy healing touch. While things are going along smoothly, it is easy to fall into the trap of believing we can do it ourselves. It is easy to be misled by the notion that we do not need God. It is easy to trust in ourselves more than in God. But in times of brokenness we see the truth. We see clearly that we can do nothing on our own and we need God for everything, and through this we find the amazing blessing – we discover the kingdom of God.

Family

Being a father has brought me some of the greatest joy of my life. Yet, when our children suffer, I suffer. I suspect I share this will all parents. When our children suffer through illness, we suffer. When our children suffer through bad choices, we suffer. When our children's bad choices reveal illnesses, we suffer. And, particularly in the last two examples, many parents suffer in silence for fear of tainting their children's reputation or future. It is a vicious trap many parents find themselves in.

Lori and I have experienced a degree of spiritual brokenness. There was a time when our lives spiraled deeper into dark suffering. But through that suffering we grew closer together and closer to God.

Over the years I have been amazed at how God reveals Himself when we are at our low points. He comforts us when we think we cannot go on. He lets us know that He is with us when we need Him the most.

I recently had the opportunity to visit my son while he was in jail. Well, I did not actually see him, I communicated with him by videoconference. I went to the jail, signed in, went to a computer screen with a telephone-like handset, and saw his image on a small video screen while we spoke to one another. It was fantastic to see him, but it was awful. It was great to see that he was not beaten up, that he was not bruised on his face. It was awful that he was in there, and it was awful that I could not help him, and it was awful not knowing how long he would be there, and it was awful that we could not really talk because it was all being recorded. But it was really good to see him. It was good in the most awful way imaginable.

Four months later Lori was diagnosed with an aggressive soft tissue sarcoma in her thigh. Through radiation treatments, surgery and chemotherapy, she stood on her faith in God. We both did. We knew then as we know now that God is with us, that God loves us, that God has the power to do all things, that He is sovereign, and He knows us and our needs.

Through it all, God revealed His grace and His mercy and His holy healing touch. God answered prayer after prayer. When we trust in God He responds. Many are only able to truly trust God after all other options have been exhausted and they are so low that they are forced to trust Him.

And I know, in all likelihood, you have experienced similar brokenness. Our situations may be different, but our brokenness is similar. I mention our experience, not because it is unique, but because it is common. We share the pain, grief, loneliness and desperation that come with brokenness, and we have the opportunity to share in God's comfort, relief and peace. I know, based on personal experience, so long as we turn towards one another and towards God, spiritual brokenness allows us to grow closer to God and closer to one another than would be possible without it.

We also share the possibility of relief that is available simply by allowing yourself to be vulnerable to brothers and sisters in Christ. At a certain point we realize that we are helpless when relying on ourselves, on our own power, on our will, and when we give all that up and simply rely on God we are blessed. In that place of brokenness, when we turn to God, we grow closer to God. In that place of darkness and total need we feel His holy Presence and we receive His special blessing. "Blessed are the poor in spirit, for theirs is the kingdom of heaven."

A friend recently sent me a Charles Spurgeon quote that said,

> "There is no greater mercy that I know of on earth than good health except it be sickness; and that has often been a greater mercy to me than health.... It is a good thing to be without trouble; but it is a better thing to have trouble, and know how to get grace enough to bear it."[28]

Our lives are all, to some extent, chaotic. I recall a sermon Bill Morgan preached where he referred to our lives as being "messy." He described one particular Saturday morning when he could not sleep. He got up extremely early and went to the Waffle House. He said for some it was early morning, for others it was late night. He described the boisterous tables filled with young people in festive spirits continuing from the night before, and the tables filled with others on their way to work or to the hunt, and the hard working, grace-filled waitresses who did their best to serve everyone with hospitality, regardless of their condition, and his own messy condition that forced him up so early. He concluded that everyone has, to some extent, a messy life. We are all in need of God's grace, and each other's love.

And if we each lead lives characterized to some extent by messiness, we should allow ourselves to be vulnerable to one another so we can each give and receive God's love. When we acknowledge the messiness of our own lives, it may allow us to see others as people who God loves.

No matter what may be happening in your life, please know that God loves you. No matter what you may have done, please know that God loves you. His love and redemptive spirit and forgiving heart are without end. And if you are able to accept that truth for yourself, please know that it is true for every other person also. Acknowledging this should change how you view every other person you encounter. They too were created in God's image.

While God loves each of us, we must not confuse love with universal approval. God hates sin and while He is merciful and patient, He is also wrath. If I want to experience the kingdom of heaven, I need to search for any seeds of arrogance and eradicate them from myself. As arrogance diminishes we move closer ptokhos in spirit, we begin to see other people as beings created by God, in God's image and who are loved by Him, and we begin to allow God's love to flow through us. We gradually, bit by bit, grasp the kingdom of God.

Polyps

I am reminded of a time when I saw the fear, concern, and terror of being a parent through my parents. It was really my father who showed it most visibly. When I was 21 my brother, who is three years older, was diagnosed with osteosarcoma, a type of bone cancer. He is fine now, but for years he suffered through multiple surgeries in an effort to save his leg and chemotherapy, which at the time seemed barbarically experimental. Less than two years after his diagnosis, while I was home from college for a short visit I had some medical procedures performed and the doctors were shocked to find a bunch of polyps in my colon. They were not expecting to find polyps in someone so young. They removed the polyps, sent the tissue to be analyzed for cancer, and asked that I call them on a specific day for the results.

My father is a very hard worker and he always took his job seriously as the consummate professional. I knew at a very early age never to call my father at work. There could not possibly be an emergency large enough to bother him at work, but he was home every night to play catch with us and to coach our teams. So, I am not saying he was absent, it's just that I knew not to bother him at work. And he never called in sick. He never missed a day at work, and he never came home during the day. He left home early each morning for work and came home after work.

On the morning the polyp lab results were scheduled to be ready, he rushed into the house at about 10:30 and asked what the doctor had said. I was still in bed. I was not really awake yet. And the thought of calling the doctor had not occurred to me. I mean, at 22 I felt bulletproof. In my mind, nothing bad could possibly happen to me. I knew my brother had cancer, but I had not entertained the notion that anything similar would happen to me. So the thought of the polyps, and the possibility of colon cancer had not registered in my mind. But I was shocked that my father was home from work at 10:30 in the morning. I remember wondering why was he home? He was acting panicked, did he get fired? What was going on?

He insisted that I call the doctor immediately. So I did. I was incredibly annoyed at the demand, but I called. I remember standing in the kitchen, pushing the buttons on the wall-mounted phone with a long, long cord leading to the handset. It was one of those cords long enough to walk around the entire house talking on the phone. When I relayed the good news to my parents they were both so relieved. They cried and hugged me, and before that moment I failed to realize the extent of their anguish.

Looking back, it had been a miracle that saved my life. A series of remarkable events led to the discovery of polyps in someone who should have been too young to get them. As parents, at some time along the path, we experience brokenness for our children. My parents knew brokenness through my brother's path and braced for it in my situation, but the story is nothing unique, in fact it is very common. In that place of brokenness, when we turn to God we grew closer to God. In that place of darkness and total need, we feel His holy Presence.

Law Suit

Years ago I worked in a law firm and spent time assisting with litigation. A friend of mine, not a client, was named defendant in civil litigation for some decisions he had made at work. He is a really good guy and he firmly believed that his decisions and actions had been proper based on the circumstances. In his profession, reputation is extremely important and he had spent his career building a reputation of honor and upstanding character. But for day after day he sat listening to witnesses, some of whom he had previously considered close friends, attack his character and his judgment, and all he could do was sit there and listen to it. Each day he felt as if he was being shredded. His reputation was being dismantled before his eyes gradually, piece by piece. He saw his reputation, his career, his livelihood, all that he had worked so hard to build gradually being destroyed. The process continued through months of discovery and ultimately the trial. In the beginning he was angry, but gradually the anger faded leaving emptiness in its place. He reached the point where he was entirely drained spiritually and emotionally. His pride was gone. He hit bottom. At night when he could not sleep he knelt for hours in prayer, pleading with God for peace and comfort. And he said that God gave him an amazing sense of peace. He knew that everything would be all right regardless of how the lawsuit turned out because God's holy Presence was with him.

Ultimately he successfully defended the lawsuit, but during that time he experienced brokenness. He was poor in spirit. He was ptokhos in spirit. He had a void in his soul that only God could fill. And in that spirit of brokenness he found God as never before. He found a connection with God that he had not previously known. In that place of darkness and total need, we feel His Holy Presence. "Blessed are the poor in spirit, for theirs is the kingdom of heaven."

We are broken people living in a broken world. For many of us, we require brokenness to rid ourselves of arrogance. Through brokenness we lose our reliance on our will. Through brokenness we are able to lose ourselves and turn our lives over to Jesus Christ who does indeed save. Jesus tells us that His kingdom is not of this world. Jesus commands us to seek first His kingdom. Through brokenness, when we turn to Jesus Christ, we receive a special blessing – the blessing of possessing the kingdom of heaven. Blessed are the poor in spirit... the ptokhos in spirit... for theirs is the kingdom of heaven.

LIVING WATER & BREAD OF LIFE

As He attempts to translate His heavenly message of spiritual life using our limited language and recognizing our limited knowledge, Jesus uses different words and different imagery. He refers to eternal life, abundant life, and the kingdom of heaven while describing the quality of life available through communion with Him. He also uses images of bread and water – Jesus offers living water and He describes Himself as the bread of life. He uses symbols of daily physical sustenance to describe the spiritual sustenance available through relationship with Him.

As Jesus traveled from Judea to Galilee He passed through Samaria. At around noon He stopped at a well. A woman came to the well. Jesus asked her for some water. She expressed her surprise that a Jewish man would speak to her. Jesus said,

> "If you knew the gift of God and who it is that asks you for a drink, you would have asked him and he would have given you *living water*. ... Everyone who drinks this water will be thirsty again, but whoever drinks the water I give them will never thirst. Indeed, *the water I give them will become in them a spring of water welling up to eternal life.*" John 4:10 & 13-14

If you know Jesus and ask Him for living water, He will give it to you, and the living water will become a spring of eternal life. Spiritual life will flow with abundance if you know Jesus and ask for the living water.

While in Galilee, Jesus fed 5,000 men plus women and children with five loaves of bread and two fish. That evening He sent the crowds away, He sent the disciples away by boat to Capernaum, and Jesus went to a mountain alone to pray. As the disciples sailed, they encountered a storm and they were afraid. Jesus walked on the water to help them. The next morning the crowds found Jesus in Capernaum. They asked how He got there because they saw the disciples leave by boat without Him. Jesus replied,

> "Very truly I tell you, you are looking for me, not because you saw the signs I performed but because you ate the loaves and had your fill. Do not work for food that spoils, but for food that endures to eternal life, which the Son of Man will give you. For on him God the Father has placed his seal of approval.

> Then they asked him, "What must we do to do the works God requires?"

> Jesus answered, "The work of God is this: to believe in the one he has sent."

> So they asked him, "What sign then will you give that we may see it and believe you? What will you do? Our ancestors ate the manna in the wilderness; as it is written: 'He gave them bread from heaven to eat.'"

> Jesus said to them, "Very truly I tell you, it is not Moses who has given you the bread from heaven, but it is my Father who gives you the true bread from heaven. For the bread of God is the bread that comes down from heaven and gives life to the world."

> "Sir," they said, "always give us this bread."

> Then Jesus declared, "I am the bread of life. Whoever comes to me will never go hungry, and whoever

believes in me will never be thirsty. But as I told you, you have seen me and still you do not believe. All those the Father gives me will come to me, and whoever comes to me I will never drive away. For I have come down from heaven not to do my will but to do the will of him who sent me, that I shall lose none of all those he has given me, but raise them up at the last day. For my Father's will is that everyone who looks to the Son and believes in him shall have eternal life, and I will raise them up at the last day. John 6:26-40

Jesus uses physical images to discuss spiritual truth. Jesus offers living water that will well up to become a spring of eternal life. Jesus offers food that never spoils and endures to eternal life. Jesus is the bread of life, and whoever believes in Him will never thirst and will never be hungry. Bread and water are physical images of spiritual satisfaction, spiritual fulfillment, life abundant, and eternal life.

What must we do to receive living water? Know the gift of God, accept Jesus as your Savior and ask Him for the gift of living water. What must we do to receive the bread of life? Do the work of God, which is to believe in Jesus. Look to the Son and believe in Him.

Earlier in this chapter we saw Jesus urge us to "seek first his kingdom and his righteousness" (Matthew 6:33). As we should expect, His message here is a continuation of that message. We should seek Him, consume Him, be filled with His holy presence, allow Him to transform our spirits and our souls, and receive His holy grace.

NEW LIFE

Jesus came to earth with a multifaceted mission statement that involved nothing less than changing everything. He came to change the world order by offering Himself as the path leading to new life and bridging the chasm separating people from God. Jesus explains that His mission involved preaching and teaching, saying, "I must proclaim the good news of the kingdom of God to the other towns also, because that is why I was sent" (Luke 4:43). Later, when speaking with Pilate Jesus says, "You say I am a king. In fact, the reason I was born and came into this world is to testify to the truth. Everyone on the side of truth listens to me" (John 18:37).

He came to explain the good news of the kingdom of God and to testify to the truth. He also came as a servant offering new life. He explains this mission directly saying, "I have come that they may have life, and have it to the full" (John 10:10).

An offer of new life must be accompanied with the realization that the old life needs to be changed. An explanation that the new life is better necessarily involves an explanation that the old life is not so good. Scripture explains that the world is a sinful place where evil roams. The thought that people are trapped as hostages in a bad place gives rise to the idea of ransom, and the notion of good and bad presumes making judgment between the two. With these thoughts in mind, Jesus explains that He came "to serve and to give his life as ransom for many" (Matthew 20:28). He also says, "For judgment I have come into this world, so the blind will see and those who see will become blind" (John 9:39).

He came to serve, but He also came for judgment. He came to turn the world upside down, to change everything. He knew the change He was ushering would disrupt institutions and power structures in place, and changes at that level are rarely peaceful. He says,

> "Do not suppose that I have come to bring peace to the earth. I did not come to bring peace, but a sword. For I have come to turn 'a man against his father, a daughter against her mother, a daughter-in-law against her mother-in-law – a man's enemies will be the members of his own household.'" Matthew 10:34-36

Ultimately, Jesus' mission involves revealing God's glory to people on earth. His mission has to do with God's glory. After the Last Supper, Jesus prays an amazing prayer. He begins praying by saying,

> Father, the hour has come. *Glorify* your Son, that your Son may *glorify* you. For you granted him authority over all people that he might give eternal life to all those you have given him. Now this is eternal life: that they know you, the only true God, and Jesus Christ, whom you have sent. I have brought you *glory* on earth by finishing the work you gave me to do. And now, Father, *glorify* me in your presence with the glory I had with you before the world began. John 17:1-5

By completing the work that Jesus came to earth to do, Jesus glorified God by revealing God's glory to the world.

While His mission statement is multifaceted, it focuses on new life. He preached and taught about new life, and He offered Himself so that we might receive the gift of new life. With this in mind, it should be no surprise that Scripture portrays Jesus as extremely concerned with our spiritual life. He uses several different terms and many different images in an attempt to convey the concept. He discusses living water, bread of life, abundant life, eternal life, the kingdom of God and the kingdom of heaven as different ways of describing spiritual life – the quality of life that is available by living in communion with God.

The world is a place where evil exists and roams; yet it is also the place where God came as fully human, where Jesus taught, where Jesus revealed God's glory, and where God is glorified through Jesus and His Holy Spirit. God's holy grace, His gift of new life is available here on earth to mere humans. May you receive God's holy grace, may you accept the gift of new life, may you allow the Holy Spirit to dwell within you, may you experience His peace, joy and love, and may God reveal His glory to the world through you.

Part II. Spiritual Realm

<<<<<<◇>>>>>>

6 | SPIRITUAL REALM

"The greatest trick the devil ever played was convincing the world he doesn't exist." Verbal Kint, The Usual Suspects

While Jesus was in the wilderness, He interacted with spiritual entities.[1] The Holy Spirit led Him to the wilderness, He spoke with a spiritual entity referred to as the devil and Satan, and angels comforted Him. Spiritual beings interacted with Jesus in the same way people interact with one another.

This is not an isolated occurrence in Scripture. Time and time again we see spiritual entities interacting with people. Scripture says some angels are good and other angels are bad.[2] In Scripture we see God sending angels as messengers to people.[3] We see angels protecting people,[4] encouraging people,[5] guiding people,[6] and battling forces of evil.[7] We see Jesus engage in conversations with impure and evil spiritual entities.[8] Scripture discusses angels and other spiritual beings as if they really exist and really interact with and influence people.

Some people interpret Scriptural references to spiritual entities as figurative, metaphorical or equivalent to mythology. They believe the references are literary tools attributing spiritual characteristics to people – angels and demons are not really angels and demons, rather they are people doing good or bad, respectively. We might describe a person who lends a helping hand as an "angel," and we might refer to a person struggling through personal crisis as "battling demons." They read the stories and believe that Jesus struggled against natural forces and His own natural temptations while in the wilderness, and that the description of angels ministering to Him probably refer to people who helped Him along the way. They interpret Scriptural references to supernatural entities as literary devices describing natural things.

Others believe angels and demons are supernatural, spiritual beings that really exist in a realm we are unable or rarely able to see. They believe that when Scripture mentions angels and demons, it refers to spiritual beings that not only exist, but that in certain situations interact with and influence people.

So which is it? When the Bible talks about angels is it really referring to nice people, or is it describing spiritual beings in our midst? Is there a spiritual realm around us or does everything have a natural explanation?

I am reminded of a line from *The Usual Suspects*, the 1995 movie staring Kevin Spacey who won an Academy Award for his performance playing the character Verbal Kint. At one point Spacey's character says, "The greatest trick the devil ever played was convincing the world he doesn't exist."

After pondering the bulk of Scriptural references to spiritual entities, I believe they are real. They are part of the supernatural realm that really exists. Humans are part physical and part spiritual. We live in the physical realm defined by and limited by space and time, but we also have spiritual lives. A spiritual realm surrounds us and influences us. And one of the fundamental purposes of Scripture is to guide us toward spiritual transformation.

As I say that the spiritual realm influences us, I am cognizant of two extremes. Many refuse to believe in the spiritual realm while others believe evil spirits influence every action they make. I have encountered people who attribute every bit of trouble in their lives to demonic forces. If they trip on crack in the sidewalk, they blame it on a demonic force. The bulk of Scripture does not support that sort of interpretation, and that is not what I am saying here. As with most things, reality exists between the extremes.

But I am much more concerned about the first group. Our educational system encourages people to equate notions of the spiritual realm and supernatural entities with mythology and irrational thought. I fear that in the US, Kevin Spacey's character reveals a nugget of truth. But this is not the case in all western cultures.

HAITI

Before traveling to a country for the first time I look at the US Department of State website and the CIA World Factbook for information about the country. Shortly after booking a flight to Haiti in 2002 I researched the CIA fact sheet. At the time it said over 80% of the nation was affiliated with Christian denominations, and over 90% of the population practiced some elements voodoo.[9] If the numbers were accurate, a significant portion of the population followed Jesus Christ *and* practiced voodoo, which seemed like an incompatible combination. I was very curious to see how folks in Haiti fit the two together in their culture.

I traveled on behalf of World Hope International to investigate microenterprise programs, to witness what was working, to learn what efforts had failed, and to begin understanding why some things worked while others did not. One morning we traveled to a construction site. A new building was being erected on a vacant lot at a street corner in an urban part of Port-au-Prince. When we arrived, workers were standing in the street. A partially constructed building – four partially erected exterior walls – stood on the site. Bricks were neatly stacked in various cubes around the site. Bags of mortar were stacked on pallets. Mortar mixing equipment and trowels were ready to be used. But no people were on the site; they all stood in the street.

I asked our translator what was going on. Why were the workers not working? He told me that the site was locked. I saw no lock, no gate and no fence. I saw no evidence of the site being locked and no mechanism for locking it. So I repeated my question, thinking I had misunderstood. The translator explained that after work each day a witch doctor performed an elaborate ceremony at the site, placing a curse on each brick, each tool, each bag of mortar and the site itself. Any person who stepped onto the site would assume a curse. Following the ceremony the site was locked. No one would enter the site until the curse was removed, and on that particular morning the witch doctor was negotiating for a higher fee.

I asked whether the curse was real. Would it really cause physical problems? Had the translator experienced anything bad happening to anyone who tested curses like that? He was embarrassed to talk about the local superstitions. He said that people did not really believe that the spells worked and he tried to distance himself from it. But his actions and the actions of every other person present indicated that they believed the spells had power, so I asked a few more questions. If he did not really believe, had he ever tested a curse? He said he had not and he did not know of any curse ever being tested. I asked him to ask others whether they had first hand knowledge of the curse working. Several told stories they had heard about a friend of a friend, or a friend's relative who crossed a curse and experienced negative effects, but none had firsthand knowledge because they had never tested a curse.

They were embarrassed to discuss the topic, they did not want to seem unsophisticated to their guests from the United States, but their actions indicated that they believed the curse worked, that bad things happen to people who test it, and that black magic is real. Or at least they thought it might be real and the risk was certainly not worth stealing a brick or mortar tools, and apparently not worth entering the site to start working until the curse was removed. The site was locked because everyone believed that the curse, the black magic, the voodoo, was either real or possibly real.

The Haitians' belief in black magic made the curse an effective locking mechanism, but is it real? I recalled a conversation years earlier. A friend in college, Eric, was from Rio de Janeiro. He was extremely smart and he excelled in the petroleum engineering program. During one spring break Eric took a mutual friend home with him to Rio. When they returned, Eric described some of our friend's adventures, including his first encounter with witch doctors and voodoo. I had seen images of witch doctors and voodoo in movies and read references to them in books, but they fit in the same category as myth and fairy tales in my mind. So I asked Eric about his experience with them, and I recalled his insistence that black magic and voodoo are real. He would not explain details of his experiences, but he spoke with such passion. His passion communicated that black magic and voodoo were more than passing thoughts. He said evil spirits are real and voodoo is among the most dangerous of them. I recalled his adamant advice, his urging insistence that I stay away from the entire realm of black magic at all cost. At the time I did not expect his advice to alter my actions because, as far as I knew, I had not encountered black magic or voodoo in Golden, Colorado, but I decided to defer to his experience and follow his advice if I ever did.

The people who live in cultures in which black magic is practiced believe it is real. But is it?

The people I encountered in Haiti were very open to the existence of the spiritual realm. Buildings and construction sites were guarded by spirits, and directed by certain people who knew the right words to say. Spirits were directed and controlled by people who knew how to do so. Haitians' acceptance of the spiritual realm provided a perfect avenue to discuss the Holy Spirit.

In a rural area outside Port-au-Prince I described the locked construction site to a group of locals and asked about voodoo and what would happen if anyone crossed the curse, and the people I spoke with described all the bad things that evil spirits could and would do to people who crossed the curse. They were certain that evil spirits existed, so I asked whether they knew of the Holy Spirit. They were intrigued. They had not heard of the Holy Spirit, but as I described Him to them, one of the men said, "Oh, so there is a good spirit also? I like that." Others nodded and smiled in acknowledgement. They liked the idea of a good spirit, but it seemed as if they had not heard about Him before our conversation.

Here in the US many have convinced themselves that the spiritual realm is not worthy of consideration. If they give it any thought, which many do not, they would likely conclude it to be of no consequence. We are sophisticated, intellectual, educated, and so advanced that we have no need for things that seem irrational and unscientific. Many believe there are good scientific explanations for all things, including explanations disproving spiritual matters, and if there are not yet good explanations there soon will be.

I ponder the good Spirit and bad spirits. I do not know about the witch doctors and spells that lock construction sites in Haiti. I will continue to lock my doors with physical locks and I will continue setting my burglar alarm at night separating me from things outside. But as I ponder voodoo and Christianity and bad spirits and black magic and the good Spirit, I wonder whether it is better to discuss voodoo to the extent that we are prepared to avoid it, or is it better to live as many, many people live in the US, failing to consider the spiritual realm at all?

Our culture has done an impressive job of making the spiritual realm sound like a fairy tale, myth or superstition, and the notion of good and bad spirits sound like science fiction. *The Wizard of Oz* introduces us to good and bad witches. *Star Wars* has a good force and an evil force. *The Polar Express* and many other Christmas stories tell us if we believe in Santa Claus the magic of Christmas will become real. But the fact that fiction mimics truth does not alter the truth. An intellectual approach that eliminates the spiritual realm from serious consideration is dangerous, because God is spirit. If we equate the entire spiritual realm with mythological, unscientific, irrational thought, God may quickly be included in the bucket.

Scripture presents evil spirits, angels and the Holy Spirit as spiritual entities that really exist. Let's consider each individually.

7 | EVIL SPIRITS

*"Be self-controlled and alert.
Your enemy the devil prowls
around like a roaring lion looking
for someone to devour."*
1 Peter 5:8

FOUNDATIONAL THOUGHTS

The construction site in Port-au-Prince was locked after a man performed a public ceremony, combining specific words and actions. People who saw the locking ceremony believed that his words directed spirits, that the spirits would follow his direction, and that the spirits would harm folks who entered the locked site. The lock worked because it kept people out. The locals were open to the existence of the spiritual realm; they believed evil spirits exist, wield power, and follow the witch doctor's commands. But of course, just because some Haitians believe things like that does not make them real.

After the Holy Spirit healed her, Delores[3] suffered attacks on her soul, spirit, mind and body. Voices in her head, not her own, tried to convince her she was losing her mind. She describes it as spiritual warfare, the work of a spiritual enemy. Her

---

[3] Delores is discussed in more detail in chapter 9

experience, her reading of Scripture, and her relationship with the Holy Spirit convince her that evil spiritual forces are real and spiritual warfare is real.

I traveled to Mongolia as part of a delegation working to establish orphanages sponsored by World Hope International, a US-based non-governmental relief organization. The group included four remarkable women – Jo Anne Lyon, founder of World Hope, and three other women. One, I will call her Deborah, was from Washington, DC and was responsible for several foundations. Another was a PhD chemist who worked in the pharmaceutical industry in Virginia. The fourth, I will call her Mary, was an American living in Hong Kong. We traveled over much of Mongolia crammed into a van, bouncing along a pothole-laden asphalt road and many dirt roads.

We met with leaders across the country and discussed efforts to solve the growing problem of homeless children. We saw clean and efficiently run state orphanages built and operated on the Soviet model, and spoke with the loving people who ran them. They accomplished remarkable good with extremely scarce resources. We saw the sewer system under Ulaanbaatar where homeless kids lived. Steam pipes from the central power plant ran through sewer tunnels, providing warmth in winter and heat to warm food. We met a seven-year-old boy who cared for his younger brother. After their mother died they moved to the sewer, where they were victimized by the gangs who ran the place. Most of the kids' stories started with parents' unemployment after the Soviet Union pulled out of Mongolia, followed by some combination of parents' alcohol abuse, drug abuse, violence and death. We met a young man name Otgunbayer who a few years earlier was one of the gang leaders. We heard stories and saw evidence of tragic suffering.

Our small group traveled through Ulaanbaatar, north to the Siberian border, south to the edge of the Mobi Desert and east in the mountains. We ate together and talked after dinner, and gradually we shared stories about our lives. I understood that three of the four women were close friends united by a deep love of Christ Jesus and by many shared experiences traveling the world. I heard amazing stories of God moving in response to their prayers in many different situations on several continents. They had an intimate relationship with God. Prayer was part of their life and when they prayed, even I felt God respond.

Over the days we shared countless conversations about every topic imaginable. One evening I spoke with the three friends and our conversation veered to the subject of evil. As we discussed newspaper accounts of evil around the world, the conversation moved deeper to personal experiences. Jo Anne described flying into Sierra Leone by UN helicopter during the civil war. One of the rebels' calling cards after raiding a village was hacking limbs from victims they allowed to live. She saw countless men, women and children missing hands, arms, legs or some combination. Their limbs had been hacked from their bodies by machete wielding rebels. An entire population had lost the ability to care for themselves or one another. They were desperately in need. Many had lost hope.

Jo Anne described a boy who was thirteen when she met him. When he was eight, rebels attacked his village capturing the boy, his mother and his brothers and sisters. They told the boy to kill his mother. If he refused the rebels would kill him and his family. His mother begged him to do it, and he did. The kids were conscripted into the rebel army. The boy quickly rose to the rank of commander and he forced many to carry out similar atrocities. When Jo Anne met him, his evil acts haunted him. At the instant he pulled the trigger sending bullets into his mother, he was convinced he was beyond saving. After that, evil acts became easier and easier. Still a boy, he was a victim of evil and an instrument of evil convinced there was no path that could possibly lead him to hope or anything good.

She described World Hope's efforts to help the boy and many other lost boys sharing similar stories, and to fabricate prosthetics for the victims, providing a semblance of the hands, arms and legs they once had, and enabling them to walk and work. The prosthetic program combined with counseling, education and teaching about the forgiveness available through Jesus Christ provided the beginning of hope. She described the spirit of forgiveness overcoming the spirit of evil depicted by a man who stood on two prosthetic legs as he encountered the man who hacked off his limbs years earlier. The victim offered forgiveness and both moved toward healing.

On one trip to Sierra Leone, shortly after she arrived by UN transport, a man with two bodyguards approached her. The man cordially identified himself and said that his boss, who he named, wanted to meet Jo Anne. She recognized the boss's name. He was a rebel leader, notorious for evil beyond imagination. She agreed to go.

As the leader of rebel forces, his location was a guarded secret. So the men blindfolded Jo Anne, drove through the city for a long time making too many turns to count and back tracking and turning more before heading out into the jungle. They drove a great distance and finally stopped at the rebel leader's lair. She still had no idea why she was there. Her blindfold was removed. The leader explained that he had heard about World Hope's activities and the lives that were changed as a result. He heard about the prosthetics and about the spiritual healing taking place. He heard about forgiveness and love. She said he expressed fear. He was afraid of the power behind World Hope's actions, and he wanted to meet the person responsible for that power and learn the secret behind it.

As she told the story, Jo Anne laughed. She waved her hands toward herself as she said, "Can you believe he was afraid of me? I was praying like crazy for God's protection, and he was afraid of me." Even more amazing, Jo Anne had the opportunity to tell the man about the source of the power he saw – Jesus Christ. She spent the next few hours witnessing to him, the man notorious for his evil, about the wonders of Jesus Christ, the source of the power he had witnessed.

Jo Anne discussed seeing prostitutes as young as five held as slaves in brothels in the Philippines. She described World Hope's efforts to free young girls and women from slavery. She also described the opposition they encountered not only from the brothel owners but from government officials who protected them. People working to free girls put their lives at risk daily. It was war in every sense of the word. Freeing girls physically was only the beginning of the long process towards recovery.

The women discussed places they had traveled and other evil they had witnessed. A few stories greatly disturbed them. As they talked about what had happened, they each relived each story. The stories caused them to remember one particular event that they did not want to talk about. It greatly disturbed them to remember it. They said the event involved such evil they did not want to discuss it. As our conversation ended that night and they each drifted to their separate rooms.

Our world is filled with evil influences, and we each respond them in our own ways. I recently received a text message from a friend saying, "I'm just tired. My spirit is tired so that's hard to sleep off." Spiritual exhaustion may be the result of evil or may simply be the product of an overly busy and stressful life. My spirit is tired also. Over the past eighteen months we lost four of our five dogs, my father suffered with an extended stay in the hospital, my son was arrested on charges that could have lead to a lifetime of incarceration, and my wife was diagnosed with soft tissue sarcoma in her hamstring. She endured radiation, surgery and chemo that nearly killed her, my father is leading a healthy life again, and my son is gradually moving forward with his life but he continues to be haunted by the horrific events of one evening. I know that the drain to my spirit has been nothing like the drain to their spirits, but even I feel tired.

I am not sure whether all of the events are related to evil in the world, or whether some are simply the result of living in this fallen world. For example, is Lori's cancer the result of evil or is it simply a body's cells going awry as a result of some biological abnormality? I am not sure, but the resulting condition is certainly awful.

EXISTENCE & INFLUENCE

Does an Evil One Exist?

Without doubt, our world is broken and we are surrounded by evil influences and evil events. People do malicious things to one another. For many, pain is part of the routine human condition. People suffer physically, emotionally, economically and spiritually. Pain and suffering are ubiquitous, causing me to wonder whether suffering and acts of malice are simply part of the human condition or is some evil force or presence causing these things? Or could it be some of both? Does the natural human condition include pain, suffering and malice, and in addition to that do external evil forces exacerbate the dark human condition?

Evil was not part of the original human condition. We know this because, before the fall, God created people and said His creation was good.[1] Evil was in the world before the fall and people were tempted by it (as seen through Eve's conversation with the serpent in Genesis 3), but after the fall, people gained knowledge of good and evil and were separated from God, death entered the world, and the earth was cursed.[2] Since that time, mankind has been exposed to evil and the tragedies associated with the fallen realm, and has been vulnerable to the combined influence. Theoretically, evil is not part of the original human condition – evil is an outside force influencing humans – but determining whether evil is part of the human condition or the human condition is rendered evil though outside forces is really a distinction without a difference.

Paul describes our world as "dark"[3] with battles being fought between spiritual forces on earth and in the heavenly realms. Evidence of evil surrounds us. Many people go to bed each night hungry. Many people have no shelter to sleep in at night. Many people struggle with addiction in one of its many forms. Many suffer from and struggle with depression. Many are being attacked by cancer or other awful physical condition. Many people have been forced from their homes fleeing violence and chaos of war, with no place to go. Many are trapped in various forms of slavery around the world. While over a billion people around the world lack safe drinking water, some cities in the US fail to provide safe drinking water to the people living there. And on top of all these tragedies, day after day we read of verbal attacks, hatred, discord, murder, rape and people abusing the power afforded them through their professional position. We see suicide bombings and other acts of terrorism – in many cases people killing innocent people in the name of God. The headlines reveal evidence of evil manifesting itself through action.

While evidence of evil is all around us, what is the source of evil? What causes humans to show the opposite of love to one another? Scripture discusses evil as a spiritual force. It discusses evil as a force housed within specific spiritual beings and, consistent with our experience in the world, Scripture discusses evil as a force influencing people and attacking people.

The Haitians feared spiritual attack. In his letters, Paul is deeply concerned with spiritual attacks. His writing provides imagery suggesting and supporting the notion of spiritual warfare. He says,

> Finally, be strong in the Lord and in his mighty power. Put on the full armor of God, so that you can take your *stand against the devil's schemes*. For our struggle is not against flesh and blood, but against the rulers, against the authorities, against the *powers of this dark world* and against the *spiritual forces of evil in the heavenly realms*. Therefore, put on the full armor of God, so that when the day of evil comes, you may be able to stand your ground, and after you have done everything, to stand. Stand firm then, with the belt of truth buckled around your waist, with the breastplate of righteousness in place, and with your feet fitted with the readiness that comes from the gospel of peace. In addition to all this, take up the shield of faith, with which you can extinguish all the *flaming arrows of the evil one*. Take the helmet of salvation and the sword of the Spirit, which is the word of God. Ephesians 6:10-17

Using strong imagery, Paul says the evil one attacks people with flaming arrows. Paul urges his readers to be warriors dressing for battle, standing "against the devil's schemes" and fighting against spiritual entities. By saying "our struggle is not against flesh and blood," Paul clarifies that he is describing a spiritual struggle. He then identifies the enemies in the battle: "rulers... authorities... powers of this dark world and... spiritual forces of evil in the heavenly realms." So the spiritual enemy is here on earth and in the "heavenly realms." According to Paul, the spiritual realm is as real as the chair I am sitting on and the desk I am sitting at. The attacks are also real. While the evil one may not launch real flaming arrows at people, the attacks are nonetheless real.

Evil tries to destroy good. I have heard it said that evil is the absence of God. While this is true, if the thought creates images of evil as a vacuum, a void, an empty space seeking something to fill it, the notion is too passive. It may be true that evil is measured by God's absence in the same way that temperature is a measure of heat with cold simply representing the absence of heat, and that brightness is a measure of light with darkness representing the absence of light. But evil is not passive, and please do not let this imagery create a passive image in your mind. Evil is an active force seeking to separate you, us, everyone from good, which means separating us from God.

Scripture identifies a spiritual being that is the essence of evil, whose character represents evil and whose actions carry out evil. The devil seeks to destroy good. Peter portrays the devil, the force of evil, as a prowling lion saying,

> "Be self-controlled and alert. Your enemy the devil prowls around like a roaring lion looking for someone to devour." 1 Peter 5:8

Peter and Paul regard the devil as a real, living entity that houses evil. The enemy prowls, roars and devours like a lion. The evil known as the devil stalks and attacks. Peter uses imagery of a lion while Paul uses the image of a soldier shooting an arrow.

Both indicate an enemy is methodically plotting, hunting and attacking.

Jesus also discusses evil as a real force. In the Sermon on the Mount, Jesus provides guidance about prayer and He tells us to ask God to deliver us from evil. Jesus says,

> "This, then, is how you should pray: Our Father in heaven, hallowed be your name, your kingdom come, your will be done on earth as it is in heaven. Give us this day our daily bread. Forgive us our debts, as we also have forgiven our debtors. And lead us not into temptation, but *deliver us from evil.*" (Some manuscripts say "... *deliver us from the evil one,* for yours is the kingdom and the power and the glory forever.") Matthew 6:9-13.

During the evening of the Last Supper Jesus prayed for His disciples. As part of His long prayer, Jesus prays,

> "My prayer is not that you take them out of the world but that you *protect them from the evil one.*" John 17:15

To make these statements, Jesus must believe evil really exists and God the Father has the power and authority to protect people from it. Does evil or an evil one exist in the world? If it does not, why would Jesus pray asking God the Father to protect us from the evil one and teach us to pray a similar prayer?

While it is easy to discuss evil in abstract terms by referring to articles in the newspaper about horrific events happening around the globe, it is much less comfortable to discuss the influence of evil in our personal lives. Jesus, Peter and Paul discuss evil in a general sense and warn that evil influences individuals, but Scripture does so much more. It also describes evil forces directly, physically impacting real people, forcing us to consider evil on personal terms.

EVIL SPIRITS INFLUENCE PEOPLE

Scripture suggests that spirits interact with and influence one another. As discussed earlier, each person has a spirit. While people have spirits, other categories of spirits also exist. Scripture says some spirits exist that are not connected with people. For example, God is spirit.[4] Jesus is spirit.[5] Angels are ministering spirits.[6] Spiritual forces, including spirits associated with other people, influence each person's spirit.

Scripture records Jesus interacting with evil spirits that exhibit influence over people. The encounters help us understand how spirits influence people, Jesus' authority over the spirits, and how He exercises His authority. Remember, Jesus refers to evil and the evil one, Peter refers to evil spirits as the enemy and as a lion that prowls, attacks and devours, and Paul describes evil spirits as warriors shooting arrows. They methodically plot, prowl, hunt and attack; they are intent on causing harm; and their ultimate goal is to separate us from God. Let's look at some encounters described in Scripture.

Man in Synagogue

Jesus was in Capernaum staying in the home of Peter's mother-in-law, who was in bed with a fever. Jesus touched her hand and she was instantly healed. Matthew continues telling the story writing,

> "When evening came, many who were demon-possessed were brought to him [Jesus], and *he drove out the spirits* with a word and healed the sick." Matthew 8:16

Mark records another event taking place in Capernaum around the same time. On the Sabbath Jesus taught in the synagogue and everyone was amazed at His teaching. They had never heard anyone teach with His authority.

"Just then a man in the synagogue who was *possessed by an impure spirit* cried out, "What do you want with us, Jesus of Nazareth? Have you come to destroy us? I know who you are – the Holy One of God!" "Be quiet!" said Jesus sternly. "Come out of him!" The impure spirit shook the man violently and came out of him with a shriek." Mark 1:23-26 (see also Luke 4:33-35)

The spirit influenced the man to the extent that the spirit spoke using the man's body as its vessel. The spirit spoke to Jesus, recognized Jesus as the Messiah, and obeyed Jesus. The spirit submitted to Jesus' authority. Jesus taught with authority and He demonstrated His authority over evil spirits.

I find it a little unsettling that a man who went to church to worship was demon-possessed. Who led who to church? Is this a common occurrence? So many questions.

Legion

Jesus and the disciples crossed the Sea of Galilee and came to shore at the southeastern corner of the sea. As they walked on the shore, a man possessed by evil spirits approached Jesus. The man lived in the tombs and had superhuman strength. People could not subdue him and when they chained his hands and feet, he broke the chains. He cut himself with stones and he continuously cried out. When he saw Jesus, he ran to Jesus, fell on his knees and shouted,

"What do you want with me, Jesus, Son of the Most High God? Swear to God that you won't torture me!" For Jesus had said to him, "Come out of this man, you evil spirit!" Mark 5:1-20 (see also Matthew 8:28-34 and Luke 8:26-39)

Jesus asked the spirit to tell Him its name. The spirit said, "My name is Legion, for we are many." The spirit begged Jesus to allow it to stay in area, and asked to be sent into a nearby herd of pigs. Jesus gave it permission to enter the pigs. When the spirit entered the pigs, the pigs rushed down a hill and into the sea where they died.

As with the man in the synagogue, the spirit referred to as Legion invaded the man and exerted influence over him including speaking through him and controlling his body, voice and actions.

Boy with Epileptic Symptoms

Peter, James and John traveled with Jesus up a mountain where Jesus was transfigured before them.[7] Jesus' clothes became a glowing, brilliant white, brighter than they had ever seen. His face glowed. Elijah and Moses appeared before them and a voice from heaven spoke proclaiming Jesus to be the Son of God, the Messiah. As the four men traveled back down the mountain, they encountered a large crowd of people surrounding the other disciples. A man in the crowd approached Jesus and said he brought his demon-possessed son to the disciples but they were unable to remove the evil spirit. Jesus asked to see the boy.

> "So they brought him. When the spirit saw Jesus, it immediately threw the boy into convulsion. He fell to the ground and rolled around, foaming at the mouth... When Jesus saw that a crowd was running to the scene, he rebuked the evil spirit. "You deaf and mute spirit," he said, "I command you, come out of him and never enter him again." *The spirit* shrieked, convulsed him violently and *came out*." Mark 9:20 & 25-26

Again, the evil spirit influenced the boy's behavior, but yielded to Jesus authority. Later, when they were alone, the disciples asked Jesus why they were unable to drive the spirit out of the boy. Jesus replied, "This kind can come out only by prayer."[8]

So there are different kinds of evil spirits. The authority granted the disciples was sufficient to direct and control some kinds of evil spirits, but not all kinds. The disciples had a grant of authority, but it was limited. Sometimes they needed to appeal to God for His direct intervention.

Other Examples

In addition to detailed accounts, like the ones set forth above, on several occasions Luke tells us that Jesus "cured" people of evil spirits without providing many details. He mentions the fact in passing as if the events were so routine that they were not worthy of detailed explanation. For example, Luke explains that Jesus stayed up all night praying before selecting the twelve disciples. After that, Jesus went with the twelve to a flat plain where He preached the Beatitudes to a large crowd of people – people from all over Judea, Jerusalem, Tyre and Sidon. Between the two stories is a short transition where Luke says,

> "*Those troubled by impure spirits were cured*, and the people all tried to touch him, because power was coming from him and healing them all." Luke 6:18-19

The sentence is thrown in, as a brief transition between two stories of greater significance to Luke, as if removing impure spirits from people was routine, ordinary, and not worthy of much attention.

Later in his gospel, Luke describes a time when John the Baptist is in prison. In his anguish, John begs friends to go to Jesus and ask Him directly whether He is the Messiah. Recall that John the Baptist and Jesus share a long history. They were connected before birth: the angel Gabriel visited John's father and Jesus' mother before each birth; their mothers were related and spent time together during their pregnancies; and their ministries overlapped.[9] John baptized Jesus, he saw the dove of the Holy Spirit land on Jesus and heard God's voice call out from heaven proclaiming Jesus as the Son of God.[10] But as John sat in prison he began to wonder whether it was true. If Jesus really was the

Messiah, if He really was unveiling a new kingdom and He really was the king, why did He allow John to sit in jail?

John's friends spoke with Jesus. Jesus referred to Messianic prophecies. He told them to describe to John all the miracles that were happening – people were healed, people were raised from the dead, and the good news of God was preached to the poor – fulfilling the prophecies. As part of the story, Luke wrote,

> "At that time Jesus cured many who had diseases, sicknesses and *evil spirits*, and gave sight to many who were blind." Luke 7:21

In several places Luke mentioned the fact that Jesus exercised authority over evil spirits, but that was not the focus of Luke's stories. The evil spirits were mentioned in passing. Luke continued mentioning evil spirits and authority over the spirits in his second book, Acts. He described the authority that Peter and the other apostles demonstrated over evil spirits writing,

> "Crowds gathered also from the towns around Jerusalem, bringing their sick and those *tormented by impure spirits*, and all of them were healed." Acts 5:16

> "For with shrieks, *impure spirits came out* of many and many who were paralyzed or lame were also healed." Acts 8:7

The passages above indicate that impure or evil spirits exist, that at times they dwell within people, that at times they have been separated from people and that the apostles had authority over the evil spirits. The spirits mentioned in these passages seem to be independent entities, capable of surviving on their own, apart from people. But they are also capable of invading a person and influencing a person physically, mentally and emotionally.

How Do Evil Spirits Influence People?

Physical Influence

What do evil spirits do to people? How do they influence people? In examples above we see extreme physical influence including: (i) spirits taking over a man, using his body as an instrument for their voice while he sat in the synagogue; (ii) a spirit controlling a boy's body, causing him to exhibit symptoms similar to epilepsy; (iii) spirits taking over a man's body, speaking through him and giving him superhuman strength such that no man nor chains could subdue him; and (iv) spirits invading pigs' bodies, causing them to rush into the sea where they drown.

Temptation

We previously discussed the temptation of Jesus in the wilderness as an example of spiritual attack, demonstrating that spiritual attacks happen. Let's consider the account again looking at the methods of attack. After Jesus was baptized in the Jordan River, He travelled alone to the wilderness where He fasted for forty days. A character described as the devil, the tempter and Satan visited Jesus. They spoke with one another in the same way that two humans might have a conversation. Matthew writes,

> Then Jesus was led by the Spirit into the wilderness to be tempted by the devil. After fasting forty days and forty nights, he was hungry. The tempter came to him and said, "If you are the Son of God, tell these stones to become bread."
>
> Jesus answered, "It is written: 'Man shall not live on bread alone, but on every word that comes from the mouth of God.'"
>
> Then the devil took him to the holy city and had him stand on the highest point of the temple. "If you are

the Son of God," he said, "throw yourself down. For it is written:

"'He will command his angels concerning you, and they will lift you up in their hands, so that you will not strike your foot against a stone.'"

Jesus answered him, "It is also written: 'Do not put the Lord your God to the test.'"

Again, the devil took him to a very high mountain and showed him all the kingdoms of the world and their splendor. "All this I will give you," he said, "if you will bow down and worship me."

Jesus said to him, "Away from me, Satan! For it is written: 'Worship the Lord your God, and serve him only.'"

Then the devil left him, and angels came and attended him. Matthew 4:1-11.

The story includes the Holy Spirit leading Jesus, angels attending to Him, and the devil, the tempter, Satan tempting Him. Satan tempted Jesus.

Satan did not attempt to influence Jesus by physically controlling Him or taking over His body; Satan attempted to influence Jesus by speaking to Him. The tempter asked Jesus to prove His position, or possibly to have God prove Jesus' position. Twice Satan said, "If you are the Son of God…" Jesus refused to take the bait. He refused to engage in that discussion. He refused to treat Satan with the respect necessary to engage in that conversation because Satan is not deserving of His respect.

The tempter used three approaches. Satan tempted Jesus based on His physical needs – Jesus was hungry and Satan encouraged Jesus to misappropriate the power and authority God had granted Him for personal gain rather than for God's glory. Jesus responded by quoting Deuteronomy 8:3 and switching the conversation from physical needs to spiritual needs. We may need food for physical life, but we need the word of God for spiritual life.

Next, Satan used Scripture to tempt Jesus, quoting Psalm 91, which discusses God sending His angels for protection. Satan quoted the words accurately, but he twisted around the intended meaning.

Finally, Satan tempted Jesus by offering power and wealth in exchange for Jesus agreeing to worship and serve Satan. This sort of satanic offer is a common theme in books and movies. Think of the Oscar Wilde's novel *The Picture of Dorian Gray*, movies *Angel Heart* starring Mickey O'Rourke and *The Devil's Advocate* starring Al Pacino, and songs like *The Devil Went Down to Georgia* by The Charlie Daniel's Band and *Heaven Help the Fool* by Bob Weir. These are but a few of many. Each involves a deal where the devil offers worldly success in exchange for the person's soul.

In fiction, Satan is able to deliver the deal bargained. But does Satan have the authority to grant Jesus "all the kingdoms of the world and their splendor?" How much authority does Satan have? This leads us to something else Jesus said about the devil.

Deception

Chapter 8 of John's Gospel records a conversation between Jesus and a group of religious leaders known as Pharisees. It is a long conversation. Jesus starts by describing Himself as the "light of the world" (John 8:12). One of the religious leaders questions the validity of Jesus' statement because He offered no witness to support His claim. Jesus replies explaining that His Father supports His testimony, which leads to a long discussion about who His Father is and who the religious leaders' fathers were. Twice Jesus accuses them of wanting to kill Him. They do not dispute the claim; yet continue to discuss the identity of fathers.

Jesus said to them,

"If God were your Father, you would love me, for I have come here from God. I have not come on my own; God sent me. Why is my language not clear to you? Because you are unable to hear what I say. *You belong to your father, the devil, and you want to carry out your father's desires. He was a murderer from the beginning, not holding to the truth, for there is no truth in him. When he lies, he speaks his native language, for he is a liar and the father of lies.* Yet because I tell the truth, you do not believe me! Can any of you prove me guilty of sin? If I am telling the truth, why don't you believe me? Whoever belongs to God hears what God says. The reason you do not hear is that you do not belong to God." John 8:42-47

These are harsh words spoken by a wandering homeless man to the leading religious leaders of the day. As part of His rant, Jesus calls the devil "a murderer from the beginning," and "a liar and the father of lies" with "no truth in him." He calls the devil a murderer because he recruits people to carry out his evil plans. The devil apparently recruited the religious leaders into his plans by whispering in their ears, possibly in the same way he spoke to Jesus in the wilderness.

So Jesus, who saw Satan fall from heaven to earth like a bolt of lightning,[11] describes the devil as a liar and a murderer. Jesus says the devil is the religious leaders' father because they want to kill Jesus and they do not belong to God. This is a terrifying exchange because the Pharisees were, as a group, deeply religious people who sincerely wanted to please God by following all the established rules of the church. They went to church, they prayed, they studied Scripture, they tithed and they followed the Law and custom in intricate detail. They sought God by doing the things they thought would please God. How did they shift from pursuing God to listening to the devil? Let's look at more Scripture, the portion that leads to the passage quoted above. At the beginning of the conversation, Jesus is talking with a large group of Pharisees. Later in the conversation, the group has dwindled. John writes,

> To the *Jews who had believed him,* Jesus said, "If you hold to my teaching, you are really my disciples. Then you will know the truth, and the truth will set you free." John 8:31-32

By this point in the conversation, the group involved in the discussion has narrowed to "the Jews who had believed in him." Notice that the verb is past tense. Jesus explains to this smaller group of people that they need to follow His teaching if they are to be His disciples. This is a message very similar to other statements Jesus made, like "Whoever has my commands and obeys them, he is the one who loves me." [12] He continues explaining that people who follow His teaching know the truth and "the truth will set you free."

The "Jews who had believed" do not understand why Jesus says they need to be set free. In their mind, they are already free. No shackles or chains bind them. They come and go as they please. But as it is with so much of Jesus' teaching, He focuses on spiritual truth, not physical reality. They were spiritually bound to the devil. John continues writing,

> They answered him, "We are Abraham's descendants and have never been slaves of anyone. How can you say that we shall be set free?"
>
> Jesus replied, "I tell you the truth, everyone who sins is a slave to sin. Now a slave has no permanent place in the family, but a son belongs to it forever. So if the Son sets you free, you will be free indeed. I know you are Abraham's descendants. Yet *you are ready to kill me,* because you have no room for my word. I am telling you what I have seen in my Father's presence, and you do what you have heard from your father."
>
> "Abraham is our father," they answered.

> "If you were Abraham's children," said Jesus, "then you would do the things Abraham did. As it is, *you are determined to kill me*, a man who has told you the truth that I heard from God. Abraham did not do such things. You are doing the things your own father does."

> "We are not illegitimate children," they protested. "The only Father we have is God himself." John 8:33-41

These are upstanding citizens. Their actions, attitude and appearance suggest they are the most righteous people around. They wear the right clothes, regularly attend church, pray, study Scripture, tithe, and follow the Laws and customs of the church. They are good people by human standards.

They love the church. In fact, there is a good chance that their desire to stop Jesus is a desire to preserve the church. They very well might believe that by killing Jesus they are serving God, which is twisted beyond words. Satan can manipulate everything to harm us and to create distance between us and God – even our desire to be religious (note to self: pursue God not religion). Jesus points out their misguided, twisted thinking. Let's take another look at the passage quoted above, this time focusing on Jesus words to His Jewish listeners:

> Jesus said to them, "If God were your Father, you would love me, for I have come here from God. I have not come on my own; God sent me. Why is my language not clear to you? Because *you are unable to hear what I say. You belong to your father, the devil, and you want to carry out your father's desires*. He was a murderer from the beginning, not holding to the truth, for there is no truth in him. When he lies, he speaks his native language, for he is a liar and the father of lies. Yet because I tell the truth, you do not believe me! Can any of you prove me guilty of sin? If I am telling the truth, why don't you believe me? Whoever

belongs to God hears what God says. *The reason you do not hear is that you do not belong to God."* John 8:42-47

They are unable to understand what Jesus is saying. They cannot comprehend His message because they are allowing the devil, the father of lies, to manipulate their thoughts. They want to carry out the devil's desires. Wow. They do not agree with Jesus' assessment because they believe they are serving God, but Jesus' discerning spirit is perfectly accurate and His words are true. Imagine good, church-going people intent on carrying out the devil's desires without realizing it. This is frightening.

What does this mean for us? The passage terrifies because it describes upstanding, church-going, by every outward appearance righteous folks who want to please God and love the church so much they want to kill to preserve it. They seem to be in a good place, and in fact, they had believed in Jesus, but they allow the devil to twist their thoughts and they get off track. They were more concerned with following the rules of the church than seeking God. So, I ponder, what lies do I believe? In what ways have I fallen into the same trap?

We are surrounded by lies. Some are innocuous – marketing campaigns stretching the truth in an effort to cast a product in the best possible light – others are far worse. Yesterday I received an email advertising a hotel. I have stayed at the place several times and it is a fine place to stay, but not nearly as luxurious or filled with beautiful people as the advertisement suggested. Each photo showed the actual place, framed in the perfect angle and light to reveal the beautiful and crop the unattractive. I have stood in the hotel. I have taken in the total experience, and it seems like a different place than the one shown in the photos. Is the ad a lie? Each photo shows an image of objects that actually exist in the place shown, but constructed to reveal less than the whole truth.

Companies hire marketing and advertising experts to prepare ads like that one. Some stretch the truth farther than others, and they surround us. Television, magazines, newspapers, Facebook, Instagram … they are all fueled by advertising revenue. The existence of Instagram has created a new industry of influencers, people who have so many followers that companies pay the influencer to promote their products through Instagram photos. When I see an ad in a magazine, I know the photo is of a model paid to appear, taken by a professional photographer, and produced by a crew of professionals. I know it is part of the business designed to influence me. But Instagram suggests spontaneity and genuineness that seems violated when we are forced to wonder whether the person is holding a Starbucks cup because they like Starbucks or because Starbucks is paying them to manipulate me.

We are left wondering whether we can believe anything anymore. White House spokespeople discuss the merits of "alternative facts"[13] as they attempt to explain statements made by President Trump. "Fake news" was a hot topic during the 2016 U.S. Presidential election, and at least one well-documented news report[14] claims foreign dictators use fake news as a tool to destabilize democracy, making it an extremely cost-effective tool to accomplish goals formerly achieved through military maneuvers.

As we view the world around us through the continuously available feed of digital information, we need heightened discerning powers to filter truth from lies. But this is also true with the whispers we hear. The religious leaders who had believed in Jesus did not generate a desire to kill Jesus by reading false news on the Internet, the devil influenced their individual and collective thought and they began to believe it was a good idea. Through a twisted sequence of seemingly rational thought, good people started believing an evil plan was good. They mistook evil for good.

This is exactly what the prophet Isaiah warns against:

> "Woe to those who call evil good and good evil, who put darkness for light and light for darkness, who put bitter for sweet and sweet for bitter." Isaiah 5:20

Are there elements of your personal life where this has happened or is happening? We know from the account of Satan tempting Jesus in the wilderness that the devil knows Scripture and is skilled at using it as a tool to deceive. Have you encountered this in your life? Have you looked in the mirror to see a person who is overweight, even when your weight is fine? Or do you see some other negative image? If you've had one drink, do you think you need a second one (or third or fourth) believing the next one will make you feel even better? Do you feel discontented in your marriage, and believe that spending time with another will provide satisfaction? Do you believe progressing in your career will bring you the happiness, joy, peace and satisfaction you desire? These are but a few of the many lies Satan plants in our minds. I have heard them described as whispers or voices in our minds, but I believe they are more like planted thoughts. However they are communicated, they are lies.

As we are inundated with more and more false information, it becomes quite a conundrum trying to distinguish truth from lies. With so much false information surrounding us, it is natural for people to become jaded, refusing to believe anything. We place ourselves at risk if we believe lies, but we place ourselves at potentially greater risk if we fail to believe the truth.

Jesus calls Himself the Truth.[15] Jesus calls the devil a liar because he lies and has no truth in him. So back to the previous question: could Satan have delivered "all the kingdoms of the world and their splendor" to Jesus? Satan has no truth in him. How can you trust a liar?

WHAT DOES JESUS DO TO THE SPIRITS?

Jesus Evicts Them

Jesus commanded spirits to leave people, but with the exception of Legion that left the man and entered a herd of pigs, Scripture is silent on where the spirits went after leaving each person. In one conversation, Jesus mentioned evil spirits invading people, leaving people and wandering the earth. While Jesus spoke with the most righteous, upstanding religious people around, the Pharisees, He called them a "wicked and adulterous generation." Later in the conversation Jesus said:

> "When an evil spirit comes out of a man, it goes through arid places seeking rest and does not find it. Then it says, 'I will return to the house I left.' When it arrives, it finds the house unoccupied, swept clean and put in order. Then it goes and takes with it seven other spirits more wicked than itself, and they go in and live there. And the final condition of that man is worse than the first. That is how it will be with this wicked generation." Matthew 12:43-45 (see also Luke 11:24-26).

In an effort to describe "how it will be with this wicked generation," Jesus tells a parable about evil spirits. The surface of the parable is about an evil spirit that left a person and wandered around the earth seeking another person to invade. Jesus did not offer the parable as a true story, but is there some truth to the simple parable plot? Do evil spirits wander the earth after leaving a human?

The surface of most parables is a simple, readily accepted plot revealing deeper meaning, and the effectiveness of a parable depends on the surface plot being simple and readily accepted. If listeners are caught up questioning the surface story, the deeper meaning will never be considered and the purpose of the parable will be lost. Jesus taught a great deal using parables. He spoke about a farmer planting seeds, a shepherd searching for a lost lamb, servants serving masters, a fisherman catching fish with a net, a woman mixing yeast into dough, a mustard seed growing into a big plant, and other ordinary scenes from first century Holy Lands. Listeners readily accepted each plot as a routine occurrence.

With that in mind, Jesus' listeners must have readily accepted the existence of evil spirits dwelling within people, leaving people and wandering about the desert in search of a new host. This is consistent with how the gospels were written – Jesus driving evil spirits out of people was mentioned in passing as commonly accepted fact. It seems clear that Jesus' listeners believed in the existence of evil spirits, but of course, their belief does not make it true.

What about Jesus? Did He believe that the story represented common occurrence? I think He did, in the same way He knew a shepherd would search for a lost lamb and mustard seeds grow into big plants. He knew the plots of His parables were simple events that commonly happened, which is why the parables so effectively communicate deeper truths. In fact, for Jesus to use this particular plotline as a parable, He must have believed it to be a universal truth that all His listeners would understand, accept and move on to ponder the deeper, intended meaning. And if Jesus believed it to be true, it is true.

So if evil spirits are known to dwell within people and after being evicted to wander about seeking a new person to invade, what did Jesus do to the spirits that He cast out of people? Did He do anything to change the spirits' behavior? Did He punish them? Did he seek to rehabilitate them? Did He handcuff them in any way?

No. Well, when He ordered the spirit out of the boy with symptoms of epilepsy, Jesus told the spirit to never enter the boy again, but Jesus did not otherwise restrict it.[16] And this is a rare example of Jesus restricting evil spirits. Jesus did not nothing to the evil spirits other than remove them from their then-current dwelling. He left them free to wander about and eventually repeat their evil activity. This seems like a person who finds a snake in his home, catches the snake, carries it outside and, with the door wide open, releases it on the porch. Most people would kill the snake. Others would call a pest control expert who would remove the snake before either killing it or releasing it far away. But Scripture's silence suggests Jesus did not kill, harm or restrict the continued activity of evil spirits.

As I ponder this, I come back to Jesus saying that He saw Satan thrown from heaven like a bolt of lightning.[17] God cast Satan to earth and Jesus seems content to allow Satan and evil spirits to roam about. If Jesus' actions while in human form are an indication, God might evict evil spirits from time to time, but for the most part He allows them to proceed on earth unhindered, or so it appears.

Binding Satan

I have heard people pray asking God to "bind" evil spirits, meaning to disable the evil spirits from conducting evil activity. I believe these prayers are based on two passages from Matthew. The first is part of the account known as the Confession at Caesarea. Jesus and the disciples are in Caesarea Philippi. Jesus asks the disciples who people say He is and later asks who the disciples say He is. Peter replies saying that Jesus is the Messiah. The story continues:

> Jesus replied, "Blessed are you, Simon son of Jonah, for this was not revealed to you by man, but by my Father in heaven. And I tell you that you are Peter, and on this rock I will build my church, and the gates of Hades will not overcome it. I will give you the keys of the kingdom of heaven; *whatever you bind on earth will be bound in heaven*, and whatever you loose on earth will be loosed in heaven." Matthew 16:17-19.

In the second passage, Jesus teaches the disciples how to handle a believer who sins against another believer. Jesus says to go to the person face to face to discuss the matter. If that does not work, go again with two or three other believers to discuss the situation. As part of that teaching, Jesus says,

> "I tell you the truth, *whatever you bind on earth will be bound in heaven*, and whatever you loose on earth will be loosed in heaven." Matthew 18:18.

"Whatever you bind on earth will be bound in heaven." What does this mean? Is this a grant of unlimited spiritual authority? Jesus did not handcuff or hinder evil spirits after evicting them from a person. If Jesus did not bind evil spirits, can we bind them? Do we have some different and greater authority than Jesus had while He walked the earth as a man? Or did He have the authority and power but choose not to use it?

Jesus is God. Certainly, God can do anything and everything. If God so desires, He can infuse any human with any authority and power He can imagine, including the power to bind evil spirits. That being said, I think barring some unique, God-infused special situation, Jesus incarnate represents the highest and broadest level of authority any human can possibly hope to have. Scripture provides no evidence of evil spirits being bound except in the revelation of the end times.[18] With this in mind, we should probably not expect evil spirits to be bound, even by praying in Jesus' name.

As an ancillary thought on this point, if spirits are not bound and we are encountering the same evil spirits that were here when Jesus lived on earth as a fully human man, the spirits have a lot of experience, and we are neophytes at a game they have mastered. This is why Peter urges us to be alert, watching out for the prowling lion. Paul urges us to put on the armor of God to protect us from the devil's arrows. Jesus teaches us to pray asking God to deliver us from evil or from the evil one. If we were empowered to simply bind evil spirits in Jesus' name, Jesus, Peter and Paul would not urge caution as they do. They would say, "Just bind them."

So what do the passages mean? "Whatever you bind on earth will be bound in heaven." What does it mean? The choices we make while living on earth have eternal consequence. Peter believed Jesus to be the Messiah. He heard God the Father reveal the truth to him and he believed. He demonstrated faith through his words and action. His belief was bound through his action and words on earth. His salvation was sealed.

Similarly, a church member who refuses to listen to the church and continues to sin against members of the church fails to demonstrate his faith through word and deed. His words and action demonstrate the opposite of Peter's example. His result is the opposite of Peter's. In both situations, choices people make while living on Earth have everlasting consequence.

AUTHORITY

Earth, the world, this globe upon which we live, is the place where evil and good both exist. God is the sovereign, Creator of all things with ultimate authority over all creation. He allows evil to roam the earth and act with limited authority, and this is a necessary part of human will. Jesus warns His followers about evil, He explains that evil hates good, He promises that the world will hate people who follow Him, and He discusses the authority that evil has on earth.

God's Authority

The Bible begins saying, "In the beginning God created the heavens and the earth" (Genesis 1:1). God created everything. He created the world and everything in it. He created the heavens and everything in them. He created everything including all physical and spiritual entities, forces and beings, which means He created angels, demons and Satan.[19]

While it seems rationale to conclude that the Creator is greater than His creation, and it might be good enough to stop there and move on, time and time again Scripture proclaims God's sovereignty. Many verses say this. Here are a few:

"Yours, O'Lord, is the greatness and the power and the glory and the majesty and the splendor, for everything in heaven and earth is yours." 1 Chronicles 29:11

"Blessed be your glorious name, and may it be exalted above all blessing and praise. You alone are the Lord. You made the heavens, even the highest heavens, and all their starry host, the earth and all that is on it, the seas and all that is in them. You give life to everything, and the multitudes of heaven worship you." Nehemiah 9:5-6

"Before the mountains were born or you brought forth
the earth and the world, from everlasting to
everlasting you are God." Psalms 90:2

"For you, O Lord, are the Most High over all the earth;
you are exalted far above all gods." Psalm 97:9

[Paul's sermon in Athens] "The God who made the
world and everything in it is the Lord of heaven and
earth and does not live in temples built by hands. And
he is not served by human hands, as if he needed
anything, because he himself gives all men life and
breath and everything else." Acts 17:24-25

"He is the image of the invisible God, the firstborn
over all creation. For by him all things were created:
things of heaven and on earth, visible and invisible,
whether thrones or powers or rulers or authorities; all
things were created by him and for him. He is before
all things, and in him all things hold together."
Colossians 1:15-17

God is sovereign. He has all authority and the power and
freedom to delegate portions of His authority to anyone He
chooses.

Satan's Fall

Scripture describes Satan as an angel who was the "model
of perfection"[20] but who grew corrupt and proud. Satan wanted
to ascend higher than God, the Most High. He rebelled against
God, so God threw Satan out of heaven and down to earth.[21]

Genesis tells us that God created everything in the
heavens and on earth, and "God saw all that he had made, and it
was very good" (Genesis 1:31). If all creation was good when God
made it, what happened? How did a formerly good angel become
bad? It seems even angels are susceptible to pride, corruption and
greedy desires. We cannot blame original sin for Satan's fall

because Satan was in the garden tempting Adam and Eve. Satan appeared in the form of a snake and convinced them to eat the fruit,[22] so Satan had apparently already been cast out of heaven.

Scripture is silent on why and how Satan turned from the model angel to the leader of evil on earth, but it seems that evil on earth is necessary to ensure free will. If God desires humans who freely choose Him, they must have a choice. A choice without options is really no choice at all. People must be free to choose life with God or life separated from God. Only God is good, and life separated from God lacks good, thus is evil. The absence of God is evil, and life separated from God is evil. It follows that evil must exist for free will to exist.

Satan's Authority on Earth

Again, for reasons Scripture does not explain, God granted Satan and evil spiritual entities limited authority on earth. God threw Satan out of heaven and down to earth, where Satan and evil spirits act within the limits of authority allowed by God. In what was likely the first book of the Bible written, the Book of Job portrays Satan seeking permission from God to test Job. Satan meets with God and God grants Satan authority within well-defined limits. God allows Satan to attack everything Job possessed, but not his body.[23] Satan acts within the limits prescribed and later requests an expansion of the limits.[24] God expands Satan's authority allowing attack on Job's health, but Satan must stop short of killing Job.[25] Once again, Satan respects the limits – he acts within the scope of authority God granted. God is sovereign and God chooses to grant Satan some authority on earth.

Scripture refers to Satan's authority on earth in several ways. On three occasions Scripture records Jesus calling Satan the "prince of this world." Paul uses similar words describing Satan as "ruler of this dark world,"[26] the "god of this age,"[27] and "the ruler of the kingdom of the air, the spirit who is now at work in those who are disobedient."[28] John writes, "We know that we are children of God, and that the whole world is under the control of the evil one" (1 John 5:19). They present Satan as a spiritual being housing evil, exhibiting evil, working through people who lead lives separated from God, and ruling the earth for a limited time.

Let's take a closer look at Jesus' discussions of the "prince of this world." At the end of His earthly ministry, Jesus rode into Jerusalem on a donkey as adoring crowds followed Him. In Jerusalem He stopped and said to the crowd:

> "Now my soul is troubled, and what shall I say? 'Father, save me from this hour? No, it was for this very reason I came to this hour. Father, glorify your name!"
>
> Then a voice came from heaven, "I have glorified it, and will glorify it again." The crowd that was there and heard it said it had thundered; others said an angel had spoken to him.
>
> Jesus said, "This voice was for your benefit, not mine. Now is the time for judgment on this world; now the *prince of this world* will be driven out. And I, when I am lifted up from the earth, will draw all people to myself." John 12:27-32

Later that week, on the evening of the Last Supper, Jesus mentions the "prince of this world" twice more. After Jesus washes the disciples feet and teaches about loving service, Jesus explains that He is the way to the Father, teaches about the Holy Spirit, and then says:

> "All this I have spoken while still with you. But the Advocate, the Holy Spirit, whom the Father will send in my name, will teach you all things and will remind you of everything I have said to you. Peace I leave with you; my peace I give you. I do not give to you as the world gives. Do not let your hearts be troubled and do not be afraid.

"You heard me say, 'I am going away and I am coming back to you.' If you loved me, you would be glad that I am going to the Father, for the Father is greater than I. I have told you now before it happens, so that when it does happen you will believe. I will not say much more to you, for the *prince of this world* is coming. He has no hold over me, but he comes so that the world may learn that I love the Father and do exactly what my Father has commanded me.

"Come now; let us leave." John 14:25-31

Later that evening, Jesus teaches a lesson known as the Vine and the Branches, warns about the world's hatred, and teaches more about the Holy Spirit. As He discusses the Holy Spirit He says,

"But very truly I tell you, it is for your good that I am going away. Unless I go away, the Advocate will not come to you; but if I go, I will send him to you. When he comes, he will prove the world to be in the wrong about sin and righteousness and judgment: about sin, because people do not believe in me; about righteousness, because I am going to the Father, where you can see me no longer; and about judgment, because the *prince of this world* now stands condemned." John 16:7-11

Three times during Holy Week and twice during the Last Supper, Jesus mentions the "prince of this world." He says the prince of this world "will be driven out," "is coming" and "now stands condemned." Satan, the devil, the ruler of people separated from God, the god of this age… each term refers to a spiritual entity characterized by evil. Jesus' statements suggest that Satan's authority was about to change, but how?

Jesus' Authority over Evil

Jesus is God. He is one person of the Holy Trinity, and He has full authority over everything. During Jesus' ministry, He told His followers that he infused them with enough of His authority to overpower evil spirits saying, "I have given you authority … to overcome all the power of the enemy" (Luke 10:19). Jesus has all authority; the enemy has power; and Jesus gives His followers authority over the enemy. This provides further corroboration of Satan's power and God's authority over it.

On the evening Jesus gave Himself up for us, Jesus acknowledged the reality of evil in the world, the reality of evil housed within spiritual beings, and the limited authority of the evil one. As He acknowledged this, Jesus proclaimed authority over evil and the evil one. He knew what the evil one was about to do and He knew the evil one was condemned because Jesus has authority over it.

Forty days after His resurrection, Jesus ascended to Heaven. As Matthew describes the events that occurred immediately before the ascension, he writes,

> "Then Jesus came to them and said, 'All authority in heaven and on earth has been given to me.'" Matthew 28:18

Paul describes Jesus' authority over all things by saying,

> "That [God the Father's] power is like the working of his mighty strength, which he exerted in *Christ* when he raised him from the dead and seated him at his right hand in the heavenly realms, *far above all rule and authority*, power and dominion, and every title that can be given, not only in the present age but also in the one to come. And *God placed all things under his feet* and appointed him to be head over everything for the church, which is the body, the fullness of him who fills everything in every way." Ephesians 1:19-23

Jesus has all authority over heaven and earth. But doesn't Satan have some authority on earth?

When Satan was thrown out of heaven, God granted him limited authority over earth. When Jesus died on the cross, the game changed. Suddenly, people had a bridge to God. Through the cross, Jesus provided the bridge. Satan still has limited authority on earth, but Jesus provides the way out (which is why Jesus says, "I am the way..."[29]). Paul and the author of Hebrews describe the miracle saying,

> "Once you were alienated from God and were enemies in your minds because of your evil behavior. But now *he has reconciled you by Christ*'s physical body through death to present you holy in his sight...." Colossians 1:21-23

> "When you were dead in your sins and in the uncircumcision of your sinful nature, *God made you alive with Christ*.... And having *disarmed the powers and authorities*, he made a public spectacle of them, triumphing over them by the cross." Colossians 2:13-15

> "Since the children have flesh and blood, he too shared in their humanity so that *by his death he might destroy him who holds the power of death* – that is, the devil – and free those who all their lives were held in slavery by their fear of death." Hebrews 2:14-15

Jesus' death on the cross was a game changer. His death and resurrection created a path to God that previously did not exist and it altered Satan's authority on earth. Through the cross, powers and authority of sinful nature were disarmed, the power of death was destroyed, and reconciliation with God is available to those who follow Jesus Christ.

The World Houses Both Good and Evil

Parables Suggest This

Jesus tells the Parable of the Weeds,[30] a story about a farmer who planted good seed in a field. While he slept, an enemy scattered seeds that would grow into weeds across the field. Weeds and good crop grew next to each other until the harvest, when they were separated. This is one of the few parables that Jesus explains. He said the field represents the world, the farmer is Jesus, the enemy is the devil, the weeds are "the sons of the evil one," and the good seeds are "sons of the kingdom." In His explanation, the world is the place were Jesus and Satan each sow seeds, and where good and evil both exist until separated at harvest.

Jesus also explained the Parable of the Soils. A farmer generously scattered seeds. He threw them everywhere. Some fell on the path, some fell on rocky places, some fell on shallow soil, some fell among thorns, and some fell on good soil. Birds ate seeds on the path. The seed nestled in rocky soil grew, but the plants quickly withered because their roots were not very deep. The plants that grew among thorns were soon choked out. The seed sown on good soil produced a good crop. Jesus explains the parable saying,

> "When anyone hears the message about the kingdom and does not understand it, *the evil one comes* and snatches away what was sown in his heart. This is the seed sown along the path. The one who received the seed that fell on rocky places is the man who hears the word and at once receives it with great joy. But since he has no root, he lasts only a short time. When trouble or persecution comes because of the word, he quickly falls away. The one who received the seed that fell among the thorns is the man who hears the word, but the worries of this life and the deceitfulness of wealth choke it, making it unfruitful. But the one who received the seed that fell on good soil is the man who

hears the word and understands it. He produces a crop, yielding a hundred, sixty or thirty times what is sown." Matthew 13:19-23

Both parables portray the world as a place where God generously plants good seeds. The world is also the place where the evil one actively works to prevent God's seeds from growing. The world houses good and evil. It is the place where Satan prowls seeking people to devour. It is also the place where God showers His holy grace and the Holy Spirit dwells within children of God. I would say good and evil co-exist in the world, but that would inaccurately suggest peace. Good and evil both exist in the world, but it is a war zone.

Jesus & Believers Interact with Evil Spirits

But of course, Jesus did not offer the parables as factually accurate accounts. While His explanations describe the evil one battling God's efforts on earth, they are not historical accounts. As previously discussed, Scripture includes historical accounts of Jesus and others interacting with evil spiritual beings on earth. Jesus has a conversation with Satan while He is in the desert fasting for forty days.[31] On the shore of the Sea of Galilee, Jesus speaks with a group of demons calling themselves Legion. They recognize Jesus as the Messiah, they acknowledge His authority, and they submit to Him and beg for mercy. Jesus sends the spirits into a herd of pigs.[32] Jesus has a conversation with an evil spirit within a man in the synagogue in Capernaum.[33]

Jesus sends out the twelve disciples to preach that the kingdom of God is near. Before sending them out, He gives "them authority to drive out impure spirits and to heal every disease and sickness" (Matthew 10:1). Later, Jesus sends out seventy-two of His followers across the region, instructing the missionaries to "heal the sick … and tell them, 'The kingdom of God has come near to you'" (Luke 10:9). He instructs both groups to preach the same message and He anoints each group with authority over evil.

When the seventy-two missionaries return, they joyously tell Jesus that demons submitted to them in Jesus' name. They are amazed that their affiliation with Jesus infused them with authority, and that demons recognized their authority and submitted to it. Jesus illustrates heavenly authority over evil as something far greater than they imagine, saying,

> "I saw Satan fall like lightning from heaven. I have given you authority to trample on snakes and scorpions and to overcome all the power of the enemy; nothing will harm you. However, do not rejoice that the spirits submit to you, but rejoice that your names are written in heaven." Luke 10:18-20

The missionaries do not seem surprised by the existence of demons. They are surprised by the respect demons had for their authority. They are surprised that demons recognized them as Jesus' representatives possessing some of His authority. Jesus replies describing heavenly authority over evil – He describes the head demon, Satan, as he was cast out of heaven and thrown to earth like a bolt of lightning. As discussed above, God has authority over Satan and all the demons under him, and Jesus has infused His followers with heavenly authority "to overcome all the power of the enemy."

LIGHT & DARKNESS

God deposited Satan on earth where he roams, exercising limited authority and wreaking havoc on human lives. The place where we live is the very place Satan and his demons roam and do their work. Scripture records Satan saying he has been "roaming throughout the earth, going back and forth on it" (Job 1:7 and 2:2).

While the world is the place where good and evil both exist, and where evil battles and hates good, Jesus describes the world in contrast to heaven. To be "worldly" is to be separated from God, which is the definition of evil. Heaven is light; the world is dark. The world is the place where evil dwells, roams, works and lives in opposition to God. Jesus describes Himself as "the light of the world."[34] He also says that His followers "are not of the world," [35] and He urges His followers to differentiate themselves from the world, calling them to be "the salt of the earth … light of the world."[36] Because evil hates good, Jesus explains that the world hates Him and He warns His disciples that the world will hate them.[37] People of God must actively distinguish themselves from the world, which is tricky because they live in the world.

Similarly, Paul urges his readers to separate themselves from the world and warns that Christians will be persecuted. Here are a few of the statements Paul wrote about this:

> "*Do not conform any longer to the pattern of this world,* but be transformed by the renewing of your mind." Romans 12:2

> "In fact, *everyone who wants to live a godly life in Christ Jesus will be persecuted,* while evil men and imposters will go from bad to worse, deceiving and being deceived." 2 Timothy 3:12-13

> "Do not be yoked together with unbelievers. For what do righteousness and wickedness have in common? Or *what fellowship can light have with darkness?* What harmony is there between Christ and Belial? What does a believer have in common with an unbeliever? What agreement is there between the temple of God and idols? For we are the temple of the living God. As God has said, 'I will live with them and walk among them, and I will be their God, and they will be my people.'

> "Therefore come out from them and be separate, says the Lord. Touch no unclean thing, and I will receive you. And I will be a Father to you, and you will be my

sons and daughters, says the Lord Almighty." 2 Corinthians 6:14-18

James writes a similar message saying,

"You adulterous people, don't you know that *friendship with the world is hatred toward God*? Anyone who chooses to be a friend of the world becomes an enemy of God. Or do you think Scripture says without reason that the spirit he caused to live in us envies intensely? But he gives us more grace. That is why Scripture says: 'God opposes the proud but gives grace to the humble.'

Submit yourselves, then, to God. Resist the devil, and he will flee from you. Come near to God and he will come near to you. James 4:4-8

Jesus, Paul and James depict the world in contrast to the heavenly. The world is dark; heaven is light. The world is evil and sinful; heaven is righteous. Good and evil forces both exist in the world, but the world is known for its darkness.

God is sovereign. He creates all things, breathes the breath of life into all living things, and has all authority over all things in the heavens and on earth, physical and spiritual. God placed Jesus at His right hand with authority over all things, and gave Satan some limited authority on earth. The Holy Spirit and Satan are both active in the world. Good and evil are both active forces in the world. God's holy grace showers around us and over us, and His Holy Spirit lives within believers while Satan and evil forces try to separate people from God. The world is a battle zone where Satan prowls like a lion, shoots arrows like a soldier, and methodically and with great stealth attacks victims.

Hidden adversaries seem to freak people out. Spiders and snakes are creepy because they might be hiding in open view; they emerge from nowhere. Satan specializes in stealth attack. As Verbal Kint said in *The Usual Suspects*, part of the devil's genius plan is convincing the world it does not exist.

EVIL IN THE WORLD

Has Scripture convinced you that evil exists, and that evil is housed within spiritual entities that influence people? The devil, Satan and evil spirits are real. They really are around us. Once you accept that as true, I urge caution that you do not give them more credit than they are due. Please do not attribute everything bad that happens in your life to the influence of evil spirits because that would be giving them more credit than accurate. But beware of the possibility of their influence, guard against their influence, pray for deliverance from their influence, and be vigilant against their attacks.

Their goal is to separate you from God. Work on your relationship with God continuously so this will not happen. Pray for His wisdom and discernment to recognize their attempted influence and power, strength, wisdom and courage to repel the attacks. And study Scripture. Paul tells us that Scripture is a significant part of our armor against the attacks of evil.[38] We also know that Satan knows Scripture and he will use it in his attacks, as demonstrated through his temptation of Jesus in the wilderness.

I think of all the seemingly innocuous and common things from my childhood that were instruments of the occult. I recall the song *Aquarius / Let the Sunshine In* by the 5th Dimension. It played frequently on the radio. The melody is still fresh in my mind with lyrics explaining that astrology leads to harmony, peace and understanding – things only available through God. I recall humming along and signing "The age of Aquarius, age of Aquarius ..." and singing the other words as the radio played. I heard the song and repeated the words, and by so doing started to accept the lie as an accepted truth. Yes, it is subtle, but what a lie, and what a beautifully stealthy attack. How many have been deceived and misled by it?

Growing up we received two newspapers each day in our home and I usually read the comics. On the corner of the comic page was the daily horoscope, providing the day's forecast based on the alignment of stars. I knew the astrological sign for each member of my family and we joked about the day's forecast and what would happen to each of us that day. We did not really believe it, but we read it and joked about it.

According to Scripture, this is really bad and I have since repented from it and asked God for forgiveness and I flee from things of astrology. It is of the occult and evil, and it is nothing new. The Old Testament is loaded with warning about things such as this.

The prophet Isaiah mocks the Babylonians and their beliefs saying,

> "Keep on then with your magic spells and with your many sorceries, which you have labored at since childhood. Perhaps you will succeed, perhaps you will cause terror. All the counsel you have received has only worn you out! Let your astrologers come forward, those stargazers who make predictions month by month, let them save you from what is coming upon you. Surely they are like stubble; the fire will burn them up." Isaiah 47:12-14

I vividly remember times my brother and I stayed with my grandmother. We traveled there every year or so. While there, we played with our aunt, who is just a few years older than my brother, and our cousins who we rarely saw. On several occasions someone pulled out a Ouija board. The kids all placed hands on a device lying on a board with printed letters, and asked spirits to guide the device towards letters spelling out a message. It was creepy and the sort of thing Scripture commands us to avoid.

> Do not turn to mediums or seek out spiritists, for you will be defiled by them. I am the Lord your God. Leviticus 19:31

I attended Colorado School of Mines and had friends from all over the world. It was extremely diverse. For instance, I joined a fraternity and my pledge class contained a Jewish guy whose father had a concentration camp number tattooed on his forearm and a guy from Switzerland whose grandfather was a Nazi officer. Just to round things out, the following pledge class included a guy from Jordan who wore a gold chain necklace with a gold pendant in the shape of a map of Palestine. It was a diverse group, and after graduation my friends scattered across the globe. Some of my closest friends went to Alaska, Bolivia, Peru, London, Houston and California. After a few years we wanted to get everyone back together. Jeff lived in Houston. He organized a black tie formal and invited everyone to Houston. He picked a weekend in February, scheduled the formal on Saturday night, and encouraged everyone to come on Friday.

A group arrived Friday evening. We went out to eat at a place not far from Rice University. We walked in, put our name on the list and looked for a place to sit for the 30-minute wait. Jeff saw a large booth and motioned some of us to join him. A woman sat in the corner of the booth. Jeff asked if we could join her and she said she would love to have us sit with her and she pointed to a sign stating she was a palm reader. It was Mardi Gras and the restaurant had invited her from New Orleans to read palms as part of the festivities. Jeff asked how much it would cost. Not seeing anyplace else to sit, Jeff looked at the rest of us and shrugged as if to ask whether we wanted to stay.

Pete pulled out a bill, handed it to her and offered his hands. It was shocking how she knew all about him. His grandfather had been a long-time US Senator, and she talked about the history of influence in his lineage. And she said many other things that were strikingly accurate. It was eerie.

Jeff went next, then Todd. Nothing remarkable happened with either of them. I was kind of next. I really did not want to do it, mainly because I was too cheap to spend the money, but I offered the money and my hands. She took my right hand and looked at it. Then she looked at me and looked at my hand again. She said, "What are you doing here?" I was stunned. I did not say anything. She said, "Why are you here? You need to leave." She slid the money I had given her back across the table toward me and motioned her hand ordering me to leave.

As we got up to vacate her table our name was called to move to the dining room. I walked to the dining room and sat down, a little shaken by the incident. Someone asked me what I said or did to offend the woman. I said that I did nothing except pay and offer my hand. I wondered whether she was ordering me away from her table, the bar, the restaurant, the city of Houston, or something else? I did not know what she saw or why she said what she said. But I know from Scripture that I should not have been there. I should not have been consulting her to read my future. God strictly forbids that behavior. It is evil. It is of the devil. I repent. I pray for forgiveness.

As the Israelites camped across the Jordan River preparing to enter the Promised Land, Moses reminded them of the Law and of how they should act in the new land. As part of the instruction he said,

> "When you enter the land the Lord your God is giving you, do not learn to imitate detestable ways of the nations there. Let no one be found among you who sacrifices his son or daughter in the fire, who practices divination or sorcery, interprets omens, engages in witchcraft, or casts spells, or who is a medium or spiritist or who consults the dead. Anyone who does these things is detestable to the Lord, and because of these detestable practices the Lord your God will drive out those nations before you. You must be blameless before the Lord your God." Deuteronomy 18:9-13

Isaiah urges people of God to cry out to God rather than consult with spiritists:

> When men tell you to consult mediums and spiritists, who whisper and mutter, should not a people inquire of their God? Why consult with the dead on behalf of the living? Isaiah 8:19

Jeremiah warns Israel about astrology saying:

"Hear what the Lord says to you, O house of Israel.
This is what the Lord says: 'Do not learn the ways of
the nations or be terrified by signs in the sky.'"
Jeremiah 10:1-2

Scripture says that people who work as mediums and
spiritists should be put to death, and it also says that King Saul
was killed because, among other things, he sought the advice of
mediums.

A man or a woman who is a medium or spiritist
among you must be put to death. You are to stone
them; their blood will be on their own heads.
Leviticus 20:27

Saul died because he was unfaithful to the Lord; he
did not keep the word of the Lord and even consulted
with a medium for guidance, and did not inquire of
the Lord. So the Lord put him to death and turned the
kingdom over to David son of Jesse. 1 Chronicles
10:13-14 (see also 1 Samuel 28)

He said to me: "It is done. I am the Alpha and Omega,
the Beginning and the End. To him who is thirsty I
will give to drink without cost from the spring of the
water of life. He who overcomes will inherit all this,
and I will be his God and he will be my son. But the
cowardly, the unbelieving, the vile, the murderers, the
sexually immoral, those who practice magic arts, the
idolaters and all liars – their place will be the fiery lake
of burning sulfur. This is the second death."
Revelation 21:6-8

Evil is all around us. As a child I found it by turning on
the radio and listening to a popular song, on the comic page of
our local newspaper, and in the game closet at my grandmother's
house. Later in life I found it in a restaurant as we waited for a
table to open in the dining room. These are not places one might

go when seeking out evil or when seeking out the dark side of life. These are normal, common every day places to go and things to do.

Consider some of the practices addressed in the Old Testament: mediums, spiritists, practitioners of magic arts, and astrologers. People who consult them are doing wrong and people who offer the services are doing wrong. The services are not of God and they have been around since Old Testament times.

CONCLUSION

At the beginning of this chapter I discussed traveling across Mongolia with a group that included four women. One evening we discussed stories of evil they had encountered in various forms around the world. As the stories continued, Deborah looked at the other two and asked, "should I tell him about that time in Africa?" Jo Anne gave her that look my mother used to give me instantly communicating that I was doing something wrong and that I had better stop it immediately. Mary looked down and away, not wanting to discuss it. Deborah said something like, "just a short version, he can handle it."

After hearing the awful stories they had already shared I wondered what could possibly be worse. I was about to realize the line demarcating acceptable topics of discussion was the line between evil revealing itself through physical attack and evil revealing itself through spiritual attack.

The three traveled with a fourth woman in Africa, but I do not know where. They rode in a vintage Range Rover slowly along a rugged narrow trail through the jungle. They traveled out to a village to meet with leaders that morning and were now driving back to the town where they were staying. Rain had just stopped and water gathered in pools in the road, splashing up from the wheels. It was steamy. At a bend in the road sat a small shack of a convenience store. The driver suggested stopping for a quick break.

As they got out of the jeep they saw an elderly woman sitting on the porch floor holding a can and begging. A wooden cane sat next to her. They asked the store clerk about her. He said she could barely walk and she needed help. Deborah asked if they could pray for her. Hearing no objection, the four women gathered around her. Mary kneeled in front holding her hands. Deborah, Jo Anne and the fourth woman kneeled and stood behind her, placing their hands on her back, head and shoulders. They started praying and the elderly crippled woman leapt to her feet. As they retold the story, Mary and Deborah said it was like a cat sprayed with water, or like throwing water on a hot frying pan. She leapt to her feet, grabbed Mary's arms in her hands, looked in Mary's eyes and said words they did not understand. She then ran off the porch, behind the store and into the jungle on a walking path. She left her cane on the porch. The women chuckled recalling how quickly she moved for a crippled woman.

They were shocked by what had just occurred. They stood looking at each other silently, bewildered by what had just happened, then they went into the store, purchased soft drinks and water, returned to the jeep, and continued their journey. They had not traveled very far when the rear passenger side wheel came off the jeep. The driver inspected the situation and found that the lug nuts were gone, as if someone had removed each lug nut. He searched and found all the lug nuts, jacked up the jeep, put the tire back on, and tightened the lug nuts. They continued on their way only to have two other wheels fall off at separate times along the way.

They eventually arrived at the lodge. After cleaning up, they met for dinner. Mary was not feeling well, so she did not eat. She felt bad the next day and worse the following day. As she continued her decline, the women agreed that the old woman had put some sort of spell on her when she grabbed Mary's arms and spoke. In the short version they told me, this is where the story moved very quickly. They prayed over Mary. They prayed and prayed and prayed. Later that day, Mary vomited what appeared to be piles of worms and she was cured. She was fine the rest of the trip, and the wheels stayed on the jeep. They knew without a doubt that the women had cursed Mary and their jeep and their journey with some sort of evil spell. And they knew that God cured Mary and everything else. While evil exists in the world, God has authority over it.

As they talked about what had happened, they each relived it. Whatever happened, they did not want to talk about it and the memory greatly disturbed them. The story ended our conversation that night. They each drifted silently, in deep thought to their separate rooms.

Our world is a place of great contrast. As depicted each evening on the news and each morning in the newspaper, evil certainly exists. People do horrific things to other people, and evil spirits roam. The world is also the place were God reveals His glory. We see His glory through the wonders of nature that He creates, through people reaching out to one another with love and compassion, and through His holy word. While evil spirits exist on earth, good spirits also exist.

8 | ANGELS

If you say, "The Lord is my refuge," and make the Most High your dwelling, no harm will overtake you, no disaster will come near your tent. For he will command his angels concerning you to guard you in all your ways; they will lift you up in their hands so that you will not strike your foot against a stone. Psalm 91:9-11

Praise the Lord, you his angels, you mighty ones who do his bidding, who obey his word. Praise the Lord, all his heavenly hosts, you his servants who do his will. Praise the Lord, all his works everywhere in his dominion. Psalm 103:20-22

Are angels real? Do heavenly beings really guard people, help people and serve as God's messengers, or are angels actually just people who show loving compassion to other people? When the writer of Psalms says, "The Lord ... will command his angels" and refers to angels as "mighty ones who do [God's] bidding" is he discussing heavenly beings or people acting heavenly?

As Lori and I sat in the infusion clinic in south Denver watching a cocktail of chemotherapy chemicals drip into her, the nurse who cared for Lori was amazing. Her eyes were bright and filled with life. She provided strong words of encouragement without diminishing the suffering that the chemicals would cause. She was attentive, compassionate, and strong with words of wisdom. As we left after the first day we discussed that Dianne was an angel sent from God, and the thought of returning the next day was a little brighter knowing Dianne would be there to help.

Over the first four days of treatment, Lori's suffering continuously increased as her general well being declined. The first day following treatment, which was Friday, Lori was far worse than the day before. Friday night she was unable to eat, she threw up the sips of water she tried to get down and she was extremely weak. She was unable to get out of bed. I called the doctor suggesting that we should go to the emergency room. He encouraged me to wait until the morning when we could go to the infusion clinic in downtown Denver that was open Saturday morning. He was confident that additional fluids and a different anti-nausea medicine administered intravenously would help.

At 7:20 the next morning I helped Lori to the car. We drove downtown to the clinic. As I signed her in, Lori found a bed and collapsed in it. The nurse, Zozo, introduced herself, hooked up a bag of fluid and took a few minutes to connect on a personal level. She explained to Lori that while she was feeling awful, what she was feeling was expected. Zozo explained what Lori should expect, and that it would be all right, and she encouraged her with strong, confident words in a beautiful French accent. Her eyes were loving and compassionate, and her words were strong. We often discuss that Zozo was an angel sent from God. She was the right person at the right place with the right words exactly when Lori needed it.

As we discuss these beautiful, strong, intelligent, compassionate, loving ladies, we describe them as angels. In so doing, are we attributing qualities possessed by real, heavenly beings to mere humans, or are we describing the only angels that really exist, namely people who do good things for other people? Do heavenly angels really exist?

The question is nothing new. Scripture tells us that the debate over whether angels are real was one of the issues separating two Jewish denominations, Sadducees and Pharisees, during the time that Jesus walked the earth:

> "(The Sadducees say that there is no resurrection, and that there are neither angels nor spirits, but the Pharisees believe all these things.)" Acts 23:8

JESUS DISCUSSES ANGELS

Scripture records Jesus talking about angels as if they are His co-workers, helpers, warriors, or His entourage. They are the ones He goes to when He needs help. They are at His disposal. He calls upon them and they do what He asks them to do.

Jesus spoke about angels in reference to a time that was in the future relative to when He spoke the words. Like His holy entourage, Jesus said angels would be with Him when He comes into His Father's glory.[1] He said that He will send out His angels to "weed out of his kingdom everything that causes sin and all who do evil" (Matthew 13:41); He will send His angels to gather certain people;[2] and angels will accompany Him when He returns.[3]

Jesus spoke as if angels are real heavenly beings who are ready to help Him. As guards arrested Jesus in the garden, Peter drew his sword and struck a guard, severing his ear. Jesus restored the guard's ear, told Peter to put his sword away and said, "Do you think I cannot call on my Father and he will at once put at my disposal more than twelve legions of angels?" (Matthew 26:53). Jesus rebuked Peter for trying to help, explaining that He has helpers Peter had never seen. If Jesus was referring to an army of compassionate people, Peter would have known about them. Jesus was talking about heavenly beings that Peter had not met.

While speaking with Nathanael, Jesus went further. He promised that Nathanael would see angels saying,

"You believe because I told you I saw you under a fig tree. You will see greater things than that." He then added, "*Very truly I tell you, you will see* heaven open and the *angels* of God ascending and descending on the Son of Man." John 1:50-51

Once again we see "Very truly I tell you," Jesus code indicating the words about to be spoken are very important. Jesus always spoke the truth – He used the phrase to emphasize what He was about to say. In this situation the words do not sound figurative or metaphorical. They sound as if they should be taken at face value – Jesus promised a specific person, Nathanael, that he would some day see heaven and the angels who are there. The statement would be true if Jesus was predicting that Nathanael would some day, for some reason, hallucinate or dream and see something that was not really there. Or the statement would be true if Jesus was explaining that angels really exist and someday Nathanael would be allowed to see them. The second explanation seems much more likely given who Jesus is, His other statements about angels and the context of the discussion. Angels must really be real for that to happen.

While angels obey Jesus' commands, they also have significant standing. They are close to God – Jesus said, "Angels in heaven always see the face of the Father in heaven" (Matthew 18:10). And their opinion seems to matter in the grand scheme of things. Jesus said He will either acknowledge or disown people before the angels of God,[4] suggesting that angels are important in that process.

Jesus described angels as being at His disposal and ready to follow His commands. Scripture records two times when angels helped Him: when He was tempted in the wilderness and when He prayed in the garden on the evening of His arrest. In the wilderness angels "attended him"[5] and in the garden an angel "strengthened him."[6]

On one occasion Jesus spoke with his disciples and he said, "Whoever is ashamed of me and my words, the Son of Man will be ashamed of them when he comes in his glory and in the glory of the Father and of the holy angels" (Luke 9:26). Jesus says that He will come in His glory and that angels will be with Him and they will all be in God's glory. It does not sound like He is talking about compassionate people or fictitious characters. Angels are as real as the Father and His glory. If you believe Jesus is who He claims to be and that He words are true, it is difficult to read His statements about angels and not believe angels are real heavenly beings that really exist.

CHARACTERISTICS REVEALED THROUGH SCRIPTURE

Scripture discusses angels a lot. A word search on www.biblegateway.com states that the NIV version of the Bible uses derivatives of the word "angel" 290 times. What else does Scripture teach about angels?

Spirits

Angels are spiritual beings. Humans are part spiritual and part physical. Scripture describes angels as "ministering spirits sent to serve those who will inherit salvation" (Hebrews 1:14). Scripture does not say that angels have a physical presence, only a spiritual presence.

They experience emotions. Angels rejoice when people repent,[7] but they do not marry and do not die.[8]

Warriors

Angels are also warriors. When you imagine an angel, what image comes to mind? A few years ago my daughter joined Pi Beta Phi Fraternity for Women. Their unofficial symbol is the angel, so they had an angel party and the probationary members were required to dress like angels. Elizabeth wondered, "What should I wear? What does an angel look like?" We thought of white and large wings. We Googled images of angels and saw photos from a Victoria's Secret fashion show. This was not really how I wanted my daughter to dress for her party, but it revealed some popular notions of what angels look like – attractive women with wings and little clothing. This image seems inconsistent with descriptions of angels in Scripture, which depict them as warriors wielding swords and killing people.

Angels enforce God's judgment, which at times requires that they kill people. Paul reminds us that the Old Testament records many instances of angels killing people.[9] An angel killed the entire Assyrian army in one night.[10] An angel killed Herod because he refused to worship God.[11] After God banished Adam and Eve from the Garden of Eden, He placed "cherubim and a flaming sword flashing back and forth to guard the way to the tree of life" (Genesis 3:24).

During King David's reign, God pronounced judgment against Israel and sent an angel to execute it. The angel caused a plague to hit town after town across the nation. King David bargained with the angel to end the killing.[12]

During the Exodus, Israelites camped across the Jordan River from Jericho. Balak, the king of Moab, was very concerned. He saw how many people camped across the river. He feared that if they crossed the river there would not be enough food for everyone. So he called upon Balaam to curse the Israelites.

As Balaam traveled to meet King Balak, his donkey saw an angel standing in front of them blocking the path. The angel had a sword drawn in his hand. The donkey was afraid, so he left the path and went into a field. Balaam was unable to see the angel. He beat the donkey and forced it back to the road. Along the path the donkey saw the angel with sword drawn two more times. Once the donkey crushed Balaam against rocks as he maneuvered to avoid the angel. The last time he encountered the angel in a narrow spot on the path. The donkey could not move forward without running in to the angel, so he lay down in the path. Balaam was furious. As he beat the donkey, his eyes were opened and he saw the angel holding a sword in his hand. He fell facedown on the path. The angel warned Balaam to speak only what the angel told him to say when he spoke with King Balak.

Angels are not women with wings, not even beautiful, scantily clad women with wings. They are mighty warriors.

What Do Angels Look Like?

Scripture says that people have shown hospitality to angels without knowing it.[13] This suggests that some angels look like people, or perhaps they are able to assume physical appearance in certain situations (they are spiritual beings after all). In other places, Scripture gives very specific descriptions of angels. Some angels are described as appearing like people who shine or glow. Others are otherworldly in appearance: they look singularly like nothing on earth, but their features appear as if they combine parts from a variety of earthly creatures.

While standing on the bank of the Tigris River, Daniel sees an angel who looks like "a man dressed in linen, with a belt of fine gold from Uphaz around his waist. His body was like topaz, his face like lightning, his eyes like flaming torches, his arms and legs like the gleam of burnished bronze, and his voice like the sound of a multitude" (Daniel 10:5-6).

After Jesus is crucified, Mary Magdalene and other women walk to the tomb to care for His body. At the tomb they see an angel whose "appearance was like lightning, and clothes were white as snow" (Matthew 28:3). The men guarding the tomb "were so afraid of him that they shook and became like dead men" (Matthew 28:4).

In these situations, angels appear on earth and interact with people in a way that is very similar to the way people interact with one another. And their appearance is similar to human appearance, only shinier. Other descriptions of angels are from heavenly visions. People on earth are suddenly able to see into heaven, and they see angels. Let's look at some of their amazing descriptions.

John describes one of the angels that he saw during his heavenly vision like this:

Then I saw another mighty angel coming down from heaven. He was robed in a cloud, with a rainbow above his head; his face was like the sun, and his legs were like fiery pillars. He was holding a little scroll, which lay open in his hand. He planted his right foot on the sea and his left foot on the land, and he gave a shout like the roar of a lion. When he shouted, the voices of the seven thunders spoke..." Revelation 10:1-4

Earlier in the revelation, John saw the throne in heaven with One sitting on it who has the appearance of jasper and ruby encircled by a rainbow. Twenty-four thrones surround the throne. Lightning flashes around the thrones and they rest on a "sea of glass, clear as crystal" (Revelation 4:6). John continues describing four heavenly creatures:

In the center, around the throne, were four living creatures, and they were covered in eyes, in front and in back. The first living creature was like a lion, the second was like an ox, the third had a face like a man, the fourth was like a flying eagle. Each of the four living creatures had six wings and was covered with eyes all around, even under its wings. Day and night they never stop saying:

"Holy, holy, holy is the Lord God Almighty, who was, and is, and is to come." Revelation 4:6-8

Isaiah saw a similar scene when he glimpsed heaven. He saw the throne and angels, and heard them saying virtually identical words that John had heard. Isaiah calls them seraphim and describes them saying,

In the year that King Uzziah died, I saw the Lord, high and exalted, seated on a throne; and the train of his robe filled the temple. Above him were seraphim, each with six wings: With two wings they covered their faces, with two they covered their feet, and with two they were flying. And they were calling to one another:

"Holy, holy, holy is the Lord Almighty; the whole earth is full of his glory."

At the sound of their voices the doorposts and thresholds shook and the temple was filled with smoke. Isaiah 6:1-4

Ezekiel describes a number of heavenly visions. His first vision includes four heavenly beings. He describes the scene like this:

I looked, and I saw a windstorm coming out of the north – an immense cloud with flashing lightning and surrounded by brilliant light. The center of the fire looked like glowing metal, and in the fire was what looked like four living creatures. In appearance their form was human, but each of them had four faces and four wings. Their legs were straight; their feet were like those of a calf and gleamed like burnished bronze. Under their wings on their four sides they had human hands. All four of them had four faces and wings, and the wings of one touched the wings of another. Each one went straight ahead; they did not turn as they moved.

Their faces looked like this: Each of the four had the face of a human being, and on the right side each had the face of a lion, and on the left the face of an ox; each also had the face of an eagle. Such were the faces. They each had two wings spreading out upward, each wing touching that of the creature on either side; and each had two other wings covering its body. Each went straight ahead. Wherever the spirit would go, they would go, without turning as they went. The appearance of the living creatures was like burning coals of fire or like torches. Fire moved back and forth among the creatures; it was bright, and lightning flashed out of it. The creatures sped back and forth like flashes of lightning. Ezekiel 1:4-14.

Ezekiel describes another specific type of angel, which he refers to as cherubim. They are associated with God's glory – the author of Hebrews calls them "the cherubim of the Glory" (Hebrews 9:5). They stood in the temple as God's glory filled the temple,[14] and they departed the temple as soon as God's glory left.[15] A wheel accompanies each cherub. The wheel is alive and is part of the cherub, though not connected. Ezekiel writes:

> ... the wheels sparkled like topaz. As for their appearance, the four of them looked alike; each was like a wheel intersecting a wheel. As they moved, they would go in any one of the four directions the cherubim faced; the wheels did not turn about as the cherubim went. The cherubim went in whatever direction the head faced, without turning as they went. Their entire bodies, including their backs, their hands and their wings, were completely full of eyes, as were their four wheels. I heard the wheels being called "the whirling wheels." Each of the cherubim had four faces: One face was that of a cherub, the second the face of a human being, the third the face of a lion, and the fourth the face of an eagle. Ezekiel 10:9-14

Some of the angels look like shiny, glowing, bright humans. Some have six wings and are covered with eyes. Some have four wings and glow like hot embers. Living wheels that sparkle like topaz accompany some. Some were viewed as part of heavenly visions, others appeared as part of otherwise normal earthly scenes.

In his book *Miracles*, Eric Metaxas[16] describes miraculous stories that happened to people whom he knows personally, whom he trusts, and whom he believes to be of sound mind. He includes a story about his friend Peter who has on three occasions been afforded the opportunity of seeing angels worshiping with the congregation in Saint Thomas's Episcopal Church on Fifth Avenue in New York. Each time Peter was near the front of the church during Sunday worship service.

On the first occasion the congregation was standing singing a hymn when his eyes were opened revealing a glimpse into another realm. He saw an angel standing about thirty feet from him. The angel was about thirty feet tall, with large wings. He wore brightly colored armor, carried a sword, and stood regally observing the congregation. Peter said he was not really afraid, but struck by awe. The angel was an awesome warrior and Peter was awestruck.

The second time, Peter was seated in a similar place in the sanctuary. Once again the congregation stood to sing a hymn and once again, he was able to see into another realm. This time the angel was slightly behind him over his left shoulder. Peter glanced at him and he was much bigger than the first one. He guessed the second angel was fifty feet tall, and standing right next to him. He was too frightened to look in his direction very long, but as he glimpsed he saw that the angel wore the same multicolor armor as the first one, and the colors were brighter and clearer and more brilliant than anything on earth.

On another occasion, Peter saw an angel by the front door of the church. He said the colors were clearer and brighter than anything on earth.

Each time, Peter felt privileged to see what he saw, and he was filled with awe and wonder, and he knew with complete certainty that he was afforded a brief glimpse into another realm.

Are Angels Always Visible?

I posed the question about the appearance of angels, and some people have seen them. But the more appropriate question might be whether angels are near us and around us yet unseen? Balaam's donkey saw the angel long before Balaam's eyes were opened to see the angel. Metaxas' stories about Peter's rare vision of angels during church services in New York suggest that angels are present but people are rarely allowed to see the realm in which they exist.

Paul wrote about things in God's creation that we cannot see, saying:

> The Son is the image of the invisible God, the firstborn over all creation. For in him all things were created: things in heaven and on earth, *visible and invisible*, whether thrones or powers or rulers or authorities; all things have been created through him and for him. He is before all things, and in him all things hold together. Colossians 1:15-17

Some things are made to be invisible. But a few people have been afforded rare opportunities to glimpse the heavenly realm and briefly see the invisible.

Lots of Them

Further support for the notion that angels exist in another realm rarely seen by humans is the vast population of angels described in Scripture, which explains that lots and lots of angels exist. "You have come to thousands upon thousands of angels in joyful assembly…" (Hebrews 12:22). "The chariots of God are tens of thousands and thousands of thousands…" (Psalm 68:17). "The Lord … came with myriads of holy ones from the south, from his mountain slopes" (Deuteronomy 33:2). "A great company of heavenly host" accompanies the angel who tells shepherds that Jesus has just been born (Luke 2:13).

As guards appear to arrest Jesus in the Garden of Gethsemane, Peter draws his sword to defend Jesus. Jesus instructs Peter to put away his sword saying, "Do you think I cannot call on my Father, and he will at once put at my disposal more than twelve legions of angels?" (Matthew 26:53).

In his heavenly vision, John sees and hears too many angels to count. He describes the scene: "Then I looked and heard the voice of many angels, numbering thousands upon thousands, and ten thousand times ten thousand. They encircled the throne and the living creatures and the elders" (Revelation 5:11).

EXODUS

God used angels to help call Moses into service, and He continued using angels to help the former slaves during the Exodus in a variety of ways. One attracted Moses to a particular plot of earth so he could talk with God. Others guided the Israelites on their journey, protected them from attacking armies, instructed them on how they should live, and served as warriors against other armies.

Before he heard God's call, before the Exodus, Moses tended his father-in-law's flock. They wandered to the far side of the wilderness and came to Mount Horeb, the mountain of God, where an angel appeared to Moses "in flames of fire from within a bush" (Exodus 3:2). Moses went to the bush to investigate and God spoke to him. God called Moses by name, explained that the ground on which he was standing was sacred ground, explained the plans He had for Moses, discussed the Exodus, and promised to be with Moses.[17]

An angel of the Lord appeared in a strange form – appearing as a bush on fire yet not consumed – to get Moses' attention. Once Moses approached the bush, God spoke directly to Moses. The angel did not speak to Moses, but he played a critical role in the process.

As the Israelites walked out of Egypt, Pharaoh changed his mind. He chased after them with his army. Eventually, the Israelites stood on the shore trapped between the sea and the Egyptian army. Moses explains,

> "Then the angel of God, who had been traveling in front of Israel's army, withdrew and went behind them. The pillar of cloud also moved from in front and stood behind them, coming between the armies of Egypt and Israel. Throughout the night the cloud

brought darkness to the one side and light to the other side; so neither went near the other all night long." Exodus 14:19-20

An angel led the Israelites. As the Egyptian army approached, the angel stood between the two armies, protecting the Israelites. That night, the sea parted allowing the Israelites to flee through it.

On the other side of the sea, they travelled through the wilderness and God promised that His angel would continue leading them and guarding them, he would tell them what to do and fight for them. God said to Moses,

"See, I am sending an angel ahead of you to guard you along the way and to bring you to the place I have prepared. Pay attention to him and listen to what he says. Do not rebel against him; he will not forgive your rebellion, since my Name is in him… My angel will go ahead of you and bring you into the land of the Amorites, Hittites, Perizzites, Canaanites, Hivites and Jebusites, and I will wipe them out." Exodus 23:20-21 & 23

The angel served a variety of diverse roles. He was guard, guide and advisor. He was also judge over the Israelites and warrior against the residents of the lands they would soon travel through.

God reminded Moses about the angel twice. After the Levites tried to atone for the sin relating to the golden calf, God promised the angel would lead them to the Promised Land.[18] And as they continued along their way God reminded Moses that the angel would drive out the residents of the lands they were approaching.[19]

After the Israelites entered the Promised Land, the angel spoke to them:

The angel of the Lord went up from Gilgal to Bokim
and said, "I brought you up out of Egypt and led you
into the land I swore to give to your ancestors. I said,
'I will never break my covenant with you, and you
shall not make a covenant with the people of this land,
but you shall break down their altars.' Yet you have
disobeyed me. Why have you done this? And I have
also said, 'I will not drive them out before you; they
will become traps for you, and their gods will become
snares to you.'" Judges 2:1-3

Upon hearing this from the angel, the people of Israel
wept and offered sacrifices to God.

The angel spoke on behalf of God. While Moses was still
with them, God promised that His angel would guide and direct
the Israelites, but the angel would not forgive their rebellion
because God's holy Name was in the angel. Here, the angel
reminds the Israelites of all this, and explains how they had failed
to satisfy their side of the covenant.

Angelic activity surrounded the Exodus. Angels served
a variety of roles: God's messengers, guides, warriors and
executors of His judgment.

MESSENGERS – NAMES, POWER AND PRESENCE

After the Exodus, God continued using angels as messengers infused with His power. Scripture describes examples of God using angels as messengers to prophets, to people who would soon have children, and to others. Through the accounts we learn that angels have names, but some have names that humans are unable to understand, and we see that God entrusts angels with tremendous authority and power.

Gideon

As the Israelites settled in the Promised Land, they interacted with the locals and started acting like them. They went so far as to begin worshiping the gods that the locals worshipped. A group of locals, the Midianites, harassed the foreigners, attacked them and destroyed their crops, so some of the Israelites moved to the mountains. They lived in caves and other fortified places for protection,[20] and they cried out to God for help. In response, God used angels to recruit prophets into His service.

An angel visited Gideon as he hid from the Midianites threshing wheat in a winepress. The angel said, "The Lord is with you, mighty warrior" and "I will be with you, and you will strike down all the Midianites, leaving none alive" (Judges 6:12 and 6:16).

It was an unlikely message delivered to a man hiding from enemies. Gideon wanted proof that the angel was really an angel and really from God. He asked the angel to wait while he prepared an offering. Gideon prepared goat meat, broth and bread for an offering, returned to the angel, and placed the meal before him. As the angel touched the meat and bread with the tip of his staff, fire consumed the food. Gideon believed he was an angel sent from God. Later that night the Lord told Gideon to destroy his father's altar to Baal and Asherah pole, and he did.[21]

God sent an angel to initiate conversation with Gideon, and God continued the conversation directly. The angel explained that God wanted to use Gideon for a specific task and responded to Gideon's questions. This prepared Gideon to receive messages directly from God.

Elijah

The king of Samaria was injured when he fell. He sent a delegation to Ekron to ask the god Baal-Zebub whether he would recover. An angel told Elijah to meet the king's delegation and the angel told him exactly what to say, saying,

> "Go up and meet the messengers of the king of Samaria and ask them, 'Is it because there is no God in Israel that you are going off to consult with Baal-Zebub, the god of Ekron?' Therefore, this is what the Lord says: 'You will not leave the bed you are lying on. You will certainly die!'" 2 Kings 1:16

God sent an angel to give information and instruction to Elijah.

Daniel

Daniel saw a vision about the end times involving a ram and a goat. God sent an angel named Gabriel to explain the vision.[22] Some time later, as Daniel prayed, Gabriel visited him again saying,

> "Daniel, I have come to give you insight and understanding. As soon as you began to pray, a word went out, which I have come to tell you, for you are highly esteemed." Daniel 9:22-23

Gabriel continued explaining many things to Daniel. He was a special messenger from God speaking words of wisdom and insight to the great prophet.

Samson's Birth

An angel visited an unnamed woman. We know that she was married to a Danite named Manoah who lived in Zorah, and that she did not have a child.[23] The angel spoke to the woman saying,

> "You are barren and childless, but you are going to become pregnant and give birth to a son. Now see to it that you drink no wine or fermented drink and that you do not eat anything unclean. You will become pregnant and have a son whose head is never to be touched by a razor because the boy is to be a Nazirite, dedicated to God from the womb. He will take the lead in delivering Israel from the hands of the Philistines." Judges 13:3-5

Manoah wanted to ask the angel how to raise the boy, so he prayed asking God to send the angel back to them. The angel returned. As they spoke, Manoah asked the angel to tell him his name. The angel replied, "Why do you ask my name? It is beyond understanding" (Judges 13:18).

Manoah offered a goat and grain offering to the Lord. As the flame from the offering rose toward heaven, the angel ascended with it. Manoah and his wife knew with confidence that their visitor was an angel, and they believed the angel's words were from God.[24]

An angel whose name is beyond human comprehension announced Samson's birth, then, in response to prayer, returned to have a conversation with the man who would become Samson's father.

John the Baptist's Birth

Zechariah served as a priest. For years, he and his wife Elizabeth prayed for a child. On this particular occasion, Zechariah was chosen to enter the inner room in the temple alone to burn incense for the Lord. He entered the temple as others prayed outside. As he approached the altar, an angel appeared to him and told him about the son he and his wife would soon have. The angel said that the boy

> "will be filled with the Holy Spirit even before he is born. He will bring back many of the people of Israel to the Lord their God. And he will go on before the Lord, in the spirit and power of Elijah, to turn the hearts of the parents to their children and the disobedient to the wisdom of the righteous – to make people prepared for the Lord." Luke 1:15-19

Zechariah questioned the angel, who replied saying:

> "I am Gabriel. I stand in the presence of God, and I have been sent to speak to you and to tell you this good news. And now you will be silent and not be able to speak until the day this happens, because you did not believe my words, which will come true at their appointed time." Luke 1:19-20

After the exchange, Zechariah was unable to speak until his wife had their baby boy and they named him John. As soon as that happened, Zechariah regained his ability to speak. From the exchange we learn the following:

1. Some angels have names that can be understood by humans.

2. Gabriel stands in the presence of God. Notice that he speaks in present tense. This means that he was in the presence of God while he spoke the words. He was in the presence of God and in the presence of Zechariah at the same time. He could see both of them, but Zechariah could only see the angel; and

3. Gabriel had the ability and authority to render Zechariah silent.

God grants angels authority to act on His behalf. Angels are stronger and more powerful than people,[25] and messages spoken through angels from God are binding as if God spoke them.[26]

Jesus' Birth

Angelic visits surrounded Jesus' birth. Gabriel visited Mary to tell her she had been chosen to be the Messiah's mother. Mary was afraid when she saw Gabriel, but the angel said,

> "Don't be afraid, Mary; you have found favor with God. You will conceive and give birth to a son, and you are to call him Jesus. He will be great and will be called the Son of the Most High. The Lord God will give him the throne of his father David, and he will reign over Jacob's descendants forever; his kingdom will never end." Luke 1:30-33

Mary asked how it would happen and Gabriel explained. Mary agreed to go along with the plan.

When Joseph learned that Mary was pregnant, Joseph planned to divorce her quietly. That night an angel appeared to him in a dream saying,

> "Joseph son of David, do not be afraid to take Mary home as your wife, because what is conceived in her is from the Holy Spirit. She will give birth to a son, and you are to give him the name Jesus, because he will save his people from their sins." Matthew 1:20-21

Joseph followed the angel's recommendation. After Jesus was born, angels visited shepherds who were in the field tending flocks. Luke describes the scene as follows:

> An angel of the Lord appeared to them, and the glory of the Lord shone around them, and they were

terrified. But the angel said to them, "Do not be afraid.
I bring you news that will cause great joy for all the
people. Today in the town of David a Savior has been
born to you; he is the Messiah, the Lord. This will be
a sign to you: You will find a baby wrapped in cloths
and lying in a manger."

Suddenly a great company of the heavenly host
appeared with the angel, praising God and saying,
"Glory to God in the highest heaven, and on the earth
peace on whom his favor rests." Luke 2:9-14

Later an angel returned to Joseph in a dream. He warned
that Herod wanted to kill Jesus and told Joseph to go to Egypt.[27]

Angels were actively involved in the story of Jesus' birth.
They prepared Mary and encouraged her to commit to the plan.
They prepared Joseph and helped him navigate stormy waters as
he heard the news. They gloriously announced the birth to
shepherds and they helped the family avoid the tragedy of
Herod's ruthless plans. Angels served as God's messengers
throughout the process.

While some angels have names that cannot be understood
by humans, [28] at least one angel has a name that we can
understand. An angel named Gabriel visited the prophet
Daniel,[29] the priest Zechariah,[30] and Mary, the woman who would
become Jesus' mother.[31] Each person had a conversation with the
angel.

Throughout Scripture, angels serve as God's messengers
and through these encounters we learn about angels' names,
power and authority. We see angels serving as messengers
throughout the Exodus, we see angels delivering messages to
prophets, we see angels delivering glorious birth announcements,
and we see an angel administer punishment. God grants angels
authority and their words are binding.

<u>COMFORTERS AND PROVIDERS</u>

Hagar & Ishmael

Angels also serve as comforters and providers. Scripture records two times angels visited Hagar to encourage her, comfort her, reveal insight about her future, and provide for her physical needs.

Abram and Sarai were husband and wife. Sarai was unable to have children, so she encouraged Abram to have a child through her servant, Hagar. When Hagar was pregnant with Abram's son, Sarai began to despise and mistreat her, so Hagar fled to the wilderness. An angel appeared to her, urging her to return to Sarai and promising, "I will increase your descendants so much that they will be too numerous to count" (Genesis 16:10). The angel also told her to name her baby Ishmael and told her about the sort of man her baby would grow to become.[32] So Hagar returned to Sarai and Abram, and gave birth to Ishmael.

After Sarah (formerly known as Sarai) gave birth to Isaac, she encouraged Abraham (formerly known as Abram) to send Hagar and Ishmael away. He banished them into the wilderness with the amount of food and water they could carry. When the food and water was gone, Hagar lay Ishmael under a bush, walked away and cried. An angel appeared to Hagar and reminded her that God was planning to make Ishmael into a great nation. God then opened her eyes allowing her to see a water well. They drank water and God continued to watch over them.[33]

Elijah

Jezebel threatened to kill Elijah, so he fled through the wilderness toward Mount Sinai. Elijah was tired and hungry. He lay under a bush, prayed to God that he might die where he was, and went to sleep. God sent an angel. Scripture continues saying,

> All at once an angel touched him and said, "Get up and eat." He looked around, and there by his head

was some bread baked over hot coals, and a jar of water. He ate and drank and then lay down again.

The angel of the Lord came back a second time and touched him and said, "Get up and eat, for the journey is too much for you." So he got up and ate and drank. Strengthened by the food, he traveled forty days and forty nights until he reached Horeb, the mountain of God. There he went into a cave and spent the night. 1 Kings 19:5-9.

PROTECTORS AND RESCUERS

Lot

Lot lived in Sodom, a place known for debauchery. He saw two angels enter town and he invited them to stay with him for the night. That night, the angels told Lot that they came to destroy the town. They encouraged Lot to take his family and leave town early the following morning; otherwise they too would be destroyed. Lot and his family left just before the angels caused burning sulfur to rain over the region.[34] (I suppose this is also an example of God using angels to enforce his judgment.)

Daniel

Daniel records an angel protecting three men as they sat in a fiery furnace and one man as he sat in the lion's den. They had been sentenced to die for refusing to worship the king. King Nebuchadnezzar ordered everyone to bow and worship a gold statue made in his image. Shadrach, Meshach and Abednego refused. The king ordered guards to throw the three men into a furnace heated seven times hotter than normal. The furnace was so hot that it killed the guards who were near it. When the king looked into the furnace he saw four men standing in the fire. An angel stood with the three men protecting them.[35]

Years later, King Darius issued a decree stating that any person who worshiped anyone other than the king would be sentenced to death in the lion's den. Daniel continued to openly pray to God three times each day. Daniel was sentenced to death and placed in the lion's den overnight. The following morning the king found him unharmed. Daniel said,

> "May the king live forever! My God sent his angel, and he shut the mouths of the lions. They have not hurt me, because I was found innocent in his sight. Nor have I ever done any wrong before you, Your Majesty." Daniel 6:21-22

Apostles

Twice in the Book of Acts, Luke describes angels rescuing people from jail.

Shortly after Jesus ascended to heaven, the apostles became renowned for healing people. They often gathered in the temple to pray and people crowded the path leading to the temple to be near them as they passed by. Sick people lay near the path hoping Peter's shadow would fall on them. Across the region people heard of the apostles' power and many traveled to Jerusalem to be healed. As the apostles' fame grew, religious leaders took notice and ordered their arrest. An angel released the apostles from jail and told them to return to the temple courts to preach the Good News.[36]

Later, Herod arrested a group of believers, including James. At Herod's command, a guard executed James with a sword. After Jewish leaders approved the execution, Herod arrested Peter and surrounded him in jail by sixteen guards. Herod planned a public trial after the Passover.

The church gathered together and prayed for Peter. The night before the trial, an angel appeared in his cell. The angel found Peter sleeping chained to two guards. The angel woke Peter up and the chains fell off. He then gave Peter his clothes and led Peter out of the jail. They passed by guards who did not notice them; each door opened on its own; and they walked through unhindered. Peter said he thought it was a dream until the angel left him and he found himself on the road alone.[37]

Peter said,

"Now I know without a doubt that the Lord has sent his angel and rescued me from Herod's clutches and from everything the Jewish people were hoping would happen." Acts 12:11

PERSONAL STORIES

Over the years I have heard many people describe personal encounters with angels. Most of the stories involved supernatural protection but each one involves an evidentiary gap. The person who experienced each event has the sincere, emphatic belief that an angel reached into our space and time to guard, protect and help them. But in each situation alternative explanations exist and a person hearing the story is left asking, "How do you know it was an angel?"

Some events involve situations where events unfolded in an unexpectedly beneficial way for someone, in others some unexplainable force altered the expected course of events, but the force or agent of change was not seen. In others, the helper was seen but it could have been a person. So the following examples are far from iron-tight. People I know and believe described each one to me. I list them as examples of how some people believe angels interact with us today, and, to be clear, I believe them to be true or I would not repeat them here.

Susan

A few years ago we ate dinner with a group of friends. At the time some shows were on television involving angels, and the conversation turned to whether angels really exist. Susan said with strong conviction that she knew with certainty that angels exist. She explained telling a story that happened about ten years earlier.

At the time her kids were young – their oldest was in grade school and their youngest was a toddler. They lived in a two-story house. The den had a vaulted ceiling with an overlooking loft. One evening, Susan was in the den. She looked up to the loft and saw her toddler on the outside of the banister holding on to the railing. Susan started toward her daughter as the toddler lost her grip and fell. Susan said her daughter fell fast, but about halfway down her fall slowed and she gently came to rest unharmed on the sofa below.

Susan is convinced that an angel caught her daughter mid-air and gently placed her down on the sofa below. She did not see an angel, but she is certain that an angel protected her daughter.

Bill

I met Bill in Worthington, Minnesota at the Nels family reunion in August 1994. He was my mother-in-law's brother. We happened to sit near each other Saturday morning in the Comfort Suites conference room where folding tables and folding chairs had been arranged for the reunion breakfast. We ate eggs, sausage and biscuits on paper plates with plastic utensils, and sipped coffee from Styrofoam cups. Bill was in his 70's. He and his wife, Nellie, had flown in for the weekend from his home in Santa Barbara, California.

After we spoke for a while about the weather and how I fit into the family, he started talking about his experience in World War II. We talked for quite a while. We continued talking long after everyone else left the room. I was amazed by his stories and he seemed to enjoy telling them, which surprised other members of the family who said Bill never spoke about the war. In fact, they said he refused to talk about it when asked.

A few weeks later a book arrived at my house in the mail. Bill had mailed what on the surface looked like a high school annual. Its hard cover was 8x10, textured light blue with a green tint, and labeled "Santa Fe 35th Infantry Division – Normandy, N.

France, Rhineland, Ardennes, C. Europe." The book was about ¾ inch thick.

Bill was a Ranger in the 35th Infantry Division during World War II under General Patton. In June 1944, he traveled from England to France by boat, arriving on D-Day, he got off in Normandy, and battled his way across France, Belgium, Luxembourg, Holland and into Germany. The book chronicled the division's travels from Plymouth, England to the Elbe River in central Germany. Bill had annotated the margins with handwritten notes and photographs.

Early in our conversation Bill asked me whether I believed in angels. Without pausing for my answer, he explained why he knew angels saved him many times during his travels across Europe.

He was 22 years old as he stood in line for what he and his friends referred to as the "last supper." The night was dark and fog was rolling in off the English Channel. General Eisenhower walked down the chow line shaking hands with soldiers. He stopped, shook Bill's hand and asked, "What is your job soldier?" "Anti-tank gunner, Sir." Eisenhower replied, "Good, I know how the G.I.'s are feeling."

After dinner they boarded boats heading for Normandy. Bill did not talk about the landing, the beach, what he experienced there or how he survived it. But he described the trip inland, heading for Saint-Lo. He described traveling a narrow, winding road. Fallen soldiers lined the roadside ditch. As Bill passed by, troops gathered the fallen.

Before long he had moved to the front, which was not a distinct line. It was not a black line on a map; it was a blurry grey area where things changed quickly. And it involved hedgerows, centuries old walls comprised of rock-hard soil and tall vegetation separating fields. Some were five feet tall; others were thirty-five feet tall. They were natural barricades hindering their advance and shielding the enemy.

As the battle in Saint-Lo slowed, the commanding officer sent Bill ahead on the road leading to Avranches. They drove a six-wheel truck pulling a trailer-mounted 50 caliber anti-tank gun. Moving at night, they set up an outpost off the road behind a hedgerow. They did not pick a part of the hedgerow that would provide camouflage because they were not trying to hide; they were only trying to get off the road. So the place where they happened to be was a relatively sparse piece of hedgerow, leaving their truck and gun visible from the road.

Each night at 2 a.m., headquarters called Bill's radio to check-in. That night, Bill and one other man were alone. It was a little before 2 when they heard troops walking down the road adjacent to the hedgerow. They were not concerned – they presumed the troops were friendly, until they heard the men speaking German. Suddenly, they found themselves within a few feet of enemy soldiers, and their radio was about to sound. When headquarters called, the radio would ring a uniquely American tone, and when that happened they knew they were dead.

Several of the men speaking German stopped so close to Bill he could hear their breathing. For reasons that initially puzzled Bill, his radio was silent and the men never saw the truck or gun. The call came every night except that one, and the German soldiers should have seen the truck and gun. Bill came to believe that angels protected him that night. He believed that angels silenced his radio and hid the truck and gun.

They moved south to Laval, then east to Le Mans and on to Orleans. One night Bill's superior handed him a map and ordered him to move five miles forward. He and six other men secured the anti-tank gun, loaded into the truck, and headed in the direction ordered. Maps were not always accurate. As they attempted to follow the map in the dark, they saw a town ahead. On the outskirts of town they pulled off the road and turned off the truck. They heard men speaking German and they saw men using horses to move artillery guns into position.

A French farmer walked on the road leading a cow. They talked with the man and asked which army occupied the town. The man said the town was full of German soldiers. As they spoke with the man, three German trucks drove on the road toward them. The farmer told them not to worry. At that time of night, he guessed the trucks were food and supply trucks, and he told Bill to start his truck, drive forward thirty meters, turn around in the farmer's driveway, and leave. Bill's driver did not want to restart the truck because the Germans would hear it, but he followed the instruction. They pulled forward, turned around and drove away. If the Germans noticed them they did not respond. Bill was later convinced that the farmer was an angel.

Bill spent Christmas day 1944 in Metz, France. He expected to have a few days to rest, but that evening an order came down from General Patton. They had two hours to prepare to leave for Bastogne, Belgium to take part in what became known as the Battle of the Bulge.

They drove north into the Ardennes Mountains where a blizzard pounded. The air was below zero Fahrenheit, the wind blew hard, snow fell horizontally and they could not use headlights to stay on the mountain road. The next morning their green truck and anti-tank gun stood out on the snowy land. People from the village nearby brought white bed sheets to camouflage the equipment. Bill was later convinced that the generous provision of bed sheet camouflage was God sent.

After a month-long battle, they continued north to Venlo, Holland. Bill's parents immigrated to the United States from Holland. They spoke Dutch in his home, so he knew the language. As they entered Venlo, Bill spoke to some of the kids in their native language. The kids introduced Bill to their parents, who invited Bill to stay in their barn. The family wrote letters to Bill's parents in Sheldon, Iowa telling them that their son was with them and healthy, at least at the time the letter was written.

That night in France, when Bill was a few feet away from German troops, did an angel alter their vision rendering them unable to see Bill and his truck and anti-tank gun? That night when they drove to the outskirts of a French town controlled by German troops and a farmer walking a cow helped them, did an angel come to their aid? Did angels produce bed sheets? Bill was convinced angels were involved in each situation, and many others. We know from Scripture that angels are normally invisible to human eyes. Should we only believe they help on rare occasions that they are visible?

Bill compared his experiences in Europe to John G. Paton's experiences in the New Hebrides Islands.[4] In the 1800's, as Paton served as missionary on the islands, he endured years of near daily attacks on his life.[38] Time and time again, intervening forces outside Paton's control repelled each attack.

Bill retold a story about Paton that was very meaningful to him. Paton and his wife were in the mission one night. They heard warriors approach the building and they had reason to believe that the warriors had come to kill them. They expected the warriors to set the mission on fire and kill them as they fled. The Patons prayed. They prayed all night and they were not attacked.

Years later the chief who led the warriors that night befriended Paton, and Paton asked the chief about that evening at the mission. The chief said he planned to attack the mission and he planned to kill the Patons, but when he and his warriors arrived at the mission, they saw men surrounding the building. So they left. Paton explained that he and his wife were alone at the mission that night, and they both believed the men that the chief saw were angels sent to guard them.

Bill was convinced that angels had protected Paton, and he eventually came to believe that angels had protected him time and time again as well. Bill had also read about Captain Eddie Rickenbacker who, after crash landing his B-17 on the Pacific Ocean, survived when a gull landed on his head providing food and liquid for him and his crew. Rickenbacker credited God and His angels with his rescue.

Billy Graham wrote about Paton and Rickenbacker in his book, *Angels: God's Secret Agents*.[39] I am not sure if Bill read the book, or if Bill's discussion of the stories and the depiction of Paton and Rickenbacker in the book are coincidental, but Bill's experiences remind me of another story mentioned in Graham's book and told in detail by Corrie ten Boom in her book *A Prisoner and Yet....*[40]

The ten Boom family lived above their watch shop in Haarlem, Holland. They were devout Christians who lived lives

---

[4] Now the Republic of Vanuatu in the South Pacific

of faith by helping people in need. During German occupation of Holland during World War II, the ten Boom family allowed people who were wanted by German police to stay in their home, including members of the Dutch underground and Jewish people. They constructed false walls in their apartment upstairs to hide people during police inspections. Most of the time they had two to six people living with them, and more who stayed for a few hours until they were able to locate another safe house.

In February 1944 Corrie, her sister Betsie, their brother, father and other family members were arrested. Their father was 84 years old and died within a few days of his arrest. Corrie and Betsie lived in captivity for ten months in several facilities before being moved to Ravensbruck Concentration Camp in eastern Germany. Corrie was the sole survivor from the family.

After arriving at Ravensbruck on a cold winter night, Corrie and Betsy saw a multicolored mountain of clothing, blankets and personal effects near the entrance to a building. They saw women leaving the building with nothing more than the thin dress that they wore. Corrie and Betsy realized they would soon be asked to surrender the remainder of their possessions.

They prayed for strength and protection. Upon entering the building, Corrie hid their underwear and her Bible in the restroom. They surrendered everything else – their clothing, blanket, shoes, everything – and put on the thin dress. Corrie retrieved the underwear and Bible from the restroom and hid them under her dress. She prayed for angels to surround her so she would not be seen. On several occasions as they walked out of the building, guards carefully checked everyone for items they should not have have. Guards checked everyone around Corrie. They searched Betsy, but they did not see Corrie's obvious bulge under her dress, and she was able to carry her prized possessions to the barricks.

Corrie believed angels hid her. She believed that angels shielded her so the guards failed to see her, allowing her to keep her Bible and underwear. She knew that God sent angels in response to her prayer, yet she never saw them. Bill was convinced angels helped him in the same way, hiding his truck and gun and preventing his radio from ringing. The angels were not visible to humans, nonetheless, Bill and Corrie knew with certainty that angels protected them.

Lori

Lori lived in south Denver during her high school years. Today, the intersection of Hampden and I-25 is a densely populated area, always bustling with activity and traffic. It is hard to imagine a time of any day when traffic does not crowd the intersection. In 1980 the intersection was near the southern edge of development. While I-25 was busy all the time, roads off of the highway that far south were empty and quiet at night. Just south of Hampden, a bridge was constructed over I-25 allowing traffic on Quincy Avenue to cross over the freeway and access Monaco Street and Happy Canyon Road, a rare diagonal across the Cartesian grid.

That summer the area around the bridge and the intersection of the three roads was under construction. There were no streetlights and as the hour grew later, fewer and fewer cars traveled the roads.

Late one rainy night Lori drove her brother's old car home. She had driven through the construction zone many times, but not at night. On this night, rain caused visibility to be lower than usual – wet pavement reflected light from her headlights away from her; it did not bounce back to her so it did not assist her vision. With no streetlights and wet pavement, she had extremely poor visibility.

Lori navigated the construction cones slowly. She saw a gap between the cones and thought it indicated a turning lane. She was wrong. As she steered to the right, the car left pavement and lodged deeply in mud. She had no raincoat, no umbrella, and it was raining steadily. She got out and her first step landed in knee-deep mud. She walked to the pavement, stood in the dark, felt her clothes absorbing rain and plotted her path forward. She was about a mile and a half from home. She started walking.

It was late and dark. She was muddy, wet, cold, lonely, angry with herself, and worried about what her father would say.

There were no people and no cars within sight. Suddenly she saw her shadow in front of her, and she turned to see headlights behind her. An old pickup pulled alongside her and a man inside offered her a ride. She was terrified. She did not know whether she should get in. She knew she should not get in, but for some reason she did. The man asked her where she was headed and he drove her home.

Her house was on Dahlia two blocks from the corner of Hampden and Happy Canyon. Dahlia is a straight road. The positioning of her house offered clear visibility down Dahlia in both directions. The man drove to her house, turned up the circular driveway, stopped and let her out. She got out of the truck, took two steps toward the front door, and then turned around to see the license plate of the truck. The truck was gone. She looked up and down Dahlia and no taillights were in sight. The old pickup had disappeared.

As an interesting addition to the story, Lori could not and cannot recall the facial details of the man who drove the old pickup. If this tidbit were stated in reference to me, it would be meaningless. I routinely struggle to remember faces and names. But for Lori, this is significant. She has an amazing gift of recognizing faces and remembering names. When she sees someone she has seen before, she instantly remembers their name and how she knows them. When we go to social events I always want her next to me, otherwise I embarrass myself with names.

When we are in New York she sees so many famous people that I miss. One day in New York we ate a late lunch at a little Italian restaurant. The tables were so close our elbows nearly touched the people next to us. She kept cautiously motioning for me to look at the guy sitting next to us. He was like six inches away. I looked but it meant nothing. After he left, she explained that it was Chris O'Donnell. I thought about it and she was definitely right.

We got in a taxi heading for the Metropolitan Museum. As the taxi turned left off the avenue, the driver stopped quickly to avoid hitting an older man wearing a wool coat and a wool driver's cap. He gave an angry look at the taxi driver who had come so close to hitting him. Lori shouted, "That's Woody Allen." I looked and she was right.

We rode an elevator with a very nice lady. During the ride we had an interesting conversation. After the lady got off, Lori explained that she had played Alice on television and I suddenly recognized whom we had been talking with.

These events happen all the time. She sees people. She looks at them. She recognizes them and she never forgets. It is how she lives and a gift she possesses. But on that particular night she could not remember anything about the man who drove the old pickup truck.

Lori is convinced her rescuer was an angel sent to help her in her time of need.

Randy

One Friday night during high school, two of my friends and I were driving around bored. We drove on a country road about two miles southwest of town when we happened upon a kid we knew from high school whose pickup was stuck in a ditch beside the road. He had apparently attempted a U-turn on the narrow county road, and he went a little too far forward. His front wheels were lodged in the ditch and his rear wheels were at the edge of the road. The truck was titled at a thirty-degree angel. We knew the guy, but we were not really friends. If we had any place to be we would not have stopped, but we were bored, so we stopped.

They were trying to figure out how to get it out without calling a tow truck, which they could not afford. We were in my friend's Jeep, but neither vehicle had a towrope. I suggested we push it out. Six guys were there. I figured if five of us pushed and the driver put it in reverse, we would get it out.

We went to the front of the truck and realized that the hood of the truck was only slightly higher than our feet. The road separated two wheat fields. A ditch was dug out on both sides of the road, and the road and wheat field were at the same elevation. The truck was lodged in the ditch, lowering the height of its hood.

As we started pushing the truck, our first three steps would be down into the ditch. On the first try we all got it rocking, gave it a push as the driver gunned the engine. It backed up a foot or two before slamming back into the bank of the ditch beneath our feet. We tried it again with similar results.

I suggested that we just needed to stay with it the next time. We were taking one step then jumping out of the way. If we all pushed all the way through the ditch we could get it out. So we all agreed – none of us would jump out of the ditch. We would keep pushing the truck until it was out.

I was in the middle of the truck. Two guys were on either side of me. We told the driver to go and we started pushing and the truck successfully backed out onto the road. I was in the bottom of the ditch when the truck stopped, and I stood there alone. The others had bailed out, leaving me all alone to get squished by the truck had it slammed back into the ditch.

Now I know that I did not push the truck out on my own. First, that would have been impossible, and second, even if I could have, I did not push hard enough to accomplish a feat like that. My first thought was sadness at how guys who I thought were my friends had let me down. I wasn't angry, just let down. My second thought was that an angel had saved me. And then I had this recurring nightmare about how close I voluntarily came to serious injury or death. It was a choice I voluntarily made, and it could have cost me so much. It haunted me for a long, long time. Fortunately, an angel stepped in.

CONCLUSION

Scripture records Jesus talking about angels on many occasions and the things he says about angels indicate (i) they really exist in the heavenly realm, (ii) they sometimes appear on earth, (iii) they obey God, and (iv) they respond to Jesus when He asks them for help. Some people on some occasions have been afforded the opportunity to see angels, but these are rare opportunities. On the rare occasion that angels are seen by humans, some look like people and others have an otherworldly appearance.

Angels serve God. They obey God. They do His bidding as warriors, and when God so requests, they reach into our world to help people as messengers, guides, instructors, rescuers, providers, comforters and helpers. Whether seen or unseen, angels really exist.

But not everyone believes they really exist. I find comfort knowing that Scripture clearly reveals the disconnect between ideologies. It reveals tremendous angelic activity and a great deal of teaching about and discussion regarding angels, yet Scripture also explains that religious leaders at that time debated whether angels are real saying,

> "(The Sadducees say that there is no resurrection, and that there are neither angels nor spirits, but the Pharisees believe all these things.)" Acts 23:8

Some believe while others do not. Evidence from Scripture and experience seem clear to me. May God send His angels to protect you and lift you up.

9 | HOLY SPIRIT

"The Spirit clearly says that in later times some will abandon the faith and follow deceiving spirits and things taught by demons."
1 Timothy 4:1

In Scripture, more often than not, the Greek word pneuma refers to the good Spirit, the Holy Spirit or God's Spirit. God is one God in three persons. The Holy Spirit is one of the three. He is God, He is from heaven, He is a spiritual being, and He possesses many qualities that we may think of as personal qualities, but when we do so we are thinking of it backwards because we were created in God's image, not the other way around. He thinks, feels emotions, grieves, and experiences peace and joy. He also acts: He comforts, teaches and speaks.

Jesus spent His last evening on earth in fully human form teaching the disciples.[1] He washed their feet as a sign of love and He commanded them to wash one another's feet. Shortly after this, Jesus taught about the Holy Spirit explaining that Jesus sends the Holy Spirit from God the Father[2] to people who love Jesus and obey His commands.[3] Jesus calls the Holy Spirit the Counselor, Comforter or Advocate, depending on the translation.[4]

The Holy Spirit interacts with people. He engages people almost like people do. He talks with people, teaches people, leads people and has fellowship with people. While He is described as one person of God, He does not have a physical presence. As a spiritual being, the Holy Spirit speaks to people and through people, and He performs many other actions upon and through people. He influences people directly, internally by dwelling within their spirit. He infuses His Holy Presence directly into a person's spirit, delivering the elements of His Presence – His joy, peace, comfort, strength, power – to each person within whom He dwells.

RESIDES IN PEOPLE

God's Holy Presence is everywhere all the time. He is omnipresent, unbound by space, and unbound by time. He dwells within people who invite Him in. During the evening of the Last Supper, as Jesus taught about the Holy Spirit, He said,

> "The world cannot accept him [the Spirit of Truth] because it neither sees him nor knows him, but you know him, for *he lives with you and will be in you*." John 14:17

Keep in mind that He was speaking to His close friends, people He had traveled with and lived with for years. They followed Him. They believed in Him. They served Him. Jesus said that the Holy Spirit lives within His disciples.

Fundamental to Paul's theology is the notion that the Holy Spirit dwells within people, and as a result of that indwelling the Holy Spirit transforms human spirits. In one of his letters to the church in Corinth, Paul writes about Jesus saying,

> "*He anointed us*, set his seal of ownership on us, and *put his Spirit in our hearts* as a deposit, guaranteeing what is to come." 2 Corinthians 1:21-22

So Jesus places the Holy Spirit in our hearts. In Ephesians Paul writes a similar message. Once again he discusses Jesus saying,

> "And in him you too are being built together to become a *dwelling* in which God lives by his Spirit."
> Ephesians 2:22

This is a reference to the Holy Trinity – through Jesus people become a place for God to dwell by the Holy Spirit. In one of his letters to Timothy, Paul expresses a similar message saying,

> "Guard the good deposit that was entrusted to you – guard it with the help of the *Holy Spirit who lives in us*."
> 2 Timothy 1:14

The Holy Spirit lives within certain people. He is God's holy presence residing within people and transforming them. As one of the three persons of the Holy Trinity, the Holy Spirit is God. He is everywhere all at once, so His presence is not limited, it is not confined to the people within whom He dwells. His presence is broader than the physical limits of people.

WHAT DOES HE DO?

The Holy Spirit Enlightens Minds & Spirits

On four occasions Scripture records Jesus telling us that the Holy Spirit explains things to people. Jesus tells us that the Holy Spirit teaches, reminds, and guides people, and He testifies to us about Jesus. In the first, Jesus speaks to His followers. He warns that they will be questioned and punished because of their relationship with Jesus, but He explains that when they are questioned the Holy Spirit will tell them what to say.

"For the *Holy Spirit will teach you* at the time what you should say." Luke 12:12

The next three occur during the Last Supper. As Jesus teaches about the Holy Spirit, He explains that the Holy Spirit teaches, reminds, guides, and testifies about Jesus.

"But the Advocate, the Holy Spirit, who the Father will send in my name *will teach you* all things and *will remind you* of everything I have said to you." John 14:26

"When the Advocate comes, whom I will send to you from the Father – the Spirit of Truth who goes out from the Father – *he will testify* about me." John 15:26

"But when the Spirit of Truth comes *he will guide you* to all truth." John 16:13

Just as Jesus promised, in Acts we see examples of the Holy Spirit speaking directly to people. In one example, Peter was in Joppa on the roof of a house praying when he saw a vision of a sheet descending from heaven carrying all sorts of mammals, reptiles and birds. As he saw the vision, a voice said, "Get up, Peter. Kill and eat" (Acts 10:13). Peter argued with the voice because some of the animals were unclean according to Jewish custom and eating them would violate Jewish dietary laws. The event repeated three times. As Peter sat on the roof processing what he had seen and pondering notions of cleanliness and uncleanliness, the Holy Spirit spoke to him. Scripture says,

"While Peter was still thinking about the vision, the *Spirit said to him*, 'Simon, three men are looking for you. So get up and go downstairs. Do not hesitate to go with them, for I have sent them.'" Acts 10:19

Peter went downstairs just as two men knocked on the door looking for him. They were Gentile. By Jewish custom, Peter was restricted from interacting with them in certain ways. However, spurred by the Holy Spirit, Peter met with them, travelled with them to their master's home in a different town, and stayed with them. The Holy Spirit spoke directly to Peter, told him what to do, and he obeyed.

In another example, Acts describes Paul's missionary journeys and quotes Paul saying that the Holy Spirit spoke directly to him. As he traveled back to Jerusalem at the end of his last journey, Paul says,

> "I only know that in every city the *Holy Spirit warns me* that prison and hardship are facing me." Acts 20:23

On the final leg of his journey to Jerusalem, Paul stopped in Caesarea where he met a prophet named Agabus. Luke records the encounter between Paul and Agabus saying,

> "Coming over to us, he [Agabus] took Paul's belt, tied his own hands and feet with it and said, 'The *Holy Spirit says*, 'In this way the Jewish leaders will bind the owner of this belt and hand him over to the Gentiles.''" Acts 21:11

The Holy Spirit spoke to and through the prophet Agabus. During Paul's last sermon recorded in Acts, he told his listeners that the Holy Spirit speaks through prophets explaining that He spoke through Isaiah.

> "The *Holy Spirit spoke the truth to* your ancestors when he said through Isaiah the prophet..." Acts 28:25

Similar to his preaching, Paul wrote about the Holy Spirit in his letters. Paul explains that the Holy Spirit leads people, reveals messages to them, engages in fellowship with them, promotes fellowship between them, and speaks to them. Following are a few examples.

"For those who are *led by the Spirit* of God are the children of God." Romans 8:14

"These are the things God has *revealed to us* by his Spirit. The Spirit searches all things, even the deep things of God." 1 Corinthians 2:10-11

"May the grace of the Lord Jesus Christ, the love of God and the *fellowship* of the Holy Spirit be with you all." 2 Corinthians 13:14

"The *Spirit clearly says* that in later times some will abandon the faith and follow deceiving spirits and things taught by demons." 1 Titus 4:1

The author of Hebrews repeated the thought, writing,

"The Holy Spirit also *testifies to us* about this. First he says..." Hebrews 10:15

Jesus said the Holy Spirit speaks through people. Jesus, Paul and the author of Hebrews explain that the Holy Spirit speaks to people. He enlightens people's minds and spirits; He guides, teaches and reminds people; and He engages in fellowship with people. In Acts, Luke records real world accounts of the Holy Spirit speaking directly to people. The passages set forth above describe the Holy Spirit speaking directly to Peter, Paul and Agabus. Jesus promised it would happen and in Acts, Luke describes it happening.

The Holy Spirit Transforms Human Spirits

The Holy Spirit spoke audibly to Peter and Paul. They apparently heard Him speak to them with their ears. But this is not the only way He speaks. Much more often, He chooses to speak inwardly, bypassing our human senses. He enlightens our minds and spirits directly.

The Holy Spirit dwells within people, He provides His strength, power, knowledge and wisdom to people. God places His Holy Spirit within people. Paul equates this to an anointing – people are anointed with the Holy Spirit when the Holy Spirit enters them and dwells within them. The Holy Spirit makes people better than they are without Him. He transforms people. He gives them peace, joy and holiness. He sanctifies them. He pours out His love into them.

Paul wrote about this in four of his letters that we have available to us as Scripture. When he wrote his letter to believers in Rome, he was writing to people he had never met. Rather than writing to reinforce what he had already taught, he wrote to introduce himself and the Gospel to the church. So Romans provides a fairly comprehensive statement of the Gospel. In three different parts of the letter Paul describes the transformative power of the Holy Spirit. The Holy Spirit dwells within people, and that indwelling presence transforms them.

Paul describes the peace, hope and joy available through Jesus Christ, and in conclusion he writes,

> "And hope does not disappoint us, because *God has poured out his love into our hearts through the Holy Spirit*, whom he has given us." Romans 5:5

Later in Romans,[5] Paul discusses spiritual maturity and some of the little things that were causing division in the church, like acceptable food and drink and whether certain days of the week are sacred. Paul says that the distinctions do not in themselves matter so long as everything is done for God's glory. He recommends that each person refrain from acting in a way that is a stumbling block for others. For example, one person may choose to eat meat while another person may refrain from eating meat, each decision is fine so long as they give glory to God as they do so. If one person's decision to eat meat becomes a stumbling block to the one choosing to abstain, the meat eater should stop. Again, this should be for God's glory. Paul explains that as a person matures spiritually, the love of Jesus Christ will gradually fill them to a greater extent, and God's glory will flow through them more and more. He continues this thought writing,

> "For the kingdom of God is not a matter of eating and drinking, but of *righteousness, peace and joy in the Holy Spirit*, because anyone who serves Christ in this way is pleasing to God and approved by men." Romans 14:17-18

Righteousness, peace and joy are characteristics exhibited through people within whom the Holy Spirit dwells. Six paragraphs later, Paul concludes his discussion of spiritual maturity with a doxology:

> "May the God of hope fill you with all *joy and peace* as you trust in him, so that you may overflow with hope by the power of the Holy Spirit." Romans 15:13

As Paul concludes his letter to the church in Rome, he explains his most fundamental reason for writing the letter and for ministering to Gentiles (i.e. people who were not Jewish). The goal of his ministry was to help Gentiles be sanctified by the Holy Spirit:

> I have written you quite boldly on some points, as if to remind you of them again, because of the grace God gave me to be a minister of Christ Jesus to the Gentiles with the priestly duty of proclaiming the gospel of God, so that the Gentiles might become an offering acceptable to God, *sanctified by the Holy Spirit*." Romans 15:15-16

Paul discusses the process of spiritual transformation through the indwelling Holy Spirit in terms of spiritual maturity, indicating maturation happens gradually over time. He also describes it as sanctification, which means to make holy and is another way of referring to the same gradual spiritual transformation. Only God is holy, but sanctification describes the process of a person gradually moving toward holiness, gradually absorbing holiness and gradually releasing or removing obstacles separating the person from God. The process described as spiritual maturation or sanctification are efforts to describe the Holy Spirit transforming human spirits and souls in which He dwells.

Paul mentions the process of spiritual transformation through the indwelling Holy Spirit in his letters to the church in Ephesus and Thessalonica, writing:

> "I pray that out of his glorious riches he may *strengthen you with power* through *his Spirit in your inner being*, so that *Christ may dwell in your hearts* through faith. And I pray that you, being rooted and established in love, may have power, together with all the saints, to grasp how wide and long and high and deep is the love of Christ, and to know this love that surpasses knowledge – that you may be *filled to the measure of all the fullness of God.*" Ephesians 3:16-19

> "You became imitators of us and of the Lord, in spite of severe suffering, you welcomed the message with the *joy given by the Holy Spirit.*" 1 Thessalonians 1:6

> "But we ought always thank God for you, brothers and sisters loved by God, because God chose you as first fruits to be saved through the *sanctifying work of the Spirit* and through belief in truth." 2 Thessalonians 2:13

The Holy Spirit dwells within certain people, and when He does His presence transforms their spirits and souls. His holy presence provides strength, power, love, fullness, joy and holiness. The Holy Spirit transforms human spirits and souls.

Galatia was a region in what is now southwestern Turkey. In his letter to the churches in the region, Paul carries the thought of spiritual transformation through the indwelling Holy Spirit one step farther – he describes the characteristics exhibited by people who are on the path of transformation. He described the attributes as "fruit of the Sprit."[6] Notice that the word "fruit" is singular but he uses a bunch of words to describe it. Paul writes,

> "But the fruit of the Spirit is love, joy, peace, patience, kindness, goodness, faithfulness, gentleness and self-control. Against such things there is no law. Galatians 5:22-23

Paul discusses spiritual maturity as a process involving gradual spiritual transformation. He discusses sanctification as the same gradual process. In Galatians he introduces the notion of fruit of the Spirit, which is physical evidence of the same transformation. The Holy Spirit transforms human spirits and souls, and when He does so His fruit will be revealed through each person's behavior.

The Holy Spirit Influences Behavior

Earlier in Galatians Paul discusses righteousness through the Holy Spirit as something he hopes for, writing,

> "But by faith *we eagerly await through the Spirit the righteousness* for which we hope. For in Christ Jesus neither circumcision nor uncircumcision has any value. The only thing that counts is *faith expressing itself through love.*" Galatians 5:5-6

This supports the thought that (i) spiritual transformation is a gradual process occurring through the indwelling Holy Spirit, (ii) the little things, like the decision to be circumcised or not, or the decision to eat or abstain from eating meat, fade away as the spiritual transformation occurs, and (iii) a person transformed by the Holy Spirit will behave differently – they will demonstrate their faith through love.

In other letters Paul repeats the message that spiritual transformation reveals itself through behavioral changes. In one of his letters to the church in Corinth, Paul wrote,

> "Therefore I want you to know that no one who is speaking by the Spirit of God says, 'Jesus is cursed.' And no one can say, 'Jesus is Lord' except by the Holy Spirit.'" 1 Corinthians 12:3

The indwelling Holy Spirit influences a person's behavior. Here, Paul explains that the Holy Spirit influences people, and when they speak by the Holy Spirit their word choice changes. Immediately after writing the quote above, Paul discusses a different aspect of the indwelling Holy Spirit, which he calls "spiritual gifts." [7] As the process of spiritual transformation occurs, the Holy Spirit reveals Himself through people by granting each some unique ability or abilities. Paul mentions a list of examples including unique gifts of knowledge, special wisdom, unique faith, the ability to heal people, and a unique discerning ability among others. This is another way a person's behavior is transformed through the indwelling Holy Spirit.

In another letter to the church in Corinth, Paul returns to the same theme: a transformed heart reveals itself through changed behavior. He wrote,

> "*You show* that you are a letter from Christ, the result of our ministry, written not with ink but with the Spirit of the living God, not on tablets of stone but on tablets of human hearts." 2 Corinthians 3:3

The Holy Spirit imprints Himself on the human heart. He transforms the human spirit and soul within whom He dwells and as a result, that person's behavior is changed. Paul writes, "You show..." You show that the Holy Spirit dwells within you through your actions and behavior. Spiritual transformation reveals itself through the person's behavior.

The Holy Spirit Speaks Through People

Jesus explained to His followers that they would be persecuted because they chose to follow Him. As part of that teaching, Jesus said

> "But when they arrest you, do not worry about what you say or how to say it. At that time you will be given what to say, for it will not be you speaking, but the *Spirit of your Father speaking through you.*" Matthew 10:19-20

This is very similar to an event discussed previously. Luke records Jesus warning about persecution, saying that when they are arrested the Holy Spirit will teach them what to say. In Matthew's account of either the same event or a similar event, Jesus says the Holy Spirit will speak through the person. The distinction between the two is subtle. Whether the Holy Spirit teaches a person what to say or speaks through the person, the interaction is intimate. However, where the Holy Spirit teaches what to say, He enlightens the human spirit and mind, and where He uses the person as a vessel for His voice, it is possible that the same level of transformation is avoided. Of course, it is possible that the Holy Spirit only speaks through transformed people, rendering any distinction even smaller.

Jesus said that the Holy Spirit spoke through King David. Jesus was talking with religious leaders when He asked them whom the Messiah's father would be. They answered that the Messiah would be the son of David. Scripture continues saying,

> "[Jesus] said to them, 'How is it then that David, *speaking by the Spirit*, calls him Lord? For he says, 'The Lord said to my Lord: 'Sit at my right hand until I put your enemies under your feet.''
>
> If then David calls him 'Lord,' how can he be his son?'" Matthew 22:43-45 (see also Mark 12:36)

In that exchange, Jesus says that King David "spoke by the Spirit," which means that the Holy Spirit spoke through him.

Peter says that the Holy Spirit spoke through all of the prophets. This is consistent with Paul's discussion, mentioned above, about spiritual gifts and the gift of prophecy. Since prophecy is a gift of the Holy Spirit resulting from His indwelling, it follows that prophecy originates with God. Peter wrote,

> "For prophecy never had its origin in human will, but prophets, though human, *spoke from God as they were carried along by the Holy Spirit*." 2 Peter 1:21

On certain occasions in certain situations, the Holy Spirit speaks through people.

The Holy Spirit Prays

It is interesting to think that the Holy Spirit prays. He is God. He is one of three persons making up the Holy Trinity, yet He prays.

As God, the Holy Spirit knows everything about every person. He knows each person's soul and spirit. He knows each person's specific points of weakness and He helps him or her at their point of need. He prays for people and He helps them pray.

I mentioned earlier Paul's discussion about fruit of the Spirit – physical evidence of the spiritual transformation caused by the indwelling Holy Spirit. In Romans, Paul discusses the indwelling of the Holy Spirit that occurs when a person first believes and the hope that person has for the transformation to come.[8] As he concludes the thought Paul writes,

> "In the same way the Spirit helps us in our weakness. We do not know what we ought to pray, but the *Spirit intercedes for us* through wordless groans. And he who searches our hearts knows the mind of the Spirit,

> because the *Spirit intercedes for God's people in accordance with the will of God.*" Romans 8:26-27

Paul explains that the Holy Spirit prays for people. He also urges people to "pray in" the Holy Spirit. In Ephesians Paul writes,

> "And *pray in the Spirit* on all occasions with all kinds of prayers and requests. With this in mind, be alert and always keep on praying for all the Lord's people." Ephesians 6:18

So the Holy Spirit prays for people and He provides a place within which people may pray. The words are beautiful and the thought is appealing, but how does a person go about praying "in the Spirit?" For that matter, how do we access the Holy Spirit?

HOW DO PEOPLE ACCESS THE HOLY SPIRIT?

As mentioned earlier, on the evening of the Last Supper Jesus taught at a frenzied pace. It was His last evening on earth in fully human form, and he taught and taught and taught. John describes Jesus washing the disciples' feet and teaching about loving service. Jesus explains that He is the way to God the Father, that He abides in the Father and the Father abides in Him, and that His goal is to bring glory to the Father. Jesus then promises the Holy Spirit saying,

> "If you love me, keep my commands. And I will ask the Father, and he will give you another advocate to help you and be with you forever – the Spirit of truth. The world cannot accept him, because it neither sees him nor knows him. But you know him, for he lives with you and will be in you. I will not leave you as orphans; I will come to you. Before long, the world will not see me anymore, but you will see me. Because

I live, you will also live. On that day you will realize
that I am in my Father, and you are in me, and I am in
you." John 14:15-19

Here Jesus says the formula for accessing the Holy Spirit
is (i) loving Jesus and (ii) keeping His commands. If a person does
that, Jesus will ask God the Father and He will send the Holy
Spirit to that person. He also says that the Holy Spirit "lives with
you and will be in you" and "you are in me, and I am in you." So
Jesus and the Holy Spirit will be in that person.

A few sentences later, Jesus discusses the notion of
abiding in Jesus and allowing Jesus to abide in you. He mentions
the concept twice in the paragraph above. A couple sentences
later, Jesus says,

"Anyone who loves me will obey my teaching. My
Father will love them, and *we will come to them and make
our home with them.*" John 14:23

So each person of the Holy Trinity abides with and in
believers. Jesus and the Holy Spirit abide in them, and Jesus and
God the Father make their home with them. How glorious is that?

But here is the problem, the paradox. We cannot do any
of that without the Holy Spirit's influence. We cannot love Jesus
or keep His commands without the Holy Spirit. It is the Holy
Spirit's working within our hearts that enables us to desire Him
at all.

During His meeting one evening with the religious leader
named Nicodemus, Jesus discusses new life and entering the
kingdom of God as new birth saying,

"I tell you the truth, no one can enter the kingdom of
God unless he is born of water and of the Spirit. Flesh
gives birth to flesh, but the Spirit give birth to spirit.
You should not be surprised at my saying, 'You must
be born again.' The wind blows wherever it pleases.
You hear its sound, but you cannot tell where it comes

from or where it is going. So it is with everyone born of the Spirit." John 3:5-8

When a baby is born, what role does the baby play in the process? What choice does the baby have? None. Birth happens to the baby who has no choice in the matter. The Holy Spirit blows where He pleases, acting where He chooses to act, delivering new life to people according to His will.

Further, the message of the gospel makes no sense without the Holy Spirit's help. God's holy word says,

> For the message of the cross is foolishness to those who are perishing, but to us who are being saved it is the power of God. 1 Corinthians 1:18;

> The person without the Spirit does not accept the things that come from the Spirit of God but considers them foolishness, and cannot understand them because they are discerned only through the Spirit. 1 Corinthians 2:14; and

> But their minds were made dull, for to this day the same veil remains when the old covenant is read. It has not been removed, because only in Christ is it taken away. Even to this day when Moses is read, a veil covers their hearts. But whenever anyone turns to the Lord, the veil is taken away. Now the Lord is the Spirit, and where the Spirit of the Lord is, there is freedom. And we all, who with unveiled faces contemplate the Lord's glory, are being transformed into his image with ever-increasing glory, which comes from the Lord, who is the Spirit. 2 Corinthians 3:14-18

We need the Holy Spirit's help to see, hear, and believe. Through His teaching, Jesus reveals the holy mystery between God's sovereignty and our responsibility. Faith is a gift from God,[9] the Holy Spirit blows where He pleases,[10] and our desire to seek Him comes from Him, but we must respond. We must beg for His mercy, grace and blessing, but the Holy Spirit is sovereign God. He acts first, yet we have responsibility. He stirs hearts, causes people to wonder, ponder and ask questions, but each person must receive the gift of faith and act on it. We must believe. We must love Jesus. We must obey. He may start the process and create the possibility for us, but we must choose, and the balance is a holy mystery. When He so chooses, sovereign God, the Holy Spirit, acts first to enable us to see Jesus for who He is, to desire Him, to follow and obey Him.

What does this look like? A little later during the Last Supper, Jesus urges the disciples to abide in Him using the analogy of the vine and branches.[11] Alluding to and completing the imagery described by the prophets Isaiah, Jeremiah, Ezekiel, and Zechariah, Jesus describes Himself as the vine, and believers as branches that continue to live and produce fruit so long as they abide in Jesus. In this discussion Jesus continually references the circle of love between God the Father, Jesus, and those who obey His commands and abide in His love. They dwell within each other, love each other and the people live as He desires. Through the discussion, the images of abiding love begin to blur.

Jesus contrasts this image of love with the world's hatred, explaining that the world will hate people who follow Christ (reinforcing and expanding the concept that the gospel is foolishness without the Holy Spirit's guidance, teaching and wisdom).[12] He then returns to discussing the Holy Spirit saying:

> "All this I have told you so that you will not fall away. They will put you out of the synagogue; in fact, the time is coming when anyone who kills you will think they are offering a service to God. They will do such things because they have not known the Father or me. I have told you this, so that when their time comes you will remember that I warned you about them. I did not tell you this from the beginning because I was with you, but now I am going to him who sent me. None of you asks me, 'Where are you going?' Rather, you are filled with grief because I have said these things.

> But *very truly I tell you*, it is for your good that I am going away. *Unless I go away, the Advocate will not come to you; but if I go, I will send him to you.* When he comes, he will prove the world to be in the wrong about sin and righteousness, about sin, because people do not believe in me; about righteousness, because I am going to the Father, where you can see me no longer; and about judgment, because the prince of this world now stands condemned.

> "I have much more to say to you, more than you can now bear. *But when he, the Spirit of truth, comes, he will guide you into all truth.* He will not speak on his own; he will speak only what he hears, and he will tell you what is yet to come. He will glorify me because it is from me that he will receive what he will make known to you. All that belongs to the Father is mine. That is why I said the Spirit will receive from me what he will make known to you." John 16:1-15

On His last evening on earth in fully human form, Jesus taught many important lessons. He taught at a frantic pace. John records portions of His teaching and prayers that evening filling chapters 13 through 17 of his gospel. During that evening Jesus taught about the Holy Spirit in very plain language "so that you will not fall away" (John 16:1).

The next day Jesus was crucified. A few days later He was resurrected and for 40 days He appeared to the disciples and taught them more. At the end of all this, on the 40th day, immediately before ascending to heaven, Jesus concluded by teaching more about the Holy Spirit saying,

> He said to them: "It is not for you to know the times or dates the Father has set by his own authority. But *you will receive power when the Holy Spirit comes on you;* and you will be my witnesses in Jerusalem, and in all Judea and Samaria, and to the ends of the earth."

After he said this, he was taken up before their very
eyes, and a cloud hid him from their sight. Acts 1:7-9.

During the Last Supper, Jesus jammed a vast array of
teaching into a short period. Over and over He taught about the
Holy Spirit, and then, immediately before His ascension He
taught more about the Holy Spirit discussing His power. As Jesus
taught, the images of abiding love between God and His people
blur, and the key to accessing the Holy Spirit is love
demonstrating itself through obedience to His commands. And
then, immediately before ascending, Jesus discussed the power of
the Holy Spirit, promising "you will receive power when the Holy
Spirit comes on you." Obedience leads to love and power.

How do we access the Holy Spirit? At a different time,
Jesus gave the simplest, most commonsense formula imaginable.
We ask Him to come. We invite Him. Jesus said the Holy Spirit
is available to those who ask God to send Him:

> "If you then, though you are evil, know how to give
> good gifts to your children, how much more will your
> *Father in heaven give the Holy Spirit to those who ask him!"*
> Luke 11:13

God the Father sends the Holy Spirit to people who ask,
who truly, sincerely, humbly seek the Lordship of Jesus Christ in
and over their lives. "Blessed are the poor in spirit for theirs is the
kingdom of heaven" (Matthew 5:3). How do people receive the
Holy Spirit? They ask. But the ability to truly ask is a gift from
God. If you want His holy indwelling, beg God for mercy. Throw
yourself at His feet. Cry out for His holy grace. Give yourself to
Him.

As part of our church services the congregation regularly
recites one of the ancient Christian creeds. We often recite either
the Apostles' Creed or the Nicene Creed, which are two of the
early statements explaining fundamental Christian beliefs. The
Apostles' Creed bears its name based on the legend that the
Apostles assisted writing the words. It says, in part, "I believe in
the Holy Spirit..." The Nicene Creed evolved from the Council of

Nicea in 325 AD and says, "We believe in the Holy Spirit, the Lord, the giver of life, who proceeds from the Father and the Son, who with the Father and the Son is worshipped and glorified, who has spoken through the prophets."

As a church, as the Body of Christ, we believe in the Holy Spirit. This is fundamental to the Christian faith. But have you asked to receive Him? Have you asked for His transformation? Have you invited Him into your life? Have you begged God for His mercy and grace and forgiveness? Have you begged Him to grant you the gift of His life so that you might dedicate yours to Him?

Through individuals He chooses, the Holy Spirit plays an integral role in many lives. We see some described in Scripture, we see evidence of His indwelling in lives of individual Christians today, and in the life of the church.

DOES HE STILL DO THOSE THINGS?

Jesus made a bunch of promises relating to the Holy Spirit. Do the promises still apply today? Paul wrote a lot about the Holy Spirit. He describes how the Holy Spirit dwells within people, the ways the Holy Spirit transforms people, and the fruit and gifts associated with that transformation. In Acts, Luke describes the Holy Spirit as a central character in a number of extraordinary events. Chapter 2 of Acts describes the Holy Spirit appearing as flames as He came upon people. Acts describes the Holy Spirit speaking directly to and through Peter, Paul and Agabus and causing miraculous events. The book also depicts the Holy Spirit moving through Peter and Paul, revealing His gifts and demonstrating His power – they teach with remarkable insight, they have miraculous discerning power, and the Holy Spirit works through them by healing many. Luke describes people sitting near the path leading to the temple so Peter's shadow will pass over them as he walks by, hoping to receive some of the Holy Spirit's healing power flowing through him.[13] He describes people passing around Paul's handkerchiefs hoping to **receive healing.**[14] The Holy Spirit moved through the men in miraculous ways.

In Scripture, the Holy Spirit is constantly caught up in miraculous activity. I believe Scripture is true and those things really happened, but is the Holy Spirit still active today? Is He still capable of doing those things, does He still desire to do those things, and does He actually do those things today? Based on personal experience and hearing personal experiences of other people who I trust, I am convinced the answer is yes. God – the Father, Jesus and the Holy Spirit – is really real. He is still real today. He still acts and speaks and dwells within people today.

The indwelling Holy Spirit is the mark of a Christian. He is the distinguishing characteristic of Christians, His presence necessarily leads to spiritual transformation revealed through changed behavior, and He comes with power. That is all still true today.

EVIDENCE OF HIS PRESENCE

What happens when the Holy Spirit takes up residence within a person? The event is contemporaneous with deliverance, that instant when God imputes righteousness upon an unholy person because of their belief, faith and acceptance of Christ Jesus and their decision to follow Him as Lord and Savior. A bunch of things happen in that instant, both in heaven and within the person. In heaven, the person is reconciled with God, forgiven, accepted as His child, justified and more. The person receives new life, union with God through Christ Jesus with the indwelling Holy Spirit, and with that new life comes changes experienced by the person and noticed by people around them.

Their desires, attitude, worldview and behavior change. They begin to see people they encounter, even those they once tremendously disliked, with increasingly greater empathy and compassion. Things they encounter in the world that once seemed acceptable or even good suddenly cause twinges of pain. For instance, in certain segments of society people regularly spice their conversation with profane language, and in that setting it is not only acceptable but expected. As Christ Jesus through the Holy Spirit regenerates a person's heart, profanity begins to hurt their spirit. They feel pain, sadness, even revulsion, which is particularly acute with the profanity involves the Holy Trinity, and they are not really offended by the words so much as sad for the person saying the words because the words indicate the lost state of the speaker's spirit and soul. And they feel pain, sadness and revulsion because they love the person, and they want the person to experience the fruits of new life in and through Christ Jesus. Lyrics in music they once enjoyed hearing sound suddenly vile. Scenes in movies and television shows that once seemed fine are suddenly awful. As the Holy Spirit takes up residence within a person and they are transformed, bathed in light, they become more sensitive to darkness, and the light shining through them becomes evident to people they encounter out in the world.

Through the Holy Spirit, the word of God opens as He reveals once unavailable treasures, and prayer grows increasingly intimate and conversational as He guides, teaches and prays alongside the person in whom He dwells. The experiential transformation creates a cycle whereby change begets increasingly more change influencing every aspect of life.

We see evidence of this sort of life change throughout Scripture. Consider Moses. In response to his encounter with God at the burning bush, he changed from shepherd tending his father-in-law's flock in the wilderness to the one who delivered a nation from bondage, showing the most powerful people in the world God's awesome power.[15] Gideon, the weakest member of the weakest clan, was hiding out from the Midianites, threshing wheat in a wine press. After Jesus appeared to him, he was suddenly transformed into a mighty warrior who led an army of 300 to overthrow the vast Midianite army, and everyone knew God had delivered His people.[16]

Think about Peter. After serving Jesus for three years, traveling with Him, listening to His teaching, and seeing the kingdom of God revealed through Him day after day through amazing signs and wonders, after eating the Passover feast with Jesus, allowing Jesus to wash his feet, listening to His amazing teaching and prayer that evening, after all that, hours after the Last Supper, Peter denied knowing Jesus three times and fled in fear. He returned to Capernaum and rekindled his life as a fisherman. Post-resurrection Jesus tracked Peter down, urged him to return to the ministry, and Peter obeyed. On the day of Pentecost when the Holy Spirit was unleashed, Peter was filled with the Holy Spirit, empowered by Him and transformed through Him, and Peter stood in Jerusalem preaching the gospel of Christ Jesus to the same people who had crucified Jesus a mere seven week earlier, and thousands came to believe in Christ that day.[17] God's power was revealed through Peter's preaching and healing ministry in such mighty ways that crowds sought him to heal them, yet some were afraid of him. Rather than approach him directly, many sat near the path hoping his shadow would pass over them and provide healing.[18] God's holy word tells us "all of them were healed" (Acts 5:16). Through the Holy Spirit, Peter was completely transformed, and his transformation was evident to everyone who encountered him.

Paul was a zealous persecutor of Christians who oversaw the stoning of Stephen[19] and traveled across the region seeking out Christians to stop the gospel's spread.[20] Paul encountered Jesus Christ and his life was completely transformed. He suddenly changed from chief persecutor of those who followed Christ to the greatest evangelist the world has known, planting churches across present-day Turkey and Greece and authoring at least 13 books of the Bible.[21]

The Holy Spirit reveals Himself through the people in whom He dwells. When people encounter God through Christ Jesus and the Holy Spirit, their lives are transformed and their behavior changes. New life creates changed lives. The two are inseparable, and genuine change of that sort is evident to others. Transformed people shine His light, show His love, and reveal His life. Their behavior out in the world is evidence of the Holy Spirit's indwelling. A variety of passages lead to this conclusion.[22] Here are a couple to consider.

Jesus says,

"A new command I give you: Love one another. As I have loved you, so you must love one another. By this everyone will know that you are my disciples, if you love one another." John 14:34-35

Love revealed through action is *the* sign that people are His disciples. God is love and love is the result of His holy transformation, and out in the real world it looks like humble loving service and behavior consistent with the fruit of the Holy Spirit. It looks like washing one another's feet[23] and "love, joy, peace, forbearance, kindness, goodness, faithfulness, gentleness and self-control" (Galatians 5:22-23).

Peter writes to followers of Christ living in a society characterized by pagan beliefs, urging his readers to live holy lives, to abstain from every practice that is contrary to holiness, and to "live such good lives among the pagans that, though they accuse you of doing wrong, they may see your good deeds and glorify God on the day he visits us" (1 Peter 2:12). As followers of Christ are transformed through Him, they increasingly take on His holiness, love, light and life, and these characteristics reveal themselves as they are out in the world conducting their everyday lives.

Paul writes to Titus,

For the grace of God has appeared that offers salvation to all people. It teaches us to say "No" to ungodliness and worldly passions, and to live self-controlled, upright and godly lives in this present age, while we wait for the blessed hope – the appearing of the glory of our great God and Savior, Jesus Christ, who gave himself for us to redeem us from all wickedness and to purify for himself a people that are his very own, eager to do what is good. Titus 2:11-14

Through Jesus Christ, the Holy Spirit transforms His people, helping them grow toward holiness, changing their desires so holy activity is what they want to do, teaching them to hate worldly passions and love what is good and Godly, changing their eyes to see others as people created in God's holy image whom He loves, and influencing their hearts so that they are "eager to do what is good."

Spiritual birth is the Holy Spirit uniting with the human spirit, and transformation occurs from this union. It is a certainty, like my certainty that if I drop my pen it will fall to the floor or if I add table salt to water the salt will dissolve and the water will taste salty. New life with the Holy Spirit is characterized by change from worldly to righteous, from sinful to holy, from darkness to light; however, the change seems to be a gradual process for most.

Jesus says, "Blessed are those who hunger and thirst for righteousness, for they will be filled" (Matthew 5:6). Christianity is marked by the hunger and thirst – the pursuit – but not necessarily by righteousness, which is the goal. Following Jesus Christ is a journey not a destination. The path leads to righteousness, and transformation happens gradually along the way.

As we seek the reality of His presence around us, we should look for people who pursue Him. And we must look in the mirror and question whether we are pursuing Him. Do you hunger, thirst and pursue righteousness, or are you content living in the same way you did before you were introduced to the Holy Spirit? New birth is marked by change. If you have not changed and are not changing, you might want to consider how that can be.

Contemporary Examples

We cannot see wind, but we see its impact on objects around us. Through the window I see an inch of fresh snow covering the lawn, table and bushes. Every now and then, snow dust rises from the table only to fall a few feet from where it started. Tree branches move gently. A pine needle skids across the snow covered lawn. I see evidence of a gentle breeze, but I do not see wind. If we want to see the Holy Spirit, we should begin by looking at His impact on people around us with eyes opened to the reality of His presence.

Jesus says that the Holy Spirit acts where He chooses,[24] meaning He does not act everywhere all the time and mere humans do not control Him. While air is all around us all the time, the wind does not always blow. And sometimes the wind is blowing but we cannot feel it – we might be inside or some other barrier may separate us from the wind. In the same way, the Holy Spirit is everywhere all the time, but at times He chooses not to act and at other times He is acting but we cannot feel Him because something in our life separates us from Him, and the all-powerful sovereign One apparently chooses in that instance to respect our choices rather than barge in.

But there should be no doubt that the Holy Spirit is living and continues to transform people and exhibit His power and mighty influence through lives today. Evidence of His holy presence and mighty touch are all around us. Here are two brief examples from people I know and trust.

<u>Joe</u>

Years ago my friend Joe lived in Maryland. He had been working in Chicago. After a long week, he started driving home late Friday night. As he drove along the clock ticked past midnight and traffic thinned. Around 3 am, he was cruising across Pennsylvania on the Turnpike. He saw an occasional oncoming headlight, but none moving his direction. He listened to the radio and kept driving. Suddenly he heard a voice say "Move over!" He thought he was hearing things. He turned down the radio. The voice said, "Move over!" It sounded like someone was in the backseat speaking in a normal voice. Joe hit the brakes and steered to the shoulder. As he veered to the right, his headlights suddenly illuminated a large deer standing in the middle of the highway. He was much taller than Joe's little car. As Joe passed the massive creature, his left side mirror collided with the buck's tail, leaving a dent, a tiny reminder and constant affirmation of the event. He stopped the car on the shoulder, got out, knelt to the ground and praised God for saving his life. Joe knows that the Holy Spirit spoke to him and saved his life that night.

Delores

In 1997 friends invited Lori and me to hear a woman speak. They explained that the event was taking place in the home of a different family, who we did not know, and it felt a little odd. I wondered whether the hosts would invite us directly, but our friends assured us it was okay. On the evening of the event, we drove to the address and found a beautiful large home set several hundred feet off the road with a winding driveway. We parked, started the long walk up the driveway and grew nervous wondering if we were really invited. We almost turned around, but momentum carried us forward. Past the grand entrance, a large living room was filled with people. We knew no one. We wondered whether we were at the right place. We walked through the room filled with strangers looking for our friends who had invited us. As I scanned the room I noticed a small woman with white hair. It was her glow that caught my attention. She radiated an amazing energy.

Our friends arrived. They wanted to introduce us to Delores, so they led us across the room where we met the radiant woman with white hair. After dinner, Delores stood in front of the fireplace and spoke. She was a tiny bird of a woman yet she conveyed power and strength. She glowed and spoke with a low, firm, almost manly voice – a surprisingly low voice for a woman of her size.

Some people sat on living room furniture; others sat on metal folding chairs positioned between the sofa, chairs, ottoman and walls; others sat on the floor and many stood. Without a single note, she spoke with amazing clarity about Christ, Scripture and God's glory. Lori and I sat in the back on the last row of folding metal chairs. People sat in front of us and stood behind us.

As Delores spoke she mentioned that God had healed her, but she passed over that point as if everyone had already heard her story. For a while she focused on God's call. As she spoke my mind wandered. I thought about myself and my general awfulness and lowliness. As Delores spoke about the wondrous things God planned to do through His people, I wondered why God chooses to use people at all and I thought that there is no possible way God could use a person as low as me in His holy service. It was a thought that just would not fit in my brain – why does the Holy, the Divine use sinful people in His service? And how could God possibly use a person like me? As I pondered the questions, the chasm separating me from God's holy perfection seemed too great. I could not comprehend Him having any desire to use me.

As I was thinking those thoughts, Delores stopped speaking. After a pause, she pointed across the room directly at me and she reprimanded me for thinking those thoughts. She said, "Do not think things like that. God can use you and He will use you." After another long pause, she continued speaking to the group.

A while later, as she concluded her talk, I was disappointed she was stopping. I wanted to hear more of what she had to say. I glanced at my watch and was startled to see that she had talked for nearly an hour. It seemed like ten or fifteen minutes at most, even while sitting in an uncomfortable metal chair.

Our friends and several others came to me and commented on the fact that Delores interrupted her talk to speak directly to me. I was sort of hoping nobody noticed. I hoped that I was wrong when it seemed she spoke directly to me, but everyone noticed. We were all a little taken aback by the experience. They wondered whether I knew her, whether I had communicated my thoughts to her in advance of her talk, and how she knew what I was thinking. They asked whether that was actually what I was thinking, and I acknowledged that it was. There was no doubt that the Holy Spirit knew my thoughts and communicated my thoughts to Delores.

The crowd mingled and people started leaving. Delores approached Lori and me. We spoke for a long time and she continued to say remarkable things. I asked about her illness. She said a few things about it but she really wanted to talk about the Holy Spirit, how He changed her, and how He had used her since her healing. As one example of the changes, she mentioned her voice saying the Holy Spirit lowered it a few octaves. He lowered the pitch of her voice so she could be heard more easily when speaking to a crowded room. She mentioned many types of physical ailments that God had cured in people through her at places around the globe. She discussed the seeds of revival that were being planted as we spoke. She knew I wanted to learn more about her healing, so she gave us a copy of the book she had written about her healing – *Jesus Set Me Free*.[25]

In 1956, over 40 years earlier, Delores was diagnosed with pseudo-arthrosis, which led to severe osteoporosis. Her bones stopped absorbing nutrients from her blood and they became increasingly brittle. During early stages of her illness her spine started crumbling. She had surgeries to fuse crumbled bones in her spinal column, but the fusions failed.

Two years after her diagnosis, a woman she knew became pregnant. The woman urged Delores and Bill to adopt her baby. They agreed and named their son Christopher.

Over the years her body continued to fail and the cumulative effects of her treatment escalated. She eventually wore a body cast to support her spine. Bill built a metal frame over her bed allowing her to pull herself up using her hands. She lived primarily in bed suffering constant pain and surviving from one round of medication to the next. Her dresser was covered with prescription vials, each designed to treat a specific symptom in an escalating list of symptoms. She was taking increasingly higher doses of pain medication and the list of supplemental medications grew to help with her illness and the snowballing combination of side effects.

Eventually she could no longer hold her head upright and her pain grew beyond a level treatable with medication. Doctors performed a percutaneous cordotomy: they severed the nerves running laterally from the left side of her spine below a point about five inches above her waist. She had no feeling below that point on her left side, eliminating both good and bad aspects of feeling. The irreversible procedure was generally reserved for terminally ill patients. By embracing the procedure she accepted that her life would soon end. She was still able to walk by shuffling her feet, but she had no feeling on her left side below the middle of her abdomen, and she lacked the energy to walk more than a few feet.

Eighteen months later the procedure was repeated to severe the nerves serving her right side, eliminating all feeling below that point in her abdomen. She missed her freedom. She depended on other people to help with most aspects of daily life and her body continued to fail. One of her kidneys became severely infected and the other stopped working. Her intestines and colon stopped working. Her cardiopulmonary system was failing and her esophagus ruptured. She had a large sore on her back that would not heal. Doctors drained it every few days, but it would not go away. Muscles in her shoulder and upper back were deteriorating and separating from her bones. Her body was shutting down. She had endured so much pain she hoped that she would die. She took pills to dull her pain, to help her stomach, to help her esophagus, to help her kidneys, to help her low blood pressure and to help her sleep. The focus of her world was pills and the schedule for taking them. Her body was moving aggressively toward death.

She and Bill started planning her funeral. Christopher grew increasingly nervous about the prospect of his mother dying. Delores prayed, "God, you are going to have to show me something that will save Chris. Show me that when I'm gone he will be alright."[26]

Through a series of unexpected events, Delores was invited to attend the Methodist Conference on the Holy Spirit in Dallas on August 30, 1975. Kathryn Kuhlman was the featured speaker. Kathryn was known as a faith healer with a popular television show, but at the request of Methodist leaders she had agreed not to perform healings at the conference. She planned to limit her activity that evening to speaking.

As Delores prepared to leave for the service, Christopher asked her where she was going and why. She explained she was going to see Kathryn Kuhlman. Christopher told her that she would be healed that night, he knew it would happen, but Delores explained that those things stopped happening in Biblical times.

Delores was filled with negative feelings about Kathryn. When she saw Kathryn's program on television, Delores quickly turned the channel. **Delores thought** Kathryn was a fraud. Kathryn wore elaborate, flowing dresses and claimed to heal people, but Delores knew she was a fake and it angered her that anyone would lie about God and give false hope to suffering people. She had read articles in newspapers and magazines describing doctors' investigations exposing Kathryn as a charlatan. Delores did not really want to go to the conference, but she went to great effort and pain to attend because she thought God would answer her prayer and give her a message that would help Christopher.

She rode to Dallas lying down in the back seat of her helper's car. She was exhausted and in great pain after the thirty minute drive. Her driver stopped near the entrance and Delores was about to suggest that they return home when a man opened the car door, helped her out, into the building and to her seat.

After introductions, Kathryn walked across the stage shouting her catch phrase, "I believe in miracles!" Delores was repulsed. She did not want to hear Kathryn. She did not want to see her. She believed she was looking at a fraud, a liar. But Kathryn spoke about the Holy Spirit in ways Delores had never heard and Delores began to see and consider the Holy Spirit in a new way.

As Kathryn spoke, Delores felt what she knew to be God's holy presence. She was afraid and amazed. She had not felt anything like that before, and she knew she was experiencing God for the first time, and she suddenly knew with confidence that God is indeed alive and present and active here on earth now. Overwhelmed by awe, she closed her eyes and she saw a vision and heard the Holy Spirit speak to her. He promised her that Christopher would not be alone and He identified Himself as the Holy Spirit.

After receiving the revelation, Delores was ready to go home. She had received what she went for. Her head was exploding with pain. Her back hurt. Her arms hurt. Her legs felt like they were on fire. Kathryn finished speaking and prayed. After the prayer she said that God revealed to her that someone had received a revelation from God and that person needed to come forward to receive healing. Several people went forward.

Delores saw that as her opportunity to leave. She got up and started walking out the door praying that no one would stop her.

As she shuffled towards the aisle, a man met her and helped her walk out. She wore a neck brace and body cast. The man asked about her condition. She explained that her legs were burning, her head was exploding in pain and she needed to leave. He asked about her neck brace and body cast. In an effort to stop the questioning, she explained that she had had two percutaneous cordotomies, because that normally ended conversations like the one the man insisted on having. But the man understood what she said. He knew what the procedures entailed and he asked whether she was surprised to feel burning in her legs.

The man was Dr. O'Wellen, a medical doctor. He originally investigated Kathryn in a desire to expose her as a fraud, but he saw legitimate miracles happen; he came to know the Holy Spirit; and he attended Kathryn's services asking God to reveal people to him that needed help. That night, the doctor walked up and down each aisle praying for God to reveal the person who God was healing. He arrived to Delores just as she stood to walk out.

He helped Delores to the lobby. As they spoke about her condition and what she was feeling, the doctor suggested that Delores remove her neck brace and body cast. She did, and they walked to the stage together.

Over the next fifteen minutes, she regained feeling in her feet, legs, fingertips and over her entire body. Her pain went away and, although she does not remember it, her helper said she ran across the stage. When Kathryn prayed over her, she fell to the ground under the influence of the Holy Spirit.

The following week Delores visited the doctor who had treated her for over fifteen years. Over the previous years he had watched her body shutting down. He had performed the percutaneous cordotomies. He had drained and treated her wound that would not heal. He had discussed end of life issues with her, urging her to get her affairs in order. On that day, he tested her and confirmed that her nerves had miraculously re-connected. He was shocked that the muscles in her back and shoulder were firm, the pain in that area was gone, and the wound on her back had healed. Her body had been spiraling rapidly toward death, but was now healed. He described her condition as nothing less than a miracle.

After the service, as she said goodbye to Dr. O'Wellen, he cautioned her about the mind games Satan would play with her. Dr. O'Wellen warned her that the Evil One would try to convince her that she was not healed, that it was all in her imagination, that it was a dream. The doctor was right. Delores said that Satan put words in her mind. At times Delores thought that nothing had happened to her body, that her body was still diseased, and that she was losing her mind. At those times, she struggled to convince herself that the healing was real and her mind was sound.

One night she woke with intense pain in her esophagus. She struggled to breath and was sweating profusely in pain. A voice in her mind told her to get up, but she knew from prior experience that when she got up while feeling like that she suffered severe choking spasms. She reached for medication. The voice told her to stay away from the pills and get up. She got up, went to the bathroom, cried out to God for help, and the attack stopped.

She had read references to spiritual warfare in the Bible, but she had not really paid much attention to them. At this point in her recovery she realized she was experiencing spiritual warfare. As Dr. O'Wellen had warned, Satan was attacking her.

Through the Holy Spirit, God opened her mind to see things she had not previously seen. One day a woman came to visit Delores. The woman had visited many times before. On this occasion, as Delores and the woman sat in her living room talking, Delores saw scenes of the woman involved in a lesbian affair. She said, "As I looked at her it was as though the pages of a pornographic book were turning and I was reading the story of her life."[27] Delores did not understand why she saw the vision, she did not understand what she should do about the vision, and at the time she said nothing about it.

Some time later, the woman returned to visit Delores. On this occasion the woman opened up and told Delores about her secret life. She described the scenes that Delores had seen during their previous meeting. God gave Delores four specific things to tell the woman. Delores said it was as if God wrote four bullet points in ink on her hand. Delores told the woman that she needed to repent, meaning she needed to turn away from all activity she knew was wrong, and Delores told her three additional points that Delores forgot as soon as the woman left. God gave her the message to speak to the woman and then erased them from Delores' mind.

As she started adapting to her new life, she received invitations to speak at churches. She had no interest in telling her story to strangers. She wanted to stay at home and enjoy her new life. She wanted to work in the garden and clean her home and make dinner for Bill and Chris. She wanted to use her newfound freedom for her personal enjoyment. But God had different plans for her. He wanted her to speak about her experience. He wanted her to use her gift of new life for His glory, not for her personal pleasure.

She was invited to speak at a local church. The pastor invited Delores to the pulpit. As Delores walked up the aisle, the pastor introduced another woman who would speak before Delores. Delores stood at the pulpit as the other woman spoke. Delores heard her say things about Delores that were deeply personal and private. In intricate detail, the woman described what Delores' future would be like. Delores was angry. She felt violated and as the woman went on and on, Delores' fury grew. Delores wondered how dare she? Who did she think she was? How could she expose intimate details about Delores to a church filled with strangers?

After the woman stopped, Delores gave her prepared speech before leaving in anger. Bill and Christoher were with her. They went to lunch and as Bill and Christopher chatted as if nothing unusual had happened, Delores grew angrier. Finally she burst out demanding to know why they did not share her fury over what the woman had said. They were confused. They explained that they could not understand a word the woman had said. They said she was speaking gibberish. The family then understood that the woman was speaking in tongues. God was speaking to Delores through the woman, and Delores may have been the only person who understood.

This was all new to Delores. In many ways, Delores was being exposed to a realm she previously did not know existed. She had never been exposed to people speaking in tongues or praying in tongues, and she certainly had never heard God speak to her in that way. She had previously believed that God's healing power had ceased during the time of the Apostles, yet God miraculously healed her body. And He did so using Kathryn Kuhlman, a woman who had generated feelings of disgust in Delores. God had other plans for Delores. He baptized her in the Holy Spirit, opened her eyes to see people in a new way, gave her words of wisdom to help other people, and put her in situations to tell her story and reveal His glory through her.

It took years for her to absorb it all and to surrender her life to God. As she gradually accepted God and surrendered her will to Him, she grew and was able to help people in ways she never imagined possible. She gradually became the woman I met in 1997 – the woman who glowed revealing God's glory. His glory flowing through her was evident to a person who had never met her, had never considered that holy people might glow, and who saw her across a crowded room filled with strangers.

As Delores grew increasingly frail, she believed in God but she never imagined He would heal her. Chris believed. As Delores piled into the car heading for Dallas, Chris believed she would return healed, and she did. This is similar to the paralyzed man that Jesus healed.[28] Jesus taught in a house and the crowd filled a large area outside. Men carried their paralyzed friend on a mat to see Jesus, but the crowd was too large. They could not gain access to Jesus, so they carried their friend to the roof, cut a hole in the roof and lowered their friend down to Jesus. When Jesus saw the friends' faith, He healed the paralyzed man. Christopher believed.

For nearly twenty years Delores suffered as her body failed. She lost her personal freedom, she felt increasingly severe constant pain, and her bodily systems gradually stopped working. During the entire time she believed in Jesus Christ, she accepted Him as her personal Lord and Savior, she prayed and she believed He could and would answer her prayers. She believed in God and trusted in Him, but her faith limited God. As she prepared to die, she got her affairs in order and she prayed to God for a special message of assurance, a sign that Chris would be all right after she was gone. She believed God would answer her prayer, but she never had any idea that God would heal her. She had faith, but her faith was too small for Lord God Almighty.

God is the creator of all things. He breathes the breath of life into each of us. He is everywhere and He knows all things. He is infinite yet intimate. He knows us better than we know ourselves. He knows our needs and He loves us. He is the loving Father. And He has all authority and power in heaven and on earth. He can do anything and everything – things beyond our ability to imagine. Paul writes,

> Now to him who is able to do immeasurably more than all we ask or imagine, according to his power that is at work within us, to him be the glory in the church and in Christ Jesus throughout all generations, for ever and ever! Amen. Ephesians 3:20-21

Delores believed in God. She believed God would answer her prayer. She believed God would help give her answers relating to her son. But she never believed God would heal her physically. She believed, but her faith was too small.

This is like Martha and Mary when their brother, Lazarus, was sick, dying and ultimately placed in the tomb.[29] They knew with certainty that if Jesus had been there before Lazarus died that Jesus would have healed their brother. They knew Jesus had the power to heal and they knew that Jesus would have used His power to help Lazarus.

Jesus arrived after Lazarus had been in the tomb four days. Martha and Mary each, separately, said to Jesus, "Lord, if you had been here, my brother would not have died" (John 11:21 & 32). They believed, but they thought it was too late for their brother. They knew Jesus had power and authority, but they never imagined His power and authority were unimaginably great. Their eyes were opened when their brother walked out of the tomb.

Delores had Jesus confined to a similarly restricted box. She believed that God is the author of life. She knew in her mind – she had the intellectual knowledge that God created all things and has all power and authority in heaven and on earth – but she did not believe He would use His power to heal her. Her eyes were opened to the reality of His power, authority and love when He reached into this world, our world, her world and healed her physically. Her intellectual knowledge was suddenly converted to true intimate knowing in her heart, in her soul, in her spirit.

As Paul writes, God "is able to do immeasurably more than all we ask or imagine, according to his power that is at work within us, to him be the glory..." God has the power and authority, His power is working in you through the Holy Spirit and it is for His glory. May you know His power and authority intimately, in your heart. May you allow Him to transform you for His glory, not for your own personal pleasure, but for His glory, and may His glory be revealed through you.

CONCLUSION

The Holy Spirit is God. He is one of the three persons making up the Holy Trinity. He has always been and always will be; He has all power and authority in heaven and on earth; He is the holy Creator of the universe; and He resides within you the moment you believe. It is amazing beyond our ability to comprehend that mere humans, sin-filled, prideful, dirty humans, are offered that sort of intimate communion with the holy One.

He speaks to people and through people. He opens eyes and ears, enlightens minds, transforms spirits and souls, comforts, teaches, reveals truth, convicts of sin, influences behavior and does many more miraculous, glorious things, including praying. He prays. We can pray in Him and He prays for us, interceding on our behalf.

It is all for His glory and our good. Life is better when lived in communion with God. May His Holy Spirit dwell within you, may His love fill you and flow through you, and may His glory be revealed through you.

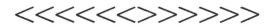

Part III. Connecting with God

<<<<<<<>>>>>>>

10 | THE BRIDGE

*In the beginning was the Word, and
the Word was with God, and the
Word was God. He was with God in
the beginning. Through him all
things were made; without him
nothing was made that has been
made. In him was life, and that life
was the light of men. The light
shines in the darkness, but the
darkness has not understood it....
He was not in the world, and
though the world was made
through him, the world did not
recognize him. He came to that
which was his own, but his own did
not receive him. Yet to all who
received him, to those who
believed in his name, he gave the
right to become children of God –
children born not of natural
descent, nor of human decision or a
husband's will, but born of God.
The Word became flesh and made
his dwelling among us. We have
seen his glory, the glory of the One
and Only, who came from the
Father, full of grace and truth.*
John 1:1-5, 1:10-14

It was now about noon, and darkness came over the whole land until three in the afternoon, for the sun stopped shining. And the curtain of the temple was torn in two. Jesus called out with a loud voice, "Father, into your hands I commit my spirit." When he had said this, he breathed his last. Luke 23:44-46

"The Word was with God, and the Word was God ... the Word became flesh and made his dwelling among us." God became flesh and lived on earth. Jesus was fully human and fully God. Take a moment and let that sink in. Jesus was fully human and fully God.

After living on earth for a time, He voluntarily died for us and conquered death.

These are the most significant events in human history because Jesus is God. If Jesus were just another man, his life and teaching may have been noteworthy. But God becoming flesh is awesome beyond our ability to imagine, God dying for us is even more so. While Jesus conquering death merely confirms His deity, it also changes the world forever. At the most fundamental level, it changes our existence and the nature of life itself.

Please allow me to say that again. Through the cross and resurrection, God changed the world forever. He built a bridge across the chasm separating humans from Him. Jesus was fully human and is fully God. He is the only bridge spanning the chasm. He is the only path connecting us with God. He is "God with us" (Matthew 1:23), "the way and the truth and the life" (John 14:6), the "resurrection and the life" (John 11:25), and so much more. Let's take a quick look at the significance of His birth and His death.

MERRY CHRISTMAS!

Merry Christmas! What comes to mind when you say, hear or read the greeting? When you hear the first Christmas carol of the season, what images fill your mind? Candy canes, Christmas trees, gathering with loved ones near a fire? Is it scenes described in the songs, like images of freshly roasted chestnuts, cold noses, and freshly fallen snow?

When greeted with "Merry Christmas," some feel happy anticipation thinking about and picking out the perfect gifts for loved ones, and getting the items home, wrapping them and waiting for the joy the gifts will deliver to people they love. For others the words reveal, rather than images, emotions, feelings, warmth hidden deeper in their soul and reveal a longing masked other times of the year. It's about sharing time with family – stopping the daily grind, stopping the chaos of daily life to share time with loved ones.

All of that is great. I love all that about Christmas. But if we stop there, if we stop with gifts and wishes of good cheer and anticipating time with loved ones, how is Christmas unique? What distinguishes it from Thanksgiving, other holidays or some pagan winter solstice celebration?

I recently bumped into a friend who says she is "not a believer." She is an amazing person. She is one of those people who is present and who helps people are in need. She will give you the shirt off her back. She described her preparations to have family come to town for Christmas. She was excited about the gifts she was wrapping, busily making plans for the Christmas feast, happily anticipating time with her family, and as she left we exchanged "Merry Christmas!" with one another.

The notion of "Christmas" is woven into our culture, so much so that in some ways it has lost its meaning. In many ways and for many people it has come to have more to do with Santa Claus than Jesus Christ. We say things like "Jesus is the reason for the season" and "we are celebrating Jesus' birthday." But those statements easily miss the supernatural awesomeness of what we are celebrating, because those statements could easily be attributed to any mere human walking the planet.

God

"The Word was with God, and the Word was God ... the Word became flesh and made his dwelling among us." When you say, hear or read "Merry Christmas!" I urge you to remember that we are celebrating God coming to earth in fully human form. Jesus is God. He has always been and always will be. While on earth in the flesh, He was fully human, and He also was and is fully God. As a result, we are celebrating one of the most important, most significant, most mind-blowing events in human history.

When you think of God, what comes to mind? No matter what comes to mind, the thought is too small, too limited, and not grand enough because our mind, our knowledge, our experience, our existence are too human to comprehend God. Even our wildest imagination does not come close. God is He whom humans simply cannot fathom.

We say He is holy, divine and pure, but we are unable to comprehend the majesty intended to be communicated by the words because our language and minds are limited and our lens is clouded by sin. We say He has all power, all authority and is the Creator of all things who breathes life into each of us, and who delivers order out of chaos, but each concept is too grand for us to wrap our mind around. He is everywhere all at once. He is unbound by space and time. His vision, thinking, reasoning, judgment and discernment are perfect. His glory is beyond our comprehension.

When He desired to create the universe – including galaxies so far away we measure their distance from earth by the distance light travels in a year multiplied by as much as thirteen billion – He did so by speaking. He is transcendent and intimate – both beyond our comprehension. He knows everything. He knows you and me better than we know ourselves. He is love. He loves each of us unconditionally.

Now consider this: sovereign, all-powerful God came to earth as, not just a human, but a baby human, the most helpless of beings. God is unbound by time and space, and He inserted

Himself into His creation. God became fully human, lived on earth, and became bound by time and space. The concept simply does not fit in my brain. I cannot comprehend it.

The Divine, the Pure, the Holy left heaven and came to this place where evil roams and sin permeates souls. Pause to let that sink in. Mankind is fallen. We are sinful and we live in a sinful place. Only God is holy and a chasm separates us from God. In my limited little mind, holiness and sinfulness seem incompatible. They cannot mix. Like light and darkness, if they were to touch, one would be destroyed.

With this image in mind, how could holy God become flesh, how could holy God muck around this sinful place, how could holy God allow Himself to be exposed to mankind's wickedness? Maybe "how?" is the wrong question because God can do anything and everything. He is sovereign, He has all authority, He is the Creator of all things and He makes the rules. But what kind of God would do that and then, what kind of God would give up Himself for us? What does this tell us about God?

He is love and He loves each and every one of us. "For God so loved the world that he gave his one and only Son, that whoever believes in him shall not perish but have eternal life" (John 3:16).

Why?

After pondering the awesomeness of God coming to earth in flesh, I have so many questions without answers. With so many questions in mind, I find great comfort in the fact that Jesus tells us why He came, and by doing so He helps us to better understand God. Let's consider three of Jesus' statements explaining why He came to earth.

> "For I have come down from heaven not to do my will but to do the will of him who sent me. And this is the will of him who sent me, that I shall lose none of all that he has given me, but raise them up on the last day. For my Father's will is that everyone who looks to the

> Son and believes in him shall have eternal life, and I will raise him up at the last day." John 6:38-40

Jesus explains that He came from heaven. He pre-existed His coming to earth. John begins his Gospel writing, "In the beginning was the Word..." (John 1:1). Jesus was not created; He is the Creator; He was in heaven before He came to earth in flesh; and He came on a mission. He came to do the will of the Father, which involves keeping those the Father gives Him, and giving the gift of eternal life to "everyone who looks to the Son and believes in him."

> "The thief comes only to steal and kill and destroy; I have come that they may have life, and have it to the full." John 10:10

> "I have come into the world as a light, so that no one who believes in me should stay in darkness." John 12:46

Jesus came to give the gift of full life, the gift of life abundant. He came as light transforming the darkness of world.

Jesus is fully God and was fully human. He left heaven, came to earth as a human, and He did so to do the Father's will, to provide eternal life, to provide full, abundant life, and to serve as light in the darkness. He came offering each of us the most amazing Christmas gift possible, the gift of His light and life.

And this tells us even more about God. He did this for us, for you and me, for every human who has ever been and who ever will be. We often say that God is love, which is true, and that God loves us, which is also true, but this puts tangible meat on the bones.

GOOD FRIDAY

God demonstrated His love for us by becoming flesh and living on earth, but to accomplish His entire goal, to become the bridge offering a path to reconciliation between us and God, Jesus had to suffer physical death. He had to lay down His life for us. On the evening before doing this, Jesus said, "Greater love has no one than this: to lay down one's life for friends" (John 15:13). Later that evening as He met with Pontius Pilate, Pilate explained that Jesus was being accused of claiming to be king. He asked Jesus whether he was a king. Jesus responded saying,

> "My kingdom is not of this world. If it were, my servants would fight to prevent my arrest by the Jews. But now my kingdom is from another place."

> "You are a king, then!" said Pilate.

> Jesus answered, "You are right to say I am a king. In fact, for this reason I was born, and for this I came into the world, to testify to the truth. Everyone on the side of truth listens to me." John 18:36-37

"For this I came into the world...." Jesus knew that He needed to take on the weight of the sin of the world. He needed to suffer in ways we cannot imagine. The holy One needed to experience the world's depraved wickedness, and the path leading to His goal involved being condemned to die. Death was part of His purpose. "For this I came into the world...."

Pilate sentenced Jesus to be flogged and crucified. The soldiers went to great lengths to torture, insult and mock Him. After the flogging, they adorned Him with a scarlet robe and a crown of thorns, and they knelt before Him calling out "Hail, king of the Jews!" (Matthew 27:29) before striking Him over and over with a staff. Then, they led Him to Golgotha where they crucified Him.

Scripture describes remarkable events as Jesus died. The sun stopped shining from about noon until three in the afternoon,[1] the curtain surrounding the holiest of places in the temple was suddenly torn in two,[2] and the earth shook, rocks split, tombs broke open and holy people were raised to life.[3]

As Jesus hung on the cross, a soldier checked to see if He was still alive. The soldier thought Jesus was dead. To verify, he "pierced Jesus' side with a spear, bringing a sudden flow of blood and water" (John 20:34).

From a human perspective, Good Friday seems anything but good. An innocent man was falsely accused for purely political purposes, put on trial with trumped up charges, hurriedly tried with no opportunity for a proper defense, and immediately thereafter tortured and executed. His arrest, trial and execution all took place in less than twenty-four hours. Viewed through our human lens, He was railroaded. No justice was served that day, and the events reveal the worst vile, evil inclinations of humanity. Yet we call the day Good Friday. Why?

Jesus was God Incarnate and through His death we are offered reconciliation with God. Through Jesus we are offered forgiveness of our sins. As horrific as the entire situation was, the result is glorious. Through His death, He is "the way"[4] and "the gate"[5] to God.

Peter describes it like this:

> When they hurled their insults at him, he did not retaliate; when he suffered, he made no threats. Instead, he entrusted himself to him who judges justly. He himself bore our sins in his body on a tree, so that we might die to sins and live for righteousness; by his wounds you have been healed. For you were like sheep going astray, but now you have returned to the Shepherd and Overseer of your souls. 1 Peter 2:23-25

John describes it like this:

> God is light; in him there is no darkness at all.... But if we walk in the light, as he is in the light, we have fellowship with one another, and the blood of Jesus, his Son, purifies us from all sin. 1 John 1:5-7

> But if anyone does sin, we have one who speaks to the Father in our defense – Jesus Christ, the Righteous One. He is the atoning sacrifice for our sins, and not only ours but also for the sins of the whole world. 1 John 2:1-2

> This is how we know what love is: Jesus Christ laid down his life for us. 1 John 3:16

HAPPY EASTER!

Scripture tells us that late on that Friday afternoon Joseph, a wealthy man from Arimathea, sought permission from Pilate to bury Jesus' body. With Pilate's permission, Joseph took the body, wrapped it in linen and burial clothes, and placed it in the Arimathea family's unused tomb.[6]

Early on that Sunday morning, which became known as the first Easter, a group of women went to the tomb to anoint Jesus' body with spices and perfume and prepare it for a proper burial. When they arrived, the stone that had once sealed the tomb was rolled away from the entrance and the tomb was empty. Two angels appeared saying,

> "Why do you look for the living among the dead? He is not here; he is risen! Remember how he told you, while he was still in Galilee: 'The Son of Man must be delivered into the hands of sinful men, be crucified and on the third day be raised again.' Then they remembered the words." Luke 24:5-8

Over the following forty days Jesus appeared to His followers to convince them that He truly lives, to continue teaching them, to encourage them, and to provide assurance. While He taught, Jesus explained that He would return to heaven where He would sit at the right hand of God the Father.[7] After appearing over forty days, with His followers watching, Jesus ascended to heaven.[8]

I AM

Throughout His ministry, Jesus explained who He is but many who heard His words were unable to hear His message. As we struggle to comprehend the Father, Jesus and the Holy Spirit, we must understand that struggling to understand God is nothing new. Problems with this go back to the beginning of Scripture.

Think about Moses.[9] He encountered God through a bush that was on fire but not consumed, which is one of the most amazing miracles in the Bible, and God called Moses to free His people from the most powerful nation on the planet at the time. In response, Moses asked how he should go about communicating who God is to Pharaoh. Moses saw the burning bush. He stood on holy ground. He spoke with God. He heard God's call and he wondered how he should describe God to Pharaoh, and because in that time and place a person's name conveyed information about the person – it explained a person's purpose and character, and in some respects knowledge of a person's name provided a degree of power and influence over that person – Moses asked God, what's your name?

God answered, "I AM WHO I AM. This is what you are to say to the Israelites: I AM has sent me to you" (Exodus 3:14).

That is the only place in Scripture where God's first person name is recorded. It is as if God, by providing an intentionally cryptic response, was explaining that mere mortals are incapable of knowing the holy, the divine, the immortal One. God's name is "I AM." Its like the time Samson's father, Manoah, asked an angel his name, and the angel replied, "Why do you ask my name? It is beyond understanding" (Judges 13:18). We humans think we are so advanced, so intelligent, so smart, yet so much is beyond our ability to comprehend.

How do we comprehend God? His light is too bright, His glory is too magnificent, His presence is too grand for mere mortals to grasp. Jesus knew our difficulty and He taught a great deal about who He is. He had already taught that people are dead until they hear His word and believe, and at that point they cross from death to life (see John 5:24). With the notion of life and death in mind, He explains that He is the life, the source of life and the path to life. Through Him and in Him we gain life, new life, abundant life, eternal life, and He tries to communicate that truth to us in a variety of ways.

Hundreds of years after Moses, with a nod to God's first person name equating to a claim of divinity, Jesus describes Himself to us in a series of "I am" statements.

> Then Jesus declared, "I am the bread of life. Whoever *comes to me* will never go hungry, and whoever *believes in me* will never be thirsty." John 6:35

Just as God provided manna in the wilderness each morning during the Exodus, thereby sustaining life, Jesus is the bread of new life, abundant life, eternal life, spiritual life.

> When Jesus spoke again to the people, he said, "I am the light of the world. Whoever *follows me* will never walk in darkness, but will have the light of life." John 8:12

In his beautifully poetic introduction to the gospel, John describes Jesus writing, "In him was life, and that life was the light of all mankind. The light shines in the darkness, and the darkness has not overcome it" (John 1:4-5). Life is light, and Jesus is both.

> "Very truly I tell you," Jesus answered, "before Abraham was born, I am!" At this, they picked up stones to stone him, but Jesus hid himself, slipping away from the temple grounds. John 8:58-59

Religious leaders understood Jesus' claim of eternal existence while employing God's first person name for Himself.

They heard the words and understood His intent – He was asserting His divinity, which in their minds equated to blasphemy, so they reached for stones.

> Therefore Jesus said again, "Very truly I tell you, I am the gate for the sheep." John 10:7

Jesus is the opening through which we access life, and He is the good shepherd who nurtures, guides and protects His sheep.

> "I am the good shepherd. The good shepherd *lays down his life* for the sheep." John 10:11

> "I am the resurrection and the life. The one who *believes in me* will live, even though they die; and whoever lives by believing in me will never die. Do you believe this?" John 10:25-26

> Jesus answered, "I am the way and the truth and the life. No one *comes to* the Father except through me." John 14:6

Jesus is the resurrection. He converts death to life. He provides new life, abundant life, eternal life. He is also the way to life, life itself and the truth.

> "I am the true vine, and my Father is the gardener. He cuts off every branch in me that bears no fruit, while every branch that does *bear fruit* he prunes, so that it will be even more fruitful…. I am the vine; you are the branches. If you *remain in me* and I in you, you will *bear much fruit*…." John 15:1-2 & 5

God came to earth in the flesh. While describing who He is, He invites us to make use of everything He offers. He invites us to "come to" Him, "believe in" Him, "follow" Him, "remain in" Him and "bear fruit." He lays down His life, provides spiritual sustenance and light, and serves as our path to the kingdom of heaven.

Jesus offers a simple invitation. While Jesus makes the invitation in several ways on different occasions, He does not insist, He does not twist our arm, He does not beg.

Do You Believe?

For each of us, the question is whether we truly believe. It is like when Jesus met Martha and Mary on the road in Bethany. He explained to them that He is the resurrection and the life and He asked them "Do you believe this?" (John 11:26). Do you *believe*? Do *you* believe?

Martha and Mary believed in Jesus, they believed He was the Messiah, they believed He had the power to heal their brother, but their belief was too small – they believed Jesus had to be physically present to heal their brother, and they never imagined Jesus would bring their brother back to life after he had been in the tomb for four days. They believed, but their belief was too small.

Do you believe? This is the question. Because when you know with absolute, 100% certainty that the answer is yes, it will change your life. Because God is really real and this whole Jesus thing and this whole Holy Spirit is really real.

The other day I sat across the table from a friend who regularly attends a Christian church. As he told a story, for emphasis, he used an expression that grieved my spirit. It burned my ears. It tortured by soul. He said a word that started with "God" and ended with a curse and it grieves me still just thinking about it. If the eyes of his spirit were opened to see God, if He knew in his soul that God is real, if he had truly experienced God's glory, He could not and would not ever speak that way. And so, in my grief, I wonder, what can I do to help him? I pray for God to use me as His vessel. I pray for Him to give me the words to say. I pray for God to enlighten the eyes of my friend's spirit.

CONCLUSION

As you celebrate Christmas, take some time to marvel at the magnitude of what Jesus' birth represents. It represents God coming to us, God assuming bodily existence, God seeking relationship with us, God offering His love, God revealing the way to us. He desires to give each of us, yes you and me, the gift of abundant life, His light, and His eternal life. Accept His gift, marvel at His loving grace, praise His holy name, and express awe for His majesty. When you say, hear or see "Merry Christmas!" think of God's glory. Think of the holy gift it represents.

And as you celebrate Easter, consider that God Incarnate, the holy, pure, divine Creator of all things who is sovereign and who has always been and who always will be, gave Himself up for us on the cross. He assumed the weight of the world's sins and sacrificed Himself on the cross, offering the path for us to be reconciled with God. And then, to demonstrate His deity, He rose from the dead.

These are the most significant events in the history of mankind. Our society has done a terrific job of merchandizing Christ out of Christmas and God out of Easter, and of blinding us to the revelation of God's glory.

> Yet to all who received him, to those who believed in his name, he gave the right to become children of God – children born not of natural descent, nor of human decision or a husband's will, but born of God. The Word became flesh and made his dwelling among us. We have seen his glory, the glory of the One and Only, who came from the Father, full of grace and truth. John 1:11-14

His glory surrounds us. May He enlighten your eyes to see.

11 | PRAYER

*"If you then, though you are evil,
know how to give good gifts to
your children, how much more
will your Father in heaven give
the Holy Spirit to those who ask
him!" Luke 11:13*

In some respects, prayer is a state of being. It is entering God's holy presence. It is longing for God. It is opening your spirit to receive God. It involves speaking to God, listening to God, singing, praising, worshiping and other activities, but at its root, prayer is a state of being in which we open ourselves to God's holy presence. Viewed differently, prayer is the avenue through which we experience God, His presence, His holy grace. Through this lens, prayer is the conduit and a certain state of being is the result. While I believe the concepts merge on deeper inquiry, we usually discuss prayer as the avenue leading to a result, and that is how I will use the word.

I have experienced a small taste of what I am about to describe. If what I am about to describe were an iceberg with its tip above the water and mass below, I have possibly experienced the fresh snowfall on the top of the tip, but have not yet explored its depths. If what I am about to describe were a feast, I have caught a whiff of the aroma. I have entered the house on Thanksgiving, experienced the wonderful aroma and sampled a spoonful as the meal was being prepared, but have not yet enjoyed the full feast. I know the feast exists because I smell it and I have enjoyed a small taste, but please do not interpret what I am about to write as a claim of possession – I describe what I have glimpsed, the aroma I have briefly experienced and that which I seek.

Picture your spirit as a light bulb. The Holy Spirit is electricity. Prayer is the wire connecting the bulb to the outlet. The bulb emits light when connected with electricity. Prayer is the conduit accessing the Holy Spirit, connecting our spirit to the Holy Spirit, and energizing, illuminating and providing vitality to our spirit.

Earthly images are inherently lacking when used to depict heavenly matters, and the light bulb image has problems. For starters, the Holy Spirit enters our spirit the moment we first believe.[1] I use it nonetheless because prayer is a supplemental conduit. Prayer enhances the presence of the Holy Spirit within our spirit and enhances the transformation of our spirit and soul. Through prayer, the eyes of our spirits are opened allowing us to, with gradually increasing ability, be sensitive to the spiritual realm around us. We are continually showered with God's love and grace, but we must receive the gifts. Prayer connects us to God and His love and grace.

Our love grows as we receive more and more of the Holy Spirit, and the natural result will be that we view the world differently – with gradually increasing awareness we view the world through a lens similar to Jesus' eyes. While in human form, Jesus was sensitive to the spiritual presence of people around Him: He recognized when people were in need and when they were hurting. When we look at people do we see people created in God's image and know that God loves them? Do we sense the inevitable connection between loving God and loving our neighbor, realizing that they are not really two commands but so inseparable that they act as one? Prayer enhances our spiritual awareness and our connection with the Holy Spirit, such that some day we will answer, "yes."

Prayer allows us to feel intimacy with God and causes us to seek God with increasingly greater fervor. Through prayer our relationship with God, the Holy, the Divine, grows and He unveils His power. With increasing awareness we gradually realize that God is really present, really who He claims to be, and sincerely interested in us. And we realize that He manifests Himself in powerful ways as He acts in response to prayer.

Our spiritual transformation forces us to consider the world around us with new eyes and we call upon His Holy Power to act in the world. We pray for God to intercede on behalf of other people. We pray for healing, total physical, spiritual, emotional, psychological, relational healing. We pray for God to take care of physical needs. We pray for God to provide comfort, strength, wisdom and protection for people around us. We pray for God's glory to be revealed through His actions.

Faith and prayer go together. It takes a certain amount of faith, or possibly desperation, to pray. Prayer begins with belief that (or at least acceptance of the possibility that) God exists, that God hears our prayer, that God listens, that God cares about us and about what we have to say, that God is capable of responding to our prayer, and that God will indeed respond. When we realize that God has answered our prayer, our confidence and trust in Him grows. Answers to prayer are for God's glory. To the extent we realize that God actively works in our lives, our faith grows. Enhanced faith glorifies God and causes us to seek God more and pray more and the cycle perpetuates itself.

God wants us to communicate with Him. Pause for a moment and let that statement sink in. God wants us to communicate with Him. He is God. I am nothing in comparison. He is holy, divine and pure. He is all-powerful and all knowing. He is the Creator of all things – He created everything out of nothing; He spoke and the heavens were created. He breathes the breath of life into each of us. He is not bound by space or time. He is everywhere at once all the time. His mind has perfect clarity. He does not make mistakes. His character is without taint or flaw. Our wildest imagination cannot begin to imagine all that He is.

But based on the glimpse of God that we have, in comparison to Him, we are nothing. We are mere mortals. Consider each description of God above and think about who we are. We are not holy, not divine, and not pure. We have limited knowledge and power. Our ability to create is limited to manipulating that which God already created. We are most definitely limited by space and time. Our ability to think is not perfect, we make mistakes and our character is flawed.

In light of who God is and our relative nothingness, I am continually amazed that He desires relationship with us. He wants us to commune with Him and when we pray He listens and responds. Through Christ Jesus and His imputed righteousness, we are made something we do not deserve. Compared to God we are nothing, we deserve nothing from God, we have no right to His favor, but through Christ Jesus, the only mediator between people and God, [2] because He considers us worthy of His relationship, we are made special.

When God speaks remarkable things happen. In the beginning God made the universe out of nothingness by speaking.[3] We are nothing, but through the bridge of atoning reconciliation made possible through Christ Jesus, we are made something, and when God speaks to us miracles happen.

When we pray our words do not need to be fancy, but our prayer needs to be genuine, sincere, rooted in humility and brokenness because of our flawed existence, and rooted in reverence and awe of God because of who He is. When approached like this, prayer naturally involves praise and worship, and is filled with thankfulness for all that God has done.

Scripture describes prayer as calling on the name of the Lord. The first prayer mentioned in Scripture occurred after Adam and Eve's first grandchild was born. Their third son, Seth, had a baby boy named Enosh. Immediately after this, Scripture says, "At that time people began to call on the name of the Lord" (Genesis 4:26).

Prayer is calling on the name of the Lord, it is crying out to God, it is talking with God. The prophet Joel uses similar wording in his prophecy predicting the outpouring of the Holy Spirit, and he connects the outpouring with prayer:

And afterward, *I will pour out my Spirit on all people.*
Your sons and daughters will prophesy, your old men

will dream dreams, your young men will see visions. Even on my servants, both men and women, I will pour out my Spirit in those days. I will show wonders in the heavens and on the earth, blood and fire and billows of smoke. The sun will be turned to darkness and the moon to blood before the coming of the great and dreadful day of the Lord. *And everyone who calls on the name of the Lord will be saved....* Joel 2:28-32

The Holy Spirit is poured out on all people, but not everyone notices, not everyone calls on the name of the Lord. Some connect with Him; others do not. Like electrical wiring connecting a light bulb to the source of energy, prayer connects us with the Holy Spirit in life changing and life saving ways.

Scripture provides many examples of the Holy Spirit pouring out in response to prayer. Jesus prayed during His baptism. Scripture tells us, "And as he was praying, heaven was opened and the Holy Spirit descended on him in bodily form like a dove" (Luke 3:21-22). The last paragraph of Luke's gospel explains that Jesus ascended into heaven. After that, the believers "stayed continually at the temple, praising God" (Luke 24:53). If we move forward to Acts chapter 2 we learn that nine days later, during the festival known as Pentecost, the Holy Spirit was unleashed. So the believers were praying for nine days in the temple, and during that time of prayer the Holy Spirit was unleashed. In Acts chapter 4 we once again find the believers meeting together to pray, and "After they prayed, the place where they were meeting was shaken. And they were filled with the Holy Spirit and spoke the word of God boldly" (Acts 4:31).

I pray because I need to. I am not saying "I need to" out of a sense of obligation or an expectation of rebuke if I don't, like saying "I need to drive the speed limit." I need to in the sense that I feel better when prayer is part of my regular routine than when it isn't. It is sort of like exercise. I need to exercise, not out of obligation and certainly not because I am training for competition, but because my body feels achy and I have trouble focusing on work and sleeping if I don't. I feel better when it is part of my routine. I need to brush my teeth because my mouth feels better after old food residue is removed and that makes everything else feel better and, because it makes me feel better, I brush my teeth several times a day. I know these are lousy analogies, partly because they are physical analogies for a spiritual matter. I pray because prayer makes me feel better.

Prayer begins with faith and ends with faith strengthened. Over time, faith and prayer work together. Faith leads to prayer; prayer strengthens faith; and the two build upon each other. Eventually prayer authenticates faith.

Why do we pray? Life is better lived in communion with God than separated from Him, and prayer connects us with God. We pray because we believe. We believe that God exists, that He listens to us, that He hears our prayers, that He is capable of responding to our requests, and that He does indeed respond. And if we believe all that, we believe in miracles because God – the Pure, the Divine, the One unbound by space and time, the almighty Creator of all things – reaching in, touching our worldly realm, and altering that realm is by definition a miraculous event. When we pray for God's favor in our life, when we pray for God to act in our life, when we pray for God to act in the lives of other people, we seek God to perform a miracle; we seek a manifestation of His Glory; we seek authentication of our faith. And God responds.

SPIRITUAL TRANSFORMATION

God responds by revealing the Holy Spirit. Certainly the Holy Spirit dwells within each person the moment they first believe,[4] but through prayer our awareness of Him grows and our relationship with Him is enhanced. Prayer is the primary avenue through which we connect with the Holy Spirit, and is fundamental for the transformation of our spirits.

Jesus promises that God will send the Holy Spirit to people who ask, saying:

"Which of you fathers, if your son asks for a fish, will give him a snake instead? Or if he asks for an egg, will give him a scorpion? If you then, though you are evil, know how to give good gifts to your children, how much more will your *Father in heaven give the Holy Spirit to those who ask him!*" Luke 11:12-13

So we pray to receive the Holy Spirit and through the Holy Spirit our spirits are transformed. Most of the prayers prayed by Jesus and Paul that are recorded in Scripture focus on spiritual matters. Paul urges us to contemplate spiritual matters during prayer, through prayer and beyond prayer, and to view spiritual matters as they influence the physical realm around us. The spiritual realm influences the physical at its most fundamental level. Paul urges us to expand our vision and with this enhanced and broadened view of the world, to recognize the phenomenal power of prayer.

In his letter to the church in Ephesus, Paul urged believers to guard against spiritual attack saying, "Put on the full armor of God so that you can take your stand against the devil's schemes" (Ephesians 6:11). He continued, explaining that the elements of armor include the truth, the Gospel, righteousness, faith, salvation and the Holy Spirit. After listing individual elements of armor, Paul discussed prayer. Prayer helps everything else. Prayer is presumed to take place; it is the umbrella under which the elements of armor reside. He said, "And pray in the Spirit on all occasions with all kinds of prayers and requests" (Ephesians 6:18). Prayer enhances our connection with the Holy Spirit who protects and strengthens and shields our spiritual self.

I recently visited our county jail for a Bible study with some inmates. We started our meeting with prayer and hymns and then I asked what they wanted to discuss. Many of the men were concerned about matters relating to forgiveness, healing their relationships with family members, and trusting their salvation in Jesus Christ. Our discussion turned to questions regarding prayer – how should we pray, what should we request in prayer, and what should we expect in response to prayer?

A man who appeared to be in his thirties carried a small paperback Bible that was tattered. A small portion of the original paper cover remained. The pages were worn, the margins were covered with pencil writing, and the corners were dog-eared. He discussed faith and prayer, and he read the first few passages from James:

> "Consider it pure joy, my brothers and sisters, whenever you face trials of many kinds, because you know that the testing of your faith produces perseverance. Let perseverance finish its work so that you may be mature and complete, not lacking anything. If any of you lacks wisdom, you should ask God who gives generously to all without finding fault, and it will be given to you. *But when you ask, you must believe and do not doubt*, because the one who doubts is like a wave of the sea, blown and tossed by the wind. That person should not expect to receive anything from the Lord. Such a person is double-minded and unstable in all that they do." James 1:2-8

He said each time he had been incarcerated; he desperately wanted to get out of jail so he could return to his life. Each time, he turned to Scripture, not to meet Jesus or to grow in faith, but to learn the magic words to say so his prayers would be answered. He compared his pursuit at that time to a scene from a movie where the actor discovered an old book of magic spells. She dusted off the book, opened it, read a few lines from the book and something magical happened – the words read from the book transformed the physical world and her wish became reality. He read the Bible seeking magic words he could say that would convince God to reach into our world and free him from jail.

He started attending weekly Bible studies in jail and he read Scripture, all the while seeking the magic words. Gradually he began to realize that he needed to change. He realized that if he was allowed to leave jail before he changed, he would likely go back to the same old life that led him to all his previous times in jail. And so he focused on the transformation that he needed in his life. He started praying, not for release from jail, but for faith, perseverance and wisdom. He wanted to understand Scripture. He wanted to know God better. He sought relationship with the Holy Spirit.

The man gradually developed the understanding that his problems were spiritual, not physical. He was in jail, but jail was not his fundamental problem. He believed that jail was a symptom of his deeper foundational problem, and that if he worked on his spirit, his physical situation would take care of itself. While not every problem is spiritual, many problems have spiritual foundations with physical symptoms. Through prayer we connect with God and He gradually transforms our spirit.

Often spiritual problems manifest themselves as physical situations and we sometimes look for physical solutions to spiritual problems. I have heard it said that every problem is, at its foundation, a spiritual problem. A physical impediment to freedom, like a jail cell, certainly has the appearance of a physical problem, but the inmate saw it as a symptom of problems at the foundation of his spirit. In a similar way, are all problems spiritual? They are related to Adam and Eve's horrific choice and the resulting curse of creation, but are they spiritual?

The notion reminds me of the book *Zen and the Art of Motorcycle Maintenance.*[5] Phaedrus ponders whether everything is illusory. Reasoning that if all our experience, knowledge and information relating to the world are revealed through our senses, it all is possibly the product of our imagination, thus illusory. After pondering the notion for a long time he concluded that the world is real – the world around him seemed too complex to be the product of his imagination.

Like Phaedrus, as I ponder the suggestion that every problem is, at its foundation, spiritual, it seems to be a stretch. I see so many problems suffered by people that appear to be physical problems, but am I missing the spiritual foundation? We live in this fallen world and pain is connected to the fallen state, so undoubtedly I am missing the spiritual root for many problems I see. But if you have cancer and are struggling with the nausea, diarrhea, exhaustion, mouth sores, bone aches and deathly feelings caused by the illness and chemotherapy, the problems certainly seem to be primarily physical. And as I watch chemo drip into my wife, who is a prayer warrior, I cannot believe her illness had spiritual roots. A mass appeared in her thigh. I have been unable to conclude that some failing in her spiritual being created the mass, because it is simply not the case. Similarly, if your employer downsizes due to economic conditions and you lose your job and as a result lose your home and you struggle to find food and a safe place to sleep, the problems are primarily physical. And it is difficult to see a spiritual foundation to an event caused by a struggling economy. A person with a strong spiritual foundation and a strong connection with the Holy Spirit might face physical problems like these with a heightened sense of peace and tranquility, rendering their reaction to the problem more peaceful, but the problems still seem to be primarily physical. Of course, I am possibly failing to see the situation clearly.

While every problem may be related to man's fall and the fallen state of creation (I cannot believe cancer existed while Adam and Eve communed with God in the garden), not every problem is spiritual. If my understanding is correct, not every problem has spiritual roots, yet we routinely struggle with many problems that have physical symptoms and spiritual foundations. Through prayer and studying His word, our relationship with God grows and our awareness of the spiritual realm grows and our spirits are transformed. As a result, our eyes are opened to see spiritual causes and spiritual solutions to many problems that we face.

PHYSICAL TRANSFORMATION

Scripture and experience confirm that prayer influences our spirits and our awareness of the spiritual realm. Does God reach into our world to touch physical matters in response to prayer? Does He influence the physical realm, the world around us in physical ways? What does Scripture and experience tell us?

The short answer is yes. God changes the physical realm in response to prayer, but not always. I have experienced prayers leading to astounding spiritual and physical transformation, and prayers prayed over and over with no apparent effect, and wondered what creates the difference.

Jesus demonstrated concern for people's physical needs. Scripture records many miracles performed by Jesus that focused on physical needs. Jesus fed over 5,000 people with five loaves and two fish.[6] He raised people from the dead,[7] cured sick people,[8] healed paralyzed people,[9] and gave blind people sight.[10] Jesus miraculously provided a coin to pay His and Peter's taxes,[11] and provided miraculous fish catches on two occasions.[12]

And Jesus instructs us to pray for God to satisfy our physical needs. He gave the disciples a template for prayer saying,

> "When you pray, say: 'Father, hallowed be your name, your kingdom come. *Give us each day our daily bread.* Forgive us our sins, for we also forgive everyone who sins against us. And lead us not into temptation.'" Luke 11:2-4

Jesus teaches us to ask God to provide our daily sustenance, which includes physical needs. By doing so, we acknowledge that our physical blessings are from God. If Jesus teaches us to ask God for physical blessings, we should trust that God answers our prayers.

Scripture records many examples of physical miracles. God healed physical ailments in response to prayers prayed by Jesus, the disciples and other believers. Does God still heal physical ailments in response to prayer? Sometimes He does. I know people who suffered physical ailments and following prayer they were healed. Here are a few examples.

Lori

I have mentioned this before, but my wife, Lori, was diagnosed with soft tissue sarcoma. It was an orange-sized mass in her hamstring. Radiation worked well as it achieved 80% kill of the mutating mass (I want to call it a foreign invader but it was even more insidious than that – it was her own cells with her own DNA going rogue). Surgeons removed the mass with clear margins. PET and CT scans revealed no indications of cancer. She was possibly cancer-free, but it was impossible to know whether sarcoma cells were travelling through her body attempting to gain a foothold in another part of her body, most likely her lungs. She could have had somewhere between zero cancer cells and the number necessary to gain a mass large enough to be detected by a scan. Given this possibility, she opted for chemotherapy to destroy any lingering cells that might have been there.

She was scheduled to receive six treatments. Each would last four days over which she would receive Ifosfamide and near-continuous infusion of Adriamycin along with other chemicals in the recipe for blasting sarcoma. Each round hit her harder than the one before it. Doctors expected her system to continue declining after each treatment, with the lowest day to occur seven or eight days later.

Her third treatment ended on Thursday, one week before Thanksgiving, so her low point was expected to occur on Thanksgiving. We prayed that the low point would happen sooner because our kids were traveling to be with us for Thanksgiving. They were both planning to arrive Wednesday.

Wednesday morning Lori felt really, really bad. She had extreme shortness of breath, racing heart, and exhaustion. She walked 25 feet from bed to sofa, lost her breath and needed several minutes to recover. We went to the clinic for blood tests to make sure she was not experiencing symptoms of serious problems. After drawing blood, a nurse checked her vital signs. She did not have a fever, but her heart rate was racing at 144 beats per minute, and the machine was unable to measure her blood pressure. The nurse pulled out equipment to measure her blood pressure manually, but she was unable to get a reading. She called a second nurse who was unable to get a reading. Lori was struggling to sit up in her chair, so the nurses found a wheelchair and helped her in it. They then wheeled her into an exam room where a third nurse tried unsuccessfully to measure her blood pressure.

The nurses were very concerned. They knew Adriamycin is very hard on hearts; she had an elevated heart rate; her blood pressure was too low to read; and she barely had enough energy to sit in a chair. She just wanted to lie down, but the nurses told her not to lie down. The nurses left to consult with a doctor. As Lori and I sat alone in the exam room I said a very short, simple prayer. It was really a faint whisper. A nurse returned relaying the doctor's order: he told us to go the Emergency Room.

I pushed Lori's wheelchair through the maze of hospital corridors to the Emergency Room, went through the admission process and as we entered the Emergency Room my cell phone started vibrating. I looked and it was a call from one of Lori's prayer warrior friends, a member of her prayer group. She never calls me. I did not answer it, but after we settled in a room I texted her explaining why I had ignored her call. She asked if she could forward my note to her prayer group and I said yes. About fifteen minutes later a nurse came to check Lori's vital signs. She hooked up the blood pressure monitoring machine and it measured without problem. Her blood pressure was a little low, but in the normal range, and her heart rate had dropped tremendously.

It was a different machine managed by a different nurse in a different part of the hospital about 30 minutes later. Lori had not been given any medication in the intervening time. I cannot think of any other difference between the attempted measurement in the ER and the clinic, except that during the intervening time a number of people were praying, and that was the difference that mattered. Her blood pressure rose from a level too low to detect to the normal range.

Over the course of the following week many other instances arose allowing God's glory to shine through her situation. We were discharged from the ER that Wednesday evening. On Thanksgiving Day Lori was able to get out of bed for a little while, but as she tried to walk from the sofa back to bed (on her own without telling anyone), she fell hitting hard on the floor. That night she had fever. We knew chemo had destroyed her white blood cell count, which was expected. A fever with no white blood cells to fight infection is a concerning combination. We returned to the Emergency Room Friday morning. Lori was admitted to the hospital and stayed for five nights receiving lots of antibiotics to fight whatever might have been causing the fever and medication to boost her white blood cell count. Time and time again God revealed His glory.

Two days after leaving the hospital, we returned to the clinic for blood tests. The nurses who had seen her ten days earlier greeted her warmly expressing their happiness and relief. One said, "I am so glad to see you. I thought we were losing you."

Praise God. He is good. Like Psalm 91:15 says, "He will call on me and I will answer him; I will be with him in trouble, I will deliver him and honor him." Praise God. He is with us and He delivers us.

You might be wondering, if God answered our prayer about low blood pressure and miraculously caused it to rise, why did He not miraculously touch her leg and cure Lori's cancer? Of course I do not know the answer, but I believe He wants to use her illness for many small opportunities to reveal His glory. He promises to be with us in trouble and to ultimately deliver us. He does not promise to remove us from trouble before we experience it. Often it is through our troubling times that He reveals His glory.

Pat[5]

Sunday mornings at our church involve a series of carefully orchestrated events. The Sanctuary is prepared starting at 7:30 am for the first service. The altar is prepared with beautiful flowers and trimmed with cloth of the appropriate color based on the liturgical calendar. Attendance pads and bulletins are placed in the proper places. A group meets at 8 to pray in the room, all while the organist rehearses, filling the room with beautiful music. At 8:15 the staff meets to review every aspect of each

---

[5] Portions of this account were described in my book *God's Glory Revealed: 52 Devotionals*, Devotional 37, "Touching the Fringe" pp.188-192.

service and to pray. After the meeting technicians verify the sound is working properly, that all microphones are working, the video feed is working and all video cameras are ready to go.

The first service begins at 9. Sunday school classes begin at 10, and the second service begins at 11.

For me, most Sundays start at 8 with a brief prayer time in the Sanctuary followed by our staff meeting and the first service. After the first service I usually talk with people briefly as they leave before hurrying to teach one of many adult Sunday school classes, which I am normally late entering and early leaving as I try to make the 11 am service on time.

On one particular Sunday I was not scheduled to teach Sunday school, so I took extra time after the early service talking with friends in the Sanctuary and hallways before slowly making my way to the Sunday school classrooms on the third floor. It was about 10:15 when I reached the top of the stairs.

Just as I did, the doors to the elevator opened revealing Pat. She asked if I had time to talk with her. I explained that, as strange as it was on a Sunday morning, I had time. Her left pupil was completely dilated making her left eyeball black. She explained that the night before she completely lost sight in the eye. That morning she saw a doctor who diagnosed her condition as central retinal vein occlusion – her main retinal vein was blocked. The doctor said no treatment is available to unblock the vein, she would not regain sight in the eye and she should receive monthly injections in the eye to prevent other problems from developing.

Pat asked if I would accompany her into her Sunday school class, interrupt the class, and ask everyone to pray for God to heal her eye. She asked specifically for me to pray for total and complete physical and spiritual healing for her, and for the Holy Spirit to transform our church and each individual in it.

A dozen or so of us prayed. We gathered around Pat, placed hands on her, anointed her with oil and prayed. Later that day she was able to see with the eye, but her vision was cloudy. I saw her the following Wednesday evening at our prayer meeting and her vision was almost back to normal. The following week she returned to her doctor. He said the injections that he previously recommended were no longer necessary. Her eye was back to normal.

God healed her eye in response to prayer. It was a rare occurrence for me to be free on a Sunday morning. It was a rare occurrence for me to be at that place at that time. But I just happened to arrive at the top of the stairs exactly when the elevator door opened. We had a divine appointment and God revealed His glory.

Kennedy[6] [13]

On June 15, 2000, the Buettner family attended a pool party for their oldest son's baseball team. After the kids swam for a while, everyone left the pool to eat on the lawn nearby. Amy helped her four-year-old son Kennedy and his four siblings get settled with food. Then she and her husband Craig sat down to eat. Kennedy was sitting on a towel eating with some older boys.

As she ate, Amy scanned the scene making sure her kids were okay and she suddenly realized Kennedy was missing. Kids were playing on bikes and riding toys. She was certain he was playing with them. She started walking around looking for him. As she looked she asked people if they had seen him. Soon everyone was looking for Kennedy.

Kennedy's brother saw Kennedy lying at the bottom of the pool. They pulled him to the surface. His body was limp, bloated and grayish blue. His father, a physician, performed CPR. Someone called 911. Men and women gathered to pray. After about five minutes of CPR, Kennedy's heart began beating erratically.

An ambulance rushed Kennedy to the local hospital and a helicopter flew him to Children's Hospital in Birmingham, Alabama. The medical diagnosis was clear. He was possibly underwater for ten minutes. Add that to five minutes of CPR and his brain had been without oxygen for as long as fifteen minutes.

---

[6] Portions of this account were described in my book *God's Glory Revealed: 52 Devotionals*, Devotional 6, "God Heals Kennedy" pp.27-31.

His chance of survival was slim, and if he survived, his brain would be severely damaged.

The Buettner family was bathed in prayer. Friends drove to meet them to pray with them in the hospital. Churches and individuals around the community prayed. Less than a week later, with tubes preventing him from speaking, Kennedy pointed to the television. He then held up four fingers, closed his fist, and held up four fingers again. He was requesting that the television be turned on to channel 44, the Cartoon Network. A week after the incident he returned home. He recovered fully.

While the story of his miraculous healing is wonderful, even more amazing is what he saw while his body slept. The four-year-old described flying with an angel who wore long white clothes. They flew through walls, through clouds, through his mother as she knelt over him praying, and to heaven. Kennedy said while in heaven he stood on glass and was invisible, and he described talking with Jesus. He described seeing a volcano with sad people and a dragon in it. He said he was not afraid.

While working to heal Kennedy's body, Jesus gave him a remarkable heavenly tour. And through it, God reveals His glory. Certainly God could have prevented Kennedy from entering the pool. God could have kept Kennedy afloat preventing the incident. God could have done so many things to prevent the situation, but had He done so, we would not be retelling the story. Through Kennedy and through many other remarkable situations, God reveals His glory.

Delores

As mentioned in the previous chapter, God miraculously healed Delores Winder. She suffered for years and ultimately had surgery to sever the nerves leading from her spine in an effort to eliminate the pain she felt continuously. After the surgeries, she lost all feeling below a certain point on her spine. During a church conference focusing on the Holy Spirit, God miraculously reattached the severed nerves and restored her body. It was a medically verified miracle. Afterward, she traveled the world speaking and praying for people. In response to her prayers, many other people were healed.

One evening I spoke with Delores and her husband, Bill. As we spoke about God's miraculous healing power, Bill mentioned that he had cataracts and was scheduled for surgery the following week. Delores laughed as she explained that God had healed many people with cataracts in response to their prayers. She recounted stories of people in various states and countries who had cataracts and following prayer the cataracts were gone. She described how she and others prayed over her husband. On many occasions they laid hands on him, anointed him with oil and prayed for healing. They knew God could heal the cataracts directly, and they believed that God would heal his. But for some reason God chose to heal him through doctors, surgery and traditional medicine. Delores said, "God wants him to have surgery. So please pray that his surgery will be successful."

For Delores, it was that simple. God often heals directly in response to prayer, but sometimes He chooses to work through intermediaries. God miraculously healed Delores and afterward He healed many people in response to her prayers, but in her husband's situation He chose to reveal His glory through a surgeon and medicine. I mention the Winders' story because it shows the same person praying the same way for the same condition, and sometimes the prayer resulted in immediate, direct physical healing and other times it did not. It removes some of the variables from the analysis. Each prayer demonstrated an identical faith in God and in God's ability to respond and in the fact that God heard and listened to the prayer. Yet some prayers resulted in immediate, direct physical healing while at other times God chose a different response.

Paul's Thorn

The Winders' story is similar to Paul's ailment that God chose not to heal. God uniquely touched Paul. While on a mission to persecute Christians he met Jesus and was miraculously transformed.[14] He changed from chief persecutor to evangelist.

After he encountered Jesus, God continued working on him. Paul says that God showed him visions and revelations, that God showed him heaven, and that he "heard inexpressible things, things that no one is permitted to tell" (2 Corinthians 12:4). And God healed people in response to Paul's prayers. [15] In fact Scripture explains, "God did extraordinary miracles through Paul, so that even handkerchiefs and aprons that had touched him were taken to the sick, and their illnesses were cured and the evil spirits left them" (Acts 19:11-12).

But Paul had some problem that he prayed about and God would not take away. Paul refers to the problem as "a thorn in my flesh" (2 Corinthians 12:7). We do not know what the problem was. We do not know if it was physical, spiritual or relational. It may have been a physical impairment or illness. It may have been temptation. It may have been a person who Paul lived in conflict with. We do not know what it was, but we know that Paul prayed three times for God to take it away, and God refused to do so.

Let's look at Scripture. After Paul describes that God had touched him in special ways, that God had revealed heaven to him and that he had heard inexpressible things, Paul explains that he boasts, not about God's revelation to him, but about his own weakness. Then Paul writes:

> To keep me from becoming conceited because of these surpassingly great revelations, there was given to me a thorn in my flesh, a messenger of Satan, to torment me. Three times I pleaded with the Lord to take it away from me. But he said to me, "My grace is sufficient for you, for my power is made perfect in weakness." Therefore I will boast all the more gladly about my weaknesses, so that Christ's power may rest on me. That is why, for Christ's sake, I delight in weaknesses, in insults, in hardships, in persecutions, in difficulties. For when I am weak, then I am strong.
> 2 Corinthians 12:19

God's power is made perfect in weakness. God chose not heal Paul because he needed the thorn to stay humble. Paul had experienced amazing things during his walk with Jesus Christ. God had used Paul in amazing ways and revealed things to Paul that were so heavenly Paul could not describe them, and this special revelation might have become the source of pride for him. God's special touch in Paul's life might have become twisted into the seed of pride, so God gave something to help him stay humble.

Jesus taught a similar message to His disciples. They had been part of Jesus' entourage as He preached and taught and healed. They traveled with Jesus. They were with Jesus as the crowds sought Him, welcomed Him and revered Him. They had a unique relationship with the One people sought. Jesus gave them special teaching, and bestowed upon them special powers and authority – they were sent out with the power to heal, and they baptized people.[16] Recognizing that this special relationship could become the source of pride, Jesus taught the following known as the Parable of Two Men who Prayed:

> To some who were confident in their own righteousness and looked down on everybody else, Jesus told this parable: "Two men went up to the temple to pray, one a Pharisee and the other a tax collector. The Pharisee stood up and prayed about himself: 'God, I thank you that I am not like other men – robbers, evildoers, adulterers – or even like this tax collector. I fast twice a week and give a tenth of all I get.'
>
> But the tax collector stood at a distance. He would not even look up to heaven, but beat his breast and said, 'God, have mercy on me, a sinner.'
>
> I tell you this man, rather than the other, went home justified before God. For everyone who exalts himself will be humbled, and he who humbles himself will be exalted." Luke 18:9-14

Even our relationship with God, our pursuit of the Holy, and our desire for righteousness can become our downfall by turning into the seed of pride. Jesus spoke to people who were "confident in their own righteousness" and urged them to stay humble. Paul says that God gave him a unique reminder, the ailment that Paul described as the "thorn in my flesh," to help him stay humble.

When Paul prayed to God asking Him to remove the thorn, God heard his prayer and answered his prayer. God said "No." While God healed many people through Paul's prayers, and even healed some who touched his handkerchiefs, Scripture leads me to conclude that God chose not to heal some of the people who Paul prayed over. It is clear that Paul prayed and God did not remove his thorn. Based on statements in his letters there were other situations where Paul probably prayed for people who were ill and God chose not to heal them in the time frame he might have hoped and expected.

In his letter to the churches in Galatia, Paul mentions that he was sick when he first preached to them and that his sickness caused them some problems.[17] In Paul's letter to Timothy, Paul suggests that Timothy drink a little wine to help his stomach and his "frequent illnesses."[18] In his last letter to Timothy, Paul asks him to give a special greeting to his friend Trophimus who was sick when Paul last saw him in Miletus.[19]

And Paul mentioned one more person who God healed after allowing his sickness to reach the point of death. While Paul was in prison in Rome, the church in Philippi sent a man named Epaphroditus to help Paul. While Epaphroditus was in Rome he became sick and almost died, but God ultimately healed him.[20]

Even Jesus was hindered in his ability perform miracles in a certain time and place. He returned to his hometown, Nazareth. As Jesus preached in the synagogue, people were amazed at his teaching, but they were unable to believe He was the Messiah because they had known Him as a child and they knew His family. They could not bridge the chasm separating their memory of Jesus before His ministry and the man who stood before them. Jesus "could not do any miracles there, except lay his hands on a few sick people and heal them. And he was amazed at their lack of faith" (Mark 6:5-6).

Jesus healed a few, but the lack of faith of the people in Nazareth hindered His ability to do more. They missed the opportunity to experience God's holy healing hand because they refused to recognize Jesus as the Son of God; they refused to seek Jesus; they refused to ask.

So we have an indication that God's miraculous provision depends on the faith of the recipient of prayers. In Paul's prayers relating to the thorn and helpers, we understand that God chose not to heal because of His will. Paul asked God to take away his thorn, and God said "No." God knew that Paul needed the thorn. The thorn helped him to stay humble. When Delores prayed for God to miraculously heal Bill's cataracts, God preferred to use surgery and medicine. When we pray, we trust that God hears our prayer and when He answers "No" or when He says "Yes, but in my way and my time," we must also trust that He knows best. But this explanation feels like a punt; it is not satisfying.

CONCLUSION

God is the all-powerful Creator of all things. He breathes the breath of life into each of us. He is everywhere at the same time. He knows everything. He has authority over everything. He is supreme. He is infinite yet intimate. He knows everything about each of us. He knows each of us better than we know ourselves. And, as amazing as this sounds, He desires a relationship with us.

Prayer enhances our connection with the Almighty, the Holy, the Divine, and prayer is a vehicle through which we engage in relationship with Him. God desires a relationship with us because He loves us and our life is improved when we connect with Him. Through prayer, God transforms our spirit and in response to prayer, God reaches into our world and transforms our physical realm. Ultimately, prayer is a state of being in which we open ourselves to God's holy presence.

Why do we pray? We pray because our life is better lived in connection with God.

12 | GOD'S PROMISES ABOUT PRAYER

"Because he loves me," says the Lord, "I will rescue him; I will protect him, for he acknowledges my name. He will call upon me, and I will answer him; I will be with him in trouble, I will deliver him and honor him. With long life will I satisfy him and show him my salvation."
Psalm 91:14-16

We know that God is the all-powerful creator of all things with authority over everything. We know He can do everything and anything. He is love and He loves us. Jesus tells us to ask and He promises that when we do we will receive.[1] Scripture also reveals that God hears and answers prayers.[2]

However, experience tells us that God answers some prayers by immediately causing the requested outcome to occur, but not others. He answers some prayers in the way we imagine He might, but in response to others He seems distant and answers come at strange times and through unexpected means. As we approach Scripture through the lens of our experience, we wonder whether some prayers are somehow better than others, or possibly whether some people are better at praying than other people.

What causes the difference? Why does God show up in expected ways in response to some prayers but not others? Is it the person who prays, the words prayed, or some other factor? Is it simply that God is random and unpredictable?

What leads to effective prayer? As I type the question I am torn over the notion of "effective" prayer. The thought of "effective" prayer troubles my soul because it seems to be a measure of whether God does what we ask Him to do in the manner and time we expect. If we measure a prayer's effectiveness by whether God fulfills our expectations or does our bidding, we possibly continue down the path wondering whether certain people or certain words are more effective at causing God to act (as if anyone is empowered to do that) or are more effective at manipulating God (as if anyone can manipulate God), and the notion feels twisted. God is not a genie in a bottle waiting for us to speak magic words so He can grant our wishes.

As we ponder the notion of effectiveness, perhaps we should first consider our expectations. If we see prayer as a state of being in which we offer ourselves to God, how should we measure its effectiveness? In this context, it seems effective prayer is measured by whether we actually commune with God, whether our spirits and souls are actually transformed, and whether we exhibit fruit of the Holy Spirit. Similarly, if prayer is the avenue through which we receive God's holy grace, effectiveness is determined by whether we connect with His holy grace. But these thoughts limit prayer to the spiritual realm. Is prayer limited to the spiritual realm or should we expect tangible, physical response from prayer?

Jesus shows loving compassion for humble people who genuinely seek Him, and He demonstrates concern for both their physical and spiritual wellbeing. There are no magic words. Genuine pursuit and a humble heart position a person to pray effectively and receive God's blessing, which includes spiritual and physical influence.

Scripture indicates that a number of factors influence the effectiveness of prayer, such as personal characteristics of the person who prays, the desires of the person for whom prayers are offered, and whether God's glory will be revealed through His blessing.

Through prayer we enter into God's holy presence, we receive His grace, we open ourselves to Him, we praise and worship Him, and we offer our thanks. We also ask, tell Him our needs, pour out our hearts to Him, and ask Him to help others. When He acts in response to our petitions we know that He heard, listened and responded to us. We know that He is really present, we know that He really cares, and through affirmation our faith grows. This causes us to seek Him all the more and the cycle continues inward and upward.

QUALITIES RELATING TO THE PERSON WHO PRAYS

People who live in relationship with God pray. Communication leads to and strengthens relationship. Scripture explains this in several different ways. It connects the concepts of abiding in God and allowing Him to abide in us with prayer. Loving God and obeying His commands are connected to effective prayer, as are humility and the pursuit of God. If our relationship with Him is such that we pray according to His will, our prayers will be effective. Similarly, Scripture discusses the desire to know God, the righteousness, faith and belief of the person who prays as significant parts of the formula for healthy prayer.

Humility, Repentance & Seeking God

One recipe for prayer that leads to God's tangible, physical blessing is provided in 2 Chronicles. After constructing the Temple, King Solomon dedicated it to God. Solomon offered 22,000 cattle and 120,000 sheep and goats to God. As He prayed, fire came down from heaven consuming the offerings and sacrifices, and God's glory filled the Temple. The festival lasted 7 days. After everyone went home, God appeared to King Solomon and said:

> "*I have heard your prayer* and have chosen this place for myself as a temple for sacrifices. When I shut up the heavens so that there is no rain, or command locusts to devour the land or send a plague among my people, if my people, who are called by my name, will *humble themselves and pray and seek my face and turn from their wicked ways, then I will hear from heaven,* and I will forgive their sin and will heal their land." 2 Chronicles 7:11-14

In our wildest imagination we cannot begin to comprehend God. God is infinite yet intimate. He is the all-powerful creator of all things yet merciful, compassionate and kind. He created the heavens so large that we measure distances in light years – the distance that light travels in a year – yet He longs for relationship with us. If we imagine His grandeur, His almighty power, His capacity for patience, His discerning mind, His knowledge, our wildest imagination falls short of who He is. How great is our God? He is greater than we can possibly know.

God is sovereign and in control. In the passage above, God explains that at times He allows suffering to encourage repentance, humility and hearts seeking Him. As discussed in the context of Paul and the disciples in the previous chapter, God's blessings may lead to conceit, pride and arrogance, so God may allow troubling situations to encourage humility.

Here, God explains that He desires people who genuinely seek Him, and He provides a prayer recipe. First, the recipe is offered to God's people – people who are called by God's name. Second, His people need to humble themselves. Third, they need to pray. Fourth, they need to seek God. Fifth, they need to repent, which means to stop doing wicked things and to turn from the wicked things they have already done. In response, God will forgive their sin and provide physical blessing upon them.

He desires His followers to live in such a way that other people know they are His. He wants us to be called by His name. He desires that we publicly advertise ourselves as His people. If you follow Jesus Christ, consider for a moment how other people know this about you. What is it that causes other people to call you by His name?

In the passage above, do you see how God draws a distinction between praying and seeking Him? They are two separate statements, indicating it is possible to pray without sincerely seeking Him. This is analogous to talking with someone but not really paying attention to the conversation – talking with your spouse while reading the paper or looking at your cell phone or watching television. Conversation without genuine presence is not really a conversation. In the same way, God instructs us to pray with genuine presence; He instructs us to pray and seek.

The recipe discusses humility and repentance. Both are spiritual qualities revealing themselves through action. God calls us to pray, seek, be humble, repent and to live our lives in such a way that we are known as His people. He also promises to be with humble people. The prophet Isaiah writes,

> For this is what the high and lofty One says – he who lives forever, whose name is holy: "I will live in a high and holy place, but also with him who is contrite and lowly in spirit, to revive the spirit of the lowly and to revive the heart of the contrite." Isaiah 57:15

The Hebrew word translated as contrite is transliterated as dakka. It means crushed into a powder.[3] Figuratively, it combines notions of humility and repentance. God, the high and holy One, the Almighty, the Infinite promises to be with people who are crushed. This is virtually identical to Jesus' promise in the Beatitudes, "Blessed are the poor in spirit, for theirs is the kingdom of heaven" (Matthew 5:3). God promises to deliver His kingdom to the poorest of the poor in spirit, and to be with those who are crushed, humble and repentant. And when people who are with Him pray, He hears and responds.

Abide, Love, Obey & God's Will

The notion of God being with us implies relationship. A collection of passages from both Old and New Testaments directly connect prayer to a person's relationship with God. The concept is cyclical and iterative. Our relationship with God grows through prayer, and prayer becomes more effective as our relationship grows.

But the concept of relationship with God who is unseen and not overly talkative is difficult to grasp, so Scripture uses a variety of images to communicate the thought. In places Scripture discusses abiding in God and allowing God to abide in us. In other places Scripture discusses loving God, obeying God, and living in accordance with His will. Each is a separate way of communicating the concept of intimate relationship with God. By looking at the passages together, the concepts harmonize to create a tapestry rich in meaning. God desires a relationship with us. He wants us to be His loving children.

How do we abide in and love God? How do we show our love to other people? Lori and I recently celebrated our 25th wedding anniversary. We drove to the Florida panhandle and stayed in a little cottage on the beach for a week. It was wonderful to be together with nothing that we needed to be doing – no obligations, no distractions, no schedule – for a full week. We had time to simply linger together and with that time we were able to talk. I heard her wit and humor. We laughed. We discussed nothing and little things and big things. We reconnected in a way that is impossible through our normal passing daily interaction – talking briefly as we get ready in the morning, or as I quickly eat lunch (usually standing at the kitchen counter), or as we go through the motions of evening chores. During our final morning at the beach, as we prepared to leave, packed our bags, loaded the car and ate our omelet at Pickles, I was so sad – not entirely because we were leaving the beautiful, peaceful place, but because we were leaving that time and place where we had the privilege of sharing uninterrupted lingering. While we were leaving a place, my sadness arose because we were leaving our time together.

I rarely remember dreams. A few days after we returned home, I had this frightening yet hauntingly beautiful dream. Lori and I were in the dream. We were about the same age that we are now, but our lives were entirely different. We were in a place that I did not recognize on the outskirts of a large city. Lori worked as a professional in the city. We talked as she drove me to the airport. I was returning home, wherever that was, and I was consumed with an awful empty lonely feeling. As she accelerated the car toward the place that would soon separate us, I struggled to formulate words to express how I felt and I struggled with the fear that if I spoke those words she might reject me and I struggled with the knowledge that if I failed to speak and the opportunity passed I would never forgive myself. I sat a foot or so away from the woman I loved, I wanted to be with her forever, yet we sped towards our separation.

That was when our dog licked my face – Fergie's quiet signal asking me to take her outside. I was instantly transported back to this world, the world where Lori rested next to me and where our dog licked my face and where I was about to make our coffee. I walked outside to the cool crisp air, my mind still in a dreamy fog trying to remember the world I departed in an instant only moments earlier, and I was so happy I was no longer there. I was so happy I could simply tell Lori that I love her and I could thank her for putting up with me for over 25 years. The dream helped me to realize in a new, clear, meaningfully real way how much I long to be with her.

But do I communicate my love to her? I hope I do. I'm not sure that I do. But I hope I communicate my love by telling her, by serving her, by doing the things she wants me to do, by listening to her, by being there for her, by supporting our family, by representing her and our family honorably before other people. I hope I communicate my love to her by acting in a way that makes it clear that I want to be with her, that I want to spend my time with her, that there is no place I would rather be. Undoubtedly I fail at this, but I will keep trying.

How is loving God different? How do we communicate our love to God? It seems that the methods of communicating love to Him are about the same. John writes, "This is love for God: to obey his commands" (1 John 5:3).

Psalm 91 ties loving God and dwelling in God to effective prayer. God promises to command His angels to guard us, and He promises to rescue, protect, deliver and honor people who abide in Him, love Him and call upon Him.

If you make the Most High your dwelling – even the Lord, who is my refuge – then no harm will befall you, no disaster will come near your tent. For he will command his angels concerning you to guard you in all your ways; they will lift you up so that you will not strike your foot against a stone. You will tread upon the lion and the cobra; you will trample the great lion and the serpent.

> "Because he loves me," says the Lord, "I will rescue him; I will protect him, for he acknowledges my name. He will call upon me, and I will answer him; I will be with him in trouble, I will deliver him and honor him. With long life will I satisfy him and show him my salvation." Psalm 91:9-16

Notice the last part: "He will call upon me, and I will answer him; I will be with him in trouble, I will deliver him..." When we pray, God answers and promises to deliver us, but He may allow us to linger in trouble for some period of time. He promises deliverance, but it may not happen when we want it. It will happen on His schedule. He promises to be with us in trouble, not to immediately remove us from trouble. He might choose to leave us in the situation for some time, allowing us to grow and allowing His greater glory to be revealed at the appropriate time.

The recipe is pretty straightforward: if we make our dwelling in the Lord and love Him and call on Him, He will answer. This is similar to the core of the Shema, which Jesus describes as the Greatest Commandment,[4] "Hear, O Israel: The Lord our God, the Lord is one. Love the Lord your God with all your heart and with all your soul and with all your strength"

(Deuteronomy 6:4-5). Loving God and dwelling in God are more than commands; they are two of the keys to effective prayer.

Psalm 91 discusses dwelling in God, which is very similar to Jesus' instruction about remaining or abiding in God. John records a remarkable volume of Jesus' teaching on the evening of the Last Supper filling five chapters of John, chapters 13-17. Chapter 15 begins with Jesus teaching about the vine and branches. Jesus describes God the Father as the gardener who prunes branches. Jesus describes Himself as the vine and His followers as branches that bear fruit so long as they abide in the vine. Jesus describes a symbiotic relationship between Himself and His followers: Jesus bears fruit through followers, who are unable to create fruit without Jesus. Fruit is only created when Jesus and His followers are connected.

At the end of that teaching Jesus says,

> "If you remain in me and my words remain in you, ask whatever you wish, and it will be given you. This is to my Father's glory, that you bear much fruit, showing yourselves to be my disciples." John 15:7-8

A portion of the first sentence, at first glance taken on its own, is wide open: "Ask whatever you wish, and it will be given you." I have heard this quoted to support the belief that God will grant any request that we choose to pray. But the promise is limited by the context of the teaching, the introductory clause of the sentence ("If you remain in me and my words remain in you..."), and the next sentence, which discusses God's glory, His fruit born through His people, and His glory revealed through His disciples. If we abide in God and allow His words to abide in us, our spirits and souls will be influenced, and our requests will also be influenced. Gradually, little by little, as we abide in Him our requests should begin to align with His will and be in pursuit of God's glory.

Psalm 91 discusses dwelling in God. Jesus discusses remaining or abiding in Him. The word translated as "remain" in the NIV version is often translated as "abide," which is a better description of the concept. Abide means to live in a place, to make the place a dwelling, to make a place a home, to nest in and get comfortable. Jesus tells us to abide in Him and to allow His words to abide in us. This means that we must allow Jesus' words to make their home in us, and we must make our home in Jesus. Where is your home? Where is your safe refuge? Where do you relax? Where do you act like yourself, without any pretense, without any concern that you will be judged?

A few years ago, I helped my son move apartments. When we started the process his home was his old apartment, and it was a little difficult to get going. There was a degree of sentimentality involved with packing each box because at that point in the process he was leaving his home, his abode, the place where he abided. We carried load after load out, and at a certain point in the process, the old apartment was no longer his home. At that point the moving process sped tremendously because he was ready to get to his home, the new place. And the final cleanup of the old place was particularly difficult because he was no longer cleaning his home; rather he was, out of obligation, cleaning the place that would soon be another person's home.

As we moved, my son's abode shifted from one apartment to the next. The transition was tied to the location of his belongings. The place that feels like home is the place where his stuff is. What is the spiritual equivalent of this? Jesus calls us to abide in Him. He calls us to make our spiritual home in Him. He calls us to dwell in Him. He also calls us to allow His words to dwell, abide, live, have their home in us.

We should allow His Holy Word to dwell within us. What does this mean? John 1:1 tells us that Jesus is the Word. We also know that Scripture is the word. Either way, the notion involves spiritual transformation revealing itself through action. If Jesus the Word abides in us through the indwelling of the Holy Spirit, our spirits and souls will be transformed. If we allow Scripture to become such a significant part of our being that it dwells within us, we will take ownership of it, we will trust in it, we will believe it to be the Truth, and we will follow it. Jesus says, "If you love me, keep my commands" (John 14:15). This statement embodies the concept of allowing His Holy Word to dwell within us.

In his gospel, John quotes Jesus connecting the thoughts of abiding in Jesus and loving Jesus to answered prayer. In his first epistle, John provides a very similar formula, and he connects the dots of loving Jesus, obeying His commands, and abiding in Him. So abiding in Him, loving Him and obeying His commands are all connected to effective prayer:

> "Dear friends, if our hearts do not condemn us, we have confidence before God and receive from him anything we ask, because we obey his commands and do what pleases him. And this is his command: to believe in the name of his Son, Jesus Christ, and to love one another as he commanded us. Those who obey his commands live in him, and he in them. And this is how we know that he lives in us: We know it by the Spirit he gave us." 1 John 3:22

Obeying Jesus Christ, following His commands, abiding in Him and allowing Him to abide in us are all connected to effective prayer. Abiding is internal. It is spiritual. Obeying and following may involve physical action. Spiritual transformation reveals itself through actions. If we love God, if He abides in us and if we abide in Him, His presence will influence our actions in the real world – He will reveal Himself through us when we love others.

Abiding, loving and obeying Jesus Christ are connected to effective prayer. Two chapters later in the same letter, John provides a slightly different formula: he connects asking according to God's will to effective prayer.

> "This is the confidence we have in approaching God: that *if we ask anything according to his will, he hears us.* And if we know that he hears us – whatever we ask – *we know that we have what we asked of him."* 1 John 5:14-15

Basic math teaches that if two separate things each equal a third thing then they must also equal one another. If a = c, and b = c, then it must follow that a = b. If "a" leads to effective prayer, and "b" leads to effective prayer, does it follow that "a" = "b"? Does obeying His commands equate to living in His will? Not exactly, but they are certainly very similar and related concepts that need to be viewed as part of the tapestry. The concepts of abiding in Jesus, allowing Jesus to abide in us, loving Jesus, obeying His commands and asking in accordance with God's will are related. They are different ways of expressing very similar and related concepts. Abiding in, loving and obeying Jesus Christ equate to harmonizing ourselves, our desires, and our prayers with God's will.

But how can we know God's will? What does it mean to ask according to His will? How do we know we are doing it? Paul wrote that we begin to understand God's will after we allow the Holy Spirit to transform our mind. This takes us back to the notion of abiding in Christ and allowing the Holy Spirit to dwell within us and allowing the spiritual transformation that results.

> "Do not conform any longer to the pattern of this world, but *be transformed by the renewing of your mind.* Then you will be able to test and approve what God's will is – his good, pleasing and perfect will." Romans 12:2

Spiritual transformation results in what Paul refers to as "the renewing of your mind," which enables us to test and approve God's will. The Greek word dokimazein, translated as "to test and approve," is also translated as to analyze, to discern, to prove, and to scrutinize.[5] Spiritual transformation through the Holy Spirit's indwelling enables us to better understand, to discern, to analyze what God's will is. However, while the words may communication images of intellectual knowledge, the knowledge referred to here is deeper and more intimate, it is knowledge held in our hearts, spirits and souls. Prayer connects us with the Holy Spirit. The Holy Spirit transforms our spirits and spiritual transformation allows us to understand God's will.

The transformation is a gradual, iterative and circular process. It happens little by little, day by day, one prayer at a time.

Prayer connects us with the Holy Spirit, who fills and transforms our spirit, which makes us want to pray more, building the connection.

Jesus, Paul, John and the psalmist connect the dots of abiding in God, God abiding in us through the Holy Spirit, loving God, obeying God, praying in God's will and effective prayer. Relationship with God leads to effective prayer, and prayer enhances our relationship with God, making it more likely that we will indeed abide in Him.

Scripture contains certain promises about prayer that hinge on our relationship with God. The quote from 2 Chronicles above begins saying, "if my people, who are called by my name..." The status of being His people who are called by His name suggests relationship. Psalm 91 discusses making "the Most High your dwelling" which suggests intimate relationship. Jesus connects the promise of John 15:7 with abiding in Him and allowing His words to abide in us, which similarly suggests intimate relationship. And the promises quoted from 1 John 3 & 5 depend on praying in a manner consistent with God's will, which requires relationship.

The passages indicate effective prayer depends on our relationship with God, which is enhanced by prayer. Another series of passages tie effective prayer to faith and belief, which are certainly connected to relationship, but the concepts are a little different.

Righteousness

Peter connects God's attention to prayer to the actions, words and righteousness of the person who prays. Jesus tells us that a person's words and actions are reflections of their spirit, meaning a righteous spirit reveals itself through righteous action.

> "Whoever would love life and see good days must keep his tongue from evil and his lips from deceitful speech. He must turn from evil and do good; he must seek peace and pursue it. For the eyes of the Lord are on the righteous and his ears are attentive to their

prayer, but the face of the Lord is against those who do evil." 1 Peter 3 (quoting Psalm 34:12-16)

Peter and the psalmist link our words and actions to the effectiveness of prayer. James provides a similar message. He ties the effectiveness of prayer to the desires and motives of the person praying, saying,

> "What causes fights and quarrels among you? Don't they come from your desires that battle within you? You desire but do not have, so you kill. You covet but do not get what you want, so you quarrel and fight. You do not have because you do not ask God. When you ask, you do not receive, because you ask with the wrong motives, that you may spend what you get on your pleasure." James 4:1-3

When you pray, do you ask exclusively for your own pleasure or for God's glory? Jesus urges us to seek God first and foremost. He also ties our words to the condition of our spirit and soul saying,

> "No good tree bears bad fruit, nor does a bad tree bear good fruit. Each tree is recognized by its own fruit. People do not pick figs from thornbushes, or grapes from briers. A good man brings good things out of the good stored up in his heart, and an evil man brings evil things out of the evil stored up in his heart. For the mouth speaks what the heart is full of." Luke 6:43-45

Our prayer life influences the condition of our spiritual self; the condition of our spirit influences our thoughts, actions and words; and our words and actions influence the effectiveness of prayer. And the condition of our spirit influences our desire to pray. Prayer leads us in the direction of holiness, which creates a desire for more prayer. It all goes together, and the foundation of it all is our relationship with God.

FAITH, BELIEF & AUTHORITY

Early one morning Jesus walks from Bethany to Jerusalem. He is hungry. He sees a fig tree by the road that is full of leaves, but the tree has no fruit. He curses the fig tree and it immediately withers. The disciples are amazed and they ask how Jesus caused the fig tree to wither so quickly. Jesus replies saying,

> "I tell you the truth, if you have faith and do not doubt, not only can you do what was done to the fig tree, but also you can say to this mountain, 'Go throw yourself into the sea,' and it will be done. If you believe, you will receive whatever you ask for in prayer." Matthew 21:21-22

Jesus demonstrates His power and authority over the tree and He tells the disciples that they may also possess that sort of power and authority. To do so, they need to (i) "have faith," (ii) "do not doubt" and (iii) "believe." And if they possess these qualities, they "will receive whatever [they ask] for in prayer."

As written, it is unclear what belief, faith and doubt are directed toward. They may be directed toward the power and authority, as if faith and belief in the existence of God's power and authority alone would unleash miraculous power on our behalf. But if we equate faith and belief with intellectual knowledge, this seems unlikely. Scripture provides examples of demons believing in God – possessing intellectual knowledge of God's power and recognizing Jesus as the Messiah.[6] They know God exists. They do not follow Him, but they believe that He exists and they believe in His power and authority. So faith and belief in God or Jesus, in and of themselves, are not sufficient to enhance prayer if the concepts are equivalent to intellectual knowledge.

In Mark's version of the same event, it is Peter who is surprised by how quickly the fig tree withers. Jesus says,

> "Have faith in God," Jesus answered. "I tell you the truth, if anyone says to this mountain, 'Go, throw yourself into the sea,' and does not doubt in his heart

but believes that what he says will happen, it will be done for him. Therefore I tell you, whatever you ask for in prayer, believe that you have received it, and it will be yours. And when you stand praying, if you hold anything against anyone, forgive him, so that your Father in heaven may forgive you your sins."
Mark 11:22-26

This version is very similar, but here the emphasis is on believing in God's provision. The first sentence commands faith in God. The second sentence focuses on believing that God will respond to prayer by granting the request. The third sentence focuses on believing that you have already received the request at the time the prayer is prayed. Again, faith, belief and lack of doubt are the critical elements. The statement involves belief, but the focus has shifted from belief in God's power and authority to faith in God and belief that He already has or will respond to the prayer.

Jesus explains that loving God and loving other people are the two most important commandments. [7] Here Jesus connects the same concepts to prayer. He begins discussing our relationship with God, and in the last sentence He discusses relationships between people. The effectiveness of our prayers has to do with our earthly and heavenly relationships.

Earlier I said that prayer is simply crying out to God. But in the passages above, Jesus speaks directly to the fig tree and in each version Jesus directs the listener to speak directly to the mountain. He does not say, "ask God to move the mountain." He says, "you can say to this mountain... and it will be done."

This implies a grant of authority from God to the person, and Jesus' words indicate the grant is based on faith and belief. Jesus explains that God the Father has given Him "all authority in heaven and earth" (Matthew 28:18). Jesus sent 72 messengers across the region to preach. After they returned, Jesus explained "I have given you authority to trample on snakes and scorpions and to overcome all the power of the enemy; nothing will harm you" (Luke 10:19). God granted authority to Jesus, and Jesus has the ability to grant authority to people. And Jesus teaches us to pray with authority by speaking directly to mountains and trees.

This is similar to Moses at the Red Sea. At the beginning of the Exodus, the Israelites were leaving Egypt and the Egyptian army gave chase. The Israelites came to the Red Sea, trapped by the approaching army. God told Moses to take his staff in hand and stretch it over the sea. He did as instructed and the water parted. After the Israelites crossed the sea on dry land, God instructed Moses to stretch his hand over the sea. When he did, the sea collapsed on the pursuing army.[8]

God instructed Moses to deal directly with the Red Sea. Moses did not ask God to part the sea; rather God instructed Moses to part the sea through use of temporary authority that God granted him. God has granted authority to certain people at certain times to cause miraculous events by direct communication to a sea and a fig tree. What does this mean for us? Have we been similarly granted authority for certain use?

So if I tell a mountain to move and it fails to happen, does that mean that I lack faith? Or does it merely mean that God wants the mountain where He originally put it? Or does it only work if the person speaks to the particular mountain on the outskirts of Jerusalem that Jesus pointed out as He spoke? Or, like Moses, does it only work when the person acting or speaking does so within the limited confines of authority communicated by God to the person?

The story began with Jesus cursing a fig tree. He saw a fig tree full of leaves. It appeared fruitful, but on closer inspection the tree had no figs. Consider the story in light of Jesus' teaching about the Vine and the Branches in John 15. Jesus is the vine, people who follow Him are the branches, and fruit is produced through the branches so long as they are connected to the vine. People are capable of producing fruit while connected with Jesus, and followers who do not abide in Jesus are like branches that wither, are cut from the vine and disposed in fire. In this teaching, people are capable of producing fruit only while they enjoy a spiritual connection with Jesus Christ. Fruit is the result of abiding in Jesus and allowing Jesus to abide in us.

The fig tree had the outward appearance of fruitfulness, but it did not produce fruit. Jesus changed the appearance of the tree. It did not bear fruit, so it would no longer look like it did. The story is a parable about our spiritual connection with God.

We need to be cautious. We need to make sure we are not like the fig tree, portraying an appearance of fruitfulness while generating bareness. Do we live our lives creating an appearance of holiness when we are really separated from the Holy? Do we try to look as if we have a deeper connection with Jesus than we really have? Do we go to church for an hour on Sunday and live the rest of the week like non-believers? Jesus cursed the barren fig tree, and He taught that branches connected with Him bear fruit and branches that fail to bear fruit will be cut off. So we each must ask ourselves, is Jesus producing His fruit through me?

Jesus cursed the fig tree. One of His friends asked him how He caused the tree to wither. His answer was a statement about prayer, faith, moving mountains, and implied authority from God. Jesus had just caused a real, live, physical fig tree to die by speaking to it. And He told His friends that they could move a mountain by speaking to the mountain if they had faith and did not doubt.

Luke records a similar teaching about faith and moving physical objects. The disciples ask Jesus to increase their faith. Jesus responds saying,

> "If you have faith as small as a mustard seed, you can say to this mulberry tree, 'Be uprooted and planted in the sea,' and it will obey you." Luke 17:6

It certainly seems as if Jesus is talking about moving a real, physical mountain and a real, physical mulberry tree. He says, "this mountain" and "this mulberry tree," as if He is pointing to each as He speaks. But the message may have more to do with spiritual mountains. I am confident that Jesus is not advocating that we attempt to recklessly employ faith and God's grant of authority to change the topographic or botanic landscape. In certain circumstances, the authority may lend itself to physical obstacles, but more often than not, the mulberry tree and the mountain are physical symbols of spiritual matters.

I heard Dr. Jim Dixon of Cherry Hills Community Church in Denver, Colorado preach on these passages. He described a church that was expanding. They bought land and planned to build on it. The back of the lot was a large wooded hill, but they did not need the entire lot so they were not worried about the hill. They hired an architect who prepared plans, sought bids for the construction, obtained capital commitments and bank financing, and built their new church and a parking lot. The city building inspector reviewed the building and refused to grant a certificate of occupancy because the parking lot was too small for the size of the building. They needed additional parking spaces, which meant they suddenly needed to remove the hill to make room for the parking lot expansion, but they had spent all funds available to them. They had a building and bank debt, but they were unable to use the building.

During the Sunday church service, the pastor called a church meeting to be held that evening. He said that he was planning to pray that night for God to move the mountain. He explained that he believed that God led them to the location, that God wanted them to make use of the building for His glory, and that God would move the mountain and provide a parking lot. He invited everyone to attend but said he only wanted people to come if they truly believed God would hear their prayers and act by moving the mountain.

A small group met that night. They prayed all night for God to act.

Monday morning a representative from a local construction company called the church. He asked for the pastor. He asked the pastor if they owned the lot with the new building on it and the pastor acknowledged that the church owned it. The representative went on to explain that they had performed studies of soil characteristics in the area, and they needed soil with a specific chemical makeup to provide certain compaction qualities. The hill on the lot was exactly what they needed. He asked if the company might be able to buy the soil from the church. The company bought the soil, removed the soil, and left a flat place where the hill once was. The church used the proceeds from the soil sale to pay for the parking lot expansion.

I believe the story because Dr. Dixon would not have preached using a fabricated story. I believe that events like that can certainly happen because God is capable of doing anything and everything that He wants to do. But I believe, more often than not, the mountains are spiritual.

The spiritual focus of the passage from Mark above is supported by the last two sentences. "Therefore I tell you, whatever you ask for in prayer, believe that you have received it, and it will be yours." If we believe we have already received it yet we still ask, it must be something that is not physically obvious. The last sentence continues the spiritual focus by discussing forgiveness.

The message involves authority and spiritual wholeness. Who would God entrust with a grant of His authority? It seems rationale to believe God grants authority to people with whom He has a relationship.

While I practiced law I worked with many clients on matters relating to transfer of authority. As part of estate planning it is common to draft powers of attorney providing a grant of authority in the event a person is incapacitated. The documents allow another person to represent you, to stand in your place if certain events arise for so long as the problem continues. So the client must ponder, if I am in a coma, who do I trust enough to take care of my affairs? Who do I trust with my bank accounts? Who do I trust to pay my bills? Who do I trust to work with the doctors to plan my health care decisions? Who do you trust with grants of authority like that?

That level of trust is earned gradually over a long-term relationship because the person granting authority must be confident that the authority will be used consistent with his or her will. The grantor must know that the person acting on his behalf will act in accordance with his desire, or at least with his best interest in mind, and not out of self-interest or in pursuit of selfish pleasure. That level of trust is not gained quickly. I imagine God's grant of authority requires a strong relationship also.

Faith and belief involve relationship with God. They are connected to effective prayer and authority from God.

The act of praying is simply crying out to God. Anyone can pray and everyone should pray. Prayer does not involve magic words or require unique physical positioning. However, Scripture associates effective prayer to certain qualities possessed by the person who prays and, as a general statement, people who have a strong relationship with God are more likely to pray effective prayers. The word "relationship" is mine. Scripture discusses humility, repentance, seeking God, abiding in God, loving God and obeying God. It discusses righteousness, faith, belief and authority.

Scripture suggests that effective prayer depends on these qualities and experience confirms that the existence of these qualities depends on prayer. They go together in a giant iterative, cyclical circle. Prayer is ever transforming and prayer continuously propels people who pray toward God.

QUALITIES RELATING TO PERSONS PRAYED FOR

People who are the subject of prayer have free will and make choices influencing the effectiveness of prayers prayed on their behalf. I pray for my children. I ask God to protect them, to send His angels to watch over them, to place a hedgerow around them hindering the influence of bad things. I ask God to take away any satisfaction they might experience from bad choices and to encourage them to seek Him. As I pray for all this, I know God hears my prayers and I know He has all authority and power to do exactly as I ask and much, much more. And God acts, but He also grants human will. If my children try over and over to break through the hedgerow, they will break free. If one of them continuously seeks places and situations where bad things happen, God will allow his or her choices to result in negative consequences. Choices made by the people we pray for influence the effectiveness of our prayers.

A man in his twenties visited our prayer service recently. As we discussed prayer concerns and prayed, it became evident that he desired prayer over his life. He was in the midst of significant change – he recently relocated to our town, moved into a house, was looking for a job and seeking healthy relationships, all while battling addiction. So we gathered around him, placed hands on him and prayed. After a long time filled with lots and lots of prayer, one of the prayer warriors began praying in a heavenly language and then he said, "God's armor is protecting you from the top of your head to the soles of your feet. He is protecting you and only you can remove that protection."

This was God speaking directly to the young man through the prayer warrior. God reminded the young man, and each of us, that He is with us and He is protecting us, but our choices matter. We have free will. If we seek Him He will respond, but He will not force His protection upon us. If we so choose, we can remove His protection from our lives.

Jesus says,

> "Those whom I love I rebuke and discipline. So be earnest, and repent. Here I am! I stand at the door and knock. If anyone hears my voice and opens the door, I will come in and eat with him, and he with me." Revelation 3:19-20

Jesus knocks but each person must open the door. God's holy grace rains down upon everyone but we must accept the gift and open it. Each person must make his or her own choice.

As mentioned in the previous chapter, Jesus taught in His hometown synagogue, and those who heard Him were amazed by His teaching and wisdom. They were amazed by the miracles He performed, yet they wondered how He gained the ability that He demonstrated. They remembered Him as Joseph's son and they knew His family. In response to all the information they possessed about Him – the evidence of God's glory revealed through His teaching and miracles, combined with their knowledge of His family and His past – Scripture tells us:

And they took offense at Him.

Jesus said to them, "A prophet is not without honor except in his own town, among his relatives and in his own home." He could not do any miracles there, except lay his hands on a few sick people and heal them. He was amazed at their lack of faith. Mark 6:3-6

Jesus performed some miracles in Nazareth, but not as many as He desired, and He was amazed by their lack of faith. The section above discusses the connection between faith of the person who prays and the effectiveness of prayer. Here, Jesus' miracles are connected to the faith of the people He desired to heal. I imagine if the people were asked, "Do you want to receive God's holy healing grace?" their answer would have been, "Yes." I believe they desired God's grace (who wouldn't?), but they doubted the authority of the messenger. They lacked faith in Jesus Christ because they knew too much about His family and His past, and their diminished faith blocked miracles.

In a similar way, the desires of the people for whom others pray influence the effectiveness of our prayers. Each person has a choice.[9] God is not going to answer a prayer if the result would be contrary to the recipient's desires. We each have freedom; we each have our will; and we each make our own choice.

Freddie and Joe

I mentioned Freddie and her son in chapter 1. Freddie is a prayer warrior. She seeks God. She desires intimate relationship with God, her life is bathed in prayer, and when she prays God responds. Freddie was a child with dark skin growing up in Alabama during the 1950s and 1960s. She experienced the ugliness of racism and many of the horrors that people are capable of bestowing upon one another. About ten years ago she was living comfortably with her husband, Joe,[7] in a Washington, DC suburb. One morning as she sipped coffee on her patio, she heard God call her move to Tuscaloosa, Alabama to start a radio ministry. She knew nothing about broadcasting. She was not a minister. She had no desire to move back to Alabama. Yet, they obediently followed, trusting that God would provide funding for the ministry and that He would work out all the details.

While furniture shopping for their new home they met Nola working in a furniture store. After they left the store, Nola felt strongly compelled to invite them to church. So she ran out of the store, chased them through the parking lot and invited them to church. Nola extended the invitation, Freddie accepted, and then asked which church. She then learned that it was a large church in downtown Tuscaloosa. As a child Freddie had walked on the sidewalk in front of that particular church, only to have white male ushers scold her for walking on their side of the street. The ushers did not want people with her skin color walking on "their" sidewalk, much less sitting next to them in the pews. She could not imagine being welcomed into that church, but she had already accepted the invitation, so they went.

Freddie and Joe are now leaders at the church. Freddie is involved in every prayer ministry available and in many mission outreach efforts, in addition to managing her weekly radio ministry. Joe is involved in prison-focused ministries and prayer ministry. They pray all the time. When people in church desire prayer, they call on Freddie and Joe to pray for them because they have been specially anointed as people of prayer.

Freddie's adult son experienced a number of health issues and ultimately fell into a coma. She prayed over her son begging God to heal him. She prayed for total, complete physical and spiritual healing. During the entire time her son lay in the hospital, she prayed. She knew that God has the power to heal. She knew that God loves her son. She knew that God heard her prayers, but her son never recovered. He did not awake from the coma. He died.

---

[7] I mentioned another story about Joe in Chapter 9.

She was traumatized. Why did God not answer her prayers? She believed. She trusted in God's sovereignty, His power, His authority, and His love. She did not doubt. She believed He would answer her prayers, and she prayed the answered prayer would reveal God's glory. But her son died.

As she grieved and questioned God, a young man visited her. He had been in a coma in the same hospital at the same time as her son. After the young man recovered, he felt compelled to see Freddie and explain that while he was in the coma he had a choice. He could return to earth or move on to heaven. The young man wanted to continue living on earth. He told Freddie his experience suggesting that her son may have been given a similar choice.

Of course we do not know what happened. There are so many unanswered questions, but the young man's story provided comfort to her as she grieved.

Do recipients of prayer have a choice? Paul explains that each person has a choice, and that God will judge people based on the choice each person makes, writing:

> God will "repay each person according to what they have done." To those who by persistence in doing good seek glory, honor and immortality, he will give eternal life. But for those who are self-seeking and who reject the truth and follow evil, there will be wrath and anger. Romans 2:6-8

John also suggests that each person has a choice. He instructs us to pray for other people, but that some people will continue living in such a way as to render the prayers ineffective.

> If you see any brother or sister commit a sin that does not lead to death, you should pray and God will give them life. I refer to those whose sin does not lead to death. There is a sin that leads to death. I am not saying that you should pray about that. All wrongdoing is sin, and there is a sin that does not lead to death. 1 John 5:16-17

As we recognize that every person has a choice, we should continue to pray for everyone. John wrote, "I am not saying that you should pray about that." He does not instruct us to refrain from praying, rather he not commanding us to pray for certain people. But we do not know who such a person is. How can we possibly know who will make certain choices? So we continue praying for other people and we continue serving them as we acknowledge their choices and their personal will matter.

I recall hearing a story. I do not know where I heard it. I may have been driving and listening to the radio. I may have read it. I am not sure. But I recall a man discussing how he left home as a teenager to enter the country and western music industry. He joined a band, traveled around the United States performing in bars and other venues, and lived the rock and roll lifestyle. He was raised in a Southern Christian home and he knew that his mother prayed for him every day.

He rarely went home. When he did, his mother asked him to go to church with her. Each time he refused, until one particular time. For some reason he agreed to go with her. During the service she approached the chancel rail, she knelt and prayed, then returned to her seat next to her son. After the service as they walked out he noticed wet drops on the railing where she prayed. He knew she had been crying while she prayed, and he believed the tears were for him. He said the teardrops moved him deeply. They did not encourage him to immediately make different choices, but gradually over the years he made different choices and he always knew that his mother was praying for him.

While we know that the will, choices and faith of the people for whom we pray are part of the equation regarding the effectiveness of our prayers, we continue praying for them. We ask God to continue to pound on their hearts so they will become fertile soil for His holy seed, and we ask for God's protection over them while the process continues. God's holy grace is showering over all of us continuously, like rain falling on everyone. We never know when a person will stop, receive the free gift of God's grace, open the gift and choose a new and refreshed life through relationship with Him.

QUALITIES RELATING TO THE SITUATION - GOD'S GLORY

God intervenes in our world to reveal His glory to people. He routinely works through ordinary, natural channels. He also intervenes in miraculous ways where, maybe just for an instant, He suspends or alters the laws of nature. When we pray and experience God's answer, we know that He heard us, listened to us, reached into our world, and acted in response to our request. When He reaches into our world and acts, He does so to reveal His glory to everyone who has eyes to see and ears to hear, and our experience of His glory strengthens our faith. Experiencing His glory gives confidence that He will continue to be with us in the future.

When was the last time you experienced God's glory?

God's Glory Revealed through Ordinary Events

If we look for it, we will see that He routinely reveals His glory through ordinary events as well as miraculous ones. The psalmist writes, "The heavens declare the glory of God; the skies proclaim the work of his hands" (Psalm 19:1).

Last night I saw the most amazing sunset. As the Sun neared the horizon, two large clouds hovered high in the sky. The lower one was a blended spectrum of lavender, from dark shades to light hues. The cloud above it revealed bright pink, peach, orange, yellow, cream and blends of them all that I cannot describe. Its western edge highlighted whisps of bright yellowy white. As I watched, the higher cloud moved slightly to the east revealing an incredible crescent moon. I turned to look at the to the darkened eastern sky and saw a cloud illuminated like a strobe light by distant lightning strikes. I stood in the yard taking it all in. God brought His art gallery to me.

God is the creator and He acts through His creation. Where do you see His holy hand at work?

As we read Exodus, we understand that the former slaves saw God's hand at work in their daily lives. They saw God's provision as they collected manna, captured quail, carried water and cooked their meals.[10] They saw God's provision for them throughout each day, even though they had to work to obtain the gifts. Is the food you eat today, the air you currently breathe, the water you drink a gift from God? Is your occupation a gift from God providing not only daily sustenance, but also opportunities to serve Him?

I have been reading a fascinating book on the history of the Old Testament. The authors provided a scientific explanation for manna, saying that certain desert insects eat tamarisk twigs and excrete a sticky substance that accumulates overnight.[11] I am not sure whether the explanation is scientifically accurate, but assuming it is, does it influence your thinking?

Does the scientific explanation cause you to see God's fingerprints more clearly on the gift of manna, does it cause you to wonder whether God really provided the manna, or does it have no influence on your view? For some, science enhances their view of God's hand at work. They see His holy fingerprints in the precision of order, and the intricacy of design and function. Others desire to see God purely through miraculous, supernatural events defying scientific explanation and expectation. Of course, some fail to see God at all.

Do you see God's hand at work? If so, do you see Him in ordinary events following the natural order of things, in the miraculous where the laws of nature are suspended, or both? I know the beautiful colors in the clouds are the result of suspended water vapor creating shadows and reflecting and refracting light from the Sun. I also know the vapor, the sunlight, and the interaction between them are part of God's creation, and I see God's holy hand at work through the glorious scene in the sky.

God is the creator and He acts through His creation. He acts through you and me, and He paints with water vapor and sunlight in the sky. The former slaves of the Exodus saw God's hand in their daily life because they had eyes to see Him and His work. Where do you see evidence of His presence? May you have eyes to see God's hand at work in the world around you, and when you do, praise God!

GOD'S GLORY REVEALED IN RESPONSE TO PRAYER

God also intervenes in miraculous ways. Miracles are a component of God's marketing plan. They advertise, point to and reveal God's glory in ways that we lowly humans are able to comprehend, and this is important beyond my ability to explain. Our spiritual health is eternal. Witnessing God's glory as it is revealed helps people move along the path toward God.

Some fail to see God's glory in ordinary events. Similarly, not everyone sees God's glory through miracles. Each person sees the world around her or him through a unique lens. If a dozen people witness an automobile accident, investigators will hear a dozen different accounts of the event. We each see events differently, interpret the events in our own way and remember the events through our individually unique system. In the same way, each person sees, remembers, analyzes and interprets miraculous events in his or her own unique way. Some will see God's hand at work while many will simply see strange or interesting events with natural explanations – they will see nothing miraculous.

Imagine that a close friend encounters a life-threatening illness. She goes to the hospital and her friends learn of her illness. Her friends ask everyone to pray for her. Lots of people pray for healing. They pray for the doctors and nurses. They pray for the medicine to help and cause no harm. They pray and pray and pray, and after a few weeks your friend leaves the hospital healed. She returns home, goes back to work, and resumes life.

Events like this play out many times each day in hospitals around the world. Who or what healed your friend? Was it the doctors, nurses, medicine and the wonders of medical science? Was it God intervening in our world in a miraculous way? Was it God using the doctors, nurses and medicine as His instruments of healing, and intervening as necessary to achieve the desired result?

As mentioned with a few examples in the previous chapter, I am familiar with situations where people have been healed and doctors are unable to provide a natural explanation for the healing. In these situations when most people hear the facts they either (i) do not believe that the facts are true, (ii) are amazed and happily surprised that the medicine and doctors caused some wonderfully unexpected result, or (iii) believe God intervened in a miraculous way.

Much more routinely, people are healed through events that occur as predicted by medical science. In these situations, I believe God intervened using doctors, nurses and medicine to achieve His desired outcome because God commonly reveals His glory through His creation. If we fail to see God's hand at work, we fail to recognize the power of prayer and we miss the point of God's decision to act in response to our requests. We miss the revelation of God's glory. We miss the opportunity to grow in faith as a result of this encounter with the Divine.

When God reaches into our world and acts, the ripple effect of that intervention should touch many more lives than just the person healed. It should impact every other person who experienced God's grace directly through the event and every person who subsequently heard about the miraculous intervention. This is part of the reason we need to pray for one another, and part of the reason we need to gather together as a community in prayer. When we involve others and when we pray together, the ripple effect is enhanced – God's glory will be revealed to more people than if we kept our needs to ourselves.

When little Kennedy was miraculously healed, the entire chain of events was bathed in prayer. The instant his lifeless body was pulled from the pool, people started praying and they continued praying long after he was healed. They prayed, God responded and His glory was revealed. Had no one prayed, yet Kennedy was healed, would the events reveal God's glory? God's glory would have been on display, but few if any would have noticed. Prayer gives us eyes to see.

GOD'S GLORY REVEALED – REQUESTING OTHERS TO PRAY

Lori's immediate reaction to her sarcoma diagnosis was a desire to be left alone. She really did not want to talk about it with anyone. After the news sank in, she still did not want to talk about it because she did not want to burden people with the information. She did not want people to feel the need to react to it. She avoids being the center of attention, and she did not want her diagnosis to glare a spotlight on her. She wanted to tell family and her closest friends, but no one else.

We talked and prayed about it and through Scripture God revealed the importance of community prayer in His mighty work. If more people prayed, more people would experience God's glory as He responded. If, by reaching out and touching our world, God desires to reveal His glory as widely as possible, we reasoned that we should spread the prayer request as widely as possible. So we asked everyone to pray. We put her name on the church prayer list and we asked other people to put her name on their church prayer lists. We asked everyone we could think of to pray for her. She received cards from people across the United States who prayed for her. And as God responded to the prayers, we spread the word of God's glory widely. He responded in so many ways and it is our prayer that many came to see God in a new and refreshed way, that their eyes saw His glory as He responded to their prayers.

One of the passages that spoke to us was the account of Jesus raising Lazarus from the tomb. God orchestrated the events to widely reveal His glory. When Jesus was around Jerusalem He often stayed with His friends Martha, Mary and Lazarus in their home in Bethany a few miles south of Jerusalem. They were close friends.

While Jesus was preaching, teaching and healing in the region where John the Baptist preached, north of the Dead Sea and east of the Jordan River (we do not know exactly where He was, but it was at least 20 miles from Bethany), Lazarus became sick. Martha and Mary sent Jesus a message telling Him that Lazarus was sick. As soon as Jesus heard the news He said, "This sickness will not end in death. No, it is for God's glory so that God's Son may be glorified through it" (John 11:4).

Two days later He told the disciples "Lazarus is dead, and for your sake I am glad I was not there, so that you may believe. But let us go to him" (John 11:14-15). So Jesus waited two days before starting His long walk to Bethany to attend to His good friend. Why did He wait? So God's glory might be revealed.

When Jesus arrived, Lazarus had been in the tomb four days. Many mourners were in Bethany from Jerusalem and places across the region. Jesus went to the tomb, which was sealed with a stone. Jesus asked people to open the tomb by moving the stone. Martha asked whether Jesus was sure He wanted to move the stone because the smell would be bad.

> Then Jesus said, "Did I not tell you that if you believe, you will see the glory of God?"
>
> So they took away the stone. Then Jesus looked up and said, "Father, I thank you that you have heard me. I knew that you always hear me, but I said this for the benefit of the people standing here, *that they may believe that you sent me.*" John 11:40-42

Then Jesus called to Lazarus and Lazarus walked out of the tomb. He was still wrapped with strips of linen and still had the burial cloth around his head.[12]

Jesus explained that the miracle occurred so that God's glory might be revealed and people might believe. God reached into our world and intervened in a tangible way with the stated purpose of revealing His glory. People who saw the event and attributed it to God experienced God's glory and their belief was strengthened and their faith was enhanced.

With this in mind, why did Jesus wait? Had God healed Lazarus immediately after he started feeling sick, it would have been great for Lazarus and his sisters and everyone else who mourned his death, but the amount of glory it revealed would have been muted. Had God healed Lazarus immediately after he died, people might have said that he wasn't really dead and a good sleep healed him. But by waiting until he had been in the tomb four days, there was no explanation available other than God's mighty hand acting in response to Jesus' prayer.

We may not understand God's timing. When we ask God to help, it may seem like He is ignoring our request when in fact He is waiting for the perfect time to act.

As discussed in the previous chapter, we must be careful not to underestimate God's power. Martha and Mary had faith. They were confident that Jesus could heal Lazarus, and they were confident that Jesus would have healed him had Jesus been in Bethany before Lazarus died. When Jesus entered town they met Him on the road separately and they each said, "if you had been here, my brother would not have died" (John 11:21 and 11:32). They had faith, but their faith was too limited. They thought Jesus had to be physically present to heal their brother, and they did not imagine that Jesus could or would return Lazarus to life. They believed, but their vision of Jesus and their understanding of His power were too small.

Look at Jesus' prayer. He prayed for the benefit of people hearing the prayer, which included many mourners from across the region. He wanted them to know with certainty that the miracle was God's, and that God sent Jesus. He prayed so the listeners would not be confused on those points. The entire episode was orchestrated to reveal God's glory to lots of people who would then travel back to their homes and tell the story. Through the telling and re-telling, God's glory rippled across the land and His glory continues to be revealed as we study Scripture describing the event.

GOD'S GLORY REVEALED THROUGH MIRACLES

Jesus said, "…if you believe you will see the glory of God" (John 11:40). Jesus prayed to God out loud to help people believe that God sent Jesus, but not everyone believed. Some people saw the stone being moved, heard Jesus pray, and saw Lazarus emerge from the tomb wearing burial linens, but they still did not believe that God sent Jesus. They saw the events and heard the words, but they did not see the glory of God. They missed the point. Jesus said that the whole event – His delay responding, the four days in the tomb, all of it – was so people could see God's glory and so Jesus would be glorified.[13] And some missed it. God's glory is revealed to people who believe.

Martha and Mary prayed to Jesus. They asked for His help. They knew He could help and they believed He would, but His timing and His unlimited power surprised them. Ultimately, God answered their prayer in a manner that revealed His glory to the maximum extent possible. God's response to prayer has to do with Him revealing His glory.

Why does God answer some prayers by causing the requested outcome to occur, but not others? Part of the analysis has to do with the spiritual condition of the person praying, but the Winders' experience and Paul's letters indicate that there is more to the analysis than that. Part of the analysis has to do with the desire of the person for whom we pray. It also has to do with God's larger plan, which we may see bits and pieces of but we will never be able to fully comprehend. When we pray for God to reach into our world and influence events, we are praying for a miracle.

In the account of Lazarus, Jesus said the miracle was for the revelation of God's glory and for the furtherance of God's glory. Other Scriptural accounts of Jesus' miracles revealed God's glory also. Each miracle served a purpose greater than the miracle itself. They revealed God's presence, power, action and love in the world. They revealed God's glory to the witnesses that day and to everyone who has heard and read the stories since.

When Jesus fed over 5,000 people with five loaves and two fish, people were amazed and some of them believed Jesus was the Messiah as a result of the miracle.[14] When Jesus and the disciples were on a boat during a storm and the storm stopped in response to Jesus' command, the witnesses were amazed at His authority and power. They believed that God's glory functioned through Jesus.[15] When Jesus encountered a demon-possessed man, He sent the Legion of demons into a herd of pigs and the pigs drowned. Everyone who heard the story was afraid of Jesus and they told Him to leave the region.[16]   When Jesus healed Jairus' daughter,[17] the sick woman,[18] the paralyzed man,[19] the leper,[20] Peter's mother-in-law,[21] and performed the other miracles recorded in Scripture, some witnesses to the events saw God's glory through Jesus and they believed in Jesus more than they did before the events.

Miracles reveal God's glory. They point to God and serve to increase the faith of some people who witness or later hear about the miracle. As Jesus said before raising Lazarus, miracles are for God's glory and to glorify Jesus through them.

When we pray for God to intervene in the world, we are praying for a miracle. Miracles are for God's glory. Perhaps some prayers are answered "no" because "yes" would not serve God's glory or because "yes" would not otherwise fit within God's greater plan or because the person for whom we intercede has desires contrary to our prayer. The person praying may have solid faith, they may not doubt, they may be righteous, they may dwell in close relationship with God, and they may satisfy every other possible obstacle to effective prayer, yet the prayer is answered "no" for other reasons.

CONCLUSION

God desires relationship with us. He is the good Father and we are His children. He wants us to know Him intimately; He wants us to dwell in Him, to know His love and as a result of the spiritual transformation that this causes, He wants to reveal His glory through us. He wants fruit to be born through us. Prayer enhances our relationship with God and assists in the spiritual transformation that we need. Prayer is essential if we desire to grow towards the Holy, Divine and Pure.

God makes a lot of promises about prayer in Scripture. As we view Scripture through the lens asking about effective prayer, several general principles emerge. We see that an association exists between effective prayer and the relationship shared between the person who prays and God; we see that people for whom we pray have free will and choices influencing the effectiveness of prayer; and we notice an association between effective prayer and the revelation of God's glory.

May God's Holy Spirit transform you, may God's glory be revealed through you, and may you introduce the joy, peace, love and power of Jesus Christ to world around you.

13 | How Should We Pray?

"Day and night they never stop saying, 'Holy, holy, holy is the Lord God Almighty, who was, and is, and is to come.'" Revelation 4:8

Prayer connects us with God. Prayer plugs us into the energy, life and love of the Holy Spirit. God loves us and like the perfect Father that He is, and He hears, listens to and answers prayer, but how should we pray? How should we approach the infinite, almighty, holy God?

I have met many people who claim to struggle with prayer. They wonder whether they are doing it the right way, whether they are placing their body in the correct position, whether they are saying the right words. Some ask whether certain requests are offensive to God. Others wonder whether they are worthy of approaching God. Prayer is simply calling on the name of the Lord or crying out to God, and because the benefits of prayer on our lives are so wonderfully transformative, I am convinced that this is one of the Deceiver's great tricks. He convinces us that prayer is difficult and that we are doing it improperly to keep us from praying.

JESUS PROVIDES A PRAYER STRUCTURE

So how should we "call on the name of the Lord"? The men who spent the most time with Jesus during His ministry asked Jesus a similar question. Jesus responded with what is now known as the Lord's Prayer.

> He said to them, "When you pray, say: "'Father, hallowed be your name, your kingdom come. Give us each day our daily bread. Forgive us our sins, for we also forgive everyone who sins against us. And lead us not into temptation.'" Luke 11:1-4

The importance of the first word of the prayer template cannot be exaggerated. Jesus instructs us to refer to our Lord, God as "Father." This is revolutionary. Who are we? What right do we have to approach God, the Almighty, the Creator of all things, the Holy, the Divine, and after we have approached Him, by what right do we call Him by such a familiar name? This is an audacious concept. But Jesus instructs us to do so, and by this, Jesus encourages us to engage in the type of relationship with God worthy of the title, "Father."

Who has the right to use the word "Father"? His children have the right. If we call God "Father," we must first be His children. Who are God's children? Scripture tells us that followers of Jesus Christ who are led by the Holy Spirit are children of God,[1] and Jesus explains who His siblings are saying, "whoever does the will of my Father in heaven is my brother and sister and mother" (Matthew 12:49). By calling God by the name "Father," we proclaim that we are His children and by doing so we proclaim that Jesus Christ is our Lord and Savior and that we are his brothers and sisters. We claim relationship with Him.

While the first line includes significant claims on our part and is audacious in its familiarity, the second line reminds us of the awe and reverence we need to maintain for the One we are approaching: "hallowed be your name." The first line urges us toward thoughts of familiar, possibly even friendly images. The second brings us back to the reality that God is the Almighty,

Holy and Divine. We must never forget that we are nothing compared to Him, and but for His holy grace, we would not be worthy to approach him.

I have heard that ancient people in the Jewish faith hallowed God's name by not speaking it. When they spoke about God they used circumlocutions. When writing they used four Hebrew characters (the Tetragrammaton is transliterated as YHWH) to refer to God the sovereign Creator. According to legend, as scriveners copied Scripture onto scrolls they stopped when encountering YHWH. Before writing the letters, they bathed, changed clothing, obtained a new writing instrument and then proceeded. The letters were sacred and the act of writing the letters was sacred. In most English versions, YHWH is translated as "LORD," using small caps. While they wrote it carefully, taking strict precautions to maintain its sacredness, they did not speak YHWH. Instead, they spoke other Hebrew words when referring to God, such as Adonai and Elohim. They did not speak His name because His name was considered too holy for them to utter. "Hallowed be your name" reveals shadows of the concept to us.

As I understand it, Jesus was not telling us to avoid speaking God's name. He was instructing us to treat His name and everything that His name represents with sacred respect and reverence. The first two lines of the Lord's Prayer create a wonderful balance between our relationship with God as the loving Father and our relationship with God filled with reverence and awe. We call Him "Father," and we hallow His holy name.

"Hallowed be your name" also reminds us that if we want to identify with His holy name, we must live lives worthy of that identity. If we call ourselves followers of Christ, children of God, God's people, Christians or some similar label, yet carry on our lives in a manner unbefitting of that designation, how can we pray the words? And if we pray the words while living in open rebellion to God, how can we expect God to answer our prayer? This line forces us to realize that our character matters, that our actions matter, that how we live our lives matters, that those qualities affect and reveal our relationship with God, and that it all influences our prayer life.

In the third line Jesus instructs us to pray, "your kingdom come." Some people pray asking God to transport them from earth to heaven where His holy presence resides, focusing on the afterlife, but that is the opposite of Jesus' instruction. Jesus says to pray asking God to send His kingdom here. God's kingdom is the place where He reigns and where His glory is revealed. With this in mind, the prayer is for God's glory to be revealed here on earth.

As discussed previously, Scripture records Jesus teaching a great deal about God's kingdom. He tells us to seek first God's kingdom.[2] In the Beatitudes Jesus explains that God's kingdom belongs to people who are poor in spirit: humility, brokenness and loss of arrogance position us to receive God's special blessing described as God's kingdom.[3] Jesus also taught that we play a role in God's plan of bringing His kingdom to earth. Through His teaching about the vine and branches,[4] Jesus taught that He bears fruit through His followers, meaning we have responsibility. So praying "your kingdom come" is not exclusively a prayer asking God to act, it is a prayer reflecting our desire for personal transformation, our commitment to act in response to the transformation, and our recognition that it is all for God's glory.

When we ask God to "give us each day our daily bread" we acknowledge His provision for us, we trust and believe that He is concerned about our physical wellbeing, and we remember that the physical things sustaining us – our food, shelter, possessions and health – are truly gifts from Him. By asking for "daily bread" we must repeat this recognition, trust and belief each day.

Jesus then instructs us to pray about sin, forgiveness and temptation. The prayer forces us to acknowledge that we are sinful, that we have sin in our lives, and if we truly seek forgiveness, we must first identify what is separating us from God and remove the obstacle, whatever it may be. As we seek forgiveness from God, we acknowledge that we must forgive others. As we ponder sin in our lives and our need for forgiveness, we are forced to recognize that sin impacts our relationship with God and our relationships with other people.

And then there is temptation. As we ask God to steer us away from temptation we acknowledge that certain situations, things or people tempt us. There are things we should not do, places we should not go, people we should not associate with, things we do not need, and other temptations around us. As we acknowledge that God desires a fatherly relationship with us, as we hallow His name, pray for His kingdom to come and seek His daily sustenance, we must also recognize the sin-filled world in which we live. As we strive to grow closer to God, we must remember that growing closer to Him involves growing away from many worldly influences that separate us from Him. While the prayer is a request for God to lead us in a certain direction, it implies responsibility on our part. We must follow His guidance.

The Lord's Prayer reveals that prayer involves personal reflection, praising and worshiping God, acknowledging our needs, reflecting on God's provision, reflecting on our relationship with God and other people, and dealing with temptation and sin. Jesus jammed quite a bit into a six-line prayer.

So how do we pray? Praying the Lord's Prayer is terrific. Another possible approach is to make the Lord's Prayer your own by incorporating the concepts of the template into your own personalized prayer. But remember, prayer is simply calling on the name of the Lord. There are no magic words; it involves speaking the condition of your heart.

JESUS TEACHES TO PRAY PERSISTENTLY

Immediately after providing the prayer template, Jesus continues teaching about prayer. Scripture continues saying:

> Then Jesus said to them, "Suppose you have a friend, and you go to him at midnight and say, 'Friend, lend me three loaves of bread; a friend of mine on a journey has come to me, and I have no food to offer him.'

And suppose the one inside answers, 'Don't bother me. The door is already locked, and my children and I are in bed. I can't get up and give you anything.' I tell you, even though he will not get up and give you the bread because of friendship, yet because of your *shameless audacity* he will surely get up and give you as much as you need. Luke 11:5-8

In the parable Jesus says, "because of your shameless audacity he will surely get up and give you as much as you need." While teaching about prayer, He uses the words "shameless audacity." So how do we pray? We pray with persistence and shameless audacity.

Jesus teaches us to pray boldly and persistently, and Scripture records Jesus repeating the same words in prayer three times,[5] yet He also warns against praying by mindlessly repeating empty words. Jesus said, "And when you pray, do not keep babbling like pagans, for they think they will be heard because of their many words" (Matthew 6:7). So we should pray with audacious persistence and it is fine to repeat the same prayer using the same words, but Jesus cautions us not to "keep babbling like pagans." This has to do with the condition of our hearts and the sincerity of prayer. Repeating empty words for the sake of speaking is of no value. We should honestly unveil our hearts to God when we cry out to him. Bold, persistent repetition of genuine need is appropriate and good.

In the next breath, Jesus tells us to keep knocking and to keep seeking.

JESUS TEACHES TO ASK, SEEK & KNOCK

"So I say to you: Ask and it will be given to you; seek and you will find; knock and the door will be opened to you. For everyone who asks receives; the one who seeks finds; and to the one who knocks, the door will be opened.

"Which of you fathers, if your son asks for a fish, will give him a snake instead? Or if he asks for an egg, will give him a scorpion? If you then, though you are evil, know how to give good gifts to your children, how much more will your Father in heaven give the Holy Spirit to those who ask him!" Luke 11:9-13

Jesus commands us to ask, seek and knock, and then states a promise, "Ask and it will be given to you... For everyone who asks receives..." The first paragraph above includes no condition, it is a command combined with a promise. A person who asks receives, a person who seeks finds, and the door opens for a person who knocks. But the object is not discussed. The passage does not say that we will receive exactly what we request. It says we will receive, but it does not say what we will receive. Jesus commands us to ask, seek and knock, and He promises to respond.

Recall our discussion about 2 Chronicles in the previous chapter. God promises, "if my people, who are called by my name, will humble themselves and pray and seek my face and turn from their wicked ways, then I will hear from heaven..." (2 Chronicles 7:14). His promise is tied to humbly praying and seeking. Jesus commands us to pray and seek and knock. Praying and seeking God go together. As we should expect, the promises running through Scripture fit perfectly together.

Through this connection, the directive to ask and seek and knock seems to refer to God and spiritual things. The second paragraph in Luke's quote of Jesus above discusses the object of the command to ask, seek and knock. Jesus compares physical objects requested from human fathers to spiritual objects requested from our heavenly Father. When children ask their human fathers for good things, most human fathers, even though they are sinful and evil, will respond by giving good things. If human fathers treat their children in a loving manner, how much more will God the Father treat His children with love? Our heavenly Father, who is love and compassion, gives the best gift possible when His children ask Him for good things – He gives the Holy Spirit.

So how do we pray? We seek God, we knock on His door, we ask Him for good things with bold audacity and persistence, and He will give us the Holy Spirit.

PRAYING IN JESUS' NAME

Jesus spent the evening of the Last Supper with the disciples, and He taught amazing lesson after amazing lesson described in John 13-17. They eat the Passover meal, which we now refer to as the Last Supper. During their time together that evening, Jesus washes the disciples' feet as a demonstration of serving one another with humility, He explains that He is the way to God, and He teaches about the Holy Spirit. He teaches about our relationship with Jesus, the Father and the Holy Spirit, explains that the world will reject Him and His followers, and teaches about prayer.

As part of His teaching about prayer that evening, Jesus says,

> "Very truly I tell you, whoever believes in me will do the works I have been doing, and they will do even greater things than these, because I am going to the Father. And I will do whatever you *ask in my name*, so that the Father may be glorified in the Son. You may *ask me for anything in my name*, and I will do it." John 14:12-14

Later that evening, Jesus explains that He will soon be leaving the disciples and that they will soon grieve. He continues saying,

> "I will see you again, and you will rejoice, and no one will take away your joy. In that day you will no longer ask me anything. Very truly I tell you, my Father will

give you whatever you *ask in my name*. Until now you have not *asked for anything in my name*. Ask and you will receive, and your joy will be complete." John 16:22-24

In each passage Jesus says, "Very truly I tell you," indicating the importance of the words about to come. Each time, immediately following that introduction, Jesus twice mentions the notion of asking in His name. In the first quote above, Jesus says He will respond to the request. In the next, Jesus says God the Father will grant any request made in Jesus' name. As a result, it is very common to hear people conclude prayers saying something like, "In Jesus' name I pray, Amen."

Let me begin by saying that there is nothing wrong with ending a prayer in that manner, but does merely saying the words constitute praying in Jesus' name? Do you think Jesus was telling us that these are magic words, like "abracadabra," and by saying the magic words the request, any request, will be automatically granted? Of course not.

So what does it mean? To pray in His holy name means much more than simply saying the words. They are not magic words. In our culture, a name is really merely a means of identifying a person. But in times and places recorded in Scripture, a person's name described who the person was. The name revealed traits about the person's will, character, personality and purpose. God changed Abram's name to Abraham to reflect his new identity as the father of many nations.[6] His new name reflected his new purpose through God. Hannah named her baby boy Samuel because she asked the Lord for him and God answered her prayer.[7] By combining two Hebrew words, Samuel means "heard of God"[8] indicating God's answer to Hannah's prayer and foretelling Samuel's prayer life. Jesus changed Simon's name to Peter, which means "stone" in Greek, saying "on this rock I will build my church...."[9] Peter's new name identified his new purpose, his new life in Christ. There are many other examples in Scripture. Names in Scripture reveal something about a person's character, will and purpose.

In some situations, the word "name" stands for the entire person. When Scripture describes praying as "calling on the name of the Lord" it means calling on the Lord or the person of the Lord. It does not mean simply calling on the word used to designate or identify Him.

So a person's name might be used to represent the person's character and will. In certain times, places and situations, stating a person's name carries with it notions of agency. In the Book of Acts some people tried to drive evil spirits out of others:

> They would say, "In the name of Jesus, whom Paul preaches, I command you to come out." ... One day, the evil spirit answered them, "Jesus I know, and I know about Paul, but who are you?" Then the man who had the evil spirit jumped on them and overpowered them all. He gave them such a beating that they ran out of the house naked and bleeding.
> Acts 19:13-16

The way they invoked the name of Jesus implied a degree of authority the men did not possess. They said "in the name of Jesus," but the words alone did not produce the desired results because they falsely indicated familiarity, agency, and alignment of will and purpose. Similarly, praying in Jesus' name means that our purpose, will, character and being are aligned with Him.

So how do we pray in Jesus' name? We align ourselves with Him, we submit ourselves to Him and we ask for His glory to be revealed through us and through that which He grants. These things are only possible if we allow the Holy Spirit to dwell within us and transform our spirits and souls. It is His life, His holy presence within a person that allows a person to pray in His holy name.

EXAMPLE OF JESUS' PRAYER

After the Last Supper, as the evening of amazing teaching was drawing to an end, Jesus prayed the prayer recorded as John 17. A single prayer fills the entire chapter. Jesus taught His disciples to pray using what we know as the Lord's Prayer, but how did Jesus pray? Let's consider His prayer a little at a time.

Jesus Prays to Be Glorified

After Jesus said this, he looked toward heaven and prayed:

> Father, the hour has come. *Glorify* your Son, that your Son may *glorify* you. For you granted him authority over all people that he might give eternal life to all those you have given him. Now this is eternal life: that they know you, the only true God, and Jesus Christ, whom you have sent. I have brought you *glory* on earth by finishing the work you gave me to do. And now, Father, *glorify* me in your presence with the glory I had with you before the world began. John 17:1-5

This first paragraph records Jesus praying for Himself. He speaks to God, referring to Him as "Father," just as He instructed the disciples to do. He uses derivatives of the word "glory" four times. He asks God to glorify Jesus, which would in turn bring glory to God. Jesus says that He brought God glory on earth by performing the work that God gave Him to do. Jesus had a lot of work to do while He was on earth, and by performing the tasks God called Him to do Jesus brought glory to God. Ultimately, Jesus' mission was to bring God glory to earth by revealing His glory to people. His goal was to introduce the glory of God to people, and on this last evening just prior to His arrest, Jesus proclaims that His mission is nearing completion.

We discussed God's glory briefly in the context of His image and miracles. How did Jesus bring God's glory to earth? God's glory is His being, His character, His holiness, divinity, purity, wholeness and love revealed to people either directly, through His creation, or through His actions. Jesus brought glory to God by doing the work God called Him to do.

But what is God's glory? God's glory is seen when we recognize and acknowledge who He really is. The prophet Isaiah saw a vision of heaven. He saw the Lord sitting on a throne. Flying above Him were heavenly beings, each with six wings. They say to one another,

> "Holy, holy, holy is the Lord God Almighty; the whole earth is full of his glory." Isaiah 6:3

God is holy and His glory fills the earth. His glory is the manifestation of His holiness. It is always present, but people do not always see it. At times God renders the revelation of His glory in such an obvious way that most people present see it. For instance, God revealed His glory directly to the shepherds when an angel appeared to them and announced the birth of Jesus Christ. Luke writes:

> An angel of the Lord appeared to them, and the glory of the Lord shone around them, and they were terrified. Luke 2:9

As another example, God revealed His glory directly to the people of Israel during the Exodus through the cloud pillar. Look at two passages from Exodus.

> While Aaron was speaking to the whole Israelite community, they looked toward the desert, and there was the glory of the Lord appearing in the cloud. Exodus 16:10

> When Moses went up to the mountain, the cloud covered it, and the glory of the Lord settled on Mount Sinai. For six days the cloud covered the mountain, and on the seventh day the Lord called to Moses from within the cloud. To the Israelites the glory of the Lord

looked like a consuming fire on top of the mountain.
Then Moses entered the cloud and went on up the
mountain. And he stayed on the mountain forty days
and forty nights. Exodus 24:15-18

Scripture provides examples of God revealing His glory
directly by allowing people to view heavenly scenes. He also
reveals His glory through people who commune with Him.

After Moses was on Mount Sinai bathing in God's glory,
his face glowed. God's glory reflected off Moses' face. His face
was so radiant that the people of Israel were afraid of him, so
Moses covered his face with a veil.[10] God's glory is revealed by
and through people who commune with Him. As the Holy Spirit
transforms a person's spirit, that person is transformed and God's
glory is revealed through that person. Paul wrote:

Now the Lord is the Spirit, and where the Spirit of the
Lord is, there is freedom. And we, who with unveiled
faces all reflect the Lord's glory, are being transformed
into his likeness with ever-increasing glory, which
comes from the Lord, who is the Spirit. 2 Corinthians
3:17-18

I think of paintings representing holy people and
depicting holiness through a glow around their face or over their
head. I am reminded of many paintings in the National Gallery
of Art showing this, like Botticelli's *Madonna and Child* showing
golden halos over each head, and Lippi's *The Adoration of the Child*,
showing a prominent halo over the angel and smaller halos over
Mary and baby Jesus, and many other paintings. Artists depict
God's glory revealed through certain people by painting a Godly
glow shining in the form of a halo.

Have you seen people who look like this? During many
trips to the National Gallery of Art in Washington, DC, I admired
the art and the talent revealed through it, but I sort of chuckled at
the halos. I understood that they represent holiness, but I did not
understand why each artist would choose to set apart some
people in that manner. And then I saw a person who glowed

because God's glory shined through her, and the paintings suddenly made sense. It was when I first saw Delores, the tiny bird-like gray-haired woman filled with the Holy Spirit standing across the room crowded with people. She glowed. I have heard that word used to describe brides on their wedding day, but this woman stood out from the crowd because of her angelic glow. If I were tasked with painting the scene, a golden halo enveloping her would have been a good way to depict her glow. God's glory glowed through her. God reveals His glory through people who commune with Him.

As we have discussed, God's glory is also revealed through His miracles. When Jesus healed the blind man by putting mud on the man's eyes, Jesus said that the man was blind so that "the work of God might be displayed in his life" (John 9:3). And when Jesus raised Lazarus from the tomb, Jesus said that the event happened for the revelation of God's glory. Jesus said, "This sickness will not end in death. No, it is for God's glory so that God's Son may be glorified through it" (John 11:4). And later, immediately before calling Lazarus out of the tomb, Jesus said, "Did I not tell you that if you believed, you would see the glory of God?" (John 11:40). And God revealed His glory when Lazarus walked out of the tomb after lying in it for four days.

So what is God's glory? It is God's character revealed through direct revelation of His holy presence, through the glow radiating from people who commune with Him, through the majesty of His creation, and through His mighty works on earth. Jesus brought God's glory to earth. He was the physical manifestation of God's glory as the only perfect human, ever, and He revealed God's glory through His miraculous works, teaching and being – by doing the work God called Him to do.

But let's get back to the prayer. Jesus prays with a conversational tone. It is very matter of fact, discussing things that both Jesus and God the Father already know. With this in mind, it seems that this prayer is for the benefit of the disciples who hear it and for us who read it, much more than for Jesus who prays it.

Jesus concludes the prayer for Himself saying, "And now, Father, glorify me in your presence with the glory I had with you before the world began" (John 17:5). Jesus is God, and He possessed the glory, He was the glory before anything was created.

Jesus explains God's grant of authority to Him, He defines eternal life, He explains that He is about to complete His mission on earth, and He asks God to give Him back the glory that He possessed much earlier, before the world began. It is a recital of fact with one request, which may also be a recital of fact – "and now, Father, glorify me" does not sound like a prayerful request, but a command or a statement of something that He knows will soon happen.

Jesus Prays for His Disciples

Jesus continues praying for His disciples.

I have revealed you to those whom you gave me out of the world. They were yours; you gave them to me and they have obeyed your word. Now they know that everything you have given me comes from you. For I gave them the words you gave me and they accepted them. They knew with certainty that I came from you, and they believed that you sent me. I pray for them. I am not praying for the world, but for those you have given me, for they are yours. All I have is yours, and all you have is mine. And glory has come to me through them. I will remain in the world no longer, but they are still in the world, and I am coming to you. *Holy Father, protect them by the power of your name*, the name you gave me, so that they may be one as we are one. While I was with them, I protected them and kept them safe by that name you gave me. None has been lost except the one doomed to destruction so that Scripture would be fulfilled.

I am coming to you now, but I say these things while I am still in the world, so that *they may have the full measure of my joy within them*. I have given them your word and the world has hated them, for they are not of the world any more than I am of the world. *My prayer is not that you take them out of the world but that you protect them from the evil one.* They are not of the world, even as I am not of it. *Sanctify them by the truth;* your word is truth. As you sent me into the world, I have sent them into the world. For them I sanctify myself, that they too may be truly sanctified. John 17:6-19

Jesus continues the conversational tone and quality of the prayer. He continues reciting facts that both He and God know, and He explains that He is saying those things for the benefit of the disciples. He wants the disciples to "have the full measure of joy within them." And Jesus asks God to do two things for the disciples. Jesus asks God to protect them. He asks God to protect them by the power of His name, which tells us that God's name has power. He also asks God to protect them specifically from the evil one.

Jesus then asks God to sanctify them by His truth. He then explains that God's word is truth. To be sanctified is to be made holy, so God's holy word is the source of holiness. Through God's word people are set aside, consecrated, made holy.

On the evening of the Last Supper, immediately before His arrest, Jesus prays for the disciples asking God to protect and sanctify them. After that, He prays for us, future believers who believe in Jesus Christ through the disciples' message.

Stop for a moment and consider this. During that evening 2,000 years ago, Jesus knew what was about to happen. During the Last Supper Jesus acknowledged that Judas would soon betray Him and He dismissed Judas from the meal.[11] Jesus knew that He would soon be arrested and crucified. He knew what was about to happen, which explains the frenzied pace of His teaching that evening. Before leaving for the garden, Jesus prayed for other people. He did not pray for Himself exclusively; He prayed for others. Specifically, He prayed for the disciples and for future believers, which includes you and me.

Jesus Prays for All Believers

> My prayer is not for them alone. I pray also for those who will believe in me through their message, that *all of them may be one*, Father, just as you are in me and I am in you. *May they also be in us* so that the world may believe that you have sent me. *I have given them the glory that you gave me, that they may be one as we are one* — I in them and you in me — so that *they may be brought to complete unity*. Then the world will know that you sent me and have loved them even as you have loved me.
>
> Father, I want those you have given me to be with me where I am, and to see my glory, the glory you have given me because you loved me before the creation of the world.
>
> Righteous Father, though the world does not know you, I know you, and they know that you have sent me. I have made you known to them, and will continue to make you known in order *that the love you have for me may be in them and that I myself may be in them.* John 17:20-26

Jesus prays for unity – unity within the Body of Christ, and unity between each individual believer, Jesus and God the Father. And He prays that God's love will be in us. He prays for us. Isn't that amazing? On His last evening, shortly before His arrest, Jesus was concerned about us; He prayed for you and me 2,000 years ago more or less.

How does His prayer compare to the prayer template that He gave the disciples? So you will not need to flip back to a previous page, the prayer template known as the Lord's Prayer that Jesus gave to the disciples is as follows:

> He said to them, "When you pray, say: 'Father, hallowed be your name, your kingdom come. Give us

each day our daily bread. Forgive us our sins, for we also forgive everyone who sins against us. And lead us not into temptation.'" Luke 11:1-4

Both prayers start by referring to God as "Father." Jesus does not praise God, but then, Jesus is God, so we need not necessarily follow His example on that point. Probably better to follow the template with respect to praise. We definitely need to honor and praise God and to humble ourselves in prayer.

When Jesus prayed, He did not specifically say, "your kingdom come," but He did pray about God's glory. In the first paragraph He mentioned God's glory four times, and He stated that He had brought God's glory to earth by completing the work God called Him to do. Where is God's kingdom? It is where His glory is. God's kingdom and His glory are connected.

Jesus did not ask God to provide daily bread. He did not ask God to forgive His sins, but we would not expect Jesus to ask this on His behalf because He is sinless.

Jesus did not pray about temptation, but He requested God to protect the disciples. He asked that God protect them by the power of His name and that He specifically protect them from the "evil one." And He asks for God's help that we might dwell in unity together and in unity with God the Father and Jesus.

While Jesus did not directly pray the Lord's Prayer, He covered many of the same points as He prayed for Himself, the disciples and us, the future believers.

So how do Jesus' prayers help us learn how to pray? His prayers focus on spiritual matters. He prays for unity, He prays that future believers, including us, will be united as one together and one with God. And He prays that through the unity of believers the world will know God's glory, will know that Jesus is the Christ and will know God's love. He prays that God's love will be in us. His prayer focuses on spiritual matters and our spiritual selves. His example encourages us to pray for other people, to pray for unity between other people, to pray for unity between other people and God, and to pray that other people intimately know God's glory.

PAUL'S PRAYERS

Paul's prayers also have a spiritual focus. It is possible that the prayers Paul wrote as part of his letters were different from the prayers that he spoke, but his letters describe the prayers he prayed for the people to whom he wrote and the prayers he requested that they pray for him. While the record is certainly not complete, it provides glimpses into Paul's prayers. While he prayed for physical needs – Paul prayed that he would be able to visit the believers in Rome,[12] he prayed for safety as he traveled to Jerusalem with the love offering that he spent years collecting from churches he helped form,[13] and he prayed for God to take away his thorn[14] – the bulk of his prayers focused on spiritual matters.

Paul frequently started his prayers by praising God and thanking God. When he wrote to the believers in Rome he started by saying, "First, I thank my God through Jesus Christ for all of you, because of your faith…" (Romans 1:8). In 1 Corinthians he started his prayer saying, "I always thank my God for you because of his grace given you in Christ Jesus" (1 Corinthians 1:4). In 2 Corinthians he wrote, "Praise be to the God and Father of our Lord Jesus Christ…" (2 Corinthians 1:3). In his letter to the church in Ephesus he wrote, "Praise be to the God and Father of our Lord Jesus Christ, who has blessed us in the heavenly realm with every spiritual blessing in Christ" (Ephesians 1:3).

After praising and thanking God, Paul often wrote about his prayers for spiritual transformation. He asks God to transform the readers' spirits and souls. Let's look at a few of his prayers.

> May the God who gives *endurance* and *encouragement* give you the same *attitude* of mind toward each other that Christ Jesus had, so that with *one mind* and *one voice* you may glorify the God and Father of our Lord Jesus Christ. Romans 15:5-6

> May the God of *hope* fill you with all *joy* and *peace* as you *trust* in him, so that you may overflow with *hope* by the *power* of the Holy Spirit. Romans 15:13

I always thank my God for you because of his grace given you in Christ Jesus. For in him you have been *enriched* in every way—with all kinds of *speech* and with all *knowledge* – God thus confirming our testimony about Christ among you. Therefore you do not lack any *spiritual gift* as you eagerly wait for our Lord Jesus Christ to be revealed. He will also keep you firm to the end, so that you will be *blameless* on the day of our Lord Jesus Christ. God is faithful, who has called you into fellowship with his Son, Jesus Christ our Lord. 1 Corinthians 1:4-9

Praise be to the God and Father of our Lord Jesus Christ, the Father of *compassion* and the God of all *comfort*, who *comforts* us in all our troubles, so that we can *comfort* those in any trouble with the *comfort* we ourselves receive from God. For just as we share abundantly in the sufferings of Christ, so also our *comfort* abounds through Christ. If we are distressed, it is for your comfort and salvation; if we are comforted, it is for your *comfort*, which produces in you patient endurance of the same sufferings we suffer. And our hope for you is firm, because we know that just as you share in our sufferings, so also you share in our comfort. 2 Corinthians 1:3-7

I keep asking that the God of our Lord Jesus Christ, the glorious Father, may give you the *Spirit of wisdom and revelation*, so that you may know him better. I pray that the *eyes of your heart may be enlightened* in order that you may know the *hope* to which he has called you, the *riches of his glorious inheritance* in his holy people, and his incomparably great *power* for us who believe. Ephesians 1:17-19

I pray that out of his glorious riches he may *strengthen* you with *power* through *his Spirit in your inner being*, so that *Christ may dwell in your hearts* through faith. And I pray that you, being rooted and established in *love*, may have *power*, together with all the Lord's holy people, to grasp how wide and long and high and deep is the love of Christ, and to know this *love* that surpasses knowledge – that you may be *filled to the measure of all the fullness of God*. Ephesians 3:16-19

And this is my prayer: that your *love* may abound more and more in *knowledge* and depth of insight, so that you may be able to *discern* what is best and may be *pure* and *blameless* for the day of Christ, filled with the fruit of *righteousness* that comes through Jesus Christ—to the glory and praise of God. Philippians 1:9-11

For this reason, since the day we heard about you, we have not stopped praying for you. We continually ask God to fill you with the *knowledge of his will* through all the *wisdom* and *understanding* that the Spirit gives, so that you may live a life worthy of the Lord and please him in every way: bearing fruit in every good work, growing in the *knowledge* of God, being *strengthened* with all *power* according to his glorious might so that you may have great *endurance* and *patience*, and giving *joyful thanks* to the Father, who has qualified you to share in the inheritance of his holy people in the kingdom of light. For he has rescued us from the dominion of darkness and brought us into the kingdom of the Son he loves, in whom we have *redemption*, the *forgiveness* of sins. Colossians 1:9-14

In the last prayer quoted above, Paul prays that the reader's mind, soul and spirit will be transformed through the indwelling Holy Spirit. He prays that they will be filled with the Holy Spirit's knowledge, wisdom and understanding, that the attributes will grow within them, that their actions will demonstrate the indwelling Holy Spirit and that they will bear fruit. And Paul urges them to give thanks to God for His holy salvation and everything that comes with it. Paul's prayer focuses on spiritual qualities.

Considering the body of prayer above, over and over Paul prays that others might receive spiritual transformation. He asks God to replace their spirits with His Holy Spirit. He uses a variety of words, but the theme is spiritual transformation. Paul asks God to give others the attitude of Jesus Christ, the spirit of unity, joy, peace, hope, love, knowledge, wisdom, understanding, strength and endurance. He reminds his readers that God has already enriched them. God has already given them His holy speech, knowledge and other spiritual gifts.

Paul's prayers for the Ephesians are direct appeals for transformation. He asks God to give His Holy Spirit of wisdom and revelation and to enlighten people's spirits such that they might know the hope and wonderful gifts and power available for them through God. He asks that God give them His strength, power and love through His Holy Spirit as He dwells within them, and that through the Holy Spirit they would fully understand, fully appreciate and be filled with the love of Jesus Christ.

How do Paul's prayers help us learn how to pray? While Paul prayed for physical protection and he prayed for God to remove his thorn, the vast majority of his prayers written in letters interceded for the spiritual transformation of his readers. His example encourages us to pray for spiritual transformation, to focus on spiritual needs of people around us, and to see the wonderful spiritual gifts available from God.

PREPARING OURSELVES FOR PRAYER

While prayer is simply communicating with God, it transforms the person who prays. As a result of that transformation, we begin to view the world differently. We begin to see other people as bearing God's image, which encourages us to pray for them. A great deal of prayer involves asking God to help other people and through prayer the spirit of the person who prays continues to be transformed.

Prayer sets a cycle in motion. It enhances the relationship between God and the person who prays; it transforms the lives of those who pray; and in certain situations it transforms the lives of those for whom prayers are offered. After accepting the transformation, people naturally praise God. Spiritual transformation merges with the revelation of God's glory. The cycle begins with God and ends with God.

Focus on God & Resulting Humility

As we focus on God, our worldview changes. We are reminded of who He is and who we are in comparison, so our view of ourselves changes. We are reminded that He is the almighty, omniscient creator of all things who loves everyone, so our view of the world and people around us changes. As we focus on God and encounter Him, it is natural to praise Him and to gain humility. When we focus on God's awesomeness our ego tends to melt away. Scripture urges us to humble ourselves before God, promising that He will revive us and lift us up when we do:

> "Build up, build up, prepare the road! Remove the obstacles out of the way of my people." For this is what the high and lofty One says – he who lives forever, whose name is holy: "I live in a high and holy place, but also with him who is contrite and lowly in spirit, to revive the spirit of the lowly and to revive the heart of the contrite." Isaiah 57:14-15

> Humble yourselves before the Lord, and he will lift you up. James 4:10

> Humble yourselves, therefore, under God's mighty hand, that he may lift you up in due time." 1 Peter 5:6

When we encounter God, praise follows. When we praise God we find humility. Praising God and personal humility go together.

Sometimes a spirit of brokenness is necessary for us to seek God, to desire an encounter with Him, and to place us on the path towards humility. Scripture is filled with teaching about pride and humility – pride blocks our relationship with God while humility allows us to recognize our dependence on God. Jesus taught about the impacts of pride on prayer. One example is known as the Parable of Two Men Who Prayed. We discussed the parable earlier in the context of sources of pride. Let's consider it again focusing on the impact of pride.

> To some who were confident in their own righteousness and looked down on everyone else, Jesus told this parable: "Two men went up to the temple to pray, one a Pharisee and the other a tax collector. The Pharisee stood by himself and prayed: 'God, I thank you that I am not like other people – robbers, evildoers, adulterers – or even like this tax collector. I fast twice a week and give a tenth of all I get.
>
> But the tax collector stood at a distance. He would not even look up to heaven, but beat his breast and said, 'God, have mercy on me, a sinner.'
>
> I tell you that this man, rather than the other, went home justified before God. For all those who exalt themselves will be humbled, and those who humble themselves will be exalted. Luke 18:9-14

Both men went to church to pray. From my worldly perspective, the first man appears righteous. He was a member of a religious order dedicated to proper living. As a Pharisee, he likely wore the right clothing, associated with the right people, and lived his life according to the Law. He fasted twice each week and tithed. He seems like a model church member, yet Jesus condemned his prayer.

The second man was a Jewish man who collaborated with Roman occupiers. He was a traitor who probably profited from taxes paid by his neighbors. Most of his fellow churchgoers probably viewed and treated him with scorn. Yet Jesus said he went home right with God.

The message contrasts outward appearance and people's perception with spiritual truth. The first man prayed for other people to hear as he discussed how good he was. The second man prayed to God in humility.

Humility opens the door for us to see our dependence on God. So long as we are proud, even satisfied with what we are accomplishing on our own, we fail to realize that we need God. Humility is essential for an intimate relationship with God.

I spoke with a close friend yesterday who is struggling with many problems. The common roots of the problems are his need to use mind-altering substances and his pride. When he is clean his life seems good, he seems happy, he does well, he seems healthy. But when things are going well, he wants to reward his hard work and success with a few beers, which leads to other things and he quickly finds himself in a low, dark, lonely place. Two months ago his life was moving along perfectly. He had been clean almost a year. He was doing well in every aspect of his life. He was taking classes in college and doing well, he had a good relationship with an amazing girl, he worked out every day, he went to church every week, he prayed and read Scripture most days, and he was actively involved in a sober community. He looked healthy and seemed happy. After working a few long days in a row and completing a big project at work, he rewarded himself with a few beers. A few days later, a friend found him on the floor of his apartment at the end of a bender, surrounded by needles and drugs, lucky to be alive.

The cycles of his life indicate he is an addict, but he cannot wrap his mind around that identity. He attends the anonymous meetings – Alcoholic Anonymous, Cocaine Anonymous, Narcotics Anonymous and others – and he introduces himself as an addict, but he does not believe the words. Each time he is clean he believes he can use a little and keep everything under control, thinking something like, "I can do it this time, it is only a matter of self control."

He is not an overtly arrogant person. In fact, he seems shy and humble. But pride and arrogance lie at the foundation of his problem because he believes he can do it on his own. He believes he can intentionally expose himself to temptation, taste the forbidden fruit and control the consequences of his choices, but he cannot. And when he sits in the anonymous meetings he feels superior to everyone else because, in his mind, they are addicts and he is not. If he does not see the pride in his life, if he does not see that he is arrogant, if he does not find humility and seek help from others and bow before God in total, complete submission, chances are high that he will soon make a choice that ends his life.

My friend is beautiful, witty, smart, funny and he will take the shirt off his back to help people in need, but because of his disease – his addiction – his arrogance and pride are leading to his destruction. More often than not, people diagnosed with cancer or other purely physical diseases seek treatment and humble themselves to receive the treatment necessary to improve their chances of a longer life. Addiction certainly has physical roots but it is tied so closely with the mind, choices and the pursuit of pleasure that many people see it as belonging in a different category than illnesses like cancer, and this hinders some from seeking the help they need and finding the humility they need to accept their diagnosis.

Pride is sly. It is a stealthy adversary. It creeps in and we fail to notice. If people are too prideful to admit that they have a disease, or too prideful to seek help when they know they have a disease, and through it all fail to see the pride in their lives, we must each ask ourselves how does pride creep in and influence my life?

The psalmists and the authors of Proverbs discuss pride and humility a lot. Old Testament prophets warn that pride blocks people from God and urge listeners to humble themselves. In fact, this is one of the themes of the story of Israel. When the people of Israel humbled themselves and sought God, things were good. When they were prideful and when they trusted and depended on their own abilities, things were not good. Consider this passage from Ezekiel:

> This is what the Sovereign Lord says: "In the pride of your heart you say, "I am a god; I sit on the throne of a god in the heart of the seas." But you are a mere mortal and not a god, though you think you are as wise as a god...." Ezekiel 28:2

As Ezekiel continues speaking on behalf of God, we learn that God does not like it when we have pride in our heart.

> "Because you think you are wise, as wise as a god, ... You will die the death of the uncircumcised at the hands of foreigners." Ezekiel 28:6 & 10

In contrast, Scripture also has many examples of people who, in their brokenness, cried out to God and God answered their prayer. Hannah is a good example. She grieved. She was broken. And in her brokenness she prayed:

> As she kept on praying to the Lord, Eli observed her mouth. Hannah was praying in her heart, and her lips were moving but her voice was not heard. Eli thought she was drunk and said to her, "How long are you going to stay drunk? Put away your wine."

> "Not so, my lord," Hannah replied. "I am a woman who is deeply troubled. I have not been drinking wine or beer; I was pouring out my heart to the Lord. Do not take your servant as a wicked woman, I was praying here out of my great anguish and grief." 1 Samuel 1:12-16

Hannah poured out her heart to the Lord. She was broken in spirit. Out of her desperate need, she cried out to God, she emptied herself to God.

We are broken people living in a broken world. For many of us, we require brokenness to rid ourselves of arrogance. Through brokenness we lose our reliance on our will. Through brokenness we are able to lose ourselves and turn our lives over to Jesus Christ who does indeed save. Jesus tells us that His kingdom is not of this world. Jesus commands us to seek first His kingdom. Through brokenness, when we turn to Jesus Christ, we receive a special blessing – the blessing of possessing the kingdom of heaven. "Blessed are the poor in spirit, for theirs is the kingdom of heaven" (Matthew 5:3).

Brokenness is not necessary for prayer, but humility is and for some of us brokenness is a means of discovering humility. In this way brokenness and prayer are united. Through brokenness we discover the kingdom of heaven, and when we encounter the Holy, the Pure, the Divine in a new and refreshed way our natural response is praise.

The reverse is also true. If we feel distant from God, praise and worship will strengthen our connection with Him. He will feel closer. Please know that God is with you all the time. If we feel distant from God, it is not because He is absent; rather, it is because we are (or something in our lives is) blocking ourselves from Him.

Praising, Worship & Thanksgiving

Whether I feel isolated from God or I feel so close to Him that I smell the perfume of His presence and feel Him surrounding me, I often start praying by praising God. I know it sounds more than a little hokey, but at times I think of something similar to a scene from a movie – no particular movie, but there are many to choose from – where a king summons a common person to appear before him. The king has complete, unfettered authority. He can do whatever he wants with impunity. He can cause the person great pain or he can grant great reward. Because the commoner's wellbeing, future and life hang in the balance, he approaches slowly, tentatively, and kneels before the king showing reverence, awe, respect and humility. The person shows total and complete subservience to the king. At times I have found it useful to emulate that sort of subservience as I approach God at the beginning of prayer. As I approach God with that sort of awe and reverence, it seems a little odd to begin by saying, "Father." I believe this is appropriate.

Sometimes I imagine the heavenly beings that John describes in Revelation 4 and Isaiah describes in Isaiah 6. Heavenly beings surround God's throne. One has the head of a lion, another has the head of an ox, another has the head of person, and the fourth has the head of an eagle. Each has six wings and the heavenly beings are covered all over with eyes, even under their wings. They never stop saying, "Holy, holy, holy is the Lord God Almighty, who was and is and is to come!"[15] They never stop! Forever and ever they continually sing praises to God.

The beings live in heaven, they live in the presence of God, they are continually surrounded by God's glory, they are not exposed to sin, and they continually sing praises to God. Realizing that heavenly beings never stop praising God causes me to wonder, would I be better off if I would follow their lead? Here I am, living in this sinful world. How much more should I sing God's praises? Not only is this a wonderful way to start praying, it is a good habit to develop. If I, as I carry on through my day, say "Holy, holy, holy, who is the Lord God Almighty, who was and is and is to come!" over and over and over, it changes my attitude, it changes my view of the world around me, it changes my response to ugly things, rude people and bad situations that I encounter. It affects my worldview.

This is why I love to start our prayer meetings singing the hymn "Holy, Holy, Holy." It begins nearly quoting the Heavenly beings, saying "Holy, Holy, Holy, the Lord God Almighty." The hymn reminds me of the heavenly beings continuously praising God. It is a wonderful way to start a time of prayer.

For me, praising God naturally leads to thanking God for everything that He has done, is doing and will do. As I praise Him, my appreciation of His blessings grows. I begin to recognize His influence in places and situations previously hidden. Praise opens my eyes and recognition leads to thanksgiving.

If we believe that God is the Creator and that He is still actively involved in our world, we see His hand in the world around us. Through those eyes, it is easy to give thanks to Him for His works. Thank God for the blessings He has bestowed upon you. Thank Him for the day. Thank Him for the breath you are breathing. Thank Him for giving you life. If you have eaten, thank Him for the food you ate. If you have not eaten, thank Him for the food He will provide. Thank Him for providing the Holy Spirit within you and around you. Thank Him for the prayers He has answered, is answering and will answer. Thank Him for everything good in your life. Thank Him for opening the eyes of your spirit, for revealing His glory to you and through you, and for His angels' protection. Thank Him for the freedom you enjoy to worship in peace. Thank Him for all that and more.

Fasting

As we ponder how to prepare ourselves for prayer, we must consider fasting. Throughout Scripture, prayer and fasting are linked. Fasting presumes prayer – without prayer, fasting is simply going hungry, foregoing pleasure, or doing without something we desire. Prayer transforms the act of voluntary self-denial into fasting. While fasting requires prayer it also supplements prayer by underscoring the link between our spiritual selves and our physical selves.

The Psalms connect fasting with prayer.

> ... I put on sackcloth and *humbled myself with fasting*. When *my prayers returned* to me unanswered, I went about mourning as though for my friend or brother. I bowed my head in grief as though weeping for my mother. Psalm 35:13-14

In the Sermon on the Mount, Jesus discusses fasting. He does not command us to fast but He speaks about fasting as if it is something that His listeners do and as we read His words we become His listeners. Fasting is presumed, not ordered.

> *When you fast*, do not look somber as the hypocrites do, for they disfigure their faces to show others they are

fasting. Truly I tell you, they have received their reward in full. But *when you fast*, put oil on your head and wash your face, so that it will not be obvious to others that you are fasting, but only to your Father, who is unseen; and your Father, who sees what is done in secret, will reward you. Matthew 6:16-18

The early church in Antioch connected prayer and fasting. They fasted and prayed, placing hands on Paul and Barnabas as they prayed.

Now in the church at Antioch there were prophets and teachers: Barnabas, Simeon called Niger, Lucius of Cyrene, Manaen (who had been brought up with Herod the tetrarch) and Saul. *While they were worshiping the Lord and fasting*, the Holy Spirit said, "Set apart for me Barnabas and Saul for the work to which I have called them." So after they had *fasted and prayed*, they placed their hands on them and sent them off. Acts 13:1-3

Later in Acts Luke records another example of the early church connecting fasting with prayer. Before appointing elders to the churches, Paul and Barnabas fasted and prayed.

They preached the gospel in that city and won a large number of disciples. Then they returned to Lystra, Iconium and Antioch, strengthening the disciples and encouraging them to remain true to the faith. "We must go through many hardships to enter the kingdom of God," they said. Paul and Barnabas appointed elders for them in each church and, with *prayer and fasting*, committed them to the Lord, in whom they had put their trust. Acts 14:21-23

Fasting is one way to prepare for an encounter with God. It is analogous to cleaning your house for dinner guests. It is analogous to ceremonial cleansing of priests under the Law of

Moses. But we must be careful with fasting. It is easy for us to attempt to turn it into a bargaining chip. If we are not careful we begin to think crazy thoughts. We might think that God owes us for the sacrifice we are making by fasting, by giving up something, by our self-denial, as if we are doing it for Him and not for ourselves. If we are not careful, we might be tempted to twist things around in this silly way. Fasting is not something done for God; it is done for ourselves that we might discover God in a new and refreshed way. It is not an act attempting to earn God's favor (He already showers us with His love and loving grace). It is about our spiritual improvement, not God's (God is already perfect).

But I hear your argument. You say that in the quote from Matthew above Jesus says, "But when you fast ... your Father ... will reward you." Doesn't this suggest that fasting is done to earn God's favor? And the answer is, it depends on what you seek. The reward is a closer relationship with Him, a more fulfilling prayer life, something closer to life abundant. If that is the reward you seek, then yes. Otherwise, you might be disappointed.

EXTERNAL FOCUS OF PRAYERS

Most prayers spoken by Jesus and written by Paul recorded in Scripture are prayers for other people. Jesus prayed briefly for Himself, but even that prayer seemed more of a summary of fact designed to help His listeners, the disciples. Paul prayed briefly for himself, and he asked others to pray for him, but with the single exception of his prayer for the thorn, even Paul's self-focused prayers and requests for prayer were intended to help other people. He asked others to pray for his safe passage to Jerusalem so that he could safely deliver a love offering to the church there.[16] He asked others to pray for his safe passage to Rome so he could minister to believers there.[17] Even Paul's requests for prayers for himself were motivated by a desire to serve others and to glorify God.

When Paul was held in captivity in Rome, he described himself as "an ambassador in chains"[18] and he asked his readers to pray for him. What do you think he asked them to pray? Did he ask them to pray for angels to break the chains and release him? No. Did he ask them to pray to soften the hearts of the people in power so they would release him? No. He asked them to pray that his chains would not hinder his ability to serve God. He asked that God would continue to use him to effectively proclaim the Gospel while he was in captivity. He did not ask for a change of his physical condition, he asked for God to continue using him while he was in prison. He wrote:

And pray in the Spirit on all occasions with all kinds of prayers and requests. With this in mind, be alert and always keep on praying for all the Lord's people. Pray also for me, that whenever I speak, words may be given me so that I will fearlessly make known the mystery of the gospel, for which I am an ambassador in chains. Pray that I may declare it fearlessly, as I should. Ephesians 6:18-20

Paul prayed that, regardless of his circumstance, God would continue using him, and that his efforts would be effective for God's purpose. He did not ask God to change his circumstance, he asked God to continue using him while he was in his situation. His focus was on God and other people.

Think about your current situation. God can use you for His glory where you are. Pray that God will open the eyes of your spirit allowing you to see the opportunities before you. Pray that God will empower you to boldly serve Him. Pray for His discerning Spirit, His wisdom, His knowledge and His words. And pray for other people.

As I look over our church prayer list, the vast majority of prayer concerns are about issues relating to physical health. The list includes praise and celebration for the birth of a healthy baby girl and her healthy mother, and praise for a once-broken wrist that healed earlier than expected. It includes requests for prayer in sympathy for the family of a young mother who passed away from complications relating to cancer, and sympathy for a young man and woman after their baby's stillbirth. It includes prayer requests for new members to the church, prayer requests for the safety of specific military personnel and for safe travel for others. By far the largest category of prayer requests is for health and healing of people suffering physical ailments. 51 prayer requests are for serious health concerns: a boy who has had leukemia most of his life, several women with breast cancer, a man with advanced skin cancer, a woman with lymph cancer, a woman with cancer in her leg, a woman with brain cancer, a man with cystic fibrosis, a man with Parkinson's disease, a man who is in intensive care after being shot during a mugging, several people with heart problems and many more.

Most of the prayer requests on our prayer list are physical concerns, yet most prayers in Scripture focus on spiritual concerns. Scripture reveals in many differing ways that God is also quite concerned with our spiritual selves – it discusses spiritual transformation, spiritual life and its examples of prayer focus on spiritual matters. But God gave us bodies and designed us to have physical needs. He loves us and He wants us to use our entire beings for His glory. Scripture also includes many examples of miracles involving physical healing, which illustrate that He is certainly concerned with our physical selves.

God is sovereign. He is above all other power and authority on earth and in heaven. He created the heavens and earth by speaking. He breathes the breath of life into each of us. He certainly has the power to heal. And He loves us. He loves you, which suggests that He possibly has the inclination to heal.

The prophet Jeremiah records a scene depicting God's sovereignty. God sent Jeremiah to a potter's house. As Jeremiah watched the potter, he worked clay into the shape of a pot but as he worked the clay it became misshapen. The potter destroyed what he was working and started over with clay, eventually forming a pot that pleased him. After describing the scene, Jeremiah writes,

> Then the word of the Lord came to me: "O house of Israel, can I not do with you as this potter does?" declares the Lord. "Like clay in the hand of the potter, so are you in my hand, O house of Israel. If at any time I announce that a nation or kingdom is to be uprooted,

torn down and destroyed, and if that nation I warned repents of its evil, then I will relent and not inflict on it the disaster I had planned. And if at another time I announce that a nation or kingdom is to be built up and planted, and if it does evil in my sight and does not obey me, then I will reconsider the good I had intended to do for it. Jeremiah 18:5-10

God is sovereign. He has all power. And Scripture reveals God using His sovereign power to heal. We are familiar with the many stories of Jesus healing and the Holy Spirit healing people through the apostles. God also healed people in the Old Testament.

King Hezekiah was sick nearing death. The prophet Isaiah went to the king and informed him that the Lord said the king would soon die. In response to the prophet's words, the king wept and prayed saying, "Remember, O Lord, how I have walked before you faithfully and with wholehearted devotion and have done what is good in your eyes" (2 Kings 20:3). God spoke once again to Isaiah, instructing him to return to the king to tell him,

> "This is what the Lord, the God of your father David, says: 'I have heard your prayer and seen your tears; *I will heal you.* On the third day from now you will go up to the temple of the Lord. I will add fifteen years to your life. And I will deliver you and this city from the hand of the king of Assyria. I will defend this city for my sake and for the sake of my servant David.'" 2 Kings 20:5-6

While Scripture provides many examples of God miraculously healing people, it also tells us that God allows righteous people to experience death as a means of sparing them from evil and providing them peace and rest. Isaiah, the prophet who spoke to King Hezekiah, writes

> The righteous perish, and no one ponders it in his heart; devout men are taken away, and no one

understands that the righteous are taken away to be spared from evil. Those who walk uprightly enter into peace; they find rest as they lie in death. Isaiah 57:1-2

Does God have the power to heal? Absolutely. Does God heal in response to prayer? Absolutely. But at times He chooses not to heal. At times He chooses not to heal devout, righteous people who pray for healing, allowing them to enter His eternal rest instead.

Recognizing God's sovereignty, authority, power and love, how do we respond? What are we to do? We pray honestly. We cry out to God telling Him the desires of our heart. We praise Him, worship Him, thank Him, we ask Him to help others in need, and we pray that His glory will be revealed through His mighty act. We pray for healing, total physical and spiritual healing. Following is a prayer that I prayed asking God to intervene on behalf of a man in the hospital. I wrote it down a while back to help me remember what to pray. It is an illustration, one example, which undoubtedly contains many flaws. I replaced the man's name with "Jim."

Father,

Praise your holy name. You are holy. You are divine and pure. You are all-powerful. You created the heavens and earth by speaking. You spoke and you formed everything out of nothing. You formed each of us. You breathe the breath of life into each of us. You have power over life and death. There is nothing you cannot do. And you know everything. You know each of us better than we know ourselves. You know each hair on our heads. You know our needs better than we do. We know that you love us. You are love and you love us. And you are everywhere all at once. You are here with us now. You love Jim and you are the mighty healer.

Thank you for your love. Thank you for your presence with us here, now. Thank you for Jesus and the Holy Spirit. Thank you for your daily sustenance. Thank you for this beautiful day. Thank you for your life. Thank you for your mighty healing touch.

We know with complete certainty that you can heal. We ask you to heal Jim. We ask for complete and total, physical and spiritual healing. We know that you can do this, we know that you love Jim, and we ask for your mighty healing touch. We ask, not only for Jim's benefit and for our benefit, but that your glory might be revealed through your mighty act. We promise, when you heal Jim, it will be for your glory. We will not forget this prayer. We will not forget that it is you who performed the healing.

We understand that you might use all the means at your disposal. We know you can heal all on your own without any help from earthly means. If that is consistent with your will please heal directly. It appears you have chosen to use doctors and nurses and medicine for your glory. We pray for the doctors. Give them your wisdom, your discerning spirit, your clarity of mind and judgment, your ability to solve problems, and your patience and love and peace. We pray for the nurses. Give them your joy, your comfort, your patience and your strength. We pray for the medicine. May it do good and cause no harm. Please cause any bad elements in the medicine to pass through Jim without causing harm, and allow the good elements to heal.

I offer a special prayer for Jim's family and friends. Give them your comfort, your peace, your holy assurance that you are here and you are in control, your strength, wisdom and discerning spirit. Open the eyes of their spirit that they may see, open their ears that they might hear, open their minds that they might understand, open their hearts to feel your love.

Thank you. Thank you for the healing you have performed, you are performing now and the healing you will do in the future. Praise your holy name.

In Jesus' name we pray, Amen.

SHOULD WE PRAY ALONE OR TOGETHER?

Yes. We should pray alone and we should pray together. Scripture encourages us to pray alone and together, and it provides examples of both. James wrote,

> Is anyone among you in trouble? Let him pray. Is anyone happy? Let them sing songs of praise. Is anyone among you sick? Let them call on the elders of the church to pray over them and anoint them with oil in the name of the Lord. And the prayer offered in faith will make the person well; the Lord will raise them up. If they have sinned, they will be forgiven. Therefore confess your sins to each other and pray for each other so that you may be healed. The prayer of a righteous person is powerful and effective. James 5:13-16

In a single paragraph James encourages us to pray alone and together and provides specific examples of each.

JESUS' PRAYER LIFE

Jesus taught a great deal about prayer. He told stories depicting various aspects of prayer and just before providing a template for prayer He said, "When you pray" pray like this.[19] His teaching presumes that His listeners pray and presumes we will pray, and He lived a life of prayer. Let's look at His prayer life: how He prayed, when He prayed, and some of the events surrounding His prayers.

As we look at how Jesus lived, we see that it is important to find time to be alone in prayer every day. Jesus was always finding time to be alone in prayer. He got up early, while it was still dark, to sneak off alone to pray. He stayed up late and stayed out alone at night in prayer. On certain occasions He prayed all night alone. His life was bathed in prayer.

Jesus is God. He is pure, divine and holy. He is without sin. While Jesus was on earth in human form, He needed prayer all the time. If Jesus needed prayer, how much more do we need to pray? As I ponder this, I imagine images of the Holy, the Divine descending to earth, the place where Satan and his demons roam, and suddenly finding Himself submersed in sin, mucking around through the ugliness of the world, swimming through filth. The sinless One was surrounded by sin. He needed to continuously reconnect with God through prayer to maintain His supply of holiness, to wash off the filth of the world. If Jesus needed this, how much more do we need it?

Jesus regularly sought time and space where He could be alone to pray. Scripture indicates this was part of His normal routine:

> "Very early in the morning, while it was still dark, Jesus got up, left the house and went off to a solitary place, where he prayed." Mark 1:35

> "Yet the news about him spread all the more, so that crowds of people came to hear him and to be healed of their sicknesses. But Jesus often withdrew to lonely places and prayed." Luke 5:15-16

> "Once when Jesus was praying in private and his disciples were with him, he asked them, "Who do the crowds say I am?" Luke 9:18

> "About eight days after Jesus said this, he took Peter, John and James with him and went up onto a mountain to pray." Luke 9:28

> "One day Jesus was praying in a certain place. When he had finished, one of his disciples said to him, 'Lord, teach us to pray, just as John taught his disciples.'" Luke 11:1

Other passages explain that Jesus sought time alone in prayer in response to and in preparation for significant events. Jesus prayed all night before selecting the twelve disciples,[20] He sought time alone in prayer before His arrest,[21] and He sought time alone in response to John the Baptist's murder.[22]

Herod Antipas imprisoned John the Baptist because he spoke out against Herod's decision to marry his brother's wife. At the request of Herod's niece and stepdaughter, he ordered the beheading of John the Baptist. When Jesus heard the news, He left in a boat on the Sea of Galilee seeking a solitary place to pray. He grieved the loss of His friend and relative, John the Baptist, and He fled the crowds desiring to be alone in communion with God.

A crowd of people walked along the shore tracking the boat carrying Jesus. When the boat stopped on the shore, a large crowd of people was there. Jesus left in search of time alone to commune with God, but He was unable to get away. They followed Him. After arriving at the shore, what did Jesus do? Did He rebuke the crowd? Did He send them home? Did He explain that He was grieving the loss of His friend John the Baptist? Did He publicly speak out against Herod, calling for rebellion? What did Jesus do?

He responded with supernatural grace. He showed compassion and love. He stopped fleeing and began ministering to the people, healing those who were in need and, when He saw that they were hungry, He asked the disciples to feed them. The disciples answered that they only had five loaves of bread and two fish, not nearly enough to feed so many people.

> "Bring them here to me," [Jesus] said. And he directed the people to sit down on the grass. Taking the five loaves and two fish and looking up to heaven, he gave thanks and broke the loaves. Then he gave them to the disciples, and the disciples gave them to the people. They all ate and were satisfied, and the disciples picked up twelve basketfuls of broken pieces that were left over. The number of those who ate was

about five thousand men, besides women and children. Matthew 14:18-21.

Jesus was grieving and He wanted to be alone in prayer, but people sought Him so He ministered to them and prayed a different prayer – He prayed for them to be fed. He prayed for a miracle and five loaves of bread and two fish fed thousands. We do not know how many people were present – if we assume each man came with a wife and two children it would be 20,000 people. We do not know how many were there, but it was a large crowd.

Look at His prayer. He took what God had already provided, thanked God for it, and trusted that God's provision would continue. And God continued to provide.

After the brief detour and miracle meal, Jesus continued on His mission to find a quiet place away from people to commune with God. He dismissed the crowd, sent the disciples away by boat, and He walked alone to a mountainside to pray.[23]

In response to the horrific news of John the Baptist's death, in response to being confronted personally by the sin of this world, Jesus sought time alone in prayer.

Jesus also went away alone to pray before significant events, like choosing His disciples and preparing for His arrest and crucifixion, but Scripture suggests that finding time alone with God was part of Jesus' regular routine. The fact that He left everyone to pray and that prayer was part of the stories tied to significant events, would be like describing that He ate that day or He was breathing at the particular moment. Time alone with God in prayer was part of His regular routine, so of course it was tied to the significant events recorded in Scripture.

When Jesus was deciding whom He would name as His disciples, He prayed all night. He sought communion with God. He sought God's holy guidance. Scripture explains:

> "One of those days Jesus went out to a mountainside to pray, and spent the night praying to God. When morning came, he called his disciples to him and chose twelve of them, whom he designated apostles..." Luke 6:12-13

After the Last Supper, after the prayer quoted as John 17, before His arrest, Jesus walked with the disciples to the Garden of Gethsemane on the Mount of Olives. He left the disciples and went a little further to be alone in prayer. Matthew, Mark and Luke each record the event.[24] In his first sentence describing the event, Luke wrote,

> "Jesus went out *as usual* to the Mount of Olives, and his disciples followed him." Luke 22:39

So Jesus regularly went to the Garden after dinner to pray, which may explain how Judas knew where He would be.

It was part of Jesus' regular routine to seek time alone with God. He got up early to be alone with God, He stayed up late to be alone with God, and while in Jerusalem He regularly prayed in the garden on the Mount of Olives. If Jesus needed time alone with God in prayer, how much more do we need it?

COMMUNAL PRAYER IN THE EARLY CHURCH

We also need to pray together. When Jesus prayed for future believers, He prayed that the believers would be as one, He prayed that we would have complete unity, and He said that through the church's unity the world will know that Jesus is the Messiah.[25] The best way to build unity is to pray together. To be clear, the sort of prayer I have in mind here is true, genuine, heart-driven prayer. While I am not knocking standing in a church service and reading a printed prayer together, this is not the sort of group prayer that I have in mind here. I am thinking of the same sort of prayer that people pray alone locked in their prayer closet, possibly with tears and sincere emotion. People who sincerely cry out to God together develop a spiritual intimacy that can be created in no other way. Prayer breaks down barriers between people. Praying together allows people to be who they really are; it removes the masks that they wear the rest of the time.

While communal prayer is critical for unity, and it is wonderful when done right, like most other good things, we humans are able to take most good things and destroy them. Not everyone is comfortable with the sort of spiritual intimacy that group prayer creates, and not everyone is worthy of the trust that this level of exposure relies upon.

A group meets in our sanctuary to pray before Sunday church service. While people are praying, other folks are doing physical work preparing for the church service. One morning as we prayed, a woman was arranging flowers on the altar filling the space with sweet fragrance. Another woman replaced used candles on the altar. A man was inserting a special announcement bulletin in each hymnal in the pews. Hymnals rest vertically on a shelf fastened to the back of each pew and the bulletins were left protruding high above each book begging to be grabbed. The organist practiced filling the room with amazing music. While the amazing, sacred, consecrated room was physically prepared for the church service, we filled the room with prayer. We prayed praising God, thanking God for His Holy Presence, thanking God for His protection over the room and people traveling there to worship, thanking the Holy Spirit for filling the room, inviting the Holy Spirit to reveal His Holy Presence as never before within each person who would come to worship in the room, and much, much more.

As we prayed, a woman walked by carrying a bowl of mints. She was carrying them from the church office behind the altar through the sanctuary to the front door so people could grab some mints along with their bulletin as they entered the church. When she walked past with the bowl of candy, I sensed sadness about her. I knew her father passed away eight weeks earlier and she had good days and bad days. When she returned, I stopped her and asked if we could pray together. I called over a prayer warrior and the three of us prayed. Later that day she stopped me and, with tears welling in her eyes, thanked me for suggesting that we pray together. She told me that she really needed that boost, that support, that showing of love from us and God's love that she felt through the prayerful connection.

Prayer enhances our connection with the Holy Spirit. Of course, Jesus would have seen the woman's heart and her need without having been told of her recent loss, but I know myself, and had I not been praying I would not have noticed her sadness. I would have gone through the moment in my usual self-absorbed fashion. And while the prayer was nothing eloquent, it allowed us to connect in a meaningful, spiritual way as humans, it allowed us to grow closer to God, and it allowed us to feel God's presence in a real and meaningful way.

I turned around and noticed a couple sitting on a pew across the room. Five days earlier the woman had back surgery. I sat by them and asked how she was feeling. She said not well. Her pain was worse. The doctor said the procedure appeared to be successful, but her pain was worse. Four of us held hands and prayed together. We praised God. We thanked Him for His protection, we thanked the Holy Spirit for His presence with us and in us, and we prayed for total physical and spiritual healing. We thanked God for the healing has caused, is causing and will cause in the future. Through that prayer we developed a spiritual connection that has changed our relationship.

Genuine, sincere, heart-filled prayer creates bonds of unity. We see many examples of this in the Book of Acts and Paul's letters. Before looking at some of the descriptions of unity in the early church, please realize that the early church was not perfect. Division and dissension existed in the early church as individuals charted the new path forward. They were not always aligned. We see evidence of this in Paul's letters and in John's Revelation as they provided guidance to the church.

I mention this because at times we might be tempted to see the early church as a model of perfection unobtainable today, which is not the case. It was not perfect, but when individuals came together as a unified church wonderful events took place. God worked through them in miraculous ways and this happens today when believers join together in unity.

The last paragraph in Luke describes Jesus ascending to heaven followed by the believers returning to Jerusalem where they "stayed continually at the temple, praising God" (Luke 24:53). In the beginning of Acts, Luke describes the ascension in greater detail, describes their return to Jerusalem, and then says "They all joined together constantly in prayer ..." (Acts 1:14). Nine days after the ascension, while the believers were together, the Holy Spirit was unleashed.

> When the day of Pentecost came, they were all together in one place. Suddenly a sound like the blowing of a violent wind came from heaven and filled the whole house where they were sitting. They saw what seemed to be tongues of fire that separated and came to rest on each of them. All of them were filled with the Holy Spirit and began to speak in other tongues as the Spirit enabled them. Acts 2:1-4

So the believers were together over the course of nine days, praising God and praying, and the Holy Spirit appeared, came upon them, filled them and influenced their behavior. They not only felt the Holy Spirit, they saw evidence of His presence. Immediately following this, Peter preached his first sermon and about 3,000 people came to know Jesus Christ that day.

Consider for a moment how bold and brave Peter was at that time. Jesus rode into Jerusalem on a donkey, was arrested and crucified. Less than two months later, Peter stood in the temple in Jerusalem preaching the Good News of Jesus Christ, likely to many of the same people who had only recently called for Jesus to die. And he preached a message so convicting that 3,000 people came to believe in and know and desire to follow Jesus Christ. The bravery, audacity and power demonstrated through Peter and the influence of his words were supernatural. They were the result of the Holy Spirit.

It was a miraculous day and it began with the Body of Christ meeting together in unified prayer and praise. Luke tells us that they continued meeting together, saying:

> They devoted themselves to the apostles' teaching and to fellowship, to the breaking of bread and to prayer. Everyone was filled with awe at the many wonders and signs performed by the apostles. Acts 2:42-43

The apostles preached and taught and performed miraculous acts, and the believers continued meeting together in prayer and praise. Not long after Pentecost, Peter and John happened upon a man who had been lame since birth. The man begged at the temple. Peter healed the man and the man ran into the temple praising God. Everyone recognized him. A crowd formed in the temple, amazed by what they saw. Peter addressed the crowd, preaching about Jesus Christ, and the temple guard arrested Peter and John.[26]

The next morning Peter and John appeared before the Sanhedrin. Caiaphas, Annas the high priest, and the full Sanhedrin were present – the same men who only a couple months earlier declared Jesus guilty and called for His execution. They questioned Peter and John, ordered them to stop preaching the name of Jesus Christ, and released them.

They went directly to the place where believers were gathered together praying. Peter and John told the group what had happened, and they all immediately prayed together and after they prayed, "the place where they were meeting was shaken. And they were all filled with the Holy Spirit and spoke the word of God boldly" (Acts 4:31). While they prayed together, the Holy Spirit showed up in miraculous fashion. He shook the building and He empowered all the believers.

About 14 years later,[27] King Herod Agrippa I executed the apostle James, son of Zebedee and John's brother. Jewish leaders applauded the act, so the king ordered Peter's detention. While Peter was chained in prison, a group of believers prayed in the home of Mary, Mark's mother. That night, as they prayed, an angel rescued Peter from prison.[28] Believers gathered together in prayer and their prayers were answered in miraculous ways.

The early church prayed together. They understood the power of communal prayer, and because they prayed together they experienced the power of the Holy Spirit together. As followers of Christ, we need to pray together. Jesus prayed for our unity, He prayed that we would be one in the same way that the Father, Jesus and the Holy Spirit are one, and He prayed that the church's unity would testify to the world about Jesus. The best way to build unity is praying together.

Should we pray alone or should we pray with others? Yes. I urge you to make time to regularly be alone in prayer, and to regularly pray with other believers.

CONCLUSION

How do we pray?

We begin by remembering who God is and who we are by comparison. We focus on His awesomeness. He created everything in heaven and on earth, He breathes the breath of life into every living being, He is all-powerful and all knowing, and He is not bound by time or space. His mind, rationale and judgment are perfect. He does not make mistakes. He is infinite yet He is intimate. He is pure, divine and holy. He is love. He loves you and knows you better than you know yourself. And, as mindboggling as this is, He desires relationship with you. He wants you to talk with Him and listen to Him. He wants relationship.

When we focus on all that and simply cry out to God, we engage in prayer. That is how we pray, because how can you focus on God's awesomeness without praising Him and thanking Him? How can you recognize His holiness and our sinfulness without falling at His feet in humility? When we approach God, the Almighty, the Divine, the Holy, with absolute humility and cry out to Him, we are praying.

God's holy grace rains over us. It is a free gift that we must receive and open. Jesus promises that when we seek we will find, when we knock the door will be opened, and when we ask we will receive. May you commune with God through His Holy Spirit. May you receive His holy grace. May God's glory be revealed through you.

14 | My Journey with Prayer (so far)

*"In the same way, the Spirit helps
us in our weakness. We do not
know what we ought to pray for,
but the Spirit himself intercedes
for us with groans that words
cannot express. And he who
searches our hearts knows the
mind of the Spirit, because the
Spirit intercedes for the saints in
accordance with God's will."*
Romans 8:26-27

We know that God loves us. If prayer is simply crying out to God who loves us, why are some intimidated by it? Why is it something we must learn how to do? In my experience, feeling comfortable praying is a progression. My prayer life has changed drastically over the years, but as I ponder the simplicity of prayer and my struggles over the years with it, I realize the progression has really been with the transformation of my inner being. As I have allowed God to transform me, prayer has become more natural. I still have a long, long ways to go, but I think of the progression in phases. By mentioning the following I am not suggesting that this is a "normal" progression and I am not recommending the following as suggested steps, rather I am simply recording what has happened along the path I have journeyed so far.

PHASE 1 – OBLIVIOUS TO PRAYER

For years I never thought about prayer, or God for that matter. The thoughts did not occur to me. I never pondered God so I never considered communicating or building a relationship with Him. Even when my brother discovered cancer had invaded his femur and he underwent surgeries and chemotherapy and endured extended time in the hospital, even during all that when people approached me to say that they were thinking about us and praying for us, I did not think about praying myself. Their statements about prayer equated, in my mind at the time, to "thinking about" us. It was nice and cordial. They cared enough to consider the pain my brother was experiencing; they cared enough to communicate concern and demonstrate compassion. That was all. It was like a birthday card sending wishes of good cheer.

At the time I wondered whether their kind thoughts helped in any way. It was nice to know they were thinking about us, but did the thoughts help? Was there some sort of telepathic force allowing compassionate thoughts to influence other people?

PHASE 2 – PRAYING LIKE PHARAOH

Early in our relationship, Lori and I often went to church together. I had not attended church regularly in many years, but I enjoyed going with her because it made me feel like I was doing something good. I am not sure who I was trying to please. It was not other people at the church because I knew no one there. I must have been trying to please Lori and her parents, trying to cause them to like me, trying to trick them into thinking I was better than I was. I may be wrong about my motivation for attending church back then, but I am confident I was not attending to worship God, or to build a relationship with God, or in any way seeking God. Whatever my motivation, it was focused on me, not God.

As our relationship progressed to marriage, going to church each Sunday became part of our weekly routine. We moved and met new friends who attended church, and over time we were around people in social settings who mentioned praying. In social settings one person might ask another how they were doing in a way suggesting that they were struggling in some way unknown to me. After they talked the first person would often say that he or she was praying for the other person.

When Lori struggled with health issues later diagnosed as a thyroid disorder, when she experienced difficulties while pregnant with our second child, Henry, and when he became sick nearing death during his second month on earth, during times like these many, many people told us that they were praying for us. At the time we were attending church regularly, most of our friends attended church with us, I regularly read Scripture, and I was beginning to ponder God, but I did not pray.

As the chaos of life swirled around us, I continued moving forward day after day without any direction other than the need to continue earning a paycheck to support the financial needs of our young family. Work, Lori and responsibilities associated with our young family were my foundations.

Because people who prayed surrounded us, I felt comfortable asking them to pray. My prayer life was like Pharaoh's prayer life. Yes, Pharaoh from the Exodus. My prayer life resembled the prayer life of the man who thought he was god, the man who enslaved the Israelites and refused to let them go, even after many plagues. My prayer life resembled his.

When Moses first approached Pharaoh, Moses asked Pharaoh if the Israelites could take a few days off to worship God in the wilderness near Mount Sinai. Pharaoh asked Moses about the Lord and continued saying that he did not know Moses' God.[1]

The conversation was the prologue to the plagues. Through the plagues, Pharaoh encountered God and saw that He was much more powerful than Pharaoh imagined any god could be. When Pharaoh saw God's power, Pharaoh asked Moses to pray for him, his family and his people. Pharaoh did not pray himself because in his mind he was himself a god, and apparently one god should not pray to another god.

But all this took some time. At first, Pharaoh thought he was dealing with a god who possessed power similar to Pharaoh's power. When Pharaoh first asked Moses to perform a miracle, Aaron tossed his staff to the ground and the staff became a snake, which was a nice trick, but Pharaoh's sorcerers replicated it. Aaron's snake ate the snakes created by sorcery, but that did not convince Pharaoh that the Lord was anything special.[2]

At Moses' command, Aaron touched the Nile River with his staff and the water turned into blood. Everything in the river died and the people had no water to drink. But Pharaoh's magicians copied the trick, so Pharaoh still did not believe the Lord's power was special.[3]

But when the frogs came, even though Pharaoh's magicians also made frogs appear, Pharaoh met with Moses and Aaron and said, "Pray to the Lord to take the frogs away from me and my people" (Exodus 8:8). Moses prayed and all the frogs died and Pharaoh began to believe in God's power.[4]

Pharaoh's sorcerers were unable to replicate the subsequent plagues. Gnats came followed by flies and Pharaoh once again asked Moses to pray to the Lord for him. After Moses prayed, the plagues of flies and gnats stopped.[5]

The plague of livestock came and all the livestock owned by Egyptians died, followed by the plague of boils and the plague of hail. Once again Pharaoh asked Moses to pray for him saying, "Pray to the Lord, for we have had enough thunder and hail" (Exodus 9:28).

Then came the locusts and Pharaoh once again asked Moses to pray saying, "Now forgive my sin once more and pray to the Lord your God to take this deadly plague away from me" (Exodus 10:17).

Then came the plague of darkness and the plague of the firstborn, and still Pharaoh refused to humble himself before God. He asked Moses to pray, but Pharaoh would not humble himself. He requested others to pray, but he refused to pray himself. Pharaoh saw God's power, but he was unwilling to humble himself before God; he was unwilling to worship God; he was unwilling to pray. Yet, Pharaoh saw God's power and asked Moses to pray on his behalf.

Like Pharaoh, I was perfectly content asking other people to pray for me. I mean, if they were taking care of it why did I need to bother praying myself? What was wrong with delegating this task? The ability to delegate was one of the things that helped me progress in my career. What was wrong with delegating prayer? Had I given it any thought, I probably would have fashioned an argument along those lines. Like Humphrey Bogart's character in *Casablanca*, Rick, I did not give it enough thought to formulate an argument. Louis said to Rick, "You despise me don't you Rick?" Rick (Bogart's character) replied, "If I gave you any thought I probably would."

What it really meant was I was unwilling to humble myself before God. I was too proud to bow before God, to admit that I need Him, to admit that He is in control, to admit that He is who He is. God was not god of my life. Something else was. It may have been my job, my marriage, my family, myself, my pride or, most likely, a combination of those things. Whatever was god of my life, the idol that I worshiped, even though I went to church most Sundays, taught adult Sunday school and studied Scripture, it was not God.

PHASE 3 – BEGINNING TO PRAY

I am not sure how or when – it was a gradual process – but at some point along the way I started to take the notion of having a relationship with God a little more seriously. I was studying Scripture daily and teaching Bible studies. I enjoyed studying Scripture and I felt a strong connection with God through Scripture. I grew comfortable praying at the end of Bible studies and Sunday school classes, but as I think back, I was praying to the other people in the class, not God. The prayer was an extension of my teaching.

On occasion I prayed alone, but not often. Most of my prayers while I was alone focused on asking God for something that I needed. If I struggled at work I asked for guidance and I asked God to help me. When Lori and I happened upon struggles in our marriage, I asked God to help us. I prayed for other people while I was in front of people, like leading a Sunday school class prayer, but not while praying alone.

Around this time I was invited to attend meetings of the Tuscaloosa Prayer Network. My boss and friend, Mike, was a supporter of the group, and he invited me to attend with the thought that I might be able to assist with the business structure of the group. The group was an affiliation of local pastors. They counseled each other, worked together on mission outreach and ministry, and they prayed for one another and for each other's churches.

After I attended meetings over the course of a year, the group invited me to attend a prayer summit. Pastors from around the southeastern United States gathered for a weekend of prayer. I did not want to go, but I went out of obligation to the group and my boss.

I had no idea what to expect, but the title of the weekend filled me with dread. Friday evening seemed like a long church service with extra prayer. We sang hymns, prayed, listened to speakers, prayed, then sang more and prayed more. It was surprisingly nice.

Saturday was a blank schedule. We were scheduled to meet all day, but nothing was on the agenda. A full day meeting without an agenda filled me with dread and thoughts about all the things I should be doing on that particular Saturday. I left Lori and our two young children at home. Not only had I caused inconvenience for Lori, I was missing a weekend with my family; I had a long list of things to do around the house; I had work to do; and if I was planning to take a weekend off from everything, I could think of many places I would have picked other than a church camp for a prayer summit with a bunch of pastors.   As I pondered the blank itinerary and thought awful thoughts, my dread veered towards anger.   So I walked in the meeting room that Saturday morning in the wrong frame of mind.   My thoughts were focused entirely on myself and the sacrifices I was making to be there.   If I thought about God it was fleeting.

The room could have held hundreds, so there was plenty of space for the 50 or 60 people who attended to spread out.   This provided a great sense of comfort for me because I did not want to reveal my sense of intimidation and discomfort about being there.   I could easily fake short prayers.   I could pray to close a Sunday school class.   I could stand in front of the church and pray before the offering was collected.   I could pray before meals.   I could do those things because I could write and memorize the words in advance, like giving a speech, and in fact it was giving a speech because I was praying for the audience not for God.   I could pray like that, but it suddenly felt fake.   I suddenly realized that I had been faking it.   As I sat in the room looking around at the people who came there because they wanted to be in a community who prayed together, I felt like a phony through and through.

So as the moderator started us off singing a few hymns and then instructed us to pray for twenty minutes for the health of our churches, I really tried.   But I had no idea where to begin.   After thirty seconds or so I was tapped out.   I had nothing left to say.   And the folks around me were praying.   They were really praying.   We were close enough to hold hands, but we were miles apart.

During lunch, one of the participants approached the moderator suggesting that we pray for the young people in our communities.   She discussed the crime and gang violence and lack of opportunity for young people, and she urged us to pray over them for at least an hour that afternoon.   So we did.   Well, they did.   I prayed a little and watched a lot and prayed a little.   Many of them wept as they prayed.   Some stood shouting as they beat their chest and looked upward.   Some lay prostrate on the floor.   Most sat bowing or knelt and leaned their elbows on a chair.   They called out to the Lord in an intimate and real way that I had never witnessed before. It was raw. It was for God. And they were not at all ashamed of what they were doing. It was all for God.

I left feeling about the way I might feel after leaving an interesting movie. I had entered a new and unfamiliar world for a brief time before returning home to my life. I thought about it some. It did not immediately change my life or me, but the experience gradually influenced my prayer life. I sought to pray more intimately. I had seen real, raw, intimate prayer. I did not really know how to pray like that, but I knew I wanted to pray in a new and better way.

PHASE 4 – EXPOSURE TO POWERFUL PRAYER

At the prayer summit I saw men and women engaged in real prayer. A little while later I felt the energy of the Holy Spirit through prayer and feeling Him made all the difference.

During this period, in a variety of places and situations, I met a number of true prayer warriors. They each introduced me to a connection with God through prayer that I had not experienced until then. Through them I felt new experiences, and through the experiences I realized that a previously unknown realm of prayerful power and existence was available. I felt what I described at the time as a bolt of energy combined with peace, comfort, and joy. It was like an internal glimpse of the Divine, the Holy. They were experiences like no other and they caught my attention. In an effort to explain, I will briefly describe one.

Woman in Mongolia

I was one of eight people from the US in Mongolia facilitating the formation of a new orphanage. Before the trip I knew one of them – Mike, the same friend who took me to the prayer summit. We travelled about 30 miles east of Ulaanbaatar to a small village in the mountains. The air was fresh and crisp, carrying the scent of pine trees, wet grass and willows near a stream – a combination of smells that took me back to childhood days of trout fishing near Lake City, Colorado. The village was a scattered collection of small wooden buildings and homes nestled between hills and a stream. We travelled there to visit a small piece of land with a building as a prospective orphanage site. Since it was Sunday, we planned a church service in the building.

Some members of a Christian church in Ulaanbaatar travelled with us. It was a small caravan. They brought a couple guitars. When we arrived a handful of people from the village were waiting to greet us.

We toured the property and small building, and asked some questions about how an orphanage would operate in the village. Could they hire employees from the village? Where would relocated workers live? Where would they get food? Was adequate water and electricity available, particularly in the winter? Did the roads stay open during the winter? We asked a number of operational questions, and then I asked what was apparently a crazy question – I asked about property ownership and evidence of title. If we pay money to the guy who claims to own the property, how do we know he owns it and how would we tell the world that we now own it? Questions about evidence of property ownership were problematic in former Soviet countries at the time.

I asked several times, "What time will we start the church service?" The answer was something like, "We will start when we start." Apparently, in places where few people have watches, precise church starting times do not exist. Gradually, over the course of the morning, more and more people wandered to the building and when thirty or forty people were present the leaders deemed it to be time to start. They passed out pages with a few hymns printed in Mongolian, and the congregation sang a song. Folks from the US who knew the songs sang in English and the locals sang in Mongolian.

During the second song I noticed out the window a woman walking slowly up the road. She walked slowly, with great deliberation and difficulty, using a walking stick. The songs had finished and the leader was speaking when the woman entered the room. She asked a question I could not understand. I guessed she was confirming she was in the right place. She sat heavily into an empty chair next to me. She seemed exhausted. Her foot was bleeding through her sock. She sat quietly leaning forward with her hands on her walking stick.

Our travelling companion, a pastor from the US, gave a sermon with translation. The pastor said a sentence in English and the translator struggled to slowly translate the sentence. Back and forth they went, one sentence at a time for twenty minutes or so. I was hypnotized by the rhythm. By the time the translator finished repeating each sentence I had forgotten what the pastor had said. One sentence at a time, the sermon dragged on painfully. Without translation it probably would have been a good sermon, but translation interruptions destroyed it.

After the sermon, the leader spoke in Mongolian. The woman with the bloody sock interrupted him. She stood and spoke. The leader was embarrassed by her breach of decorum. Here he was, the leader in front of his foreign guests, and the woman was not respecting his authority. I could not understand their words, but his expression and body language said he was urging her to be quiet. But she refused to stop. Once she had the floor she sat back down and continued speaking. After she finished, the interpreter explained. Her son had struggled with a difficult life. Jobs were few. Drugs and alcohol were plentiful. He had been injured working in a mine a few miles down the road. While he was in the hospital, he met Jesus and Jesus had changed his life. She heard that Christians would be in the village that day, so she started walking early that morning to meet the Jesus who had saved her son. She wanted to meet Jesus. She wanted to say thank you.

One of the women in our group asked the Mongolian woman if we could pray with her. She did not understand. The American woman called over a translator and repeated the question. She said something while nodding "yes." Her expression said something like, "look I walked a long way to meet Jesus, and I will say yes to whatever that takes."

The American who initiated the conversation pulled a chair in front of the woman, sat and took the woman's hands in hers. Her three friends stood near the two women. They placed their hands on the Mongolian women's shoulders. They asked me to join them, so I placed my hand on her shoulder as well. The first American woman started praying, and the other three joined in. I do not remember whether I spoke or not.

An amazing energy flowed through the group. My body became significantly hotter. I felt a strange sensation. I'm not sure how to describe it – a feeling of intense joy and peace and warmth. The Mongolian woman started crying and laughing. I felt God's Holy Presence inside me in an amazingly new way. I believe she felt what I felt, only I was on the periphery and she was the epicenter. I am pretty sure the Mongolian woman found what she was seeking.

I walked out of the building dazed. A member of our group who had been outside saw me. He asked what had happened. He said that I looked different than before. I certainly felt different. I think about how Jesus was walking through a crowd and his robe brushed past many people, but a woman touched his robe with purpose and He felt it.[6] He stopped and asked who had touched him. While many had brushed against him, only one had purposefully touched him and He felt a transfer of energy. I think about Moses encountering God and his face glowed such that he had to cover it as to not scare his companions.[7] I had experienced the Divine and His energy in an amazing new way, and apparently His energy revealed itself through my physical presence for a brief time.

I had not only encountered God in a new way, I had encountered prayer warriors – people whose prayer connected with God in a way resulting in physical manifestation of His Holy Presence. They were in a room with other people, but they were praying to God as if they were in the room alone. They were not praying to other people, they prayed to God and God alone. They prayed with power and authority, and God responded to their prayer. I had a taste, a glimpse, a brief encounter with a new realm.

I realized that prayer can be powerful and that through prayer a connection with the Holy, the Divine is possible. I had read about people connecting with God through prayer, but I did not understand the words until I experienced the feeling.

While my experience helped my belief, I did not know where to go. I did not know what to do next. There seemed to be such a wide chasm between me and the prayer warriors, I wondered whether achieving what they possessed was even possible.

After returning to the US, I organized a small prayer group. After Sunday school, a handful of people stayed to pray. We helped each other as we each struggled to pray. We prayed for the church, for people in the church with needs that we knew about, for the church service that was taking place as we prayed, and for many things. We prayed together for about an hour each week. It helped me tremendously in many ways and our friendship instantly became deeper, stronger and rooted. Praying together removed superficial layers separating us and we grew closer.

PHASE 5 – SEEKING GOD

I hesitate to write this because this is where I am. Sometimes I feel as if I am on the right path heading in the right direction. Other times I feel lost. But I am gradually feeling more comfortable praying. I am gradually building a relationship with God. I am gradually making room for the Holy Spirit to dwell within me and gradually allowing Him to transform me. At least I pray that I am.

I am beginning to realize that prayer focuses on God and His glory, not on me and not on my pleasure. I am beginning to seek God and to ask Him to reveal His glory through me and to use me in little ways as He seeks to transform the world. I am beginning to see other people as beings created in God's image and I am gradually becoming more intentional about taking the time to understand their needs, additional time to pray for them, and sometimes I am able to provide some physical help also. I have noticed that if I linger after meetings, wonderful conversations happen and I am able to see new opportunities to serve and pray.

Life is a journey, a process. May you seek God, may you invite the Holy Spirit to dwell within you, may you allow Him to transform the eyes of your spirit, and may you allow the love, peace, joy and hope of Jesus Christ to be revealed through you. May God reveal His glory through you and may you serve as light to the world.

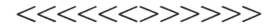

Part IV. Our Purpose

<<<<<<<>>>>>>>

15 | GOD'S GLORY REVEALED

Therefore, I urge you, brothers and sisters, in view of God's mercy, to offer your bodies as a living sacrifice, holy and pleasing to God – this is your true and proper worship. Do not conform to the pattern of this world, but be transformed by the renewing of your mind. Then you will be able to test and approve what God's will is – his good, pleasing and perfect will. Romans 12:1-2

On that beautiful Sunday afternoon, as we walked on the lawn of the Augusta National Golf Club toward the parking lot, Casey posed a question that I failed to answer. The foundation has been prepared. I can now answer the question and we can now discuss the point of it all – love. God's glory is revealed through people who serve Him. It begins with God and ends with God served. As we allow God to transform our spiritual selves, His love invades us and our worldview changes. We gain new eyes to see people as beings bearing God's image, and we gain a new desire to serve. When we allow God's love to flow through us, God's glory is revealed to others, and those who experience God's glory are in turn changed. It is all about love.

I have shared Scripture and stories about spiritual life, God's desire for us to allow Him to transform our spirits, the avenues through which we may connect with God, and revelations of God's glory. As wonderful as it might be to experience God's glory, to bask in His light, to commune with Him, and to experience the change, He does not offer His gift of grace purely for our pleasure. He offers His gift of grace to transform us and through that transformation, to position us for His service. He reveals His glory to the world in many ways including through His creation, through His word and through His people. If we desire satisfaction, if we desire a full, enriched, meaningful life, if we desire life abundant, we must allow God to transform our spirits and souls, we must allow God's love to fill us and flow through us, and we must act in the world revealing His love and His glory.

It is all about love, but what is love? As I write the question images of photos from the 1960's come to mind with people holding handwritten "make love, not war" posters. The word "make" leads thoughts towards some rock and roll connotation of promiscuity labeled as love, which is in stark contrast to the purity of love revealed in Scripture. God is love.[1] Love encompasses His character. God is holy, pure, and divine. To have love is to have God and His character. Jesus tells us that we reveal our love for God when we obey His commands.[2] Scripture describes what love looks like saying, "Love is patient and kind... It always protects, always trusts, always hopes, always perseveres" (1 Corinthians 13:4,7). Scripture clarifies that love is the result of the Holy Spirit dwelling within us by listing love as one characteristic of fruit of the Spirit.[3]

Love's purpose is unity. By loving God, we gain His love and our unity with God grows. As a result, we desire to share His love with the world around us, building unity in the world one relationship at a time. God is love. Through His indwelling, His love transforms us and prepares us to share His love with the world – allowing His glory to be revealed through us to the world.

It sounds so simple. Why do we make it so difficult? Sometimes we just need to show sincere compassion to other people.

COMPASSION

In the mid-1980's Jo Anne's[8] primary occupations were mother of four and pastor's wife in Grand Rapids, Michigan. She focused on keeping the home running, attending to the congregation, and all the important but typically behind the scenes tasks like cleaning preschool floors after vacation Bible school. A local television station was planning to film a documentary on hunger in western Michigan and Ethiopia. They invited Jo Anne to travel with them to Ethiopia to help.

She had seen images of starving people on the news and in newspapers. She had seen photos of emaciated bodies and children with distended bellies, but in Ethiopia they visited feeding camps where she encountered seas of starving people. Thousands of people surrounded each small medical facility they visited. Nurses went into the crowd seeking the few that they could help. People sat waiting. The sight of starving people was similar to the images Jo Anne had seen, but now they were not merely images on television, they were real, living humans. The news accounts had prepared her for the sight of individuals, but not for the magnitude of suffering, not for the smell of rapidly progressing death, and not for the silence. The starving people squandered no energy, not even the small amount of energy

---

[8] I mentioned my friend Jo Anne Lyon in chapter 7. We traveled together in Azerbaijan and Mongolia, and I have represented the organization she founded, World Hope International, in Haiti and Zambia. While we were together, she spoke about a pivotal moment in her life and she chose to describe the event early in her book, *The Ultimate Blessing: Rediscovering the Power of God's Presence*, Wesleyan Publishing House (2003).

required to utter a sound. They were a silent sea of human suffering.

She was from the most powerful nation on the planet and had traveled halfway across the globe to help a television crew prepare a documentary, but she encountered human need that she was woefully unprepared to help. She felt completely helpless. She was overwhelmed by the need. She felt as if she had nothing to offer them. They needed food and she had none to offer. They needed medical attention and she could not help.

So she prayed. As she prayed, she recalled Scripture about Jesus showing compassion to the crowds[4] and it occurred to her that she had something to offer – her love and compassion. She found an interpreter and through the interpreter she told the people around her that she was not a doctor, she could not offer medical help, but she was there to tell the story of their suffering to people in the U.S. in an effort to get help to them.

Jo Anne said the response was immediate. She was no longer viewed as an administrative official deciding whom to help; she was a human offering compassion and love to them all. They smiled, offered their hands and touched her face. She broke through her sense of helplessness and realized that God provided what she needed to give them – her presence, her concern, her compassion and her love. And she could be their voice. They lacked the energy to speak, but she could speak for them. She could tell their story, and her presence communicated that they had value, their lives were significant enough for her to travel a great distance to meet and to spend time with, and they were important enough to have their story told. Her presence conveyed respect, compassion and hope to a suffering sea of humanity.

Her story sounds a little like Jesus. He was not walking through crowds surrounding a feeding center in Ethiopia, but He showed compassion to the people who crowded around Him. Matthew writes,

> Jesus went through all the town and villages, teaching in their synagogues, proclaiming the good news of the kingdom and healing every disease and sickness.

When he saw the crowds, *he had compassion on them*, because they were harassed and helpless, like sheep without a shepherd. Then he said to his disciples, "The harvest is plentiful but the workers are few. Ask the Lord of the harvest, therefore, to send out workers into his harvest field." Matthew 9:35-38

Jesus showed compassion to people He encountered who were in need, and He calls His followers to help them. He calls you and me to help them.

Why are workers few? If Christianity is the world's largest religion,[5] and each Christian is called to serve others, why are the workers few? One possible reason is our sense of helplessness and inadequacy. Jo Anne's feeling of helplessness and inadequacy almost won. She almost shied away from the opportunity. It would have been easy for her to flee the field and hide behind a camera, using it as a shield blocking her from the people whom she felt unable to help. But she broke through her helplessness, she discovered power and she offered everything she was capable of offering at the time – she simply engaged as a human to other humans in need. She offered love, compassion and her voice, nothing more but nothing less.

LOVING SERVICE

Compassion requires genuine relationship, which requires physical and emotional presence. Jesus showed His compassion through His loving presence. God's children reveal His glory as they show His love by their presence, through their service and by explaining their experience with God to others. Jesus commands us to love one another as He loves us, which includes word and action.

This message is woven through the New Testament. On the evening of the Last Supper, Jesus demonstrates loving service.[6] He removes His outer clothing and wraps a towel around Himself, assuming the wardrobe and position of a slave.

He proceeds to wash the disciples' feet, a job normally reserved for a slave. He then commands His disciples to do the same saying,

> "Now that I, your Lord and Teacher, have washed your feet, *you should wash one another's feet.* I have set you an example that you should do as I have done for you. Very truly I tell you, no servant is greater than his master, nor is a messenger greater than the one who sent him. Now that you know these things, *you will be blessed if you do them.*" John 13:13-17

Once again, we see Jesus use the phrase "Very truly I tell you," Jesus code indicating something very important is about to come. It is a parable in action. Jesus is not instructing the disciples, or us, to literally wash each other's feet. He is, however, explaining that we should assume the position of slave and serve one another by allowing God's love to flow through us.

The first step involves lowering our perception of ourselves and of our status, and humbling ourselves before other people. We discussed earlier the idea of humbling ourselves before God, which is the natural response to acknowledging who He is and who we are by comparison. But humbling myself before other people has been, at least for me, entirely unnatural. It is beyond counter-intuitive. It is almost unthinkable. I recall choosing teams to play one another during elementary school recess. The teacher would pick two captains and each captain would choose one player at a time, taking turns until everyone was on a team. I imagine most people were offended if they were not chosen early in the process. I was offended if I was not one of the captains. I always desired a position of respect and prominence.

This has continued through my career and, honestly, it has served me well in my career. The desire for respect and prominence and the willingness to work hard to achieve and maintain them are essential to achieve the so-called American dream. So it is counter-intuitive that I should humble myself below other people and serve them. Wouldn't it be just as good if I helped raise their economic condition by helping them advance in their career? While that seems like a perfectly rational answer, and it possibly is for them, it would not help me become the person I need to be.

I recall times serving in our local soup kitchen. The servers stood on the kitchen side of the serving table. The patrons stood on the dining room side. As I served people in genuine need, the barrier of the serving table physically separated me from them. I served them, but I was separated, in my own part of the world, interacting with each person across the serving table for the instant that it took to place some food on the tray and pass it down the serving line. And after cooking, serving food, cleaning the kitchen and dining room, I got in my car and drove home feeling good about myself, patting myself on the back for having done something good, and checking the item off my to do list.

While that sort of service is better than not serving at all, I did not offer compassion because I was not emotionally present, I was hiding behind the serving table and I served more to satisfy my sense of obligation than love. I served food, but I offered nothing else – I failed to offer compassion or love. After living a lifetime of striving to move to the top of every organization I have been affiliated with, how can I learn to humble myself below patrons of a soup kitchen?

My son helped me. In his brief twenty-six years, he has taught me many lessons and has exposed me to many parts of the world that I had no idea existed. He has genuine compassion for people regardless of where they live or how they dress or what color their skin is. When he was just a little guy I would ask him where his shoes were or where his jacket was, he would tell me that he gave them to a friend in need. I wasn't entirely happy about his decision because his compassion meant he no longer had a jacket or shoes, but I was happy that he did not seem selfish.

One Saturday morning when he was thirteen years old, he asked if he could go to a friend's house. He said his friend's brother would pick him up. I allowed it. About fifteen minutes after they left my son called me. He asked if I could pick him up from a parking lot about two miles from our home. Police had pulled them over and they were arresting the driver of the car.

When I arrived at the parking lot my son was handcuffed and sitting in the back of the patrol car, his little blond head barely visible through the rear window. The tiny young girl of a police officer explained what had happened, but my head was spinning out of control, I was suddenly dizzy, I could barely stand up and I could not listen to her words. Soon I was introduced to the juvenile legal system.

Years later he was arrested again. This time he spent time in jail, and I learned new lessons. I learned that he needed underwear. I gathered some underwear from our home and drove to the jail. During my first trip to the jail I learned that underwear needed to be in a factory-sealed bag. After a trip to the store, I learned that they needed to be all white. After a second trip to the store, I learned that the only person who receives articles of clothing leaves at a certain time that I just missed. I learned how to set up an account that allowed him to call me and I learned how to set up an account allowing him to buy merchandise from the jail store and I learned that when I went to the jail to see him we saw each other through a video screen, and, fortunately, the judge provided the opportunity for me to learn how to arrange for a bail bond. I studied criminal law and criminal procedure in law school, but through my son I learned so much more about the reality of it all.

We did not know how long he would be in jail for a bunch of reasons I will not bore you with. As it turns out, he was not in jail very long, but it was long enough for him to conclude that many saw him as sub-human because he was an inmate. He believed that others saw him as no longer worthy of dignity or respect. The first time a local pastor visited the jail for a Bible study, my son went primarily to experience a change of scenery. When the pastor returned, my son went because the pastor treated him like he was fully human and the pastor's compassion meant more to my son than I would have ever imagined.

When I heard how much the pastor's visits meant to my son, I started going to our local jail to minister to the inmates (my son was in a different facility far away at the time). Through my experience, my son's descriptions of his experience and my love for him, my view of inmates changed. I grew. I became able to see each inmate as fully human, as a person worthy of dignity, respect, compassion and love – a person exactly like my son who I love.

And my worldview changed. I initially noticed the change while reading the newspaper. I read about horrific events, tragedies involving someone killing another and leaving innocent people suffering in the wake on all sides of the tragedy. Before the change, I would quickly read the stories as a reminder of why I lock my doors at night and avoid certain parts of town. But afterward, I found myself weeping over the newspaper for the victim, for the perpetrator, for all the innocent people involved, for the loss, for the evil on display, for the people caught up in awful situations, and for their horrific decisions. I see everyone involved as humans created in God's image. While some made awful choices and others were thrust into the wake of ugliness through no fault of their own, they are all worthy of my compassion and love.

When you see news footage of a line of shackled inmates in orange jumpsuits being led by guards, what do you see? Do you see criminals? Do you see convicts? Do you see sub-human monsters? Do you see people bearing God's image? Do you see human beings worthy of your love? I see people who could be my son who I love beyond words, and I know, no matter what they have done, God loves them and they are worthy of my love.

Through my son, I discovered new eyes to see people as bearing God's image; I discovered humility toward other people; and I am beginning to learn how to humbly serve other people. I am learning how to offer myself free from status, as merely one human reaching out to another human with compassion and in love.

I believe this is what Paul was expressing in one of his letters to the church in Corinth. He was describing the gap between my service at the soup kitchen and my transformed eyes. Paul describes love as "the most excellent way" (1 Corinthians 12:31) and says that it does not matter how smart we are, or how much faith we have, or how much we give to the poor, or how much we sacrifice for others, if we do not have love. If we do all the right things but do not have love, the acts are empty and we are nothing. Love must be the foundation of it all. Following is what many refer to as the Love Chapter:

And now I will show you the most excellent way.

If I speak in the tongues of men and of angels, but have not love, I am only a resounding gong or a clanging cymbal. If I have the gift of prophecy and can fathom all mysteries and all knowledge, and if I have a faith that can move mountains, but have not love, *I am nothing*. If I give all I possess to the poor and surrender my body to the flames, but have not love, *I gain nothing*.

Love is patient, love is kind. It does not envy, it does not boast, it is not proud. It is not rude, it is not self-seeking, it is not easily angered, it keeps no record of wrongs. Love does not delight in evil but rejoices with the truth. It always protects, always trusts, always hopes, always perseveres.

Love never fails. But where there are prophecies, they will cease; where there are tongues, they will be stilled; where there is knowledge, it will pass away. For we know in part and we prophesy in part, but when perfection comes, the imperfect disappears. When I was a child, I talked like a child, I thought like a child, I reasoned like a child. When I became a man, I put childish ways behind me. Now we see but a poor reflection as in a mirror; then we shall see face to face. Now I know in part; then I shall know fully, even as I am fully known.

And now these three remain: faith, hope and love. But the greatest of these is love. 1 Corinthians 12:31-13:13

We often hear the chapter quoted during weddings as a reminder of what love looks like and of how fundamental love is between two people committing their lives to one another. It also applies to how we view a line of inmates in orange jumpsuits, how we view a homeless man asking for change, how we view soup kitchen patrons, and how we view every other example of human being, even those who may not share our social standing.

How can we learn to love each of them? If we do all the right things but do not have love, we are nothing. Love is patient, kind, and it keeps no record of wrongs. Given this definition, love is difficult to offer even between husband and wife, yet Jesus commands us to offer love to strangers. How can we do this? It takes Christ. It takes the indwelling of the Holy Spirit. It requires new eyes through His transformation.

We cannot do it on our own. We must surrender ourselves and allow Jesus Christ to work on us and flow through us. The task appears impossible when viewed through our human eyes, yet Scripture explains it is possible through the indwelling Holy Spirit.

AS JESUS LOVES US

After Jesus washes the disciples feet during the evening of the Last Supper, Jesus reinforces His call to loving service by saying,

> "A new command I give you: Love one another. *As I have loved you*, so you must love one another. By this everyone will know that you are my disciples, if you love one another." John 13:34

He demonstrates loving service by washing feet and He commands love. Now, the command to love one another is not new, and it was not new when Jesus spoke the words. It is as old as Leviticus[7] and Jesus explained early in His ministry that the command to "love your neighbor as yourself" is the second most important commandment.[8] So why did Jesus describe it as new?

He said, "As I have loved you...." He had just demonstrated loving service through a parable in action by assuming the position of a slave and washing feet, and He was about to demonstrate His love by laying down His life for us. By saying, "As I have loved you," Jesus changed the command in a radical way, and if you think it through to its core, the only possible way any human may come close to loving the way Jesus loves is by allowing His love to flow through them.

Later that evening Jesus continues teaching about loving service, and He explains that loving service is only possible through connection with Him. As discussed previously, He teaches about the vine and the branches explaining that Jesus is the vine and His followers are the branches.[9] So long as followers abide in Jesus, so long as they stay connected with Him, so long as they allow His sustenance and love to flow through them, they bear His fruit. If they are disconnected from Jesus, they wither and die. Jesus relies on His followers to bear fruit and His followers depend on Him for spiritual life – it is a perfectly symbiotic relationship. Just as a vineyard exists to produce grapes, disciples of Christ exist to produce God's fruit in the world through loving service.

As He teaches about the vine and branches, Jesus weaves the ideas of unity between people, unity of Jesus Christ and the Father, Christ's love, the Father's love and loving God. Jesus explains that we demonstrate our love for God the Father and Jesus Christ by keeping His commands, and Jesus repeats His command to love one another two more times.[10] Over and over Jesus urges us to stay connected with Him, to love Him, to love one another, and to bear fruit.

Later that evening, Jesus prays the long prayer discussed earlier and recorded as John 17. In His prayer, Jesus says that He glorifies God by completing the work God called Him to do.[11] We are each called to serve. By serving God we glorify God and we reveal God's glory to the world, but our work must be His work, initiated by His call, sustained by His love, and performed for His glory. It is for His glory, not our own.

While our life is certainly improved through God's spiritual transformation, and our life is better when lived in communion with God, His transformation enables us to serve, gives us a heart to realize all people are created in God's image, gives us ears to hear His call, provides eyes to see opportunities, and instills a desire to serve.

WITNESS – THE CALL

Following Christ presumes service. Early in His ministry, Jesus meets Peter (called Simon at the time) and his brother Andrew. As they fish on the Sea of Galilee, Jesus calls to them saying, "Come, follow me, and I will send you out to fish for people" (Matthew 4:19). Jesus invites the men to follow Him, and in His next breath He explains that if they choose to follow Him they will serve others. Following Christ is inseparable from service.

In the passage from Matthew quoted above, Jesus says, "The harvest is plentiful but the workers are few. Ask the Lord of the harvest, therefore, to send out workers into his harvest field" (Matthew 9:37-38). There is so much work to do and not nearly enough workers. Jesus tells us to pray for workers. He says every follower is called to be a worker, but there are too few.

Later in His ministry Jesus returns to harvest imagery for another call to service. Jesus and the disciples travel from Jerusalem to Galilee. They choose a route through Samaria. At noon one day they stop at a well. Jesus stays near the well while the disciples go into town to buy food. A Samaritan woman approaches the well carrying her water jar. Jesus talks with her about spiritual life using the analogy of living water[12] and He tells her directly in clear words that He is the Messiah.[13]

The disciples return with food and Jesus talks about spiritual food saying,

"My food," said Jesus, "is to do the will of him who
sent me and to finish his work. Do you not say, 'Four
months more and then the harvest'? I tell you, open
your eyes and look at the fields! They are ripe for
harvest. Even now the reaper draws his wages, even
now he harvests the crop for eternal life, so that the
sower and the reaper may be glad together. Thus the
saying, 'One sows and another reaps' is true. I sent
you to reap what you have not worked for. Others
have done the hard work, and you have reaped the
benefits of their labor." John 4:32-38

Jesus says, "My food is to do the will of him who sent me
and to finish his work." Spiritual life is life lived in union with
God, and spiritual food involves work. Do you seek spiritual
fulfillment? Do the will of Him who sends you and finish His
work.

Jesus says, "I tell you, open your eyes and look at the
fields! They are ripe for harvest.... I sent you to reap..." Without
explanation, He mentions that the crop has to do with eternal life.
Experiencing Christ leads to spiritual life, spiritual life leads to a
desire to serve, and Jesus calls His disciples to serve.

How does the reaper harvest "the crop for eternal life"?
What does that mean? God showers His holy grace on everyone.
His holy grace is offered to people who do not know God or Jesus
or the Holy Spirit and some are receptive to it. God's grace causes
them to ponder spiritual matters, to ask questions about God, to
be receptive to spiritual discussions. The Holy Spirit prepares
them so they are receptive when the word is presented to them.
Then He sends people, His disciples, to present the word, to
explain the word and to reap the crop that He started.

I think of a woman in Azerbaijan I met about fifteen years
ago. She worked in an office in Baku. A friend invited her to a
weekly Bible study and over time she gradually came to know
Jesus Christ. I am not sure what the climate is like now, but it is a
Muslim nation and at that time if authorities caught a local with a
Bible or proselytizing or worshiping Jesus Christ, he or she would
be detained and possibly jailed. I heard of interrogation, and

people losing jobs and homes and freedom, all because they worshiped Jesus Christ.

The Bible study was a guarded secret. In the former Soviet country, most people lived in Soviet style apartments. The group met in homes. They moved to a different location each week and they were careful not to have too many people at a meeting, otherwise neighbors might become suspicious. They softly sang hymns. They studied Scripture and prayed. And they were on guard, constantly attuned to the risk. They carefully communicated where they would meet next and they were careful while walking to the meeting with a Bible buried deeply in their bag – if they were stopped and searched, possessing the Bible would be bad.

She developed the habit of praying and reading Scripture each day and attending the weekly Bible study. She sang hymns under her breath as she walked to her job in a large office building. One day during her coffee break as she sat in the break room, a woman co-worker that she recognized but did not know approached her and started asking her questions about her life. The co-worker explained that she saw something different about the woman and she wanted to learn what it was.

Terrified, she left the break room and returned to her desk. Was the co-worker a spy? How did she know? What did she know?

Day after day, time and time again over the next few months the co-worker continued to pester her, asking her questions and bothering her during breaks. Finally, one day the woman invited her co-worker to the Bible study. She gave her the address and time. She prayed the co-worker would not send the police.

The co-worker arrived to the meeting that night as the pastor read Acts chapter 2, the story of the Holy Spirit descending like flames on believers. As the co-worker heard the words, she started sobbing uncontrollably. When she was able, she explained that for months she had had a recurring nightmare. Flames engulfed her home but did not burn it. She suddenly understood the dream was Jesus reaching out to her. She understood that Jesus had reached out to her through the recurring dream and He had orchestrated events for her to attend the meeting that particular night when Acts chapter 2 would be read.

The woman communicated her experience with Jesus primarily through her presence, through her actions, by how she lived her life. It involved few words. It involved significant risk, but she served her role in the process. She reaped, witnessed and offered loving service in her own way, and the pastor served his role. They each took a relatively small step in the process to harvest the crop prepared by the Holy Spirit. The Holy Spirit did the heavy lifting. He planted the crop, He nurtured the crop, He set the stage, and He helped the woman and the pastor as they each served in their own way.

As followers of Christ, they were each called to serve Him, they were each called to witness about Him, and they each received the power of the Holy Spirit to help them accomplish the task.

WITNESS – THE POWER

The Holy Spirit delivers power. After Jesus' ministry on earth, after everything described in the gospels, after the teaching and miracles, after His arrest, torture and crucifixion, after His resurrection and forty days of post-resurrection teaching, Jesus prepares to ascend to heaven. His parting words are

> "It is not for you to know the times or the dates the Father has set by his own authority. But *you will receive power when the Holy Spirit comes on you*; and *you will be my witnesses* in Jerusalem, and in all Judea and Samaria, and to the ends of the earth." Acts 1:8

At the end of His ministry on earth, Jesus repeats the message conveyed when He first called Peter and Andrew. He uses different words, but both statements involve a command to serve. As they fished on the Sea of Galilee, Jesus said if they chose to follow Him, they would be choosing to fish for people. As He prepares to ascend to heaven, He says, "You will be my witnesses."

How does an invitation to fish equate to a call to witness? And how does the command to love one another as Jesus loves us encompass the call? As I ponder the questions, I think about the ways Jesus demonstrated love. While fully human on earth, people were attracted to Jesus like fish to a shiny lure. Crowds followed Him. They wanted to be near Him. They would not leave Him alone because He cared for them, He provided for them, He healed them, He taught as they had never been taught, and He revealed genuine compassion. A fisher of people should attract people and some of the people who are attracted will hear the fisher's message. They will listen to and hear the fisher's witness.

Fishing for people involves living our life in a way that other people notice because it reveals God's glory. The fisher inspires others because of the hints of holiness he or she reveals. When others are interested to learn more, verbal witness is the next step, and it is all enveloped within love – the love that Jesus has for us.

That is what Jesus did, and He promises that His followers will be empowered to do greater things. Jesus promises,

> "Very truly I tell you, whoever believes in me will do the works I have been doing, and they will do even greater things than these, because I am going to the Father." John 14:12

This promise was demonstrated through Peter and the apostles. Jesus originally invited Peter to follow Him and called Peter to become a fisher of people. As Jesus prepared to ascend, He called Peter to be His witness, and He promised that the power of the Holy Spirit would come upon him. Nine days later, at the festival known as Pentecost, the Holy Spirit descended on believers who were praying together in the temple.[14] Peter, freshly infused with the Holy Spirit, preached to the crowds who gathered around him and 3,000 people came to know Jesus Christ during a single sermon.[15]

The apostles were anointed with special healing power and God healed many people through them.[16] God performed such signs and wonders that people were a little afraid of them, but they wanted to be near them. Peter regularly prayed in the temple. Many brought sick friends and family and placed them on mats along the path Peter walked, hoping his shadow might fall on them and provide healing.[17]

Peter witnessed through the way he conducted his life. He lived his life for Jesus Christ, and it showed. He carried himself in a manner befitting of an association with Jesus Christ, and God anointed him with the power of the Holy Spirit. People wanted to be near him because God's love flowed and God's glory was revealed through him. As a fisher attracts fish, Peter attracted people and he served as a witness by telling people about his experience with Jesus Christ.

Jesus calls each believer to serve as His witness and He calls all believers to serve others with love, but Jesus does not send anyone out alone. He promises that the Holy Spirit is with us and He promises we will receive power when the Holy Spirit comes upon us. His call is combined with a gift. His call comes with the power necessary to fulfill the call.

So how do we do this? Are you like me? Does the story leave you wondering how you can apply this to your life? How do I drink spiritual water? How do I eat spiritual food? How do I reap spiritual crops? How do I fish for people? I know I am not Peter and I am certainly not Jesus, so how do I serve the way they served? How do I serve as Jesus' witness? How do I love in the way Jesus loves me?

Jesus says His followers will do greater things than He did because He is with God the Father. But how do we get started?

As the account of the woman in Azerbaijan and the examples in Scripture suggest, loving service involves presence, words and action. The story of the Samaritan woman at the well provides another example. John concludes her story writing,

Many of the Samaritans from that town believed in him because of the woman's testimony, "He told me everything I did." So, when the Samaritans came to him, they urged him to stay with them, and he stayed two days. And because of his words many more became believers.

They said to the woman, "We no longer believe just because of what you said; now we have heard for ourselves, and we know that this man really is the Savior of the world." John 4:39-42

The Samaritan women experienced Jesus and she told others about her experience. That is how she reaped, served and witnessed. She simply experienced Jesus, sought out other people and told them about her experience. We are called to act in a similar way. We should experience Jesus Christ and simply describe our experience with Him to others.

How is this greater than the works of Jesus? Jesus said we will do greater things than He did. How is this greater? He may have performed amazing miracles, taught amazing lessons, described the kingdom of heaven, and opened His arms to people in need, but when we speak of our experience with Jesus Christ in our lives today, we speak of His on-going presence, continuing power and continuing activity in the world, which is extremely important. Jesus is with God the Father in heaven, helping us, sending His Holy Spirit to us, showering us with His holy grace, and the world needs to hear about our experience with Him and of His holy healing grace.

WITNESS – FACING FEAR

Whether real or merely perceived, serving as Christ's witness often involves risk and each witness must overcome fear. As we saw above with the woman in Azerbaijan, witnessing may involve few words and efforts to avoid detection, but it often begins with a person who takes the time to genuinely engage another in sincere conversation, and it often involves love revealing itself through compassion and relationship.

I heard a story on the radio about David, an American evangelist in Turkey who has been detained and arrested on many occasions, and of how each time God has used him to reach people in amazing ways.[18] He said it has happened so many times that now, when the police come for him, he is excited to see what God is about to do.

Pause for a moment to allow that thought to sink in. Turkish police are knocking at his door. He knows he will likely be detained or arrested. He knows he is about to be led to a jail cell for an unknown period of time, and he is excited to see what God is about to do through him.

David said on one occasion police led him to a holding cell and fortunately they allowed him to keep his Turkish language Bible. When he walked in the cell the first man he saw asked, "What are you in for?" David replied, "God sent me here to meet you." David said he knew nothing about the man, but David soon learned that he was a Kurdish atheist who had been living in the red light district of Istanbul. The police originally detained the man for a minor offense, but he refused to give the police his true name and he had no identification, so they detained him until they could determine his identity. When they learned who the man was, they realized he was wanted for a long list of criminal activity. A few minutes before David entered the cell the man had been told that he was about to be sent to prison for ten years.

As they spoke, David handed the man his Bible. The man opened it and his eyes happened to rest on the story of the woman accused of adultery, which begins by explaining that the law called for death by stoning.[19] The man stopped reading. He did not want to learn anything about a religion that called for punishment like that for something he had done many times. David urged him to continue reading to the end of the story. When he read that Jesus refused to condemn the woman and saved her life by suggesting that the person without sin throw the first stone, the man said, "I like this Jesus." He was attracted by Jesus' compassion.

The man who had been convicted of many crimes read about Jesus, and his eyes just happened to fall on the account of Jesus showing mercy and compassion to a person who, according to the law of the time and place described in Scripture, deserved death by stoning. Intrigued, he sat down with the Bible and continued reading. David sat and spoke with other men. As they spoke, David said, "The truth will set you free." The man reading the Bible said, "Its true. What he just said is true. I am reading the words right here. It says, 'the truth will set you free.'" [20] Everyone present was amazed. What a coincidence that he would be reading the words at the very moment that David spoke them during an unrelated conversation. They must have wondered whether the meeting really was a divinely orchestrated engagement.

The man continued reading the Bible. The next morning he said that God came to him in a dream and told him that God had sent David to him to tell him about Jesus. Later that day he was taken away to prison to begin his ten-year sentence.

On another occasion David was taken to the immigration agency's detention facility. Some problems had arisen during his visa renewal process, so he was detained. He described the center as a melting pot of people from Muslim countries. People from all over Africa, the Middle East, Pakistan, Afghanistan and India were there.

He was placed in large holding cell. The cell next to his was the ISIS cell, which was concealed with a curtain. Nobody spoke with ISIS guys. Everyone was afraid of them.

David was being held on an upper floor. When he went to the restroom, through the window he saw his wife standing in line on the ground below. She was waiting to be inspected so she could visit him. He called to her through the window in English. Another man in the restroom, who was from Afghanistan, also spoke English. He had worked for a US relief organization, and he engaged David in conversation.

David learned that the man had fled Afghanistan seeking a safer place to live. He was with a group of about 50 men who had traveled across Afghanistan, Iran and Turkey. They were in a bus nearing Istanbul when they were stopped and detained. They had been out in the elements for a long time with no opportunity to bathe, so they smelled really bad.

When David saw his wife, he asked her to reach out to church members and ask for clothing for the men from Afghanistan. The next day she arrived with 50 pairs of underwear, socks and assorted items. Amazingly, the guards allowed her to give the sack of clothing to David, who gave it to the Afghani man, who felt like Santa Claus with a sack of gifts for the other men.

The act of kindness led to questions. Men asked David where the clothing came from, why did he give it, what did he want in return, and similar questions. David explained that the gifts were from the Christian community in Istanbul, and the clothing was simply offered to show the love of Jesus Christ to the men. The questions provided an opportunity for David to talk about Jesus.

He said that men in the deportation center were not criminals, but they each had a heart-breaking story to tell. They were each fleeing horrific situations desperately seeking a better life somewhere, anywhere. David said that many were interested in learning more about Jesus, but few expressed their interest in front of others for fear of losing face. Many came to David in private to learn more about Jesus.

As word spread that an American was talking about Jesus, and that the Afghani man was helping the American, the ISIS guys took notice. The interviewer on the radio asked David about this, mentioning that ISIS seems to hate Americans and Christians and that David had two big strikes against him. Answering, he spoke about faith and fear, and he mentioned the story from the Old Testament about Daniel and the lions' den.[21] He said that on that particular night, the night when Daniel was in the den, the lions' den was the safest place in the city because that is where the angels were working to protect Daniel. David knew God had sent him to the deportation center as His witness, he trusted that God would protect him, and he knew that if God allowed him to die, he would be joining God in glory and that would be ok also.

Confirming his view of heavenly protection, David and the Afghani man were each separately released before ISIS harmed either. After his release, the Afghani man knew nothing about Istanbul and had no place to go. The first night, as he looked for a place to stay, he was mugged and beaten. Fortunately he held onto his cell phone. He found a WIFI signal, located David through Facebook, and sent him a message. David was too far away to help that night, but David called a friend in the area who went out, found the man, and allowed the man to stay in his home that night. The next day, David picked the man up and took him to his home.

The man was impressed and intrigued by how much the small Christian community in Istanbul had done to help him. He saw a Bible on David's bookshelf and started reading it. As David and his family slept, the man read the Bible all night. David invited the man to attend church with him and he went. He was amazed at the contemporary style of worship. He had never heard music in church, and the preaching was a message of love, and the people were filled with joy. He was amazed by how friendly everyone was and how happy they were to worship together. He said it was nothing like the images of Christian worship that he had expected.

The man from Afghanistan soon came to know Jesus Christ, but it all started with relationship, genuine compassion and expressions of love. Words and theology came later. David started by simply talking with the man, and when he saw a need, he did what he could to help with the need. The man experienced Christ's love through the community of faith – through their gifts, their loving community and their worship. Later, when the opportunity arose, David spoke to him about Jesus Christ.

So David is excited when the police come to detain or arrest him because he knows God is about to do something amazing.

The mere thought of serving as God's witness often causes fear or anxiety. We worry that we will not have the correct answer to questions or that we will say the wrong thing or that we will be rejected. It is easy for us to think "I am not a Bible scholar so I am not prepared to serve as witness." Thoughts like that are simply wrong. Serving as witness involves nothing more than explaining your experience. What did you see, hear and experience? What was your life like before you met Jesus and how is it different now? You do not need to be a Bible scholar to discuss your life and your experience. And if your listener rejects your message, he or she is rejecting God the Father, Jesus Christ and the Holy Spirit, not you.

WITNESS – LIVING A LIFE WORTHY OF HIS ASSOCIATION

Followers of Christ are called to witness and serve others with love. Our witness involves not only our words, but also how we represent Christ through our life. If the character of our existence is unworthy of association with Christ, our words will not achieve the desired result.

Think about the man in Gerasene who met Jesus. Jesus and the disciples traveled across the Sea of Galilee, landing on the southeastern shore. As they left the boat, a demon-possessed man ran to Jesus, kneeled before Him and shouted at the top of his lungs

> "What do you want with me, Jesus, Son of the Most High God? Swear to God that you won't torture me!"
> Mark 5:7

Jesus ordered demons out of the man. After he was set free from the demons, the man wanted to follow Jesus. He wanted to join the group and travel with Jesus, but Jesus had a different mission for the man. Jesus said,

> "Go home to your family and tell them how much the Lord has done for you, and how he has had mercy on you.' So the man went away and began to tell in the

Decapolis how much Jesus had done for him. And all the people were amazed." Mark 5:19-20

The man saw Jesus, recognized Him for who He is, acknowledged His authority and power, kneeled before Him and begged for mercy. Jesus freed the man from demons, gave the man a new life, and sent him on a mission. It was obvious to everyone he encountered that he was a new person leading a new life, and when he told people about his experience with Jesus, they were amazed.

Most often, witnessing for Christ involves both words and actions because words are cheap without action to support them. Sometimes, communicating relationship does not involve words – we can communicate our relationship with Christ simply by how we live – but explaining the Gospel requires words. If you follow Jesus Christ, how do other people know that you do?

The man in Gerasene was freed from demons, and his new life reflected his experience with Jesus Christ. Everything about his presence indicated new life. He had been completely wild – living in the tombs, breaking chains and screaming continuously. After meeting Jesus he moved back home and was civilized. Jesus instructed the man to tell others about his experience with Jesus, and we are led to believe he did.

There was something about the woman in Azerbaijan that was different. Her changed presence attracted her co-worker, like a fish to a shiny lure. She witnessed first by simply being the changed person in Christ that she was, and second by taking the bold step of inviting her co-worker to the Bible study.

Peter lived his life in such a manner that people knew he was holy. They knew he would be at the temple praying, they knew if they asked him for help he would help, they knew he would tell them about his experience with Jesus Christ when asked – that is how he lived his life.

If you follow Jesus Christ, what distinguishes you from every non-believer around you?

Witness – Intentionality

Jesus explains that His followers are not of the world, yet God sends them into the world.[22] If people are to be useful for God's service, they need His power, they need His transforming presence, and they need His sanctification.[23] Jesus acknowledges that the world is a place of great contrast.[24] It is the place where evil exists, where Satan and his demons roam looking for people to devour. It is the place that Paul describes as the "dominion of darkness"[25] and "this dark world."[26] It is also the place where God showers His holy grace, where He sends His Holy Spirit and where His angels protect. God sends His people out into the dark world to serve as light in the darkness, to transform the world one relationship at a time.

Recognizing this, Jesus prays. He prays for God to protect His followers from the evil one and to sanctify them by His truth. Jesus says, "My prayer is not that you take them out of the world, but that you protect them from the evil one" (John 17:15). Christ's followers are called to be in the world as God's servants, so Jesus prays for protection.

I hear stories of saintly people like Mother Theresa and quickly conclude that they are special, and I could never be like them. I hear of people who are out in the world working in remarkable ways spreading love. I know folks who heard God's call, quit their job, sold everything and moved to a far away land to serve Him.

I think of my friend David who opened his home to me in Mongolia. Years earlier he was happily living his life in the States. He had a good job, a nice home with a loving wife and two kids. One Sunday he went to church and heard a missionary speak about the mission field, and David's heart burned with a desire to serve. He felt the call and as he and his wife prayed and pondered over the following months, they grew certain that God was calling them to Mongolia to help street children. Eventually, they sold their possessions and moved to Mongolia following God's call.

I think of Jo Anne who quit a meaningful counseling career to launch World Hope International with a clear vision and conviction of God's call, but nothing else. She had no funds and no donors, but she was certain of God's call. In worldly terms, she took a huge risk. In her mind she was simply following God's call and she knew He would provide. As a result of her faith in action, countless lives have been changed through the efforts of World Hope International.

They amaze me. I don't think I could do what they did and, in reality, so long as I tried to do it on my own, that conclusion would be accurate. But if God called me to do something like that, He would provide everything necessary to satisfy the call. I would need to step out in faith and follow His call, and I am not suggesting for an instant that it would be easy, but He would provide.

We hear stories about remarkable, saintly people allowing God to perform amazing acts of grace through them, but nobody can be a saint on their own, and those who we consider to be saints are not doing it on their own. They are allowing God to act through them. They are allowing themselves to be His vessels. They are allowing the Holy Spirit to transform their spirit, and that transformation allows the Holy Spirit to reveal His love through the people who seem saintly to us. Through the Holy Spirit this power is available to everyone. Jesus promises that we will receive power when the Holy Spirit comes upon us.[27]

Jesus prays for His followers and He calls each believer to loving service and to witness, but that does not mean we all need to move to Africa or Mongolia or some other far away place. Opportunities to reach out with loving service and to witness surround us every day, but if we are not intentional we will miss them. Take time to look around. Schedule extra time in your day so that you can linger a bit. Go to your next meeting or appointment early and talk with people you see. After your meeting linger, take time to talk on a personal level with people around you. Leave for work a little early so, if you happen to see someone in need along the way, you have time to help. Be intentional in your scheduling to position yourself for loving service.

Recently my friend Joe was driving to work. He noticed an SUV stuck in the ditch on the side of the road with a woman and two girls inside. As the traffic zoomed by, Joe stopped to see if he could help. He was driving a pickup and he had towropes. After a few minutes he had them out of the ditch and they were all on their way. From Joe's perspective it was not a big deal. It took a few minutes out of his day. In fact, when I asked him if he minded me sharing the story he had forgotten all about it. To him, it was such a small event that he had forgotten about it. But to the woman in the SUV heading to work and to the girls heading to school, Joe was a hero that day. It was a big deal to them.

What if he was late for work and did not have time to stop? Or if he was so busy thinking about other things that he did not notice? He would have missed the opportunity to offer loving service. We need to be intentional about allowing time so we are in a position to serve, we need to be intentional about looking for opportunities, and when we see them, we need to act.

Recently another friend, a small white-haired woman in her 60's who prays all the time, told me about a morning running errands around town. She prays every morning but on this particular morning she prayed asking God to use her. She prayed specifically asking Him to use her as His hands and feet. Then she went about her day. She was in the grocery store pushing her cart down the aisle and she passed a young man pushing his cart. She felt a tug at her heart and she knew God wanted her to talk to the man. But she did not do it. She passed him again and she said nothing. Several more times she passed him, but she never spoke. As she stood in the checkout line his cart was directly behind her, but she did not speak. She never acted on the opportunity she felt certain God had placed before her, in direct response to her prayer no less, and she did not act because she felt awkward. She was not afraid of the man; she did not fear for her safety; she just felt awkward approaching a stranger.

She left the store, went to her car, put her groceries in the car, sat in the driver's seat and cried. She cried out to God saying she was sorry and pleaded for another chance. She continued around town running errands. A little while later she stopped at the fabric store. When she walked in she immediately saw the same young man across the store. She approached him, explained what had happened and asked if there was anything she could do for him. He did need some help and she knew exactly where to send him.

Opportunities to serve surround us. We must avail ourselves to God, we must seek His eyes and His ears to identify the opportunities before us, and we must pray for His courage and power to act when we see them.

CONCLUSION

So what's the point of it all? Love. The point of it all is love, which necessarily involves God because He is love. If we choose to follow Christ, we will offer ourselves in loving service to others, and we will each serve as His witness. Our combined call to love God and to love other people summarizes the message of Scripture. It is also the point of it all, and when we allow His love to flow through us, His glory is revealed to the world.

Through the first thirteen chapters we discussed life, the importance of spiritual life, and our need to seek spiritual transformation through God. All of that is important. It is the foundation that must be implemented through action out in the world. While it might be wonderful to think righteous thoughts and possess the proper philosophy and theology, it is all empty if not demonstrated through action in the world. With this in mind, Jesus calls us to assume the position of a slave and offer loving service to the world.

Jesus showed compassion to the crowds and He calls us to show compassion. He demonstrated loving service and He calls us to lead lives of loving service. He taught openly about the kingdom of heaven and while He calls us to be His witnesses, He promises to give us the power to do so through His indwelling Holy Spirit. He offers the gift of new life, He offers the satisfaction of life abundant, and He promises to provide everything we need to live out the life He calls us to live.

May God give you His rest, peace and comfort, may His Holy Spirit fill you and transform you, may you know life abundant, may you be whole and satisfied, may His love flow from you, may He enlighten the eyes of your spirit to see opportunities in your path to serve Him, and may God's glory be revealed through you.

16 | LOVE & JUDGMENT

*A new command I give you:
Love one another. As I have
loved you, so you must love one
another. John 13:34*

We are each a sinner living in this sin-filled world, deserving God's wrath. On our own, each person receives just compensation, and the wages of sin is death.[1] God is patient, merciful and kind, but He judges, and each human on his or her own deserves condemnation. God's wrath is the just verdict for each of us, but through Christ Jesus we are released from the verdict we deserve, we are saved, set free.[2]

God's holy word shows us what His wrath looks like. It looks like a flood destroying every creature on earth save eight humans and two of other creatures.[3] It looks like sulfur fire raining from heaven.[4] It is awful beyond our ability to imagine, without earthly comparison.

If the notion of deserving God's wrath seems harsh, that indicates a misunderstanding of God's holiness and our depravity. On our own we are dead, we are filthy, we have evil inclinations, our mind is hostile to God and His holy word appears as foolishness.[5] On our own we simply cannot please

God and we have no business even imagining that we could handle His holy presence.

Apart from God through Christ Jesus, people tend to worship and serve created things.[6] They exult themselves and by doing so, in their minds, they bring God down. Directing their worship to the created realm with humans at the upper echelon, through their cloudy, sinful, evil vision, they see themselves as holy, righteous and deserving of life. But having exchanged truth for lies, they are blind and utterly helpless apart from God.

Through Christ Jesus we gain life. Through Christ Jesus we are saved. Through Christ Jesus we are cleansed. Through Christ Jesus we avoid the wrath we deserve. Through Christ Jesus we gain communion with the holy One. And we did nothing to deserve any of it. We could never deserve His holy gift of grace. We deserve it as much as a baby deserves being born. It is a miracle that happens, but we do not deserve it.

We were filthy, evil, dead wretches, granted new life through Christ Jesus. Our debts were larger than we could ever pay, yet He wiped them clean as a matter of grace. How could we ever look down on others in judgment? How could we ever see others in any way except through eyes filled with love, compassion and a genuine desire that they too might be granted life by His holy, loving grace?

Paul writes,

> You, therefore, have no excuse, you who pass judgment on someone else, for at whatever point you judge the other, you are condemning yourself, because you who pass judgment do the same things. Now we know that God's judgment against those who do such things is based on truth. So when you, a mere human being, pass judgment on them and yet do the same things, do you think you will escape God's judgment? Or do you show contempt for the riches of his kindness, forbearance and patience, not realizing that God's kindness is intended to lead you to repentance?
> Romans 2:1-4

If it is so simple, why do we get it wrong so often? Jesus urges us to assume the position of a slave and to offer loving service to people around us. Jesus commands us to love one another as He loves us. Jesus tells us to be light in the darkness.[7] He calls us to show compassion, to enter into genuine loving relationship, and to reveal His love and glory to the world.

Yet we often desire to place ourselves on a pedestal, looking down on other people as we strut our Superiority Dance.[8] We get confused on the whole judgment thing, and as a result many, many people in the world see Christians as anything but loving. Why do we often express judgment rather than love? It is remarkable how we struggle with this and more remarkable how much harm we do to Jesus Christ's name in the process.

If God is love, if the greatest commandments are loving God and loving other people, if the core of Jesus' message is love, and if each Christian is called to loving service, how is it that #lovewins is a message filled with anti-Christian sentiment? "Love wins" sounds like the fundamental message of the Body of Christ, yet much of the world sees Christians as judgmental, hateful, exclusionary, and lots of things other than loving. I have encountered many people from around the globe who refuse the label "Christian" while readily embracing the term "follower of Christ." Why do we get love wrong?

A few years ago I met some friends in downtown Denver to watch the Pac-12 championship football game on television. My alma mater, the University of Colorado, was playing in the game. As we watched the game and talked, my friend Eric shared the story of his recent tragic loss. Seven months earlier his brother had been beaten to death in Idaho solely because he was homosexual. He was 49 years old, a Boise State University employee, homosexual and lonely. He desired companionship and he answered an ad published on the Backpage website. He arranged to meet a man who got in his car and directed him to a secluded place where another man was waiting. The two men viciously beat Eric's brother. After he lay helpless on the ground they repeatedly kicked him with steel-toed boots, breaking ribs and battering his skull. They took his clothes, possessions and car, and left him to die in the cold Idaho night. He walked to a house and found people who helped him. He lived long enough to arrive at the hospital and to identify his attackers.

Eric talked about his brother. He said he loved his brother and described sadness and loss and grief. He told stories about growing up together and he described his brother's struggles with loneliness and he described the awful things he heard from people claiming to be Christians who passed judgment on his brother's lifestyle, offering ridicule and condemnation rather than anything close to love. Their antagonistic words exacerbated Eric's grief, and for what purpose? Why would anyone offer anything other than love and compassion and support to Eric and his family, especially in response to their loss? Eric grieved. How could anyone offer anything other than love? I do not understand.

UNDERSTANDING THE MESSAGE

It is possible the people who offered condemnation rather than compassion misinterpreted Scripture. There are two threads of Scripture that, at first glance, appear to be in conflict. Jesus commands us to love one another as He loves us, He teaches a great deal about judging others explaining we should not do it, He says that He did not come to condemn the world but to save the world,[9] and He says that He passes judgment on no one.[10] However, He blasts certain people, particularly religious leaders, with harsh judgment, He offers gentle correction to ordinary people, and He says that He came to the world "for judgment."[11] How do we reconcile these potentially inconsistent lines of thought?

As we walk through each day we are forced to make a myriad of decisions involving judgment – from what time to get up in the morning to what we will eat for lunch and thousands of other things. Riding with a person learning how to drive reveals how many choices a driver makes during even a short, routine drive. For instance, the decision to pull out of the neighborhood involves assessing the speed of oncoming cars, the distance necessary to get up to speed, the traffic flow in the path immediately in front of you and many other factors that must be properly judged to avoid collision. Our life involves judgment and choices, and if you are the person designated to help the driver learn, you must help them see the world in the way necessary to perceive the danger surrounding them and help them learn how to safely chart their way driving through traffic. If you are the driving instructor, you have the authority and obligation to make judgments and to help the new driver learn how to make similar judgments.

We must make discerning judgment as we chart our own path in the world, and at times our position and authority obligates us to offer gentle correction, which is the result of judgment. At the same time, Jesus tells us not to judge other people. We are called to be light to the world, Jesus tells us to love one another as He loves us, and He commands us to love God and to love other people. The difficulty lies in understanding our position and authority as they relate to other people who are out in the chaotic world making their choices as they chart the path for their own life. How should we respond when we see other people making poor choices?

Reciting the question posed by rubber bracelets in the 1990s, what would Jesus do? When He saw vendors in the temple, He violently drove them out. He offered harsh rebuke and physically forced them out. On many occasions He offered harsh rebuke to religious leaders. When He encountered a woman accused of adultery, He saved her life and gently suggested that she leave her life of sin.

How do we reconcile His commands with His actions? Are His actions only proper for the sinless, pure, divine, holy God, or are they examples for people, sinful as we are, to replicate? How do we chart the proper path forward? Let's consider Scripture.

COMMAND TO LOVE

Jesus commands us to love one another. He gives the instruction and He calls it a command. He could not possibly be clearer or more emphatic in His message. Jesus says,

> "A new command I give you: Love one another. As I have loved you, so you must love one another." John 13:34

> "My command is this: Love each other as I have loved you. Greater love has no one than this, that he lay down his life for his friends. You are my friends if you do what I command." John 15:12-14

Paul explains that love lies at the core of what it means to be a follower of Christ. He describes love as "the most excellent way" and "the greatest of these."[12] He says that even if a person possesses all sorts of outward evidence of righteousness like gifts of teaching, prophecy, knowledge, faith and giving, if they do not have love they have nothing.[13] Without love, everything else is rendered hollow, incomplete, and worthless. Love is foundational. To be Christian means to be filled with love and to treat others with love.

JUDGMENT

Jesus is equally clear and emphatic when telling us not to judge other people. He says,

> "Do not judge, or you too will be judged. For in the same way you judge others, you will be judged, and with the measure you use, it will be measured to you." Matthew 7:1-2

"Do not judge, and you will not be judged. Do not condemn, and you will not be condemned. Forgive, and you will be forgiven." Luke 6:37

Further, in the following passages Jesus says that He did not come to judge or condemn people:

"For God did not send his Son into the world to condemn the world, but to save the world through him." John 3:17

"You judge by human standards; I pass judgment on no one." John 8:15

So Jesus clearly commands us to love one another, He orders us not to judge other people, and He says that He did not come to the world to condemn it or to judge people. Paul provides a similar message writing,

Accept the one whose faith is weak, without quarreling over disputable matters.... You, then, *why do you judge your brother or sister?* Or why do you treat them with contempt? For we all stand before God's judgment seat. It is written, "As surely as I live," says the Lord, "every knee will bow before me; every tongue will acknowledge God." So then, each of us will give an account of ourselves to God. Therefore, *let us stop passing judgment on one another.* Instead, make up your mind not to put any stumbling block or obstacle in the way of a brother or sister. Romans 14:1, 10-13

The message is exceedingly clear – love others and do not judge. If Scripture stopped here, it would be very straightforward, but it continues and becomes a little more difficult to understand.

Jesus also says,

"For judgment I have come into this world, so that the blind will see and those who see will become blind." John 9:39

So Jesus did not come "to condemn the world" and He passes "judgment on no one," yet He says "for judgment I have come into this world." How do these statements fit together? And like a bad ad on television, I will say, "but wait, there's more!" because Jesus expresses judgment of other people on many occasions.

JESUS EXPRESSES JUDGMENT

Twice Jesus violently drives people out of the temple. John records Jesus clearing the temple before the Passover early in His ministry. Using cords fashioned into a whip He violently drives vendors and money exchangers out of the temple saying, "Get out of here! How dare you turn my Father's house into a market!" (John 2:16). At the end His ministry, again shortly before Passover, Jesus rides into Jerusalem on a donkey, enters the temple and drives all the vendors out saying, "It is written, 'my house will be called a house of prayer, but you are making it a 'den of robbers'" (Matthew 21:13).

He sees activity He deems inappropriate, and He expresses rebuke through aggressive action and strong words. Jesus blasts religious leaders, calling them all sorts of awful sounding names. He expresses judgment toward them and rebukes them. He treats them with scorn and contempt because they are arrogant and they hold themselves out to the public as if they are righteous and holy, but they, like everyone, are actually sinful. Jesus calls them "whitewashed tombs" because they look the part, they dress properly and they act righteous, but on the inside they are dead and rotten.[14]

Chapter 23 of Matthew lays out some of His most striking rebukes known as the Seven Woes. Once Jesus says, "Woe to you, blind guides!" Six times Jesus says, "Woe to you, teachers of the law and Pharisees, you hypocrites!" After each "woe," Jesus explains a specific thing that they do wrong. For example, they slam the door leading to the kingdom of heaven in people's faces, they lead followers to hell, they neglect justice, mercy and faith, they are more concerned with outward appearance than inner truth, and more.

Jesus also expresses judgment toward ordinary people. An example of this is His interaction with the woman accused of adultery. At dawn one morning Jesus heads to the temple to teach. As a crowd gathers to listen, religious leaders present to Jesus a woman accused of adultery, a crime carrying a sentence of death by stoning. The religious leaders ask Jesus what they should do with her. They are trying to trap Jesus because if He instructs them to stone her, it will undercut His teaching about love. But if He instructs them to do anything else, He will show disrespect for the law. He chooses to do neither. Instead, He says, "If any one of you is without sin, let him be the first to throw a stone at her" (John 8:7). He shifts the focus from the woman to individuals crowding around her in judgment. The woman may have sinned, but so had each of them.

The crowd and religious leaders disperse, leaving Jesus alone with the woman. Had Jesus stopped talking and simply walked away with the others, the story would have been consistent with the love and don't judge narrative. But Jesus continues and as He does He expresses judgment.

Jesus asks her, "Woman, where are they? Has no one condemned you?" She replies, "No one, sir." "Then neither do I condemn you," Jesus declares. "Go now and leave your life of sin" (John 8:10-11).

Jesus does not condemn her, but He offers corrective judgment. He does not sentence her to death, but He expresses judgment about her choices and lifestyle, and He tells her to change her ways. He does not judge the person, but He judges her decisions and actions. Is this splitting hairs or is it fundamental?

Jesus expresses judgment. He rebukes religious leaders and He offers corrective advice to normal folk, each of which certainly involves judgment. He commands us not to judge other people, and He says He did not come to earth to judge people, yet He seems to judge. How do we reconcile these thoughts that seem at first glance to be in conflict and how should His actions and commands guide us as we try to live as His servants?

As a jumping off point, we should remember that God is love and Jesus is God, and through His judgment we see that love does not mean universal approval.

MAKING SENSE OF THE APPARENT CONTRADICTION

Discerning Right from Wrong is Essential

Some of the decisions we must make minute by minute to chart our course through each day relate to evil in the world, and each of these decisions involves judgment about good and evil, and right and wrong. As mentioned several times before, we live in a world of contrast. It contains evidence of God's glory and forces of evil. As a result of the contrast in the world, Jesus explains that judgment is essential, saying the statement quoted above,

> "For judgment I have come into this world, so that the blind will see and those who see will become blind."
> John 9:39

The world contains both good and evil, and we must learn to discern the difference. Jesus came with a diverse mission statement, which included the task of changing the world. The first step toward that goal was exposing the darkness of the world. If people fail to see sin they cannot possibly realize that they need salvation. If people fail to see that the world is dark they will probably not seek the light. He came to provide spiritual transformation and spiritual eyes to see. Discerning light from darkness, discerning righteousness from evil, discerning truth from deceit, discerning right from wrong each requires judgment.

For judgment Jesus came into the world, and we must acquire and use similar discernment.

Jesus sits at the right hand of God the Father Almighty[15] and He is tasked with judging,[16] but He did not come to earth as a human to judge people.[17] While on earth as a man He neither judged nor condemned people; rather, He offered them love and compassion. He came to change the world and to expose the darkness of the world, but He did not come to judge people, and He commands us not to judge other people. Jesus says,

> "I have come into the world as a light, so that no one who believes in me should stay in darkness. If anyone hears my words but does not keep them, I do not judge that person. *For I did not come to judge the world, but to save the world.* There is a judge for the one who rejects me and does not accept my words; the very words I have spoken will condemn them at the last day. For I did not speak on my own, but the Father who sent me commanded me to say all that I have spoken. I know that his command leads to eternal life. So whatever I say is just what the Father has told me to say." John 12:46-50

While Jesus did not come to judge the world, He did come to be light in contrast to darkness. He came to expose darkness, which involves identifying its existence and distinguishing between light and darkness, which involves judgment. Distinguishing between good and evil influences in the world, and discerning between good and bad choices is not equivalent to judging a person, even the person who may have made bad choices (which includes each of us).

The distinction is subtle but extremely important. If we desire to be light to the world we must act like light, which means we must make good choices about how we live. We must distinguish good from evil, right from wrong, righteousness from sin, and we must make choices leading toward God. This involves judging the world around us, judging situations, and judging where our choices will take us. So we must be discerning, but discerning the world around us does not mean we have license to treat other people with judgment or condemnation. We must make discerning choices for our own lives, and we must treat other people with love, not judgment nor condemnation.

LOVE AND JUDGMENT ARE NOT MUTUALLY EXCLUSIVE

In certain situations love involves correction. A driving instructor must help new drivers learn to see the world around them with new eyes. They must identify dangers and learn how to properly respond, which involves judgment. The instructor must gently correct students to help them learn.

Loving correction is proper only where the appropriate relationship, position and authority are in place. If a teacher loves her students, she will correct them, guide their thinking and teach them the path toward success in the field of study. Parents love their children and correct them along the way, teaching them right from wrong. Teachers and parents should judge thoughts and actions, and they should provide corrective feedback. Their position obligates them to do so, and if they fail in their obligation they are failing to love.

While certain positions confer authority and obligation, they are limited grants. Authority only extends to the scope of the position. If you are a math teacher and your student is struggling with math, you should certainly provide correction. If your student is struggling with grammar, you might leave that to the English teacher. Teachers are presumed to possess relationship, position and authority as to their students within a limited realm. In most situations, parents possess relationship, position and authority as to their children, but not other people's children.

Given the proper relationship, position and authority, love involves correction, but it never involves judging the person. It is one thing for a math teacher to say, "You are struggling in math, let me help you." It is an entirely different to say, "You are struggling in math, therefore you are an awful person."

Providing loving correction appropriate for the situation, relationship and authority is not equivalent to judging the person.

If you see someone doing something that you believe is worthy of correction, what should you do? It depends on your relationship, position and authority with respect to that person. Sometimes love requires correction, but only after the appropriate relationship has been established. By saying "appropriate relationship," I mean (i) that a relationship exists, (ii) you are in a position of authority as to the subject matter of the correction, and (iii) you live your life in such a way that you are able to engage in the discussion. How does this fit with the example presented by Jesus?

Religious leaders treated Jesus with apparent authority. They bestowed authority upon Jesus by how they interacted with Him. For example, they allowed Jesus to teach in the temple, which is where He was teaching when religious leaders presented a woman accused of adultery to Him. By presenting the accused before Jesus, they deemed Him to possess the position and authority of a judge. And if there was any doubt about His position and authority, doubt was removed when everyone, including the religious leaders, followed His suggestion and walked away.

This may have been the woman's first encounter with Jesus. Whether it was or wasn't, she would have naturally assumed that Jesus had the position and authority conferred upon Him by the religious leaders and by the crowd gathered to hear Him speak. Given the entire setting, including the way everyone around Jesus treated Him and deferred to Him, He was in a position to correct the woman accused of adultery because He had just demonstrated His love, position and authority by saving her life.

Jesus demonstrated loving compassion to people who had done lots of things wrong, and He often urged them to change their behavior. Like a loving teacher, He demonstrated love through gentle correction, not condemnation of the person.

And He blasted religious leaders. I say that love sometimes involves gentle correction, but the Seven Woes sounds harsh and angry, not gentle and loving. Jesus had position and authority to speak the way He did to them because the religious leaders treated Him with position and authority. They granted Him the authority, and sometimes an expression of anger is appropriate to get a person's attention.

But consider this – even Jesus' harsh rebuke and displays of anger were projections of His love. Because this may be hard for us to see, Matthew concludes chapter 23, the chapter listing the Seven Woes, quoting Jesus as follows:

> "O Jerusalem, Jerusalem, you who kill the prophets and stone those sent to you, how often I have longed to gather your children together, as a hen gathers her chicks under her wings, but you were not willing."
> Matthew 23:37

He offers compassion and love, even to people whom He rebukes. Love does not equate to universal approval, and Jesus offers love to everyone.

APPLYING THE TEACHING

What do we do with this? We are called to love. We are ordered not to judge people, but at times love involves judging thoughts and actions and it involves gentle correction, and as we live our lives in this world filled with contrast we must continuously discern good from evil. Peter writes,

> The end of all things is near. Therefore be alert and of sober mind so that you may pray. Above all, love each other deeply, because love covers over a multitude of sins. Offer hospitality to one another without grumbling. Each of you should use whatever gift you have received to serve others, as faithful stewards of God's grace in its various forms. If anyone speaks, they should do so as one who speaks the very words of God. If anyone serves, they should do so with the

strength God provides, so that in all things God may be praised through Jesus Christ. To him be the glory and the power for ever and ever. Amen. 1 Peter 4:7-11

As we chart our course through each day and seek to balance the demands, this is where we get it wrong. At times we err toward judgment and get out of balance. When in doubt, err toward love and compassion, not judgment, "so that in all things God may be praised through Jesus Christ" (1 Peter 4:11). I offer a few suggestions:

1. Love other people. When you see other people, remember that God creates each person in His image. Remember that God loves each person and each person you encounter is worthy of your love and compassion. Remember that Christ Jesus bestowed His holy grace upon you through no doing of your own, that you did not deserve the new life He gave you, that you were filthy and He cleansed you.

2. If you see someone involved in activity you believe to be inappropriate, before you express any judgment consider the basis for your judgment (why is the activity inappropriate, what is the appropriate standard?), consider your relationship with the person, consider your position relative to the person, and consider your authority relative to the person. If in light of the total situation offering guidance is appropriate, do so with gentleness, respect and loving compassion so that "in all things God may be praised through Christ Jesus" (1 Peter 4:11).

3. Pray. Praise God, thank God, seek God. Pray for guidance, pray for God's discerning spirit, pray for wisdom, pray for other people, pray for the ability to see each person as someone created in God's image, pray for God to enlighten the eyes of your spirit. Pray and pray and pray more.

If we begin a new relationship with rebuke, the new relationship will quickly end. New relationships must begin with honest compassion, open arms and sincere demonstrations of love. My friend Gustavo runs an art gallery in Paris. He is also a musician and an ordained pastor who ministers to the art community there. Gustavo has discussed many examples of times he allowed friendships to develop for a long time before revealing his Christian faith, and on many occasions his friends told him that had they known he was Christian earlier in their relationship they would have stopped the relationship immediately because of their negative preconceived ideas of Christians and Christianity. Gustavo routinely encounters people whose perception of Christianity is that it is more about judgment than love. But they get to know Gustavo as a person first. They develop friendship, and then they discovered his faith. With the basis of relationship and trust in place, they ask about his faith. Many have come to know Jesus Christ through the gradual process.

Gustavo shared the conflict he often has faced when he sees new friends engaged in activity he knows to be unhealthy, but he knows that if he tries to be a corrective influence too early in the relationship, it will kill the relationship. So he must be patient and allow the friendship to develop and allow them to gradually over time ask questions. He knows it is God's prevenient grace working on them, and he knows that he is merely God's servant following His will in His time, and he knows that as they come to know Christ, and grow in Him, they will be convicted of the sin in their lives and their lifestyle will change. Sometimes being light in the world places us in uncomfortable positions, surrounded by things we know are wrong and activities we know are inconsistent with God's will. In the same way that it is not all on Gustavo to act with correction, it is not always on us to be a corrective force because the Holy Spirit convicts and corrects.

Presence, patience, love and compassion are critical elements to Gustavo's ministry, along with an understanding that, as my good friend Nancy is found of saying, it is all in God's time. We each called to be light to the world. We are each called to loving service, which begins with relationship. At the appropriate time, with the appropriate relationship, gentle loving correction may be appropriate, but it must not be rushed.

CONCLUSION

Our struggle on this point not only harms our witness and ourselves; it taints other people's perception of Jesus Christ and of the people who associate with His name, and that is inexcusable. When we inappropriately express judgment, we taint Jesus' holy name and we drive people away from Him. When unsure about your position, authority or relationship, it is much better to err on the side of love welcoming people in with open arms.

I pray for Eric and his family. May they find peace, comfort, wholeness and life abundant. May they experience God's love, compassion and glory revealed through the Body of Christ at work in the world.

17 | STUDY, PRAY & SERVE

His divine power has given us everything we need for a godly life through our knowledge of him who called us by his own glory and goodness. Through these he has given us his very great and precious promises, so that through them you may participate in his divine nature, having escaped the corruption in the world caused by evil desires.
2 Peter 1:3-4

Suppose a brother or a sister is without clothes and daily food. If one of you says to them, "Go in peace; keep warm and well fed," but does nothing about their physical needs, what good is it? In the same way, faith by itself, if it is not accompanied by action is dead. James 2:15-17

Last week a close friend called me. He said that all he felt like doing was sleeping. He slept over twelve hours the night before. He got up, but only made it to the sofa before assuming the fetal position for the next five or six hours. I stopped by his home after work and found him in his dark cave of a living room filled with heavy, stale, deathly air. Each window was covered and the only light came from his TV. It was on, but he had no idea what program was playing. He had not eaten all day, and he lay in a sleepy fog.

He used the dreaded "D" word, depression. He said he did not feel like hurting himself, joking that it would require too much energy. He just felt like doing nothing. I convinced him to get up and come home with me to eat some soup. As we sat in our kitchen eating chicken noodle soup that Lori made earlier, he described the previous days and his gradual downward slide. He wanted help and he planned to make an appointment with a psychiatrist. Over the course of a half hour or so he ate a few bites of soup and a few crackers before returning home.

The next morning it occurred to me that his downward slide started the day after he attended our prayer meeting. Prayer warriors had placed hands on him and prayed thanking God for blocking him from the spirit of addiction, for protecting him from harmful desires, for supporting his growth in recovery, praising God for the plans He has for his life, and so much more. I wondered whether he was experiencing the effects of spiritual warfare. It seemed that his addiction was evidence of spiritual warfare and his depression was a tactical variation from the enemy.

I posed the questions to him. I mentioned the curious timing and the spiritual nature of the conditions and raised the thought. After presenting the theory in a longer than planned monologue, he said, "I have no idea what you are saying. I hear the words. I understand the words. But I do not know what you mean."

I urged him to follow through on his psychiatrist appointment, but I also urged him to pray. We had prayed on his behalf, but I suggested he should also pray for himself. I realized that he did not have much energy or desire, so I urged him to keep the prayer simple. Simply thank God for being with him, thank God for the breath he just took, thank God for the little things, as he is able. And I urged him to, as he felt like it, continue studying and meditating on Scripture.

I sent a text to several of the prayer warriors who had prayed over him the week before, requesting prayer for depression. They replied explaining specific prayers and specific Scripture they were praying. Later that day, I called my friend. He said he was feeling a little better. He had showered, shaved and left the house to get some food. Baby steps in the right direction.

Along with physical battles, our lives have a spiritual component and unseen battles take place in the spiritual realm. It might be viewed a mere coincidence that his depression started shortly after powerful prayer for his addiction, and another coincidence that his depression weakened shortly after prayer. But spiritual battles are being waged and God responds to prayer. God is holy, divine and pure. He is unbound by time and space. He has all authority on heaven and earth. He is sovereign. He is the creator of all things. He breathes the breath of life into each of us. He is transcendent yet intimate. He knows everything about you, even things you do not know. He is love and He loves you. He is the source of satisfaction and wholeness. No matter what you have done, He loves you, He desires relationship with you, He responds to prayer, and He wants you to have His light, life, wholeness. Nonetheless, battles continue.

The evil one wants to destroy satisfaction and wholeness. This is why Paul urges us to "pray continually" (1 Thessalonians 5:17), why he urges us to "put on the full armor of God so that you can take your stand against the devil's schemes" (Ephesians 6:11), why he tells us to "take the helmet of salvation and the sword of the Spirit, which is the word of God" (Ephesians 6:17), and why he completes the thought by urging us to "pray in the Spirit on all occasions with all kinds of prayers and requests" (Ephesians 6:18). Paul sees the battles waged, he sees God for who He is, and he understands that we must continuously make use of prayer and Scripture. Prayer and meditating on Scripture are essential to our relationship with God, critical for our faith, and key components to gaining the "full armor of God."

Humans exist at the intersection between the physical and spiritual realms. We are part physical, part spiritual, and influenced by both realms. Paul's warfare analogy clearly communicates our need to continuously focus on our relationship with God.

THE CHOICE

It seems safe to say that we each desire a full and significant life. We want to feel spiritually whole, satisfied and complete. If we want this, we must choose it.

Everyone makes his or her own choice. Decisions made by our ancestors influence our lives in many ways. For instance, all four of Lori's grandparents chose to move from Holland to Iowa. Had they not each made that decision, Lori would have been a Dutch girl rather than an American with Dutch heritage. I did not choose to be born in Kansas City or to grow up in Enid, Oklahoma – my parents made choices that determined those things for me. For many the geography of their upbringing influences the careers they choose and where they settle down and build a life. A myriad of influences such as these overlap in a mosaic. While some relate to choices of our ancestors, we must each make the most important choice for ourselves. Each of us will either choose life abundant through Jesus or we will not make that choice.

If our parents enjoy a close relationship with the Father, the Son and Holy Spirit, their decision will certainly help provide a foundation for our walk of faith, but we must still make our own choice. Their acceptance of the holy One will not flow to us. And either by omission or affirmative choice, we each choose.

Holy Living Sacrifice

The first step is believing that the spiritual realm exists, that evil exists, and that God – Father, Son and Holy Spirit – also exists. God's holy grace showers over us all the time and heavenly forces are at work as we first ponder the meaning of life, the possibility of satisfaction, questions about God, and other weighty matters. Heavenly forces are also at work when we accept in our heart all that God is, we see Jesus for who He is, and we invite Him in to transform our lives.[1]

After making the choice to follow Jesus, as we seek His sustaining power, wholeness and love, the path forward involves study, prayer and service. A life of significance involves a daily routine of balancing healthy doses of studying and meditating on Scripture, praying, and offering ourselves as empty vessels to be used by God. It involves seeking God, seeking holiness, and absolute surrender to His will for our lives.

The Wesleyan Covenant Renewal Service[2] includes the following prayer:

> Lord, make me what you will. I put myself fully into your hands: put me to doing, put me to suffering, let me be employed for you, or laid aside for you, let me be full, let me be empty, let me have all things, let me have nothing. I freely and with a willing heart give it all to your pleasure and disposal.

Paul communicates a message of seeking God, seeking holiness and seeking surrender in a number of ways in a lot of places. As one example he writes,

> Therefore, I urge you, brothers and sisters, in view of God's mercy, to *offer your bodies as a living sacrifice, holy and pleasing to God* – this is your true and proper worship. Do not conform to the pattern of this world, but be *transformed by the renewing of your mind*. Then you will be able to test and approve what God's will

is – his good, pleasing and perfect will. Romans 12:1-2

This is a packed bit of Scripture. In three sentences Paul discusses God's mercy, offering ourselves as sacrifices, true and proper worship, the pattern of the world, transformation of our minds, and God's will. It is loaded.

When Paul discusses personal holiness and renewed mind, he refers to the gradual process of sanctification. Only God is holy, and while we may never be holy, we can gain steps toward holiness through the spiritual transformation that is available through Him. As we allow the Holy Spirit in, little by little, step-by-step, gradually we are transformed. In tiny increments, we are gradually rendered increasingly holy as we inch closer to God.

And as we gain some baby steps toward holiness, our transformation should reveal itself through action. Paul urges us to offer our "bodies as a living sacrifice, holy and pleasing to God" as our "true and proper worship." Holy, living sacrifice. Paul connects worship and holiness with service, and captures the entire message of the Gospel in three words – holy living sacrifice. Scripture urges us to grow toward holiness and to surrender ourselves to God while we still live. The call for holy living sacrifice equates to spiritual transformation displayed through action.

Each time we use the standard order of worship for Holy Communion, we pray offering ourselves to God as a holy and living sacrifice. Does that change your view of Holy Communion?

I love the opportunity to take Holy Communion, to dine with others at the Lord's Table. Part of the reason I love it is because when I swallow the elements and feel them go down my throat, I feel God's holy presence enter me, strengthen me and refresh me. I feel His holy presence in a new way. It is a means through which we receive His holy grace. The mystery of His spiritual presence takes tangible form and that seemingly insignificant act is the source of incredible of affirmation and inspiration.

The United Methodist Hymnal provides a basic order of worship for different types of church services, including Holy Communion. When we take Holy Communion we recreate some of the events that took place during the Last Supper. As we pray to God, we take bread, break it, and we recite the words that Jesus spoke saying, "Take, eat, this is my body which is given for you. Do this in remembrance of me."[3] We take a cup of grape juice and recite the words that Jesus spoke saying, "Drink from this all of you; this is my blood of the new covenant, poured out for you and for many for the forgiveness of sins. Do this, as often as you drink it, in remembrance of me."[4]

We continue praying saying, "And so, in remembrance of these your mighty acts in Jesus Christ, we offer ourselves in praise and thanksgiving as a holy and living sacrifice, in union with Christ's offering for us, as we proclaim the mystery of faith."[5]

Each time we take Holy Communion, as part of the regular order of worship, we renew our offer to God. We ask Him to accept us as a holy and living sacrifice. We offer ourselves as holy. We offer ourselves as living sacrifices. If we mean what we pray, we totally surrender ourselves to God. It amounts to completely offering ourselves as empty vessels to be filled according to His will.

Paul writes, "I urge you, brothers and sisters, in view of God's mercy, to *offer your bodies as a living sacrifice, holy and pleasing to God* – this is your true and proper worship."

ENCOUNTER

Think about your first encounter with God. Where were you, what were you doing when God grabbed you and forced you to realize that He is real, that He is really with you, that He is really present and really near? When did you gain intimate knowledge of Him in your soul – I am not talking intellectual knowledge, rather genuine knowing through relationship. When were your eyes opened?

For me, the process continues today. God continues to reveal and affirm His holy presence, but at some point along the way, I realized and I accepted and I knew in my heart that God is real, He is really with us, He is really present, and He is really near. At some point along the way, I remembered what I first felt standing in the church as a young boy experiencing God, and since that time I have sought Him. When I pray I seek Him, when I attend church I seek Him, and when I am out in the world I seek to take Him with me.

For a long time, I attended church for the wrong reasons. I went, I don't know, to try to convince Lori that was a better person than I am, I went because I kind of liked getting dressed up, being with people at church, experiencing the pageantry of it all, and going out to lunch. It was a brief form of entertainment between breakfast and lunch once a week. Maybe I went because it looked good to my neighbors. I don't really know why I went, but I can say with certainty that I did not go to church seeking God.

But gradually along the way, I experienced Him, and that made all the difference. I know He is really real and I pray that you do too. Because He is the source of satisfaction, He is the source of wholeness, He is life and light, and I know in my heart that God wants that for you.

If you have not experienced God in a way that makes Him real to you, I pray that you open yourself to that experience. And if you want that, please do not wait because early flames must be gently nurtured or they may be extinguished. If you feel the flame of desire, act on it.

So what does it mean to act on it? Pray – invite God the Father, Jesus, the Holy Spirit into your heart, into your life. Study Scripture regularly seeking God with a fervent desire, and offer yourself in loving service to others. Whatever you do, take Jesus with you and allow His love to flow through you. If you are a student, take Jesus to school with you. If you work, whatever your occupation might be, take Jesus to work with you. I often see students, professors, teachers, accountants, doctors, and business people. I see folks who are retired and on occasion I see people who are unable to leave bed. No matter your occupation, your position, or your situation, you can show the love of Jesus Christ to people around you.

A friend of mine is a teacher, and after years of struggling with her high school students, she decided she would pray for each class. She teaches five classes each day, so she dedicates one day each week to pray for each class. At the beginning of the semester she tells her students that she is praying for them and she invites them to give her specific prayer requests and this relatively simple act opens new avenues of connection and communication and it invites Jesus into the room with them.

Another friend is a plant foreman. He has spent his career working in a factory and he said, after he met Jesus his language changed, his temper calmed, the way he handled certain situations changed, and even though he did not tell anyone about his encounter with Jesus, his co-workers noticed his change and asked him about it. He said gradually the culture of his group at work changed. They gradually changed the music they listened to, the things they talked about during break, and the jokes they told. And the group developed a closer bond and they accomplish more at work. One man's conversion had a dramatic rippling effect and he said that he did not try to take Jesus to work with him, Jesus just tagged along as part of his new life.

As followers of Christ we are each called to serve our Master. Regardless of your occupation, you are commissioned to serve God. He calls each of us continuously into service. And whatever specific task He is calling each of us to do, His agenda, His task for us always involves love. We are called to allow His love to flow through us.

29,200 DAYS

As I spoke to my friend suffering with depression I, once again, failed in my efforts to describe spiritual life and the benefits associated with maintaining connection with the source of life. The moment my friend explained that I failed to communicate my message, I felt the same twinge of failure that I felt while standing on the lawn at the Masters – helpless, inadequate, and longing for better communication skills. It took me back to the beginning of our journey together.

We started this journey discussing life – physical life and spiritual life. We considered our spirit and soul before discussing the spiritual realm that surrounds us, which includes evil spirits, angels and the Holy Spirit. We discussed some of the ways the spiritual realm influences us, the avenues through which we connect with God, and the availability of transformation through Him. With that foundation, we discussed the point of it all: allowing God's love to flow through us as we show compassion to and we offer loving service to others.

Life is simply better when lived in union with God. Spiritual life, satisfaction and wholeness are gained through connection with God. Full life and the fruit of the Holy Spirit – joy, peace, patience, kindness, goodness, faithfulness, gentleness and self-control – are shared through union with Him, but as wonderful as all that is, His glory is not for our pleasure. His indwelling certainly makes us feel better, but that is not the point. Through relationship with Him, His holiness should gradually transform us and the gradual process of sanctification should reveal itself through our actions. His love should transform us and, as a result, we should allow His love to flow through us as we impact the world.

I understand the words and the concepts. Intellectually they fit in my brain. It's the application that is difficult.

If the average lifespan is 80 years,[6] on average we each will be on earth for 29,200 days. How many days do you have left? What will you do with each of them? What will you do of significance? How will you acquire satisfaction and fulfillment? We must each ask ourselves, what step will I take today?

God is sovereign. He has all power and authority. There is nothing He cannot do. And He loves you. Seek Him. Offer Him your praise, worship and service, and accept His gift of spiritual life. Allow Him to fill you with His peace, comfort and joy. Receive His life abundant.

May the eyes of your spirit be enlightened through God, may His glory shine through you, and may you reveal the love of Jesus Christ to the world.

ABOUT THE AUTHOR

Randy serves as associate pastor of First United Methodist Church of Tuscaloosa in Tuscaloosa, Alabama and managing partner of Druid Capital Partners in Northport, Alabama, and enjoys quiet time with family, Yolo boarding on Lake Tuscaloosa, participating in CrossFit over lunch (an elderly version), praying in the Sanctuary with close friends and strangers, praying alone in the backyard, and studying, talking about and writing about God's holy word. He has published two books of devotionals:

God's Glory Revealed: 52 Devotionals; and

For the Praise of His Glory: 52 Devotionals.

He posts and distributes a devotional most weeks through his website www.RandyLAllen.com. For more information, to see past devotionals, or to sign up to receive future devotionals by email, please visit the website.

NOTES

CHAPTER 2. Searching for the Cause of Life

[1] Merriam-Webster Online Dictionary, February 19, 2015,
http://www.merriam-webster.com/dictionary/life.
[2] Merriam-Webster Online Dictionary, February 19, 2015,
http://www.merriam-webster.com/dictionary/life.
[3] Genesis 2:17
[4] Genesis 3:5 and 3:7.
[5] John 10:10
[6] John the Baptist begins speaking at John 3:27. Some interpreters
conclude the quote after verse 30, attributing the statement recorded as
John 3:36 to John the Apostle. Others conclude the quote after verse
36, attributing the statement to John the Baptist.
[7] John 14:6
[8] See Numbers 21:8-9
[9] See John 7:50-52
[10] See John 19:38-42

CHAPTER 3. Soul & Spirit

[1] John 4:24
[2] John 10:10; John 14:6
[3] https://www.sweetmarias.com/product/honduras-belen-de-
ocotepeque-don-vasquez
[4] http://www.visionlearning.com/en/library/Earth-Science/6/The-
Composition-of-Earths-Atmosphere/107
[5] NAS Exhaustive Concordance of the Bible with Hebrew-Aramaic and
Greek Dictionaries
Copyright 1981, 1998 by The Lockman Foundation
[6] Genesis 1:21; 1:24; 2:19; 9:10

[7] Genesis 2:7

[8] There has been significant debate over whether spirit and soul are two parts of a single spiritual entity, or whether they are separate entities. Dichotomists believe people are comprised of body and soul, while trichotomists believe people are comprised of body, soul and spirit, three distinct entities. Heavenly concepts are beyond our ability to understand and our language is inadequate to communicate heavenly thoughts. While we try, our efforts will undoubtedly be lacking. With this in mind, splitting hairs between dichotomy and trichotomy is probably not a meaningful exercise. Nonetheless, I have opted the trichotomist view for this discussion because it is beneficial for us to consider the nuances between soul and spirit, whether they are two parts of the same entity or two separate entities. Trichotomists look to Hebrews 4:12 and 1 Thessalonians 5:23 for primary support.

[9] Zodhiates, Spiros (editor), Hebrew-Greek Key Word Study Bible, AMG International, Inc., (1996), Old Testament Lexical Aids, Psyche, p.1688.

[10] Id

CHAPTER 4. Image of God

[1] Genesis 1:1; Hebrews 11:3

[2] See Acts 9:1-9

[3] John 4:24

[4] Genesis 1:1, Colossians 1:16

[5] Deuteronomy 7:9, 32:4

[6] Titus 1:2

[7] 1 John 4:8, 4:16

[8] Exodus 34:6-7,Deuteronomy 4:31

[9] Psalm 11:7

[10] Zodhiates, Spiros (editor), Hebrew-Greek Key Word Study Bible, AMG International, Inc., (1996), Old Testament Lexical Aids, Selem p.1546.

[11] Id

[12] Genesis 3:17 and 23-24

[13] Romans 5:12

[14] Genesis 3

[15] Powell, Mark Allen (editor). HarperCollins Bible Dictionary, Harper One (2011), Sin p.965.

[16] Matthew 19:17, Mark 10:18 and Luke 18:19

[17] Matthew and Mark record Jesus discussing one sin that is unforgivable, saying "whoever blasphemes against the Holy Spirit will never be forgiven" (Mark 3:29 see also Matthew 12:31). I wrote what I wrote because this is extremely rare and it is better for us to go through life knowing we have the possibility of redemption and believing that everyone else does also rather than trying to decide who might fit that exceedingly rare category.

[18] Genesis 3:17, Romans 5:12

[19] John 17:17

[20] John 16:8

[21] Luke 18:1-8

[22] Morris, Chris. "Things are Looking up in America's Porn Industry," NBC, January 20, 2015. http://www.nbcnews.com/business/business-news/things-are-looking-americas-porn-industry-n289431.

[23] Matthew 14:15-21; Mark 6:35-44; Luke 9:12-17; John 6:5-14

[24] Matthew 15:32-38; Mark 8:1-9

[25] A sick woman is healed: Matthew 9:20-22, Mark 5:25-34, Luke 8:43-48. Peter's mother-in-law is healed: Matthew 8:14-17, Mark 1:29-31, Luke 4:38-39. A centurion's servant is healed Matthew 8:5-13, Luke 7:1-10. Jesus heals a sick man Luke 14:1-6. An official's son is healed John 4:46-54.

[26] Matthew 9:1-8, Mark 2:1-12, Luke 5:17-26

[27] Bartimaeus is healed Matthew 20:29-34, Mark 10:46-52, Luke 18:35-43. Two blind men are healed Matthew 9:27-31. A blind man is healed at Bethsaida Mark 8:22-26. A blind man is healed John 9:1-7.

[28] Ten lepers are healed Luke 17:11-19. A leper is healed in Galilee Matthew 8:1-4, Mark 1:40-45, Luke 5:12-15.

[29] Jairus' daughter raised from (the) dead Matthew 9:18-26, Mark 5:22-24, 35-43, Luke 8:41-56. A widow's son is raised Luke 7:11-16. Lazarus is raised John 11:1-45.

[30] Luke 5:1-11; John 21:1-14

[31] Nutrition Business Journal, NBJ's Supplement Business Report 2012, http://newhope360.com/sitefiles/newhope360.com/files/uploads/2013/04/TOC_SUMM120928.supp%20report%20FINAL%20standard.pdf

[32] ABC News Staff, "100 Million Dieters, $20 billion: The Weight-Loss Industry by Numbers," 20-20, May 8, 2012, http://abcnews.go.com/Health/100-million-dieters-20-billion-weight-loss-industry/print?id=16297197

[33] "Fitness Instructors and Instructors," Occupational Outlook Handbook, Bureau of Labor Statistics, Department of Labor, http://www.bls.gov/ooh/Personal-Care-and-Service/Fitness-trainers-and-instructors.htm

[34] Markus, Amy Dockser, "More Evidence Found of Biological Basis to Chronic Fatigue Syndrome," The Wall Street Journal, February 27, 2015; http://www.wsj.com/articles/more-evidence-found-of-biological-basis-to-chronic-fatigue-syndrome-1425063603?KEYWORDS=chronic+fatigue.
[35] Job 1:7

CHAPTER 5. Abundant Life, Eternal Life & Kingdom of God

[1] Isaiah 6:3
[2] 1 Peter 5:8
[3] Luke 23:40-43
[4] Zodhiates, Spiros (editor), Hebrew-Greek Key Word Study Bible, AMG International, Inc., Aionios p1580; Zoe p1630, (1996).
[5] See Vincent, Marvin, R., "Note on Olethron Aionion (eternal destruction)," Word Studies in the New Testament, online, http://www.auburn.edu/~allenkc/vincent.html (2-25-2015). See also Hanson, John Wesley, "The Greek Word Aion – Aionios, translated Everlasting – Eternal in the Holy Bible, Shown to Denote Limited Duration," Northwwestern Universalist Publishing House, Chicago, 1875, online, http://www.tentmaker.org/books/Aion_lim.html.
[6] "Aionion," Englishman's Concordance. http://biblehub.com/greek/aio_nion_166.htm
[7] Matthew 17:1-13
[8] See Deuteronomy 34:5, and Deuteronomy Timeline, The Life Application Bible, New International Version. Tyndale House Publishers, Inc. and Zondervan Publishing House (1991). p.279.
[9] 2 Kings 2:11. 2 Kings Timeline, The Life Application Bible, New International Version. Tyndale House Publishers, Inc. and Zondervan Publishing House (1991). p.543.
[10] John 1:1, 1:14
[11] John 3:3
[12] Matthew 13:24
[13] Matthew 13:31
[14] Matthew 13:33
[15] Matthew 13:44
[16] Matthew 13:45
[17] Matthew 13:47
[18] Matthew 18:23
[19] Matthew 20:1
[20] Matthew 22:2
[21] Matthew 13:24-30

[22] Matthew 13:31-32
[23] Matthew 13:33-35
[24] Matthew 13:44
[25] Matthew 13:45-46
[26] Matthew 13:47-50
[27] Matthew 5-7
[28] I do not know where the quote was published. It was in an email.

CHAPTER 6. Spiritual Realm

[1] Matthew 4:1-11; Mark 1:12-13; and Luke 4:1-13
[2] Revelation 12:7
[3] Luke 1:26
[4] Daniel 6:22
[5] Genesis 16
[6] Exodus 14:19
[7] 2 Kings 6:16-18; Revelation 20:1-2
[8] Mark 1:23-26; Luke 4:33-35; Mark 9:20 & 25-26
[9] The current entry in the CIA World Factbook on Haiti may be found at https://www.cia.gov/library/publications/the-world-factbook/geos/ha.html. Rather than give percentages it now says, "many Haitians practice elements of voodoo in addition to another religion, most often Roman Catholicism…"

CHAPTER 7. Evil Spirits

[1] Genesis 1:31
[2] Genesis 3
[3] Ephesians 6:12
[4] John 4:24
[5] 2 Corinthians 3:17
[6] Hebrews 1:14
[7] Matthew 17:1-13, Mark 9:2-13, and Luke 9:28-36
[8] Mark 9:29
[9] Luke 1-3
[10] Matthew 3:13-17, Mark 1:9-11, and Luke 3:21-22
[11] Luke 10:18
[12] John 14:21
[13] Zimmer, Ben. "A Clash of 'Alternative' and 'Facts,' The Wall Street Journal. January 26, 2017.

[14] MacFarquhar, Neil. "A Powerful Russian Weapon: The Spread of False Stories," The New York Times. August 28, 2016.
[15] John 14:6
[16] Mark 9:26
[17] Luke 10:18
[18] Revelation 20:1-3
[19] Colossians 1:15-17
[20] Ezekiel 28:12
[21] Isaiah 14:12-15, Ezekiel 28:11-19, and Luke 10:18
[22] Genesis 3
[23] Job 1:12
[24] Job 1&2
[25] Job 2:6
[26] Ephesians 6:12
[27] 2 Corinthians 4:4
[28] Ephesians 2:2
[29] John 14:6
[30] Matthew 13:24-30 and 13:36-43
[31] Matthew 4:1-11, Mark 1:12-13, and Luke 4:1-13
[32] Mark 5:1-13, Luke 8:26-39
[33] Mark 1:23-26 (see also Luke 4:33-35)
[34] John 9:5
[35] John 17:16
[36] Matthew 5:13-14
[37] John 15:18-19
[38] Ephesians 6:13-17

CHAPTER 8. Angels

[1] Matthew 13:49, Matthew 25:31
[2] Matthew 24:31, Mark 13:27
[3] Mark 8:38
[4] Luke 12:8-9
[5] Matthew 4:11, Mark 1:13 (see also Luke 4:10)
[6] Luke 22:43
[7] Luke 15:10
[8] Luke 20:36
[9] 1 Corinthians 10:10
[10] See 2 Kings 19, 2 Chronicles 32:21, Isaiah 37
[11] Acts 12:23
[12] 2 Samuel 24, 1 Chronicles 21
[13] Hebrews 13:2

14 Ezekiel 10:3
15 Ezekiel 10:18-19
16 Metaxas, Eric. *Miracles*. Penguin Group, 2014. pp 238-242.
17 Exodus 3:1-14
18 Exodus 32:34
19 Exodus 33:2
20 Judges 6:1-6
21 Judges 6:17-27
22 Daniel 8
23 Judges 13:2
24 Judges 13:8-28
25 2 Peter 2:11
26 Hebrews 2:2
27 Matthew 2:13
28 Judges 13:18
29 Daniel 8:16
30 Luke 1:19
31 Luke 1:26
32 Genesis 16:11-12
33 Genesis 21
34 Genesis 19
35 Daniel 3
36 Acts 5:12-20
37 Acts 12:1-10
38 See Paton, John G., *John G. Paton – The Autobiography of the Pioneer Missionary to the New Hebrides*, Vanuatu, 2013.
39 Graham, Billy. *Angels: God's Secret Agents*. Thomas Nelson, Nashville, TN, 1995. pp.7-9.
40 Ten Boom, Corrie, *A Prisoner and Yet....* CLC Publications, Ft. Washington, PA, 1947, 1954, 1970, 2020, pp.97-100.

CHAPTER 9. Holy Spirit

1 Chapters 13-18 of John describe the evening of the Last Supper.
2 John 14:16, 14:26, and 15:26
3 John 14:15
4 John 14:16, 14:26 and 15:26
5 See Romans 14
6 Galatians 5:22
7 1 Corinthians 12:1-11, see also Romans 12:3-8 and Ephesians 4:11-13
8 Romans 8:18-25
9 Ephesians 2:8

---

[10] John 3:5-8
[11] John 15:1-17
[12] John 15:18-25
[13] Acts 5:15
[14] Acts 19:12
[15] See Exodus 3-14
[16] See Judges 6-7
[17] See Acts 2
[18] See Acts 5:12-16
[19] Acts 7:57-58
[20] Acts 9:1-2
[21] Scholars debate whether Paul authored Hebrews. If he did, that would make 14.
[22] For some to consider please see Matthew 7:15-20, John 15:8-17, Romans 8:26-30, Romans 12:1-2, 2 Corinthians 3:17-18, 2 Corinthians 5:16-21, Colossians 1:9-14, Ephesians 2:1-10, James 2:14-26, 1 Peter 1:13-2:3, 1 Peter 4:1-6, 2 Peter 1:3-11, and 1 John 1:5-10.
[23] See John 13:1-17
[24] See John 3:5-8
[25] Winder, Delores and Keith, Bill. *Jesus Set Me Free.* Fellowship Foundation, Inc. (1993).
[26] Winder 13
[27] Winder 41
[28] Matthew 9:1-8; Mark 2:1-12; and Luke 5:17-20
[29] See John 11:1-44

CHAPTER 10. The Bridge

[1] Luke 23:44
[2] Matthew 27:51, Luke 23:45
[3] Matthew 27:51-53
[4] John 14:6
[5] John 10:7
[6] See Matthew 27:57-61, Mark 15:42-47, Luke 23:50-56
[7] Mark 16:19, Luke 22:69
[8] See Acts 1:1-11
[9] See Exodus 3

CHAPTER 11. Prayer

[1] Ephesians 1:13, 1 Corinthians 3:16, 6:19 and 12:13, and Romans 8:9-11
[2] 1 Timothy 2:5
[3] Genesis 1
[4] Id
[5] Pirsig, Robert M. *Zen and the Art of Motorcycle Maintenance.* William Morrow & Company, 1974.
[6] Matthew 14:15-21; Mark 6:35-44; Luke 9:12-17; John 6:5-14
[7] Jairus' daughter (Matthew 8:28-34; Mark 5:22-24 & 35-43; Luke 8:43-48); Widow's son (Luke 7:11-16); Lazarus (John 11:1-45)
[8] Sick woman healed (Matthew 9:20-22; Mark 5:25-34; Luke 8:43-48); Leper healed at Gennesaret (Matthew 8:1-4; Mark 1:40-45); Peter's mother-in-law healed (Matthew 8:14-17; Mark 1:29-31; Luke 4:38-39); centurion's servant is healed (Matthew 8:5-13; Luke 7:1-10); mute man is healed (Matthew 9:32-33); a deaf and mute man is healed (Mark 7:31-37); crippled woman is healed (Luke 13:10-17); sick man is healed (Luke 14:1-6); ten lepers are healed (Luke 17:11-19); man's ear is restored (Luke 22:49-51); an official's son is healed (John 4:46-54); a lame man is healed (John 5:1-16);
[9] Matthew 9:1-8; Mark 2:1-12; Luke 5:17-26
[10] Bartimaeus (Matthew 20:29-34; Mark 10:46-52; Luke 18:35-43); two blind men are healed (Matthew 9:27-31); blind man at Bethsaida is healed (Mark 8:22-26); a man born blind is healed (John 9:1-7).
[11] Matthew 17:24-27
[12] Luke 5:1-11; John 21:1-14
[13] If you would like to read more about Kennedy's amazing story, his parents have written about the experience. The information provided is adapted from their writing. For more information, please see the following: Buettner, Amy, "Mommy, I Saw Jesus," Christianity Today International / Today's Christian Magazine, November/December 2002, Vol. 40, No. 6, p.68, (2002); and Buettner, Dr. Craig and Buckstreet, J.C. Kennedy: A Story of God's Grace, (March 25, 2014, Amazon Digital Services).
[14] Acts 9:1-19
[15] See Acts 14:8-10; 19:11-12; 20:7-12; Acts 28:7-9
[16] Matthew 10:1
[17] Galatians 4:13-14
[18] 1 Timothy 5:23
[19] 2 Timothy 4:20
[20] Philippians 2:25-27

CHAPTER 12. God's Promises about Prayer

[1] Matthew 7:7, 18:19, 21:22; Mark 11:24, John 14:13.
[2] 1 John 5:14-15
[3] Strong's Exhaustive Concordance, 1793 – Dakka, http://biblehub.com/hebrew/1793.htm
[4] Matthew 22:37, Mark 12:30, Luke 10:27
[5] http://biblehub.com/greek/dokimazein_1381.htm
[6] James 2:19, Matthew 8:28, Mark 1:24, Mark 5:7, Luke 4:34, Luke 8:28.
[7] Matthew 22:37-40
[8] Exodus 14:15-31
[9] See Romans 2:8
[10] See Exodus 16
[11] Anderson, B.W., Bishop, S. and Newman, J.H., *Understanding the Old Testament*, 5th ed. Pearson Education, Inc. (2007, 1998).
[12] John 11:1-44
[13] John 11:4
[14] see Matthew 14:15-21, Mark 6:35-44, Luke 9:12-17 and John 6:5-14
[15] see Matthew 8:23-27, Mark 4:35-41 and Luke 8:22-25
[16] see Matthew 8:28-34, Mark 5:1-20 and Luke 8:26-39
[17] Matthew 9:18-26, Mark 5:22-43, Luke 8:41-56
[18] Matthew 9:20-22, Mark 5:25-34 and Luke 8:43-48
[19] Matthew 9:1-8, Mark 2:1-12 and Luke 5:17-26
[20] Matthew 8:1-4, Mark 1:40-45 and Luke 5:12-15
[21] Matthew 8:14-17, Mark 1:29-31 and Luke 4:38-39

CHAPTER 13. How Should We Pray?

[1] John 1:12-13, Romans 8:14 and Galatians 4:4-7
[2] Matthew 6:33
[3] Matthew 5:3
[4] John 15:1-17
[5] Matthew 26:44
[6] Genesis 17:5
[7] 1 Samuel 1:20
[8] Elliot's Commentary for English Readers and Cambridge Bible for Schools and Colleges, http://biblehub.com/commentaries/1_samuel/1-20.htm
[9] Matthew 16:18 and John 1:42
[10] Exodus 34:29-35
[11] John 13:21-30
[12] Romans 1:10

[13] Romans 15:31
[14] 2 Corinthians 12:7-9
[15] Revelation 4:8; see also Isaiah 6:1-3
[16] Romans 15:31
[17] Romans 1:10
[18] Ephesians 6:20
[19] Luke 11:2
[20] Luke 6:12
[21] Matthew 26:36-46; Mark 14:32-42; Luke 22:39-46
[22] Matthew 14:13
[23] See Matthew 14:1-23 and Mark 6:30-46.
[24] Matthew 26:36-46; Mark 14:32-42; Luke 22:39-46
[25] John 17:22-23
[26] Acts 3
[27] NIV Life Application Study Bible, Large Print, Acts Timeline, p.2344, Zondervan & Tyndale House Publishers, 2011.
[28] See Acts 12:1-17

CHAPTER 14. My Journey with Prayer (So Far)

[1] Exodus 5:2
[2] Exodus 7:1-13
[3] Exodus 7:14-24
[4] Exodus 8:1-15
[5] Exodus 8:16-32
[6] Mark 5:25-34 and Luke 8:43-48
[7] Exodus 34:29-35

CHAPTER 15. God's Glory Revealed

[1] 1 John 4:8
[2] John 14:21
[3] Galatians 5:22
[4] Matthew 9:36
[5] Hackett, Conrad and McClendon, David, "Christians Remain the World's Largest Religious Group, but They are Declining in Europe." Pew Research Center, Fact Tank. April 5, 2017. http://www.pewresearch.org/fact-tank/2017/04/05/christians-remain-worlds-largest-religious-group-but-they-are-declining-in-europe/
[6] John 13:1-20
[7] Leviticus 19:18

[8] Matthew 22:36-40, Mark 12:30-31
[9] John 15:1-17
[10] John 15:9-17
[11] John 17:4
[12] John 4:13-14
[13] John 4:25-26
[14] Acts 2:1-4
[15] Acts 2:14-41
[16] Acts 3:1-10 and 5:16
[17] Acts 5:15
[18] I was listening to "In the Market" with Janet Parshall on Moody Radio. Janet was interviewing Todd Nettleton, Media Director with The Voice of the Martyrs. Todd spoke about David Byle and mentioned a podcast available on The Voice of the Martyrs website. Later I listened to two podcasts. I included information from the following three sources. Please see "Turkey: A Habit of Miracles," May 12, 2017, and "Turkey: Opportunities in Difficulty," May 19, 2017, each of which is available on The Voice of the Martyrs Radio at https://secure.persecution.com/radio/default.aspx?pdid=6863 and "I have Decided to Follow Jesus (hour 2)," May 16, 2017, https://www.moodyradio.org/programs/in-the-market-with-janet-parshall/2017/05-2017/05.16.17-are-christians-intolerant---i-have-decided-to-follow-jesus/.
[19] John 8:1-11
[20] John 8:32
[21] Daniel 6:16-23
[22] John 15:19, 17:16-18
[23] John 17:19
[24] Matthew 5:16, Luke 11:34-35, John 8:12, John 12:36-37
[25] Colossian 1:13
[26] Ephesians 6:12
[27] Acts 1:8

CHAPTER 16. Love & Judgment

[1] Romans 6:23
[2] See Romans 2-8
[3] See Genesis 6-9
[4] See Genesis 19
[5] See Romans 1, Romans 6 and 1 Corinthians 1:18
[6] See Romans 1:24-25
[7] Matthew 5:14-16, John 8:12, John 12:36

[8] Dana Carvey played a character on the television show Saturday Night Live knows as the Church Lady. As part of each skit he mocked many Christian sayings, expressed judgment on others, accused them of being in union with Satan, and to conclude it all he danced the Superiority Dance.

[9] John 3:17

[10] John 8:15

[11] John 9:39

[12] See 1 Corinthians 12:31 and 1 Corinthians 13:13.

[13] See 1 Corinthians 13

[14] Matthew 23:27

[15] Acts 7:56, Romans 8:34, Ephesians 1:20, Colossians 3:1, Hebrews 1:3, 8:1, 12:2, 1 Peter 3:22

[16] Matthew 25:31-33; 2 Corinthians 5:10;

[17] John 3:17, 8:15, 12:47

CHAPTER 17. Study, Pray & Serve

[1] Beginning with an angel foretelling Jesus' birth to Mary and continuing with the supernatural birth announcement to shepherds, heavenly power and angelic activity surrounded the birth of God in flesh. As Scripture reveals through Simeon and Peter, heavenly forces are also at work when we recognize Jesus as God Incarnate.

The Holy Spirit gave Simeon eyes to see Jesus as God's salvation.[1] Others saw a baby named Jesus, but the Holy Spirit was on Simeon and when he held the baby, he saw "the consolation of Israel," "the salvation," "the Lord's Messiah," the Son of God. The Holy Spirit opened his eyes to see what others missed, and Simeon immediately recognized Jesus for who He is.

When Peter explained his confidence that Jesus is the Messiah, Jesus said, "Blessed are you, Simon son of Jonah, for this was not revealed to you by flesh and blood, but by my Father in heaven" (Matthew 16:17). God opened Peter's eyes to see. In the same way, heavenly forces are at work seeking to open our eyes, seeking to allow each of us to see Jesus as God Incarnate, and heaven will accomplish His mission if we only allow it to do so.

[2] "Covenant Renewal Service," United Methodist Church, Discipleship Ministries. https://www.umcdiscipleship.org/resources/covenant-renewal-service.

[3] "The United Methodist Hymnal: Book of United Methodist Worship." The United Methodist Publishing House, Nashville, Tennessee. P.10. (1989, 35th printing 2013).

[4] Id

[5] Id

[6] Well, I rounded up. The life expectancy for people born in the United States in 2016 is actually 78.6 years according to the Centers for Disease Control and Prevention. Whalen, Jeanne, "U.S. Lifespans Fall Again," The Wall Street Journal, Dec. 21, 2017, p.A3.

Made in the USA
Middletown, DE
12 August 2022

70450342R00275